Conductor Generalis,

OR

The Office, Duty and Authority

OF

Justices of the Peace,

High-Sheriffs, Under-Sheriffs, Goalers, Coroners, Constables, Jury Men, Over-seers of the Poor,

AND ALSO

The Office of Clerks of Assize

And of the Peace, *&c.*

Collected out of all the Books hitherto written on those Subjects, whether of Common or Statute-Law

To which is Added,
A Collection out of Sir *Matthew Hales* concerning *The Descent of Lands.*

The whole Alphabetically digested under the several Titles, With a Table directing to the ready finding out the proper Matter under those Titles.

THE LAWBOOK EXCHANGE, LTD.
Union, New Jersey
2002

ISBN-13: 978-1-58477-123-4
ISBN-10: 1-58477-123-2

Second printing 2006

The quality of this reprint is equivalent to the quality of the original work.

Printed in the United States of America on acid-free paper

THE LAWBOOK EXCHANGE, LTD.
33 Terminal Avenue
Clark, New Jersey 07066-1321

Please see our website for a selection of our other publications and fine facsimile reprints of classic works of legal history:
www.lawbookexchange.com

Library of Congress Cataloging-in-Publication Data

Conductor generalis, or The office, duty and authority of Justices of the Peace, high-sheriffs, under-sheriffs, goalers, coroners, constables, jury men, over-seers of the poor: and also the office of clerks of assize and of the peace, &c. / collected out of all the books hitherto written on those subjects, whether of common or statute-law to which is added, a collection out of Sir Matthew Hales concerning the descent of lands.

p. cm.

Originally published: [Philadelphia] : Printed and sold by Andrew Bradford in Philadelphia, 1722.

ISBN 1-58477-123-2 (alk. paper)

1. Justices of the peace--United States. 2. Courts--United States--Officials and employees. 3. Justices of the peace--Great Britain. 4. Courts--Great Britain--Officials and employees. I. Title: Conductor generalis. II. Title: Office, duty and authority of Justices of the Peace, high-sheriffs, under-sheriffs, goalers, coroners, constables, jury men, over-seers of the poor. III. Hale, Matthew, Sir, 1609-1676.

KF8800 .C58 2001
347.73'16--dc21

00-058810

Conductor Generalis,

OR

The Office, Duty and Authority

OF

Justices of the Peace,

High-Sheriffs, Under-Sheriffs, Goalers, Coroners, Constables, Jury Men, Over-seers of the Poor,

AND ALSO

The Office of Clerks of Assize

And of the Peace, *&c.*

Collected out of all the Books hitherto written on those Subjects, whether of Common or Statute-Law

To which is Added,

A Collection out of Sir *Matthew Hales* concerning *The Descent of Lands.*

The whole Alphabetically digested under the several Titles, With a Table directing to the ready finding out the proper Matter under those Titles.

Printed and Sold by *Andrew Bradford* in *Philadelphia*, 1722.

THE
PREFACE.

Kind Reader,

THERE are two Motives that have induced me to prefix a few Lines by way of Preface to the Reader of the ensuing Book.

One is, That it is generally expected, and a Book seems to come naked into the World without a Preface; tho' sometimes little or nothing to the Purpose: But since *Custom* has prevailed; since (I say) *Custom* will have it so, that a Man had as good go to Court without a *Cravat*, as to shew himself in Print without a *Preface*, I shall conform my self herein, and thereby prevent the Charge of Innovation.

The other Motive is, To let my Reader know, That the chief Part of this Book consists in Directions to Justices of the Peace, which are intirely from Mr. *Nelson*'s Book, entituled, *The Office and Duty of a Justice of the Peace*, some few things not relating to these Parts of *North-America* only excepted. As for Example, In *Great-Britain* there are several Statutes made to regulate *Hunting*, *Hawking*, *Fishing*, *Fowling*, and the like; the Breach of which Statutes are cognizable before the Justices either in or out of Sessions; but these Matters being free here in *America*, there was no Occasion to swell the Bulk of this Book with such things as would not be of Benefit or Advantage for the Reader to know; and therefore are here omitted.

The *Second Part*, ſhewing the Office, Duty and Authority of *Sheriffs*, &c. is a Collection from that Book ſo well known and approved of, entituled, *The Office and Duty of Sheriffs.* And in this Collection, I preſume, you will find full Directions to High-Sheriffs and Under-Sheriffs, in all the Parts of their Office, with the Name and Nature of all the *Capias*'s or *Writs*, and how, when and where they may (and may not) be executed: With Directions to Goalers concerning Priſons, Priſoners, Eſcapes, *&c.*

In the next Place the Duty of *Coroner* and *Clerk of Aſſize* is collected out of the particular Treatiſes concerning thoſe Offices.

The Directions to *Juries* and *The Deſcent of Lands*, are collected out of that eminent Judge *Hale*'s Book, entituled, *The Hiſtory of the Laws of* England.

The Whole being carefully Collected and Abridged, and having the Approbation (upon Peruſal) of ſome Learned in the Law; all thoſe Matters are here compriſed in One Volumn which lay diſperſed in four · the Bulk and Price of this Book not much exceeding any one of the four, out of which the Matters herein contained were collected.

Much might be writ and ſaid of the Uſefulneſs and Excellency of this Book; but it will be needleſs, ſince every Man that has Occaſion to peruſe it, and follow its Directions, will find the Uſefulneſs of it, and be ſenſible of the Benefit of its Rules and Directions, in the Courſe of the ſeveral Parts of the Law, wherein his reſpective Office calls him to officiate. And notwithſtanding I doubt not but this Book will meet with *Momus*, yet I hope there are ſome, who, upon finding its Uſefulneſs, will kindly accept what is here collected and offered to publick View for the Benefit of his Countrymen.

THE

THE

CONTENTS.

THE *Introduction* shews, The Antiquity of a Justice of the Peace, his Power, and what he may do in the Execution of his Office. Pag. 1.

What One Justice may do by Virtue of his Commission, Pag. 4.

The Power of two Justices of the Peace acting jointly. Pag. 6.

In what Cases a Justice of the Peace lies liable to be fined. Pag. 7.

Directions for granting of Warrants. Pag. 8, 12.

For granting of a Mittimus, Recognizance, &c. Pag. 2.

Of Sessions, and Matters properly to be done by Justices therein.

An Alphabetical TABLE *of the chief Matters contained in the ensuing Treatise.*

A

Accessaries; who are Accessaries and who are Principals. Page 6

Affray, or Fighting, 10

Ale-Houses. 1

Lisence and Recognizance thereon to keep an Ale-house or Tavern. 2

War

An Alphabetical TABLE.

Warrant for keeping an Ale-house without Lisence. 3
Warrant for suppressing an Ale-house, 4
Warrant and Commitment for selling Ale against Law. 5
Ale-house-keeper, a Certificate for continuing one, 6
Apprentices, 11
An Indenture for putting out an Apprentice by the Parish, 13
A Warrant against a Master for abusing an Apprentice, 14
A disorderly Apprentice, *ibid.*
The Discharge of an Appr. 15
Arrest by Justices Warrant, 16
Assault, 18
Attainder and *Conviction*, 19
Appeals in case of Murther, 288

B

BAIL, 21, 241
Condition of Recognizance to give Evidence, 24
Bastard Children, 27
The Woman's Examination, 28, 29, 30, 31
Warrant against the reputed Father, 29, 31, 32
Against the reputed Mother, 35
Recognizance.Supersedeas, Mittimus, &c. thereon, 29, 30
Bond to save the Parish harmless, 34
Bigamy, or having more Wives than One 35
Blasphemy, 36
Buggery, *ibid.*
Burglary, 37
Burning of Houses, &c. 41
Benefit of Clergy, 49
Bread, *Bakers*, 229

C

CErtiorari, 42
Champantry, 44
Clerk of Assize and Clerk of the Peace, 265
Church, *Divine Service*, &c. 44
Chance-Medley, 131
Clergy, Benefit of Clergy what, 49
Conjuration, 51
Conspiracy, 52
Constable, his Duty, Power, &c. 53
Warrant to remove a *Constab* 61
Coroners, 67, 278
Counterfeits, 72
Custom and *Customhouse Officers* 73
Cutting of Tongues, 74

D

DEath casual, 133
Deodand, 134
Descent of Lands, 290
Dissenters, their Declaration of Faith, &c. 44, 47
Certificate, Recognizance, &c. thereon. 48
Drunkenness, 75

E

E*Scapes*, 76, 260
Estreats, 78
Estates, their Descent, 290

Evi-

An Alphabetical TABLE.

Evidence, and *Examination*, 798,2
Extortion, 83

F

FAlse Imprisonment, 262
Felo de-se, Self Murder, 84,286
Felonies, &c. what? 86
Warrant, Examination, Mittimus, Recognizance, &c. thereon, 93, 94, 95
Ferme Covert, 96
Force Lawful, 97
Forcible Entry, 89
The Form of a Record and Precept to the Sheriff on forcible Entry, 103, 104
The Form of an Inquisition, 105
Forfeiture, 106
Forgery, 107

G

Games and *Gaming-Houses*, 109
Goalers and *Goals*, &c. 111
Good Behaviour, 114
Grand Jury's Charge, 273

H

HArvest Time, 120
Hawkers and *Pedlers*, 120
Highways, 122
Homicide, 130
Horses, 134
Houses of Habitation, 136
House of Correction, 137
Hue and Cry, *ibid.*

I

INdictment, 140
Judgment, 141
Jurors and *Juries*, 142, 297

L

LAnds, their Descent, 290
Larceny, Petty, 147
Law Terms explained, 234
Leather, 149
Lodgers, 151
Lord's Day, *ibid.*

M

Manslaughter, 285
Misdemeanors, 157
Misprison of Treason, 158
Money, 159
Mittimus, *ibid.*
Murder, 160
Millers, 228

N

NIght-Walkers, 168
Nusance, *ibid.*

O

OAths, 169, 236, 239
Officers, their Nominat. 176
Orchards, 177

P

PErjury, 178
Pick Pocket, 181
Pillory, *ibid.*
Posse Comitatus, 191
Process, 192
Prisons, 247
Prophecies, 192
Purveyance, 193

Q

Quaker, 193

R

RApe, 193
Recognizance, 194

Rescous,

Rescous, 196
Restitution, vide *Stolen Goods* 197
Riot, 198
Robbery, 203

S

SEssions, 204
Sheriffs, 235
Stolen Goods, 197
Superſedeas, 206
Squibs, 207
Suſpicion, 208
Swearing, ibid.

T

T*Reaſon*, 210
Petty-Treaſon, 219
Miſpriſon of Treaſon, 217
Tryals by Juries, 218, 297

V

V*Agrants*, 218
Verdict, 223

W

W*Ages*, a Warra. for Servants Wages, 15
Watch, 224
Weights and *Meaſures*, 226
Wrecks, 231
Women, ibid
Writs, and the Returns of them, 243
Writs explained, 234

The Second Part contains,

THE Office and Duty of Sheriffs, Coroners, Clerks of Aſſize, viz.
The Antiquity of a High-Sheriff, 235
The Oath of a Sheriff, 236, 239
The Form of an Indenture betwixt the Old and New Sheriff, 238
Office and Oath of Under-Sheriff, 239
Concerning Bail, 241
The Return of Writs, 243
Of Juries and their Returns, 245
Of Writs of Enquiry of Damage, 246, 264
Of Returns of a *Devaſtavit*, 247
Of Priſons, 247
Writs of *Fieri facias*, 248, 253
Writs of Poſſeſſion, &c. 251
Of Writs of *Elegit*, 254
Of *Reſcous*, and in what Caſe an Action lies, 259
Of Eſcapes, 260
Of Falſe Impriſonment, 262
Of Remedy againſt Sheriffs, 263
Writs of Partition, 264

The Office and Duty of the Clerk of Aſſize and Clerk of the Peace, 255, 272
The Charge to be given to a Grand-Jury, 273

A Guide to Coroners, 278
The Method of keeping his Court, 279
The Form of an Inquiſition, 283
Of Homicide, Manſlaughter, Felo-de-ſe, 286
Of Appeals in Caſe of Murther, 288

The Courſe of Deſcents of Lands and Eſtates, &c. 290

Of Tryals by a Jury, 297

Introduction.

The Antiquity of a Justice of the Peace, his Power, and what he may do in the Execution of his Office.

THE Power of a Justice of the Peace is very great, and is a main Prop and Pillar of good Government, in taking care to prevent and punish Offences, whereby the Peace is conserved, and Men maintained in their Rights, and the Possessions of their Goods and Chattels, *&c.* peaceably; whereas, were there not such Over-awing Magistrates, Offenders would be emboldened to make more frequent Depredations, and Strength and Violence would seize upon what the Weaker could no ways defend against them, were not the Law by this means very much their Aid and Safeguard. This Office is of great Antiquity, and has all along held up a venerable Esteem, and Good liking among the People; who find great Advantage and Benefit by those so Commissioned, being usually Men of Estates, Discreet and Judicious, capable of discerning Truth from Falshood, and to relieve the Injured and restrain Oppressors, to punish Criminals, and Discharge the Innocent and Faultless.

Justices of the Peace were Created, 1 *Ed.* 3. But they were first named so by 36 *Ed.* 3.

A *Justice of the Peace* is a Judge of Record, from whence called *Justices* and before 1 *Ed.* 3. they were called *Conservators*. He may take Recognizance of Peace, which none can do but a Judge of Record, *Lam.* 186. *Dalt.* 8 *Crompt* 196. *a Num.* 1.

He is called Commissioner of the Peace, by reason he is Authorized by the King's Commission, so Keeper of the Peace, or Justice

 of

of the Peace. And the Constitution of Justices of the Peace is Inherent, and Inseparable from the Crown, *Stat.* 27 *Hen* 8 And this Power cannot be Transferred, 20 *H* 7. His Warrant is not to be disputed by the Constable for any thing wherein he hath Jurisdiction of the Cause. *Dalt.* 8 *Chap.* 147. 6. *&c.* In some Cases the Testimony of a Justice of the Peace is of great Force, and in some Cases greater than an Indictment of 12 Men upon Oath, *viz.* in Case of Presentments of Highways, Force, Riot, *Dalt.* 9. *Lam.* 65.

A Justice of the Peace being assaulted, may commit the Party so offending to Prison, *Dalt.* 371. If a Justice see one about to make an Affray, and charge him to keep the Peace, and he answers he will not, he may bind him to his good Behaviour, *Dalt.* 294. A Justice of the Peace must proceed by Prescript of the Statute and Commission, *Dalt.* 22. Where the Statute referreth the Tryal to the Justices Discretion, it seemeth he may examine upon Oath, *Dalt.* 20. Every Justice of the Peace is a proper Conservator of Rivers within his County, *Lam* 189. And Justices of the Peace at Sessions are of Equal Authority, *Lamb.* 385. If a Fellon be brought before a Justice of the Peace upon Suspicion, though it appear to the Justice he be not guilty, nevertheless he may not be set at Liberty, but so that he may come to his Tryal, *Lamb.* 233. *Dalt.* 389. *Cro.* 40., *b. Nu.* 20. Otherwise it will prove a voluntary Escape in the Justice; for he is not to be delivered by any Mans Discretion, *Dalt.* 8 *Lamb.* 223.

He may Record a Demurrer upon Evidences, *Lamb* 529. He may give Day to to the Party to bring in Records, which is before other Justices, which is Pleaded by way of Justification, *Lamb.* 539.

In Absence of the King's Attorney, a Justice of the Peace may take Issue with one that pleadeth a Pardon, that he is one of the Parties Excepted, *Lamb.* 540.

A Justice of the Peace may take Money for the security of the Peace, *indeposito*, where Bail cannot be procured, and which, upon the

the Party so depositing the Money, breaking the Peace shall be forfeited to the King, *Just. Barkley*, 1 *Cro.* 446

If upon supposing an Indictment to be void, the Justices have discharged the Prisoner, paying his Fees, yet upon change of their Opinion, they may stay him any time before Judgement, *Lamb.* 540

Justices of the Peace may inquire of all manner of Felonies at the Common Law, or given by any Statute, and of all manner of Trespasses against the Kings Peace, and such Trespasses wherein Actions of the Case will lie for Trespasses or Deceit, and in the end of the Writ grounded upon the Case, it is contained, *Contra Pacem nostram*, *Crompt.* 8 *a Num.* 25.

Defaults against the Statute of 3 *Hen.* 6. *Chap.* 11. For Levying of Wages for Knights of the Shire, are to be heard and determined, by inquiry for the King, or Action for the Party before the Justice of Peace, *Lamb.* 512.

A Justice of the Peace has no need to shew his Commission, by which he is made Justice of the Peace, when he justifieth the doing of any thing as a Justice, for he is Justice of Record, and the Commission remaineth with the *custos Rotulorum* of the same County, and he is called by Commission in open Assize or Sessions, *Cromtt.* 120 *Lamb.* 387

A Justice of Peace may have his Action of the Case against the Party that calleth him false Justice of the Peace; it also seemeth that he may be Indicted, for they may inquire of all Trespasses, where a Man may have his Action of the Case, *Crompt.* 121

A Justice of the Peace certifying into the Kings Bench, that such a one broke the Peace in his Presence, the Party shall be put to his Fine, without a Traverse to the same, *Crompt.* 132 *a.*

A Justice of the Peace, who is of the *Quorum* ought to be resident in the County, 2 *Hen* 5

The Justices at *Newgate*, sit by Virtue of two Commissions, Goal Delivery, and Oyer and Terminer, 4 *Eliz Chap.* 2. And where the same Persons are Justices of Goal Delivery, and Oyer, *&c.*

They may sit the same Day and Place, and inquire by the same Jury, yet the Entry of the Records must be several, as the Indictment is, *Dalt.* 168

A Justice of the Peace Commandeth one by his Precept, under Penalty of 10 *l* to be at the Quarter Sessions next ensuing it, and he appeareth not, no *Scire Facias* shall go forth more than if there had been a *Subpœna*, however it seemeth he shall be Attached to be at the next Sessions upon Contempt, *Crompt.* 123 *a Num.* 9.

What one Justice of Peace may do by Power and Virtue of his Commission.

HE may cause all such as are fit to work in Harvest or Hay-time, and after Lisence them to go unto any other County. He may Rate the Price of deceitful Malt, to be sold by 2 *Edw.* 6, 10, He may compel one fit (in his Discretion) to be bound Apprentice, by 5 *Eliz.* 4. He may, it seems, give Directions to Watchmen, Keepers and Searchers of infected Persons, *Crompt.* 126, *b*, He may cause to be Whipped Trespassers in Orchards, Corn, Hedges or Woods not able to give any Satisfaction.

One Justice of Peace may Command Vagrent Persons to Prison, if they will not serve. He may upon his View of forcible Detainer, Record it by 15 *Rich.* He may punish Deceit in Cloath by Tenters, *&c.* He may cause High-ways to Markets to be enlarged, and cleansed of Trees and Bushes, 13 *Edw.* 1. *Chap.* 5. He may punish Keepers of Places for unlawful Games, and the Players at those Games. He may punish Prophane Swearing in his Presence, made out by Testimony or Conviction by the Party's own Confession. He may punish Offences in Water Men and Transporters of Corn. He may punish Defaults of Collectors, of Sheriffs, Amercements, and of Bayliffs of the Hundreds. Soldiers that purloin their Horse or Harness, He may prevent a Riot, stay it, and commit them that are concerned in acting of it.

He

He may cause an Unlicensed Ale-House-Man openly to be Whipped after Conviction, where there is no sufficient Distress to pay the Penalties, 2 *Carol.* 1. 3. He may upon View or Proof by two Witnesses, Warrant the Levying 20 *l.* Forfeiture for an Unlicensed Ale House, to be given to the Poor.

One Justice may demand the Peace against another Man, *Lamb.* 91. And he may punish Persons going or riding armed, contrary to the Statute of 2 *Edw.* 3.

A Justice may inquire of *Felo-de se* hid or cast into the Sea, where the Coroner cannot have the View of the Body, 3 *Inst.* 55. And he may send Writs for Fugitive Labourers, by 2 *H.* 5. He may take an Information out of the County against an Offender in the County So a Recognizance to Prosecute by assent of the Parties out of the County, but cannot use Coercive Power, *ibid.*

A Justice of the Peace Inhabiting in the Hundred where one was Robbed, may if he be at *York* or *London*, take the Party's Oath, being but an Examination, and no Act of Jurisdiction. A Justice of Peace in *London* ought to send Felons to the Common Goal, not to the Counters. He may take an Indictment of Barretry, without a special Commission.

He may bind a Cheater to his good Behaviour, *&c. Dalt.* 63. 7 *Jacobi* (1) He may convict of Drunkenness, by 12. *Jacobi* 1. He may seize the Goods of *Gipseys*, within a Month after their Arrival, *&c.* by the 22 *Hen* 8.

He may Record a Riot in his View, and commit the Rioters, or bind them to their good Behaviour; but single or alone proceed no further. *Dalt.* 195 He may punish Spoilers of Fish-ponds, and cause their Nets to be cut and burnt. 17 *Rich.* 2. He may take the claim of a Horse Stolen, 31 *Eliz* 12 He may Examine and bind over unlawful Hunters in the Night time, *&c.* 1 *Hen.* 7. He may compel a Vintner to draw a Man Wine, who demands it, and offers Payment, 24 *Hen.* 8. *Dalt.* 242. He may convict the Breach of the Lord's Day, against Stat. 29 *Car.* 2. And may allow of

Cause

Cause for Travelling in a Boat on the Lord's Day, according to the said Statute.

The Power of two Justices of the Peace acting joyntly.

TWO Justices of the Peace, upon View of a Riot or Rout, may Record the same, and with the Sheriff, or under Sheriff. 13 *Hen.* 4. *Crompt*, 16. *Num.* 9 to inquire by a *Jury*, and fine the Rioters, *Dalt.* 195. *Quære*, Two *Justices* on Complaint that a Servant departed before his Term ended, *&c.* are to examine and commit, if they see Cause. See more of *Labourers and Servants, in Office of a Constable*, *&c.* They may bind one to the Quarter Sessions to Answer his Offence against a Penal Law, *Lam.* 187. They may allow and discharge an Ale-house keeper at discretion. They may Assess all Parishes within the Hundred, proportionably, towards Controbution for the Partys charged upon a Robbery. They shall take Order to set poor Soldiers on Work, who cannot get Work *&c.*

Two *Justices* may fine the Head Officers in Burroughs and Market Towns, who are Remiss in viewing the Weights and Measures, and break and burn those that are defective; and Fine all Buyers and Sellers with Unlawful Weights, at Discretion. They may allow Surveyors, and their Servants, to make Materials in another Parish for the Mending the High ways where they are defective.

Two *Justices*, (one being of the *Quorum*.) upon Complaint of the Church Wardens, may convene before them the Bailiff and High-Constables, and take their Accounts of Forfeitures and Defaults estreated concerning High ways.

Two *Justices* of the Peace may take or Administer an Oath of the under Sheriff, Bailiff, *&c.* They may (one being of the *Quorum*) bail a Person Arrested for Manslaughter, Felony, or on Suspition of them. They may take Order about a Bastard Child laid

laid in the Parish, 18 *Eliz.* 7 *Jacobi.* They may License poor People Diseased, to Travel to the Bath for Remedy, *&c.* 39 *Eliz.* 4. They may send to a Work House prisoners brought before them by *Habeas Corpus*, according to 30 *Caroli* 2.

Two *Justices* (one of the *Quorum*, may take an Indictment and Inquisition *Lam.* 48. They may bind over one suspected of Counterfeiting Tokens and Letters, 33 *Hen.* 8. 1. They may search for Popish Books and Relicks, 3 *Jacobi.* 1 C. 5. They may punish Defaults in the Overseers of the Poor. They may punish Offenders in disturbing the Execution of the Statute against Rogues. They may send to the House of Correction persons about to leave their Family to the Parish, 7 *Jacobi* 1. *c.* 4. They may examine Offenders in Back-stalls, against the 19 *H.* 7. at the Sessions, *&c.*

Two *Justices* of the Peace (one of the *Quorum*) may reform false Measures, or Neglect of Clerks of the Market, *Dalt.* 151.

They may bind over to the Asizes, or Sessions, one suspected of Deceit, by Counterfeit Letters, and proceed in like Nature in some other Matters of lesser Moment; and for many things more fully set down and Explained, *vide the Offices of a Constable, Overseers of the Poor*, &c.

Three *Justices* (*Quorum unus*) may take Examination of those that Maim Horses, Cattle. or that destroy Nurseries, or other young Trees, and throw down Inclosures in the Night unlawfully, *&c.*

Where a Justice of the Peace lies liable to be Fined.

IN the Case of Bailing one not Bailable, and refusing to Bail one Baliable, and detaining him, he lies liable to a Fine, and to pay double to the Prisoner, 3 *Edw.* 1. 23. *Hen.* 6. In the Statute against Riots, if he does not Execute it, he is Finable 100 *l.* 13 *Hen.* 4. So in that of forcible Entry, 10 *l.* 8 *Hen.* 6. Exercising his Office before the Oath taken, *Dalt.* 14. For not

not being present at the Annual Tax of Servants Wages, 10 *l*. If a *Justice* of the Peace does not in 40 Days certifie unto the Kings bench Presentments of Extolling the Pop's Power, he forfeits 100 *l*. 5 *Eliz. c.* 1. For Imbessellng, willfully Raising, maliciously Inrolling an Indictment not found, changing an Indictment of Trespass into Felony, is Fine and Imprisonment, and loss of Office, *Lam.* 631. He may be Imprisoned for taking Bond in his own Name, and not in *Domino Regi*, the Matter concerning the King, 33 *H.* 8. *C.* 9. For conspiring with another to Indict a Stranger at the Sessions, otherwise as a thing done by him as Judge, *Crompt.* 122. *a Num.* 32. Where a Justice fails to do justice, he may be put out of Commission, and punished, 4 *Hen.* 7. So for refusing to take Surety for the Peace, when it is Tendred. *Vide Crom* Jurisdiction of Courts. For Imbezelling and Racing Records, he forfeits his Office, and may be Fined, *Vide antea.*

Directions for granting Warrants by a Justice of the Peace.

A Warrant in Writing must be under the Justices Hand and Seal his Hand at least. However it is better if it be Sealed, as the usual way is, *Dalt.* 460.

A Warrant of the Peace, or good Behaviour must contain the special Matter.

A Warrant for Treason, Murder, or such like Capital Offence, need not contain the special Matter or Cause, *Dalt.* 160.

If a Justice of the Peace, being out of the County grants his Warrant to be served in the County, the Officer making the Arrest must carry the party before some Justice of the Peace within the County. *Lam.* 91. *Dalt.* 461.

A Justice of the Peace may make his Warrants, To come before himself, yet in a Warrant for the Peace, the usual Manner is otherways.

Upon

Upon a General Warrant, an Officer may chuse to go before what Justice he pleases.

If a Justice of the Peace make a Warrant beyond his Authority, it is not disputable by a Constable, or other Officer, but must be obeyed, unless it be to do a thing out of the Justices Jurisdiction in a Cause where there is no Judge; for if in this Latter Case the Officer execute the Warrant, he is punishable. *Dalt.* 8. 465. *Lam.* 65. *Crompt.* 147. *B. Lamb.* 91. 92. *Dalt* 865.

A Warrant directed to two joyntly to arrest a Pary, he may be arrested by either of them.

A Warrant made in the King's Name, ought to be made to all Ministers, as well within Liberties as without. *Dalt.* 355

Warrants may be made either, (1) in the Name of the King, or (2) in the Name, of the Justice, and either of them must be testified by the Justice from whom they Issue, or (3) without Stile by Superscription of the Justice. *Dalt.* 395. See more of *Warrant's in the Office of a Constable in this Book*, and how they are to be Executed.

Sessions held, by one Justice of the Peace is not Good, tho' it were summoned by two, and stiled by their Names, but two sufficient Justices Warrants sealed (*Quorum unus*) The Place where Sessions is to be held is Arbitrable, and therefore though by Summons they are to be kept in one place, yet they may be kept in another, but then there can be no Amercement for Default of Appearance. *Lamb.* 383. 384. But they must be kept within the County. *Dalt.* 531. So in a Town Corporate, but not to Intermeddle.

Two Sessions at one time for one County lawfully Summoned at two Places are good, but Appearance at one shall excuse the default of an Appearance at the other, and Presentment taken before either of them shall stand good, *Lamb*, 384. But Punishable without Notice.

At a General Sessions, all Matters enquirable by Justices of the Peace, either by Statute, or their Commission, ought to be given in Charge; otherwise at special Sessions. *Lamb.* 613. and may be held three Days.

 At

At the Quarter Seſſions, Officers and Miniſters of the Court, and Jurors of the County owe their Attendance, *Lamb.* 386.

Jurors, not appearing acording to Summons, are puniſhable for loſs of Iſſues, the uſual part of Eſtreats,

Conſtables making Default are Fineable.

The Juſtices of the Peace, if need require, may keep a ſpecial Seſſions by Virtue of their Commiſſion, or by the Statute. 1 *Hen.* 5, *Chap.* 4, *Lamb*, 623, All Matters within the Commiſſion or Statute, may at a ſpecial Seſſions of the Peace be given in Charge, yet they are at Liberty to give in Charge, either all, or any of them. *Lam.* 623. 624.

If two Juſtices of the Peace, one being of the *Quorum*, make a Precept to the Sheriff for the holding a Seſſions at ſuch a Place and Day, and to return a Jury before them, other Juſtices cannot by their *Superſedeas* Inhibit it, *Crompt.* 126. *B.* But the King by his Writ of *Superſedeas* may diſcharge it. *Ibid.*

All that come to the Seſſions for publick Service, or upon Compulſion, upon Complaint, and Examination of the Matter upon Oath, ſhall be freed from any Arreſt upon Original Proceſs, *Lamb. Cro.* 190. *B. Lamb.* 402.

Indictments are many times tried the ſame Seſſions wherein the Perſons were Indicted, yea, the ſame day before Juſtices of Goal Delivery, or Juſtices of Oyer, *&c.* But in caſe of Felony it ſeems very reaſonable to be deferred to the next Seſſions, upon Cauſe ſhewn; it being ſo in an Indictment of Nuiſance generally, and *Life* is more to be valued and favoured, *&c. Dalt.* 537.

Many things of great Import cannot be done but at the Seſſions, and ſome but at ſuch particular Seſſions. *Dalt.* 537. *See further under the Title Juſtices of the Peace.*

Of Mittimuſſes and Recognizances, what they are, and how to be taken.

A *Mittimus* muſt contain the Name of the Party or Parties, his or their Offences, and the time of Impriſonment, that it may appear

appear whether the Prisoner be Bailable, or not *Lam.* 297. *Dalt.* 439.

If one be Committed without Bail or Mainprise and the Cause be expressed in the Mittimus, and yet is Bailable, other Justices may Bail him; yet *Quære*, seeing their Authority is equal, *Dalt.* 439. But if no Cause be expressed, other Justices shall not Bail him without the Pirvity of the First Justice or Justices, because the Cause of Commitment probably may not be Bailable. *Dalt.* 439.

If the Mittimus be General, the other Justices that Bail must take Notice at Peril, *ibid.* There is a Writ called a Mittimus, for removing Records of Outlawry, Judgment in the King's Bench, *&c.* unto the Common Pleas, or by an Act of Parliament unto the King's Bench, *&c.* A *Recognizance* is a Bond of Record, testifying the Recognizor to owe a certain Sum of Money to some other, and that acknowledgment of the Sum is to remain of Record, and none can lawfully take it but a Judge or Officer of Record, *Dalt.* 457.

Every Recognizance taken by a Justice of the Peace must be made by these Words [*Domino Rigi*] and great Care to be had in so doing; for it is Imprisonment for any Person to take it otherwise. For these Words *Domino Rigi*, import and imply the Recognizor to be bound to our Lord the King, and not to any other. *Dalt* 276,

Sureties in Recognizance ought to be Subsidy Men, and they must be two besides the Party himself.

It is in the Discretion of the Justice of the Peace, if he take a Recognizance, *Ex Officio*, to appoint the Number of Sureties, their Sufficiency in their Goods and Lands, and the Sum of Money, and how long the Party shall be bound.

A Recognizance for the Peace, unless the Words be expressed for keeping of the Peace, seemeth void. So it is if a Recognizance be that the Recognizor shall not Beat or maim *B.* without the expressing the keeping of the Peace, *ibid.*

A Recognizance expressing no time of appearance, but generally to keep the Peace is good. And so these few may serve to give a light

light into others; for they are many; and in the main they tend to one and the ſame thing, tho' in Circumſtances they differ.

Of Seſſions and Matters properly to be done by Juſtices therein.

THe Seſſions is the Aſſemble of any two or more Juſtices of the Peace, (*Quorum unus*) at a certain time and Place within the Limits of their Commiſſion, appointed to enquire by a Jury, or otherwiſe to take knowledge, and thereupon to hear and determine according to their Power, of Cauſes within their Commiſſion, and Statutes referred to their Charge, *Lamb.* 378.

A Seſſions held without Summons is good, but in ſuch Caſe none ſhall looſe any thing for Default of appearing. *Lamb.* 380, 381.

Summons of the Seſſions is uſually by precept written to the Sheriff, and by him to be returned, at Seſſions. *Lam.* 381.

Precepts for Summoning the Seſsions, may be made by any two Juſtices of the Peace, (*Quorum unus*) but not the *Cuſtos Rotulorum* alone; and Summons cannot be diſcharged by *Superſedeas* of all other Juſtices, but by *Superſedeas* out of Chancery, *Lamb.* 382, 383.

Of Warrants. &c.

AS For Warrants Grantable by Juſtices of the Peace, they may be ſtiled and made after ſeveral manners, *viz.*

1*ſt.* In the Name of the King, and yet the *Teſte* may be under the Name of the Juſtice, or Juſtices of the Peace who grant them.

2*dly.* Or they may be ſtiled and made only in the Name of the Juſtices ſo granting.

3*dly.* Or elſe be made without any ſuch Stile, and only under the *Teſt* of the Juſtice of the Peace, or only ſubſcribed by the Juſtice, as the Cauſe requires.

OF

Ale-Houſes; &c.

INNS were allowed for the Benefit of Travellers, who have certain Privileges whilſt they are in their Journies, and are in a more peculiar manner protected by Law; 'tis for this Reaſon that the Inkeeper ſhall anſwer for thoſe Things which are ſtolen *Infra Hoſpitium*, though not delivered to him to keep, and though he was not acquainted that the Gueſt brought the Goods to the Inn; for it ſhall be intended to be through his Negligence, or Occaſioned by the Fault of him or his Servants. So if he puts a Horſe to Paſture without the Direction of his Gueſt, and the Horſe is ſtolen, he muſt make Satisfaction.

But if a Neighbour who is not a Traveller, lodges in an Inn, and looſeth his Goods, or if the Gueſt is robbed by his own Servant in the Inn, or by any one who came thither with him, or by leaving his Goods in one Room when the Innkeeper deſired to leave them in another, in ſuch Caſes he ſhall not be anſwerable.

The true Uſe of Ale-houſes and Inns was for the Relief and Lodging of Travellers, and to ſupply the Wants of thoſe who are not able to provide great Quantities of Drink and Proviſion; and if any Ale-houſe-keeper or Inn-keeper refuſe to lodge a Traveller, The Juſtice of Peace may compel him to do it, or the Conſtable may preſent it as an Offence next Seſſions, in Order to Suppreſs it; or tho Party may have an Action on the Caſe; but they connot be compelled to Sell Victuals, unleſs the Traveller tender Money, if required.

At Common Law any perſon might build an Inn for the Reception of Travellers, and without Licence from Juſtices; but if he ſold Ale to any Perſon beſides Travellers, without Licence, he was puniſhable *Hutt.* 99.

But for the better Direction of thoſe who keep Ale-houſes, King *James*, *Anno* 16 publiſhed theſe Articles by his Proclamation, the Subſtance whereof are, *viz*.

1. That the Juſtices meet once in a Year, either in *April* or *May*, and call before any two of them (*Quorum unus*) ſuch perſons who ſell Ale, and Inform themſelves by Men of Credit, what Perſons are fit to keep Ale-houſes, and then Licence them.

2. That in Licensing they take a Recognizance, with a Condition annexed, (*ut posthac*) and no other.

3. That the Person licenced do give such a Recognizance with Sureties, *&c.* for the Performance of the Condition, to continue but for one Year; and whenever taken to expire in *April* or *May* following, then to be renewed if Justices think fit.

4. Justices may call the Clearks of the Peace, Town-Clerks or Deputies, to attend them at their Meetings, to take Recognizances, *&c.* and enter them at Sessions, that the King may be intitled to the Forfeitures, and engross the Recognizance and Condition in Parchment; which is to be the Original, and give a Copy examined to the Ale-house-keeper.

5. They should keep a Book in which the Names of all Ale-house-keepers should be kept, and they should attend the Justices with that Book.

6. That they take 18 *d.* for every Recognizance, and the Justices Clerk 1 *s.*

7. If not licensed at the Meeting, he may have a Licence afterward.

8. That none be licensed who have not a convenient lodging for a Traveller.

9. That the Justice suffer none to sell, *&c.* without Licence, and that they proceed against Brewers at Quartersessions for selling Ale or Beer to unlicensed Persons.

10. That the Clearks of the Peace in *Trinity* Term every Years carry a Brief of all Recognezances into the Office of the Patentees, that there be no Concealment.

11. Justices in Sessions to enquire of the due Execution of these Articles.

If an Inn-keeper, or Ale-house-keeper, sells in a Vessel not stamped, or refuses in bringing in the Reckoning to give the particular number of Quarts or Pints, he shall not detain any Goods, if the Guest refuses to pay the Reckoning, but he shall be left to his Action at Law.

A License to keep an Ale house.

Pennsilvania, ss. WE whose Names are hereunto subscribed, two of His Majesties Justices of the Peace for the said Province, do, according to the Statute made and provided, licence, admit and allow *A. B.* of *&c.* Victualler, to keep a common Ale-house in the House wherein he now dwelleth, for and during the Space of one whole Year next ensuing the Date hereof, so as the said *A. B.* do not suffer any unlawful Games to be used in his said House, and so as he keep good Order and Rule therein so long as it shall continue a common Ale-house, as aforesaid. *Given* under our Hands and Seals, *&c.*

A Recognizance thereupon,

BE *it Remembered*, That on the first Day of *May* in the fourth Year of the Reign of our Soveraign Lord *GEORGE*, by the Grace of God King of *Great Britain, France* and *Ireland*, &c. appeared Before us *A. B.* and *C. D.* Esqrs two of His Majesties Justice

Juſtices of the Peace for the County of, *&c.* in the Province of, *&c.* *Samuel Jones* of the Town of *Tarby* in the ſaid County-Inholder, and *John James* of the ſame place Cordwainer, and acknowledged themſelves to be Indebted unto our ſaid Lord the King in the Sum of 20 Pounds, lawful Money of *America*, to be levied upon their and each and every of their Lands and Tenements, Goods and Chattles to the uſe of our ſaid Lord the King, his Heirs and Succeſſors, if failure be made of the under-writen Condition.

The Condition of this Recognizance is ſuch, *That whereas* the above-bounden *A. B.* is by the Juſtices within named, licenſed, admitted and allowed to keep a common Ale-houſe, in the Houſe where he now dwelleth, in C. *If* therefore the ſaid *A. B.* ſhall not during the Continuance of the ſaid Licence, ſuffer any unlawful Games to be uſed in his ſaid Houſe, but ſhall during the ſaid Time maintain good Order and Rule therein, That then this Recognizance to be void, or otherwiſe to remain in full Force.

The Recognizance is to be certified at the next Quarter-Seſſion of the Peac. 5 *&* 6 *E.* 6. *c.* 25.

A Warrant againſt one for keeping an Ale-houſe *without* Licence.

To the Conſtable of &c.

New-York ſs. WHereas we whoſe Names are hereunto ſubſcribed, two of His Maieſties Juſtices of the Peace for the ſaid County, have been credibly informed, upon Oath, that *A, B.* of *&c.* doth keep a common Ale-houſe without Licence, contrary to the Statute in that Caſe made and provided: *Theſe are therefore* to will and require you to bring the ſaid *A. B.* before us, or one of us, or ſome other of His Maieſties Juſtices of the Peace for the ſaid County, to be dealt with according to Law: An hereof fail not. Given under our Hands and Seals, *&c.*

A Warrant for two Witneſſes againſt an Unlicenſed Ale-houſe keeper,

To the Conſtable of, &c.

New-York ſs. W*Hereas* Complaint upon Oath hath been made unto me, That *A. B.* of *&c.* doth of his own Authority, and without any lawful Licence, keep a common Ale-houſe, and doth ſell Ale, Beer, *&c.* in the Pariſh aforeſaid: *And Whereas* I am credibly informed that *C. D.* and *E. F.* of *&c.* can juſtify the ſame *Theſe are therefore* to require you to give Notice unto the ſaid *C. D* and *E F.* that they appear before me at, *&c.* upon Monday next at eight a Clock in the fore-noon, then and there to Teſtify what they know concerning the Premiſſes: *Whereof* they are not to fail at their Perrils. *Given under my Hand and Seal,* &c.

A Warrant for an Unlicenced Ale-hous-keeper on the first Conviction.

To the Constable, &c.

WHereas A. B. of the Parish of C. Victualler, was this present Day lawfully Convicted upon Oath before me for keeping a common Ale-house in the said County of, &c. not being lawfully licensed according to the Form of the Statute in that Case made and Provided, by reason whereof he hath forfeited to the Poor of the said County the Sum of twenty Shillings of lawful *British* Money: These are therefore to require you, or one of you, to levey the said Forfeiture by destraing the Goods and Chattles of the said *A. B.* and that you detain the same for the Use aforesaid: And in default of Payment of the said 20 *s.* within three Days after such Distress taken, that then you appraise and sell the same, to satisfy the said Forfeiture: And if the said *A. B.* shall not have sufficient Goods upon which the said 20 *s.* may be levied as aforesaid, or shall not pay the same within six Days after the Date hereof that then you the said Constable do openly whip, or cause the said *A. B.* to be whipped in the County of *C.* for the said Offence: And hereof fail not, &c.

A Warrant to levy 10 s. *on an Ale-house keeper*, &c, *for suffering to Tiple,*

To the Constable of &c.

WHereas it hath been duly proved before me this present Day upon Oath, that *A. B.* of *C.* aforesaid, Victualler. did upon the first Day of *A.* suffer *D. E.* &c. of &c. to remain and continue Drinking and Tipling in the House of the said *A. B.* in *C.* aforesaid, contrary to the Form of the Statutes in that Case made and provided: These are therefore to require you the said Constable to levy by Distress of the Goods and Chattles of the said *A. B.* the Sum of Ten Shillng, for the said Offence, for the Use of the Poor of the said Parish, and to detain the said Goods for the Space of Six Days next after such Distress taken, if the said Forfeiture of 10 *s.* shall not be paid to you within that Time; and that afterward you apraise and sell the said Goods to satisfy the said Forfeiture. rendring the Over-plass to the owner. And hereof fail not &c.

A Warrant to suppress an Ale house for Disorder,

To the Constable, &c.

WHereas we are credibly informed, that *A. B.* of *C.* &c. doth suffer rude and disorderly persons to frequent his House in the Town of *B.* now being a [illegible] Ale-house, wherein they usually commit great Disorders, to the Disturbance of those

thoſe who live near the ſaid Place: For which Reaſon we D. E. and G. F. Eſqrs. two of His Majeſties Juſtices of the Peace, (*Quorum unus*) do think it convenient to diſcharge and put away the common ſelling of Ale and Beer, or other Liquors in the ſaid Houſe. *Theſe are therefore* to require you forthwith to go to the ſaid *A. B.* and charge him from henceforth not to ſell, or ſuffer to be ſold any Beer, Ale or other Liquors in the ſaid Houſe: and that you alſo cauſe the Sign of the ſaid Houſe to be pulled down.

Two Juſtices (*Quorum unus*) may prohibit and remove common Ale-ſelling, 5 & 6 *Ed.* 6. *c.* 25. *Crompt.* 197. 198. on *contempt*, *Bond for good Behaviour*, *Impriſonment and Fine.* 1 *Bulſtr.* 109.

A Warrant and Commitment upon the Statute of 5 and 6 Ed, 6, *for ſelling Ale againſt the Command of the Juſtices*,

To the Conſtable of, &c. *And to the Keeper*, &c.

WHereas *A. B.* of *C.* hath been duly diſcharged from ſelling Ale or Beer in a common Ale-houſe within the ſaid Town of *C.* in the ſaid County, notwithſtanding which Diſcharge he hath ſince, contrary to the Command of the Juſtices of the Peace of the ſaid County, uſed to ſell Ale and Beer therein: *Theſe are therefore* in His Majeſties Name to command you the ſaid Conſtable, that you take the ſaid *A. B.* and him ſafely convey to the Common Goal at *C* aforeſaid, and to deliver him to the Keeper thereof, together with this Precept, commanding you the ſaid Keeper to receive the Body of the ſaid *A. B.* into your Cuſtody, and him ſafely to keep by the Space of three Days without Bail or Mainprize, and not diſcharge him afterwards, until he enter into a Recognizance with two Sureties, according to the Form of the Statute in that Caſe made, That he will not keep a common Ale-houſe or Tipling-houſe, or uſe commonly the ſelling of Ale and Beer. And hereof fail not. Given under our Hands and Seals, *&c.*

The Form of the Recognizance,

BE *it Remembered*, That, *&c.* (*as before in Page* 2.)

THE *Condition of this Recognizance* is ſuch, *That whereas* the above-bounden *A. B.* hath been lawfuly convicted before us *C. D.* and *E. F.* Two of her Majeſties Juſtices of the Peace for the ſaid County, for keeping of a Common Ale-houſe in, *&c.* without being allowed thereunto in the open Seſſions, or by two Juſtices of the Peace for the ſaid County; for which ſaid Offence the ſaid *A. B.* was by us committed to the common Goal of the ſaid County, there to remain for the ſpace of three Days purſuant to the Statute in that Caſe made and provided. If therefore the ſaid *A. B.*

shall not keep any common Ale-house, Tipling-house or commonly sell Ale or Beer from henceforth, without such allowance as aforesaid, Then this Recognizance to be void, or else, *&c.*

Note, This Recognizance must be certified at the next Quarter Sessions which certificate is by this Statute made to be a Conviction of the Party offending, and an Authority to the Justices in Sessions to assess 20 *s.* as a Fine upon the Offender.

But this Law did not work the Reformation intended, because the Fine was seldom levied by Reason of the Poverty of the Offenders; or if it was levied, the Person would some times run away and leave a Charge upon the Parish, which was a discouragement to the Prosecution.

Therefore by *Stat.* 3 *Car.* if they were not of Ability a Corporal Punishment was added, and an easie way of Conviction, *viz.* by one Justice out of Sessions, and a more speedy Remedy for a Fine.

A Certificate for continuing an Ale-house keeper.

To the Right Worshipful His Majesties Justices of the Peace within the lower Division of *L. &c.*

WE *Whose Names are hereunto subscribed, Inhabitants of the Parish of* H. *within the Division and County aforesaid, do humbly certifie, that the now dwelling-House of* A. B. *Victualler, is conveniently situated there for a Victualling-House, and that he is of good Name and Fame; and the said House is well accomodated for Entertainment of Travellers, and that he keepeth good Rule therein: And therefore we humbly desire your Worships that his Licence for keeping the said Victualling-house may be continued.*

C. D. and E. F.

Accessaries

Who are Principals, and in what Cases. And who are no Accessaries.

IN High Treason the Procurers before the Fact, or the Receiver of a Traitor afterward knowing him to be so, is a Principal.

In all other Fellonies, and in forcible Entries, Riots and all Trespasses, the Aiders, Consenters or Abetters, if they are Present at the time when the Fact is committed, tho' tis personal and done by one, yet these are all Principals; but if not present they are Accessaires

Accessaries before: So likewise if they be in the same House, tho' not in the view of the Felony. *Dalt.* 353. *H. P. C.* 215. 3 *Inst.* 59.

But in Murder there may be a Principal, tho' not present when the Fact is done, as where one knoweth Drink to be poisoned, and perswadeth another to drink, who drinketh and dyeth in the Absence of him who perswaded it, yet it is Murder in him. *H. P. C. ib. Dalt.* 353, 4 *Co.* 44.

The Procurers and Abettors in stealing of a Woman, and those who receive her, knowing her to be stolen, are all Principal Felons. 3 *Hen.* 7. c. 2.

So upon the Statute of 5 *Eliz.* of Forgery of Writings, all are Principals. The Presence or Absence of the Party makes the Difference betwen the Principal and the Accessary before the Fact; if present, then he is a Principal, if he encourage, advise or abet; if absent when the Thing is done, then he is Accessary before the Fact. *Moor* 666. *Dalt.* 354.

If a Felony of another Nature than what was advised, doth proceed from the Abetting or Encouragement given by any ill Man, he is likewise an Accessary to it; as if he adviseth one Man to rob another, and instead thereof he killeth him in making Resistance: in this Case the Abettor is Accessary to the Murder, because his Advice was pursued to do an ill Act, which maketh him Accessary to all the Consequences thereof. *Dalt.* 354.

So 'tis if the Advice or Command was executed in another manner, at another time, or in any Place than where commanded.

As if the Command is to rob in the High-way, and instead thereof the Person is robbed in his House; or to poison a Man, and he stabs him; or to rob him one Day, and he doth it another Time. In all these Cases he is Accessary before the Fact.

If a Man is in Confederacy with an other to Steal his own Goods, who stealeth them accordingly from his Servant with Intent to charge his Servant, this maketh him an Accessary. *Golds.* 186.

And in all Felonies which are made so by Statutes, and which were not so at Common Law, there are Accessaries both before and after the Fact. The Abettors, Aiders, Concealers and Receivers, are not named in the Statute, excepting only in Felony, for carrying away a Woman against her Will, upon the *Stat.* 3. *H.* 7. in which Case all are Principals. 3 *Inst.* 61, 62. 2 *Inst.* 1683.

When the Felony commanded is executed upon another Person.

If *A.* adviseth a Man to kill another by Poison, who knowing thereof delivereth it to another to Eat it, who eateth and dyeth, this is Murder; but the first Adviser to Poison is not Accessary to it.

So where there is a Variance in the Nature of the Offence; as if I commanded Man to rob another in the High-way, and he commits Burglary. *H. P. C.* 217. *Lamb.* 285. *H. P. C. ib. Lamb.* 285.

Also, if one doth more than is commanded; as if I command a Man to apprehend another, and instead thereof he robs him; for there must be an evil purpose of Mind continuing till the Act commanded be compleated to make a Man an Accessary before the Fact.

There can be no Acceſſaries before the Fact in caſe of Manſlaughter, for it is an Offence which follows upon a ſuddain Affray, 4 *Rp.* 44.

The Principal muſt always be named in the Indictment againſt an Acceſſary, and ought to be firſt atainted, otherwiſe the other Acceſſary connot be tried; for by the Acquital of the one the other is diſcharged *Dalt.* 359.

If an Erroneous Judgment be given againſt the Principal, yet the Acceſſary muſt be tried; but if the Principal die before Atender, or is acquitted by Verdict; or if after Conviction he hath the Benefit of the Clergy, or is pardoned; or 'tis found by Verdict that he killed another *ſe defendendo, or per infortunium*, in all which Caſes the Acceſſary is diſcharged. *Dalt.* 339.

So 'tis is if the Principal is burnt in the Hand, the Acceſſary is thereby acquited. *Dalt.* 339 359 *Cro. Car.* 567.

By the Common Law there could be no Acceſſary in one County to a Felony done in another, becauſe thoſe of a ſtrange County could not upon the Trial have any Cognizance of the Principal Offence; But this is now Remied. By the Statute 2 & 3 *E.* 6. *cap.* 24. If a Felony is done in one County, and there are Acceſſaries in another, they may be indicted as Acceſſaries.

The Law ſeemed defective in this Matter (*viz.*) That no Acceſſary could be convicted or ſuffer Puniſhment where the Principal was not attainted, or had his Clergy; and by this Means the Contrivers of Felonies, and the Receivers of Stolen Goods often went unpuniſhed. Therefore

An Act was made 1 *Annæ*, That if a Man is convicted of Felony, or ſtands mute, or challenges above Twenty of the Jury, it ſhall be lawful to proceed againſt the Acceſſary notwithſtanding the Principal had his Clergy, was Pardoned, or otherwiſe delivered before Attainder; and ſuch Acceſſary ſhall ſuffer the ſame Puniſhment, if convicted ſtands mute, or challengeth above Twenty, as he ſhould have ſuffered if the Principle had been attainted.

By this Acts he that buys or receives ſtolen Goods, knowing them to be ſtole, ſhall be proſecuted for a Miſdemeanour, and fined and impriſoned, though the Principal is not convicted; and if he happen to be convicted afterwads, that Puniſhment ſhall exempt the Receiver, &c. from being again puniſhed as an Acceſſary.

It was formerly held, that he was an Acceſſary after the Fact, who received or aided a Felon, though he did not know any Felony was done: But then the Receiver muſt dwell in the ſame County where the Felon was outlawed; and the Reaſon was, becanſe upon the Outlawry he is a Felon upon Reeord; and the Proceedings being in the County-Court, all the Inhabitants of the County ought to take Notice of it: But this was thought too ſevere, and therefore now a more particular Knowledge of the Fact is required.

Thoſe who willingly receive Felons, or relieve, aſſiſt, comfort or aid them, knowing they have committed Felony, are Acceſſaries after the Fact.

The Fact to which the Party is an Acceſſary, muſt be Felony at the very Time in which he becomes an Acceſſary; and therefore the Receiver of one who gave a mortal Wound to another, before the Death of the Party ſtruck, is not an Acceſſary to the

Murder

Murder, becauſe it wonld not be Felony in the Receiver at the Time of the Stroke given, for the Man was then living.

He who buyeth ſtolen Goods for leſs Value than they are really worth, ſeems to conſent to the ſtealing; for by an Under-value it appeareth that the Seller did not come by ſuch Goods honeſtly.

But Mr. *Dalton* makes a Difference in this Cauſe, between a Buyer, who is a Stranger and one who is an Acquaintance of the Thief: For if a Stranger buy ſtolen Goods for near the Value, he is not puniſhable; but if a Companion of the Felon buy the Goods which he ſtole for leſs Value, this he ſays, is by Covin, and makes him an Acceſſary after the Fact.

Formerly to receive Goods ſtolen, knowing them to be ſtolen, did not make an Acceſſary, unleſs he did likewiſe receive the Thief. But now

Who are Acceſſaries after the Fact.

But the *Stat.* 3 & 4 *W.* & *M. c.* 9. buying or receiving ſtolen Goods, knowing them to be ſtolen, makes an Acceſſary to the Felony after the Fact.

If the Owner hath complained to a Juſtice of Peace, or to a Conſtable. or if the Felon be taken upon Hue-and-Cry, or otherwiſe, and then the Owner takes his Goods, or compounds with the Felon, or conſents to his Eſcape, this makes him an Acceſſary after the Fact, becauſe he did once act againſt the Offender *criminaliter.*

But if in Purſuit he retaketh his Goods, and ſuffereth the Felon to eſcape before any Complaint made to the Juſtice, or without being charged, *&c.* this is a Miſdemeanor for which he may be fined, but it doth not make him an Acceſſary; becauſe *in initio* he has Liberty *agere civiliter vel criminaliter.*

A Servant is ſo by relieving his Maſter, being a Felon, or by aſſiſting him to eſcape; for he is bound to accuſe him, or to depart his Service; and ſo is the Maſter by relieving his Servant.

Husband receiving a Wife, knowing her to have done a Felony, *ſed non e converſo.*

Thoſe who receive a Man bailed for Felony,

Relieving a Felon in Priſon.

To ſend Letters or Meſſengers in his Favour; to teach him to read, or to advice him that he endeavour to perſwade the Witneſſes not to appear againſt him at his Trial,

Not to reveal a Felony, which I know is intended to be done, or ſuffering a Felon to eſcape, but giving him no Aſſiſtance.

Ex vi Termini, the Principal is to be tried before the Acceſſary, and therefore one *Cholmley*, Recorder of *Lincoln*, was turned-out of his Office for trying the Acceſſary firſt. 1 Vent. 146.

If the Principal is acquitted or convicted of Manſlaughter, or in his own Defence, or is admitted to Clergy before Attainder, or is pardoned or dieth, the Acceſſary is acquitted: But this muſt be before Attainder, for if afterwards, the Acceſſary ſhall be arraigned. Raym. 477.

If the Principal doth appear, or appearing & ſtands mute, the Acceſſary cannot be tried: If he is not attainted, the Acceſſary ſhall not be outlawed. If a Man is indicted as Acceſſary to two Principals, one of which happens to be convicted. and the other doth not appear, yet

yet the Acceffary fhall be tried, and may be condemned, if found Acceffary to the Party convicted, and may again be arraigned as Acceffary to the other when he appeareth.

If both Principal and Acceffary plead to the fame Felony, they may be tried by the fame Jury; but Judgment muft firft be had againft the Principal, and the Jury muft be charged to acquit the Acceffary, if they find the Principal not guilty.

The Acceffary fhall not take Advantage of any Error in the Attainder of the Principal. 9 *Rep.* 119. *B.*

Where now a Felony is made by Statute, which was not fo at Common Law, there may be Acceffaries, tho' not named in the Statute.

In an Indictment againft an Acceffary you muft fet forth the manner of the Felony, and that the Defendant knowing him to have done fuch a Felony, *felonice recepit*, &c. *Dalt.* 358.

If a Criminal is Indicted as Principal, and *acquited*, he cannot afterwards be indicted as Acceffary *before that Fact*, becaufe he who advifes the Thing to be done, is in a manner guilty of the Fact it felf; and being acquitted of that, he is difcharged of all Guilt before the Principal Fact committed,

But notwithftanding fuch Acquittal, he may be Indicted *as Acceffary after the Fact*, becaufe fuch an Acceffary cannot be Guilty of committing the Fact itfelf, for that was before he knew any thing of it. *Keeling* 26.

Affray

IS a Fighting between two or more, and differs from an Affault; for the one is a Common Wrong, the other is an Injury done to a particular Perfon.

There muft be a Stroke given or offered, or a Weapon drawn, or otherwife it is not an Affray. *H. P. C.* 135.

But yet a Challenge to fight by Word or Meffage, has been held an Affray; and *Anno* 16 *Car.* 2. one *Collins* was indicted for carrying a Challenge, knowing the contents, and was found Guilty, and fined 100 *l.* and committed for a Month without Bail, &c. *Sid.* 186.

What may be done on this Head (1) *By the Conftable.*

He may command the Affrayers to depart, and upon Refufal, may commit them; if they refift, he may call others to his Affiftance, and may juftifie the Wounding in fuch Cafe.

If 'tis a great and dangerous Affray, he may commit them till they find fureties for the Peace.

If any Person is wounded, he may commit the Offender, or if he will he may carry him before a Justice of the Peace, who may commit him if, he will not give Security, to appear at the next Sessions.

He may take them out of Franchise in the same County: He may pursue them into another County, but then when taken he must carry them before a Justice of the Peace, for he cannot commit out of the County.

If he is assaulted doing his Duty, or if the Affray be in his Presence, he may put them into the Stocks till he can get Assistance to convey them to Goal; or he may secure them, according to the Quality of the Offenders, till he can bring them before a Justice or to Prison, but not in his own House. *Dalt.* 38. *Lamb.* 133.

If he is hurt in the Affray, he may have an Action of Trespass.

If there is threatning to kill, to beat, or hurt, tho' this is no Affray, yet he may apprehend the Persons, and carry them before a Justice: But where an Affray is over, he cannot apprehend any one without a Warrant from a Justice, unless some Person is dangerously wounded.

If he neglect his Duty in not endeavouring to suppress and Affray, *&c.* tis presentable at Sessions, and he ought to be fined. *H. P. C.* 135

(2) *What may be done by the Justice.*

If the Affray is in his Presence, he may commit till they find Sureties.

If any Person is dangerously hurt, he may within a Year and a Day after the Hurting commit; and tis not Discretion to bail the Offender, tho' he may do it by the Law.

He may, *ex officio*, require those who strike or threaten in his Presence, to find Sureties for their Good Behaviour.

(3) *What may be done by a private Person.*

Any Man may stay the Affrayers, who are about to assemble to break the Peace, till the Heat is over, and deliver them to the Constable.

Likewise any Man may apprehend an Offender who hath dangerouslly wounded another, and carry him before a Justice, or to Gaol. *H. P. C.* 135. *Dalt.* 35.

Apprentices.

THe Children of such Parents who are not able to maintain them, may be put on Apprentices; and the Parents refusing to suffer them, may be bound over to the Sessions. *Dalt.* 107.

But this must be by the Assent of two Justices; and the Overseers of the Poor, or the

the greater Part of them, are to place out such Children, and the Law hath made them Judges of the Disability of the Parents: And one Justice may compel any Person meet to be bound. *Dalt.* 103

There is no necessity of giving Money with them; 'tis Discretionary in the Church-wardens whether they will give any or not. *Dalt.* 105.

Every Man of good Estate or Ability may be compelled to take Apprentices, of every Man who by his Profession or Manner of living must keep such Servants; for the power given to Church-wardens to place them out, doth necessarily imply, that such who are fit to be Masters must take them.

Poor Children when bound must be above Seven, and under Fifteen; for if above that Age they cannot be compelled: But they must work, or go to Service, or be sent to the House of Correction, or bound over to the Sessions, or to the Good behaviour. 7 *Jac. c.* 3.

The Man Child shall be bound till he comes to the Age of Twenty-four Years.

Above the Age of Ten Years, any Person may be bound by his own Agreement by Indenture. *&c.* and if above Twelve he may be compelled by a Justice. 5 *Eliz. Cap.* 4.

If an Apprentice do not his duty, the Master may complain to one Justice, who may reconcile them. if he can; and if the Fault shall by him be judged in the Apprentice, then the said Justice may send him to the House of Correction.

'Tis true, there is no express Authority given to the Justice to send a disorderly Apprentice thither; but it seems to be warranted upon the Preamble of the Statute 7 *Jac. cap.* 4. made for erecting such Houses to punish idle and disorderly Persons: But the safest way is to bind him over to the Sessions, and from thence he may be sent to the House of Correction.

Neither have the Justices any express Power to discharge an Apprentice, if the Fault is in him, as they have if the Fault is in the Master; but it hath been held, and so is the Law now, that the Cause in the Act, which gives the Justice, in their Sessions Power to inflict a Corporal Punishment on a bad Apprentice, is rather an Enlargement than a Restraint of their Authority. for they cannot punish a bad Master, but may discharge the Apprentice; but they may either punish or discharge a bad Apprentice, as they shall think fit.

If the Fault be fouud in the Master, then the Justice may bind him over to the Sessions, and four Justices there may discharge the Apprentice, which Discharge is to be enrolled by the Clerk of the Peace.

But the Master and Apprentice may agree to leave each other; and in such Case the Master may give Leave under his Hand to depart, and then one Justice out of Sessions may discharge him, by allowing the Cause of putting him away. 5 *Eliz. cap.* 4.

But because he cannot be made an Apprentice without a Writing, therefore he cannot be discharged but by a Writing under the Hand of his Master.

It shall be a Cause of Departure on the Masters side.

Not allowing Meat, Drink or Wages agreed on; this is a good Cause to be allowed by

On the Apprentices Side, Any departing from his Service whatsoever, refusing to do any reasonable Sevice, is a Departure in Law; but as to that Part of the Act which says, an Apprentice departing without a Testimonial, shall be whipped as a Vagabond; it must be an Apprentice in Husbandry, and one of full Age, for otherwise an Infant, who is the Son of a Gentleman, may be punish'd as a Rogue. *Winch.* 25.

If an Apprentice steal any Thing from his Master above the Value of 12 *d. not deliver'd to him to keep* upon due Proof thereof made before one Justice, he may commit him to Gaol, together with those who perswaded him to commit the Felony, and those who received the Goods, knowing them to be stole; but if under that Value, then they may be all sent to the House of Correction by one Justice; but according to Mr. *Dalton* rather by the Sessions.

An Indenture for putting out an Apprentice by the Parish.

T*His Indenture made the* —— *Day of* —— *in the* —— *Year of the Reign of our Sovereign Lord* GEORGE *by the Grace of God of* Great Britain, France *and* Ireland *King, Defender of the Faith*, &c. Annoq; Domini 1718. Witnesseth, *That* A. B. and C. D. *Church Wardens of the Parish of*, &c. *And* E. F. *and* G. H. *Overseers of the Poor of the said Parish, by and with the Consent of His Majesty's Justices of the Peace of the said County, whose names are hereunto subscribed; Have put and placed, and by these Presents do put and place* J. K. *a poor Child of the said Parish, Apprentice to* L. M. *of the same, Baker, with him to dwell and to serve from the Day of the Date of these Presents, until the said Apprentice shall accomplish his full Age of* 24 *Years, according to the Statute in that Case made and Provided: During all which Term the said Apprentice his said Master faithfully shall serve in all lawful Businesses, according to his Power, Wit and Ability; honestly, orderly and obediently, in all things demean and behave himself towards his said Master, and all his during the said Term. And the said* L. M. *doth for himself, his Executors and Administrators, covenant and grant, to and with the said Church-Wardens and Overseers, and every of them, their and every of their Executors and Administrators, and their and every of their Successors for the time being, by these Presents, That the said* L. M. *the said Apprentice, in the Art and Mystery of a Baker, which he now useth, shall and will teach and instruct, or cause to be taught and instructed, in the best Way and Manner that he can: And shall and will, during all the Term aforesaid, find, provide and allow unto the said Apprentice, competent and sufficient Meat, Drink and Apparel, Lodging, Washing and all other Things necessary, and fit for an Apprentice. And also shall and will provide for the said Apprentice, that he be not any way a Charge to the Parish, or Parishioners of the same; but of and from all Charge, shall and will save the said Parish and Parishioners harmless, and indemnified during the said Term: And at the End thereof, shall and will make, provide, allow and deliver unto the said Apprentice double Apparel of all Sorts, good and new; (that is to say) A good new Suit for the Holy-days, and another for the Working-days.* In witness whereof, *the Parties abovesaid to these present Indentures, interchangeably have put their Hands and Seals the Day and Year first above-writen.*

Sealed and Delivered in
the Presence of

C *We*

We whose Names are subscribed, Justices of the Peace of the County aforesaid (Quorum unus) *do, as much as in us lies, consent to the putting forth the abovesaid* J. K. *Apprentice, according to the Intent and Meaning of the abovesaid Indenture.*

A Warrant to put out poor Children Apprentices.

To the Church-Wardens, and Overseers of the Poor of the Parish of *A.* in the said County and to every of them.

THESE are in His Majesty's Name to command you, That on *Tuesday* the Third Day of *June* next, at Nine of the Clock in the Forenoon of the same Day, you bring unto us in Writing at the House of *A. B.* in, *&c.* the Names of all such poor Children of your Parish, whose Parents you shall not think able to maintain them, and the several Ages of such Children: which said Children, or such you shall think fit to be put forth Apprentices, you are to bring before us at the Time and Place aforesaid: And likewise that you do then and there present unto us in Writing, the Names of such Inhabitants of your Parish, especially such who have not already taken such poor Children Apprentices, to whom you shall think fit such Children may be placed: and that you give them Notice, that they are then required to appear before us to shew Cause why such Children may not be bound to them, and that you be then and there also present, and bring this Precept with you. *Hereof* fail not. *Given*, &c.

A Warrant against a Master for abusing his Apprentice.

To the Constable, &c.

WHEREAS Complaint upon Oath hath been made unto me, by *A. B.* Apprentice to *C. D.* of the Parish of *E.* in the said County, Baker, That the said *C. D.* doth not allow unto his said Apprentice sufficient Meat, Drink and Apparel; but hath often corrected him immoderately without any just Cause: *These are therefore* to require you to bring both the said Master and his Apprentice before me, or some other of His Majesty's Justices of the Peace for the said County, to be examined touching the Premisses; and further, That such Order and Direction may be taken between them as to Justice doth appertain. *Given* under my Hand and Seal, *&c.*

A Warrant against a disorderly Apprentice.

To the Constable, &c.

WHEREAS Complaint upon Oath hath been made unto me by *A. C.* Joyner, That *C. D.* now being an Apprentice unto him, is a stubborn and disorderly Servant

Servant, and doth very much misbehave himself towards his said Master: *These are therefore* to command you to bring both the said Master and his Apprentice, before me, or some other Justice of the Peace for the said County, to be examined concerning the Premisses; and farther, That such Order and Direction may be taken between them, as to Justice doth appertain. *Given* under my Hand and Seal, *&c.*

A Warrant against an Apprentice for Departing from his Master.

To the Constable, &c.

WHEREAS Complaint upon Oath hath been made unto me by *A. B.* of, *&c.* That *C. D.* his Apprentice hath lately departed from him contrary to Law: *These are therefore* in His Majesty's Name, to command you to take and bring the said *C. D.* before me, or some other of His Majesty's Justice of the Peace for this County, to answer the Premisses. *Given*, &c.

The Justice may grant this Warrant upon Complaint of the Master, and he may reconcile the Matter: But I do not see how he can punish an Apprentice by Indenture; the Sessions may.

And Action on the Case lies against him who receives an Apprentice by Indenture; and an Action of Covenant against the Apprentice himself.

The Discharge of an Apprentice.

WHEREAS *R. K. H. D. E. F.* and *G. H.* four of His Majesty's Justices of the Peace (whereof one is of the *Quorum*) for the County aforesaid, having heard and examined the Matter in Difference between *A. B.* an Apprentice to *C. D.* of *&c.* And it appearing to us upon Oath that the said *C. D.* hath not allowed his said Apprentice sufficient Meat, *&c.* and hath several times beaten him very immoderately without any just Occasion. We do therefore for the Cause aforesaid discharge the said *A. B.* from his said Apprenticeship; and do hereby under our respective Hands and Seals pronounce and declare, That the said *A. B.* is discharged from being any longer an Apprentice to his said Master. Witness our Hands and Seals, *&c.*

This Discharge should be enrolled by the Clerk of the Peace or Town-Clerk, which shall be good against the Master, his Executors and Administrators.

A Warrant For Servants Wages.

To all Constables, &c.

WHEREAS Complaint upon Oath hath been made unto me by *A. B.* late Servant of *C. D.* of *&c.* That he the said *A. B.* being lawfully hired by his said Master, and did ſerve him for the Space of &c. and that the ſaid C. D. doth now refuſe to pay the Wages which are juſtly due to his ſaid Servant for the Time he hath ſerved him *Theſe are therefore* to require you to bring the ſaid C. D. before me, or ſome other of His Majeſty's Juſtices of the Peace for the ſaid County, to anſwer the Premiſſes; and that you give Notice to the ſaid A. B. to be then and there preſent to make good his Complinat. *Given* under my Hand and Seal, &c.

By a late Act *Anno* 12 Annæ *Riginæ*, any Servant that purloins, embezels or makes away his Maſter's goods, &c. to the Value of 40 *s*. it is made Felony without *Benefit* of Clery. *Vide Felonies.*

Every Houſe-keeper in any City or Town Coporate, of the Age of 24 Years, and uſing Art or Myſtery there, may take an Apprentice, whoſe Terms ought not to expire till he is 24 Years old.

Artificers in Market-Towns not Corporate, and who are Houſholders, and of the Age of 24 Years, may take other Artificers Children Apprentice.

Arreſt by Juſtices Warrant.

ALL Perſons under the Degree of a Baron may be arreſted by a Warrant from a Juſtice of Peace, for any Miſdemeanor, or any thing done againſt the Peace. *Dalt.* 406.

A Peer may be arreſted by a Writ out of *B. R.* for a Contempt or Breach of the Peace.

A Clergy man, but not in Divine Service.

A *Feme Covert* for a Riot.

An Infant, if he cannot find Sureties for the Peace but not for the Breach of any Statute, unleſs he is therein charged.

'Tis no Arreſt for a Conſtable having a Warrant to command the Party to appear before a Juſtice of Peace, but he muſt lay hold on his Perſon. *Dalt.* 405.

Where an Affray is made, and the Offenders fly into another County, the Conſtable may purſue them.

He may break open a Door to take an Offender; but then ſome Felony muſt be committed. *H. P. C.* 93.

Seſſions may award a *Capias* againſt a Perſon Indicted, and by Virtue thereof the Officer may break open Doors.

Commitment by a Juſtice, muſt be to the Common Goal, by *Mitimus* under his Hand and Seal, containing the Cauſe; and it ought to conclude, *viz.* There to remain till he be delivered by due courſe of Law; otherwiſe 'tis void. *H. P. C.* 94.

A

A Sworn Officer need not ſhow his Warrant.

In all Criminal Caſes where any one is in Danger of Life or Member, any private Man may Arreſt another without Preſentment, Proceſs or Warrant; ſo likewiſe where a Felony is committed, every Perſon preſent muſt endeavour to take the Offender, or may be fined and committed; and in ſuch Caſe any ſuſpected Perſon, tho' upon common Fame only, may be taken; and if he make Reſiſtance, you may juſtify the Beating of him.

All theſe may be arreſted by any private Perſon; but then they muſt be brought to the Conſtable, and if he is not to be found, then to the Juſtice in order to their Committment. *Dalt.* 408.

A Juſtice of Peace may, at his Diſcretion, grant a Warrant to take ſuch whom he ſhall ſuſpect to be inclined to break the Peace. *Dalt.* 409.

So upon his own View he may commit thoſe who offend againſt Penal Laws.

Herein any Perſon aiding him, may break open a Houſe to apprehend a Felon, having a lawful Warrant; ſo likewiſe to apprehend one who hath dangerouſly wounded another; ſo where an Affray is in a Houſe, and the Door ſhut, the Conſtable may break it open; ſo upon a forcible Entry or Detainer, either upon View of Juſtices or upon an Inquiſition taken before them; ſo may the Sheriff upon an Outlawry in a perſonal Action; ſo he may upon a Warrant for the Peace or Good Behaviour, and generally in all Caſes where the King is Party. *Dalt.* 254 *Moor.* 606.

But he ought firſt to acquaint the Perſon of the Cauſe, and to deſire the Doors may be opened.

If Complaint be made to a Conſtable of a Felony done, or Blow given, tho' the wounded Perſon is not dead, if an Aſſault be made on himſelf, or where there is any Breach of the Peace done in his View he may put the Offenders in the Stocks, or ſecure them in his own Houſe till he can bring them before a Juſtice. *H. P. C.* 92.

When brought before a Juſtice, if he hath Power by any Statute to bind him over or to cauſe him to do any Thing, and he refuſes, he may commit him till he is conformable.

If he fly into another County, and is taken there, he ſhall be committed to Goal not where the Felony was done, but where taken.

Conſtable may put him in the Stocks for a reaſonable Time till he can get Help to convey him to Goal.

Goaler may make his own houſe a Goal; but a Juſtice muſt not ſend him theither, but to a Common Goal, and the Goaler cannot make his own Houſe a Goal above a Day and a Night.

At Common Law, the Goaler could not put Irons upon a Priſoner; but by the Statute of *W.* 2. *Cap.* 11. 'tis enacted, That *Carceri mancipetur in ferris.*

By a late Statute, the Priſoner muſt not be carried to a Victualling-houſe without his Conſent, ſo as to charge him with any Sum of Money for Meat or Drink, nor more taken for the Arreſt than by Law required, nor any Reward expected for keeping him out of Goal till he can find Bail or agree, nor more taken for a Nights Lodging, or other Expences, than what ſhall be allowed by the next Juſtice or Seſſions.

This

This must be at his own Expence, (if able) otherwise at the Charge of the Town where taken, who may be distrained if they refuse.

If the Prisoner refuse to be at the Charge, the Justice may direct a Warrant to the High Constable; or Petty Constable to the Town where he hath any Goods, to sell as much as will satisfie the Charges.

If the Gaoler will not receive him, the Constable must bring him to the Town where taken, who must keep him till next Assizes, and there the Gaolor shall be punish'd. *Dalt.* 413.

Where Imprisonment is directed by any *Statute*, and no Time limited when the Offender shall be committed, it must be presently; so where 'tis not limited, how long he shall continue in Custody, there 'tis in the Discretion of the Court.

He must be kept *in salva & arcta Custodia*, and if the Gaoler himself suffer him to go a broad at any Time, though he return to the Prison, 'tis an Escape, and the Gaoler may be fined; for Imprisonment is a Punishment of the Offender, as well as the keeping of him to answer his Fault.

Assault.

ASSault is derived from the old *Latin* Word *Assultus*; which signifies a *Leaping on another*, so that *ex vi termini* it cannot be perf rm'd without the Offering some Hurt to the *Person*, as by striking, *&c.* And Battery is the wrongful beating another

1. *Where Men have a natural Power over others it is Justifiable.*.

As Parents have over their Children till they come of Age, for till then they may chastise them for Offences without Breach of the Peace.

2. *It is also justifiable Where Men have a Civil Power over others.*

As the Master hath over his Servant, the School-Master over his Scholars, a Gaoler over his Prisoners, and any Man over his Kinsman who is mad; or who, being at Liberty attempteth to do any Mischief.

He may strike another to defend his Person from being wounded or beaten.

If a Soldier hurt another by Misfortune or Negligence, and not wilfully; so if two agree to play at any Game, and one is hurt, 'tis no Breach of the Peace, becanse it was by Consent.

I may justifie the beating of another, who would do Mischief to Wife, Father or Mother; for I am bound by Law to protect the one, and I owe Obedience to the others.

So may the Wife justifie the beating one who would beat or assault her Husband; so may the Father or Mother any Person who would beat their Children.

A Servant may likewise justifie the beating another, in Defence of his Master, (*& e converso*) conversò) but not of his Master's Father or Mother, &c. because he owes no obedience to them.

So where the Life of any one is in Danger by beating, or otherwise, any Person may endeavour to resist, and that by beating him who offereth the Violence. *Dalt.* 206.

So if any one would by Force wrongfully take away my Goods, whether I have a Property in them, or a bare Possession only, 'tis justifiable to resist; but the Offender must not be wounded; and if killed, 'tis Felony.

So 'tis if another endeavour to put me out of Possession of Land, or to turn a High-way, or to direct a Watter-Course, &c.

I shall conclude this Title with a remarkable Case, which was thus: One courted the Sister of Mr. *G.* a Barrister of *Grays-Inn*, and a Justice of Peace for S. and he not consenting to the Match, was sent for to an Ale-house by Mr. *M.* and one *T.* When he came thither *T.* went out of the Room to prevent any Person from assisting Mr. *G.* whom *M.* beat so much, that he broke his Arm: And for this Battery, he and *T.* were Indicted and found guilty; and *M.* was fined 1000 *l.* and *T.* 500 *l.* and both committed for a Month without Bail, and to find Sureties for their Good Behaviour for Seven Years.

Attaint, See *Jury*.

Attainder and Conviction.

THese Words are used promiscuously, and sometimes one is signified by the other as by the Stat. of 3 *H.* 7 *cap.* 1. 'tis enacted, That if any Man be acquitted of Murder upon an Indictment, or *attainted*, an Appeal may be brought if the benefit of Clergy is not had; here the Word *Attainted* must signifie *Convicted*, because after Attainder 'tis late to have the Benefit of Clergy.

But in Propriety of Speech, a Man is said to be Attainted, when after Conviction Judgment is passed by the Court; and he is said to be convicted when he confesseth the Fault, or is found guilty by a Jury, and before Judgement given.

Yet a Man may be attainted upon an Outlawry, and convicted in many Cases by his own Confession, and without a Verdict; as generally upon Penal Laws, *viz.* a Recusant indicted at Sessions, and Proclamation made for him to surrender himself to the Sheriff if he neglects to appear at the next Sessions, the Record of his Default is a Conviction and so in many other Cases.

The Punishment of a Person attainted, viz.

Loss of Life, Corruption of Blood, Forfeiture of Fee simple Estate from the Time of the Offence, so that the King shall have *Ann. diem & vastum* therein, and then it goes to the Lord of the Fee by Escheat, but the Lord may Compound with the King and have it presently.

Forfeiture

Forfeiture of Goods from the time of the Attainder only.

Before Conviction he may sell his Goods for his Maintenance in Prison. *Dalt.* 363

Before Conviction, if he is attainted of Felony and pardoned, tho' he cannot be indicted for any Felony committed before the Attainder, yet an Appeal of Robbery lies against him for a Robbery committed before, because the Party may have Restitution upon an Apeal.

'Tis true, he may be Indicted for a Treason done before the Attainder of Felony, because 'tis not only an Offence of a higher Nature, but the King upon the Conviction will be entitled to the Forfeiture of his Lands; however, if such Land was first vested in the Lord by the Attainder in Felony, it shall not be divested by any Conviction for a Treason committed before such Attainder, so as to give the King a Title.

If the Husband makes a Feoffment in Fee, then commits Treason, is Pardoned, and dies, his Widdow shall not have Dower against the Feoffee, because she is barred by the Attainder, so long as it Remains unreversed. *Leon.* 3

After Attainder, a Grant of Goods or Lands shall bind all Persons but the King and the Lord of the Fee.

After Attainder, his Body is his own till Execution, and if he is killed before that Time, his Wife may have an Appeal.

After Attainder, he may be taken in Execution at the Suit of any Subject for Debt, but may be Executed notwithstanding he may purchase Lands in Fee.

At Common Law, if a Felon was found guilty before the Coroner, or that he did fly, the Sheriff or Coroner might seize his Goods before Trial for the Use of the King, which ought to be appraised and left in the Custody of the Neighbours where the Offender lived.

The Law was the same if he did not fly, but was indicted; but then after the Appraisement, they ought not to be removed out of his House before Attainder, if the Offender could give Security that they should not be imbezel'd; if not, then they were to be deliver'd to the Neighbours, who ought to keep them duriug his Imprisoment, and he was to have reasonable Maintenance out of them till Conviction. *Dalt.* 362.

By the Statute of 1 *R.* 3. *cap.* 3. The Common Law is in this Particular confirmed, and the Party imprisoned shall recover double the Value of his Goods seized by any Officer, or taken out of his House before Conviction. *Dalt.* 363.

After Conviction, or *fugam fecit* returned by the Coroner, all the Goods, the Corn growing, the Profits of the Fee-simple Estate for a Year and a Day, and the Issues of intealed Lands during Life, and all Debts due upon any Securities, are forfeited to the King, and the Party to whom the King shall give the same, may bring an Action in his own Name to recover them.

If 'tis erroneous, the Party may appear at any Time, and reverse it by writ of Error.

At Common Law, it was an Error in Fact for the Party outlawed to be beyond Sea at the Time of the Judgment pronounced upon the Exigent; for which, the Outlawry might be reversed in all Cases.

The Advantage of this Error is taken away in Treason, by the Statute of 6 *Ed.* 6. but not wholly; for there is a Proviso, That if the Person shall yied himself to the Chief Justice

Justice within a Year and a Day after the Outlawry pronounced, he shall be admitted to traverse the Indictment.

Sir *John Hawles* tells us, That no Judgment was ever yet given upon Construction of this Statute before that of Sir *Thomas Armstrong*, in the late Reign, because a Trial was never before that Time denied to a Person outlawed, if he came within the Time limited.

'Tis true, Sir *Thomas Armstrong* did not yield himself, but was taken in *Holland*, but still within the Year; so that it seemed a great Hardship to deny him a Trial upon the Nicety of a Word.

Bail

AT Common Law, Bail was allowed for any Offences except Murder; but now by the Stat. *W.* 1. *cap.* 15. 'tis directed Where it shall be taken, and where not, which seems to be a Rule to this Day, because the Statute 1 & 2 *Phil. & Mar. cap.* 13. which gives Justices of Peace Power to bail, hath relation to this very Statute. 2 *Inst.* 190.

These Writs were directed to the Sheriff, under whose Custody the Person was detained; and he was usually replevied, that is, Pledges were taken for him in the County-Court in all Causes, except for the Death of a Man, and except a Person committed by the personal Command of the King, tho' the Commitment should be unlawful; a Person committed by the Judge for any Causes proper to his Judicature, or for the Forest, in these Causes the Sheriff was not to intermeddle in his Court, but the proper Remedy was by a *Habeas Corpus*, and Justice was done to the Party in the Great Courts at *Westminster*,

Now the Reason why Bail was taken in all other Causes, was, because *Stabat indifferenter* upon a bare Accusation, whether the Party was guilty or not; and therefore by that Statute a Person outlawed was not to be bailed, because he is attained in Law; but if upon the *Capias Utlegatum* he pleads a *Misnosmer*, or alledge any Error in the Proceedings, he might be bail'd.

A Person abjuring, is attainted by his own Confession; Approvers confess the Felony to be actually done by themselves; a Person taken with the Thing stolen; In all these Causes, *non Stat' indifferenter*, nor for breaking a Prison, for it may be presum'd that an innocent Man will not do it. Notorious Felons; he that is accused by an Approver; one who sets an House on Fire, Counterfeiting Money, both which were Offences at Common Law; and so was Counterfeiting the Great Seal, One guilty of an open and manifest Offence, and for Treason. All these were exempted from bail by this Statute, but might be bailed in *B. R.*

Likewise, if a dangerous Blow is given, the Person may be bailed till the other is dead. Bail refused, where the Person is bailable by Law, is a Misdemeanour, and finable. *H. P. C.* 97. *Styles* 182.

Bail is allowed to Accessaries to Felony, before and after the Offence, until the Principal is convict. *Dalt.* 281.

Bail is allowed to Persons Aiding Felons, suspected to be done, and not if it be actually done; but it must be by two Justices, *Quorum unus*, and they must be both present when they Bail him, and they must take the Examination in Writing, which, together with the Recognizance entred into by the Witnesses to prosecute, must be certified at next Assizes, attainted thereof by Outlawry: If he bring a Writ of Error, B. R. may bail him. *H. P. C.* 101.

Bail is allowed in Larceny to Persons indicted thereof before the Sheriff, under the Value of 12 *d.*

In Mans slaughter, bail is allowed by the Statute, 1 & 2 *Phil. & Mar. cap.* 13. by two Justices, *Quorum unus*, who must be present when they take the Bail, and it must be after Examination; but Manslaughter is not bailable if the Fact is confessed, or 'tis certainly known that he killed the Person, for it must stand *indifferenter* if Bail is allowed and therefore if it be found Manslaughter upon the Coroner's Inquest, tho' no Indictment is preferr'd, *King's-bench* would not bail, for the Statute saith, That Bail shall be allowed in Manslaughter where the Party is bailable by Law; which implies, that 'tis not to be allowed in all Cases. 1 *Roll. Rep.* 258. *Poin's* Case.

But of late some Doubts have been made, Whether a Man can be lawfully bailed for Manslaughter? Tho' my Lord *Heals* tells us, if it be a *Non liquit*, whether the Party accused did the Fact, two Justices may bail him.

In Sessions Process. Commitment thereon, upon an Indictment against any Penal Statute, by which Bail is not prohibited, may be bailed by two Justices, *Quorum unus.*

In Sessions Process. Against the Party to appear upon an Indictment for a Trespass, one Justice may bail. *Dalt.* 382.

In Trespasses, Where Life or Limb is not in Danger after an Indictment and Process thereon, the Party may be bailed by two Justices, *Quorum unus. H. P. C.* 100.

Bail taken away by Statutes, viz

Accessaries. In Treason. *per Stat. W.* 1 *cap.* 15.

Abjuring The Realm because they are guilty by their own Confession. *W.* 1.

Accountants. Found in Arrears before Auditors, till Satisfaction made.

Ale-house-keepers, Without Licence, the second Offence being Commitment to the House of Correction for a Month, suffering Tippling contrary to 1. *Jac cap.* 9.

Appeals. Of Death not bailable. *H. P. C.* 103.

Approver, These are Men who have committed Felony, and confess it; but this doth not concern Justices of Peace, any otherwise then to take his Confession and commit him, and send his Warrant for those accused. *W.* 1. *cap.* 15.

Armour. Persons riding armed contrary to the Statute of *Northampton*, committed by by Justices, are not bailable; concealed by a Recusant convict, or disturbing the Delivery of it, one Justice may commit for three Months without Bail.

Breakers Of Prisons, *W.* 1. *cap.* 5.

Surveyors and Collectors of Money for repairing Bridges, refusing to account. 22 *H.* 8. *cap.* 5.

Burning Houses, *W.* 1. *cap.* 15.

Coyning False Money, *W.* 1. *cap.* 15.

Commission Of Rebellion out of *Chancery*; Person taken thereon. *Dalt.* 382.

Counterfeiting Great Seal, *&c.* *W.* 1. *cap.* 15.

Felons, Notorious, *viz.* Those who are taken with stolen Goods. *Will.* 1. *cap.* 15.

Those who are taken freshly by Hue-and-Cry. *H. P. C.* 101.

Felony Actually done, tho' it doth not appear that the Accused is guilty. *H. P. C.* 98. Attained or convicted thereof by Confession or Indictment. Acquitted within a Year. Not to be bailed but at Discretion. That an Appeal may be had against him, 3 H. 7. *cap.* 1 *H. P. C.* 103. *W.* 1. *cap.* 15.

Forgers Of Deeds, Wills, or Writings sealed, or Court-Rolls, and those who assent to it; those who publish it knowingly, *viz.* Imprisonment after Conviction for Life, where any Man's Estate of Inheritance might have been defeated.

Fraudulent Conveyances. The Parties who put them in Suit. Those who assign Lands or Goods so to them convey'd knowing thereof Commitment for half a Year after Conviction.

Gaming, Those who keep such Houses.

Those who play at unlawful Games; Commitment, till they find Sureties not to offend again.

Inn-keepers. Who shall not sell Hay, Oats, Beans, Provender, or other Victuals for Man or Beast, for reasonable Gain; convicted the second Time; Commitment for one Month, 21 *Jac. cap.* 21.

Labourers, Going from Work before finished; Commitment for a month.

In Man-slaughter, After the Confession of the Offender, 2 *Inst.* 187 *Sedefendendo*, not bailable by Justices of Peace, but *B. R.* may bail him. *H. P. C.* 99. 161.

In Murder 'tis *Corpus pro Corpore.* Not bailable at Common Law, yet it hath been allowed by *B. R.* and adjudged, That the Sature of *W.* 1. *cap.* 15. should receive a favourable Construction, according to the Discretion of the Judges, and as the Circumstances of the Case require. *Latch.* 12.

And therefore one *Andrews* being outlaw'd for Murder, did 14 Years afterwards bring a Writ of Error, and was bailed. *Stiles* 94.

So Two were committed upon Suspicion of Murder, and when those who actually had done it, confessed at their Execution, the others who were imprison'd were bailed. *Stiles.* 98.

Acquitted thereof upon an Indictment, not to be bailed till after a Year and a Day, that the Party may bring his Appeal. 3 *H.* 7. *cap.* 1.

Perjury, In any Court of Record, or Court Baron Commitment for 6 Months.

Poor, Things relating to them, as refusing to pay Rates for them, and no Distress to be taken: Commitment till paid, and Charges.

Overseers refusing to make their Account, or to pay over to new Overseers what remains in their Hands; Commitment till perform'd.

Negligent in their Office, forfeits 20 *s.* and having no Distress to be taken, Commitment till Forfeiture paid.

Parents refusing to relieve Children, as the Justice shall assess in Sessions, Forfeiture 20 *s. per* Month; and having no Distress to be taken, Commitment till paid.

Rogues. Incorrigible, being committed, must continue in Custody till next Sessions.

At Common Law, the Sheriff or Constable might have bailed one suspected of Felony; but now that Power is given to Justices of Peace by particular Statutes, *viz.* by 1 *R.* 2. *cap.* 3. 3 *H.* 7. *cap.* 3. 1 *&* 2 *Phil. & Mar. cap.* 13.

The Sureties and Sum are left to the Discretion of the Justices, where no Sum certain is appointed by Law: But if the Crime be Suspicion of Felony, they must take very sufficient Persons for the Appearance of the Party, and bind them in a good Sum.

And if the Justices, at any Time before Appearance, shall think the Sureties taken not sufficient, they may compel the Party to give better, or commit him.

The Sureties likewise may bring the Offender before the Justices of Peace, and desire to be discharged upon his Commitment, if they are of Opinion that he will run away.

The Justices may examine the Statutes upon Oath. *Dalt.* 375.

And if they bail any Person who is not bailable by Law, they ought to be fined. See *Stat. W.* 1. *cap.* 15.

A Condition of a Recognizance to prefer a Bill and give Evidence.

THe Condition of this Recognizance is such, *That if the within bound* A. B. *do personally appear before his Majesties Justices of Gaol-Delivery, at the next General Gaol-Delivery to be holden for the within County of* Kent, *and do then and there prefer a Bill, or cause to be prefered a Bill of Indictment against* W. T. *for the matters wherewith the said* W. T. *is charged before* [The Justices within named, or the within named Justices] *and do also then and there give such Evidence as he knoweth concerning the same, as well to the Jurors that shall enquire thereof on the behalf of our Sovereign Lord the King as also to the Jurors that shall pass upon the Tryal of the said* W. T. *for the same; That then this Recognizance shall be void, or else it shall stand in full Force.*

If at the Sessions, say;

Do personally appear before his Majesties Justices assigned to keep the Peace in the within named County of Kent, *at the next General Sessions of the Peace to be holden for the said County, at* M. *in the County aforesaid; and do then and there prefer,* &c. *as* in the foregoing Condition.

A

A Condition to give Evidence.

THe Condition of this *Recognizance* is such, *That if the within bound* A. B. *do personally appear before His Majesties Justices of Gaol-delivery, at the next General Gaol-delivery to be holden for the within named County of* Kent, *and do then and there give such Evidence as he knoweth against* J. K. *concerning the Matters wherewith he is charged, as well to the Jurors who shall enquire thereof on the behalf of our Sovereign Lord the King, as also to the Jurors that shall pass upon the Tryal of the said* J. K. *for the same, That then this Recognizance shall be void, or else it shall stand in full force.*

If it be to appear at the Sessions, say;

Do personally appear before His Majesty's Justices assigned to keep the Peace in the within named County of K *at the next General Sessions of the Peace to be holden for the County at* T. *in the County aforesaid, and do then and there give such Evidence,* &c. as aforesaid.

A Condition for Felony or suspicion of Felony.

THe Condition *of this Recognizance is such, That if the within bound* A. B. *do personally appear before His Majesties Justices of Goal-Delivery, at the next General Gaol delievery to be holden for the within named County of* Kent, *then and there to answer our Sovereign Lord the King, for and concerning the* Felonious taking and stealing of *&c. wherewith he standeth charged before,* &c. *and to do and receive,* &c. *and do not depart the said Court without* Licence *for the same: That then this Recognizance to be void; or else it shall stand in full force.*

2. If it be to appear at the Sessions, say;

Do personally appear before His Majesty's Justices assigned to keep the Peace in the within named County of K. *at the next General Sessions of the Peace, to be holden for the said County at* T. *in the County aforesaid, then and there to answer,* &c. as before.

3. If the Felon be in Prison, say;

THese are *to charge and require you, That immediately you bring before me the Body of* A. B. *now in your Custody, to be bailed, as Law requireth.* Whereof *fail not.* Given *under* &c.

To acknowledge a Recognizance or Bail in the Name of a Person not consenting thereto, Felony, 21 *Jac.* 1. *cap.* 16. *Cro. Eliz.* 531. 4 & 5 *W.* & *M. cap.* 4.

Bastards

Bastards.

Bastardy is an Offence punishable as well in the Spiritual Courts, as at the Common Law.

By the Common Law, if the Husband be within four seas, that is within the Jurisdiction of the King of *England*, if the Wife hath Issue, no Proof is to be admitted to prove the Child a Bastard, (for in that Case *filiatio non probat' probari*) unless the Husband hath an apparent Improbability of a Creation; as if the Husband be but eight Years old, or under the Age of Procreation, such Issue is Bastard, albeit he be born within Marrage. Coke Lit. 244. 373. 1 *H.* 6. 3. 7. *H.* 4. 9.

So if the Husband be gelt.

An Infant born nine Months and Days after the Death of its Father, no Bastard.

If the two next Justices make not Provision for Bastard, the Sessions must settle it, as two Justices ought to have done. Roll. l. 1. 358. Noy. 142. Jones 330.

Maintenance of Bastards by Mother and reputed Father, is by these modern Laws of 18 *Eliz. cap.* 3. and 7 *Jac. cap.* 6. the former Laws were only for punishment. Jenkins 47. pl. 90.

A Woman was not questioned for having her first Bastard, on the 18 *Eliz. cap.* 3. Then she had another. She cannot be proceeded against by 7 *Jac.* (as for a second Offence) c. 4. 2. *Bulstr.* 248.

Neither Sessions nor Assizes can meddle touching Bastardy, but upon Appeal; (otherwise the two Justices must order.)

If two Justices make an Order, if Party refuse to perform, or enter into Recognizance to appear at the next Sessions, they may commit him without Bail.

If (by Practice and Design) a Child be born in a Parish, the Parish where the Practice was shall keep the Child.

Bond to pay 20 *d. per.* Week for keeping a Bastard, Defendant cannot plead that there was no Order made.

If a harlot will take the Child, whereof she is newly delivered, and cover it with Leaves, and let it lie Abroad, whereby Vermin destroy it this is Murther. 21. *Jac. c.* 27. *Cromp.* 24, *B.*

Indictment lies for conspiring to charge one with a Bastard Child, and thereby also bring him to disgrace.

An Indictment will preferred against one for Conspiring to accuse another with being the Father of a Bastard Childe.

To make an Order for a Bastard Child, there must be two Justices, whereof one to be of the *Quorum.*

An

An Order made by two Juſtices, for the Maintenance of a Baſtard Child by 12 *d. per* Week, as long as the Child ſhall continue chargeable to the Pariſh, is good.

The Juſtices of Peace's Order muſt be paid Weekly, and not Monthly.

A Baſtard Child of a Perſon able to keep it, & not like to be chargeable to the Pariſh, is not within the Statute of 18 *Eliz.*

If the Father of a Baſtard Child dies poor, the Mother muſt provide for the Baſtard if able; but if not, the Town were laſt ſetled.

Neither Seſſions nor Aſſizes can meddle touching Baſtardy, but upon Appeal.

The Seſſions cannot make an Order for keeping of a Baſtard, except upon an Appeal from the two Juſtices, which are firſt to make an Order.

If Notice ſhould not be given to the Putative Father till the Seſſions is paſt after the Order made, ſo that the Party is deprived of the Benefit of his Appeal; yet *B. R.* would not quaſh the Order, but referred it to the Juſtices in Seſſions to diſcharge or confirm it. *Stiles* 325.

This Order being a Judgment upon the Parties, is not to be reſpited without paying what is ordred, if it be a Sum in Groſs, as 'tis uſual, beſides Weekly Payments.

And none but the Juſtices have Authority to declare who is the reputed Father; but if they are unreaſonable in the Sum allowed for the Relief of the Pariſh, *B. R.* may reform it; as if they order 2 *d. per.* Week for the Maintenance of a Child.

And regularly theſe Things are required to make a good Order.

1. It muſt be made by two Juſtices, *Quorum unus.*

2. They muſt be next the Place where the Pariſh is, which is to be relieved.

3. It muſt be made at a private Meeting, and not at Seſſions.

4. It muſt be concerning a Baſtard Child, and ſo expreſſed, *and likely to be chargeable*, &c. It muſt appear how long the Father ſhall maintain it. *Stiles* 154. 1 *Vent.* 37.

5. The Place of Birth muſt be alledged, for otherwiſe the Child may be born where the Two Juſtices have have no Juriſdiction; and it muſt likewiſe appear, that it was born in the Pariſh to which Relief is ordred. *Siles* 14. 368.

6. It muſt be made purſuant to the Act, *viz.* to relieve the Pariſh in Part or in all, and for the Relieve of the Child by a Weekly Maintenance, In ſome Orders, the Word *Education* is inſerted, but that hath been excepted againſt.

7. It muſt directly affirm who is the reputed Father. *Sid.* 363.

But an Order is ill, if it doth not appear that one of the Juſtices is of the *Quorum*; if the Money is ordred to be paid *Weekly*, inſtead of *Monthly*; if 'tis ordered to be paid till the Child is 14 Years old, when it ought to be ſo long as it ſhall be chargable to the Pariſh; if the reputed Father is ordered to give ſuch Security as the Church-wardens ſhall think fit. *Syd.* 222.

So if the Order is, that one ſhall contribute half the Charges, becauſe he ſuffered a Soldier to get his Servant with Child. *Styles.* 207.

As to the Third Rule above-mentioned, the Statute of 3 *Car. cap.* 4. (by which divers Acts are continued, repealed, and ſome made perpetual) gave the Seſſions Power to examine all Things concerning Baſtardy, which the Two Juſtices had before; but what was enacted by that Law, was to continue only (in this Cause) to the next Sessions of Parliament, which being long since expired, the Two Justices have now the Original Jurisdiction again, and their Order shall bind till avoided by Appeal, 1 *Vent.* 175. 1 *Mod.* 287.

Now upon the Appeal, the Sessions must either affirm or quash the Order made by the Two Justices: They cannot make a new one; neither, after 'tis reversed, can any other Sessions make another Order, because upon such Reversal the Statute of 18 *Eliz.* is satisfied, and no other Justices can intermeddle with it; and therefore where an Order is discharged upon an Appeal, the Party who was charged is absolutely accquitted. *Vent.* 59.

An order was made, to pay such Carges as the Parish had been at; and did not say that the Child was likely to be chargeable, *&c.* yet it was held good. 1 *Vent.* 37.

'Tis true, no time is Limitted by the Statute, and therefore Exceptions have been taken to Orders to pay so much a Week for a certain Number of Years; but this Exception hath been disallowed, especially when tis also expressed in the Order for so long time as the Chid is a Charge, *&c.*

If the Child dies after the Order is made, and before the next Sessions, and no Security be given to perform the Order; then when the Party appears at Sessions, they may order him to pay the Charges, upon Proof of Serving the Order.

But if Security hath been given, then the Sessions have no further Power; but the Bond must be put in Suit, if the Condition is not performed.

The Woman's Examination before the birth of the Child.

THE *Examination of* T. W. *single Woman, taken before me* P. L. *Esq; this first Day of* July, An' Dom' 1718. *Who upon her Oath saith,* That she is a hired Servant to one *G. F.* of *&c.* at the Wages of *6 l. 10 s. per Annum* and has continued in her said Service from the second Day of *November* last: And further saith, That in the Month of *December* last, as she this Examinant was making one of her said Master's Beds in a back Room, one Mr. *J. W.* living next Door to her said Master's House, came into the said back Room to her, (no Person being present) and promising great Kindnesses to her, prevailed with her & then had the carnal Knowledge of her Body on the said Bed she was making, and has had three several Times since on the same Bed; and at one of the said Times he the said *J. W.* begot her with the Bastard-Child of which she is now pragnant, and near the Time of her Delivery. And this Examinant further deposeth, That he the said *J. W.* and no other Person whatsoever, is the only true Father of the said Bastard Child, of which she is now pragnant as aforesaid.

A Warrant againſt the Reputed Father thereon.

To all Conſtables &c.

THeſe are in His Majeſties Name to will and require you upon Sight hereof, to take and bring before me the Body of *A. B.* of whom you ſhall have Notice to anſwer ſuch Matters of Miſdemeanours as on His Majeſty's behalf ſhall be objected againſt him by the Church-wardens and Overſeers of the Poor of the Pariſh of *&c.* touching a Baſtard Child by him begotten on the Body of *C. D.* ſingle Woman, of which ſhe is now pregnant, (as ſhe hath made Oath) in Breach of his Good Behaviour, which when born is likely to become chargeable to the ſaid Pariſh; And that he find ſufficient Sureties to indempnifie the ſaid Pariſh from the ſaid Baſtard-Child when born: Hereof fail not at your Perils. Given under my Hand and Seal, *&c.*

Note, When the Perſon appeareth before the Juſtice, he muſt enter into a Recognizance with Sureties to appear at the next Seſſions, and be continued thereon until the Child is born: Or he may be bound to appear at the next Seſſions after the Child is born.

A Recognizance to appear at the next Seſſions.

THE Condition of this Recognizance is ſuch, *That whereas* the above-bounden *C. D.* is charged by *A. B.* of, *&c.* ſingle Woman, That he had carnal Knowledge of her Body ſeveral Times, and the ſaid *A. B.* is now with Child by him the ſaid *C. D.* which when born will be a Baſtard. If therefore the ſaid *C. D.* ſhall perſonally appear before his Majeſty's Juſtices of the Peace at their next Quarter-Seſſions of the Peace to be holden for the ſaid County at *M.* then and there to receive and abide what ſhall be enjoined by the ſaid Court concerning the Premiſes; and in the mean Time to be of the Good Behaviour, That then, *&c.*

Another Recognizance to appear at the Seſſions next after the Birth.

A. B. of, *&c.*——40 *l.*

THE *Condition*, &c. That *A. B.* ſhall perſonally appear at the next Seſſions of the Peace to be holden for the ſaid County after *S. R.* ſingle Woman ſhall be delivered of the Baſtard-Child of which ſhe is now pregnant, and upon her Oath charges the ſaid *A. B.* to be the Father, Which when born is likely to become chargeable to the Pariſh of, *&c.* as the Church-wardens and Overſeers of the Poor thereof have complained; And in the mean Time to be of his Good Behaviour: That then, *&c.*

A Supersedeas in Bastardy.

WHEREAS *M. K*, of, *&c.* hath before me found sufficient Sureties for his Good Behaviour and personal Appearance at the next Sessions of the Peace to be holden for the said County, after *M. H.* single Woman, shall be delivered of the Bastard-Child (or Children) of which she is now pregnant, and upon her Oath charges the said *M. K.* to be the Father, which, when born, is likely to become chargeable to the said Parish, as the Church-wardens and Overseers thereof have complained.

These are therefore to require you, upon Sight hereof, not to arrest, attach, or otherwise imprison him the said *M. K.* if for the Cause aforesaid, and no other, as you will answer the contrary: And for your so doing this shall be your sufficient Warrant. Given, *&c.*

If he do not find Sureties, then he is to be committed.

The *Mittimus* before the Birth.

To the Keeper, &c.

I HEREWITH send you the Body of *C. D.* brought before me this present Day, and charged upon the Oath of *A. B.* of *&c.* to have begotten her with Child; which Child when born, will be a Bastard: He the said *C. D.* having refused before me to find sufficient Sureties for his Good Behaviour, and personal Appearance at the next General Quarter-Sessions of the Peace to be holden for the said County, to answer the said Charge. These are therefore to require you to receive the said *C. D.* into your Custody, and him safely to keep, until he shall be thence delivered by due Course of Law: Hereof fail not. Given, *&c.*

If he give Sureties, as before, nothing further to be done till the Child be born, and then two Justices (one of the *Quorum*) are again to examine the Mother of the Bastard Child.

Here follows the Proceedings after the Birth.

The Examination of S. S. of, &c. *taken before us* J. M. *and* P. L. *Esquires, Two of his Majesty's Justices of the Peace of the said County, this Day of*——Anno Dom. 1718.

WHO upon her Oath saith, That the Female Bastard-Child, of which she was delivered the 15 th Day of *April* last was Twelve-month, about Ten of the Clock in in the Evening, in the Parish of, &c. was begotten by G. S. late Commander of His Majesties Ship C. who cruising of the Coasts of *L.* and coming a shoar there, frequented this Examinants House (she keeping a Victualling-house) and there became acquainted with her, and had the carnal Knowledge of her Body. And this Examinant further upon Oath saith, That he the said *G. S.* and no other Person whatsoever is the only true Father of her said Child of which she was delivered as aforesaid.

Jur' die & Anno supra dicto coram S. S.
J. M.
P. L.

Then the Justices are to order, (1) The Punishment of the Father and Mother. (2) The Relief of the Parish. And, (3) They may charge the Parents with the Payment of Money for the Relieve of the Child,

If the two Justices cannot agree in making their Order, it may be referred to the Sessions to be examined; but it must be again heard before the two Justices, with the Direction of the Court, because the Sessions cannot make an Original Order in Bastardy.

'Tis usual for the Justices, before they make their Order, to convene before them the Mother and the reputed Father and such Witnesses as they think fit.

A Warrant to convene the reputed Father, &c.

To all Constables, &c,

WHEREAS we are Informed, That *A. B.* of, &c. hath been lately delivered of a Bastard Child now living, and likely to be chargeable to the said Parish. And whereas the said *A. B.* upon her Examination taken upon Oath, hath charged *C, D.* to have begotten the said Bastard Child on her Body. These are therefore in his Majesty's Name to command you to bring the said *C. D.* before us on *Monday* the 10 th Day of *July* next at Nine of the Clock in the Forenoon of the said Day at the House of, &c. to be examined touching the Premises; and that you give Notice to the said *A. B.* to be there also present; And that you also give Notice to *E. F.* of, &c. and *G. H.* of &c. that they are required of us to appear at the Time and Place aforesaid, to testifie what they know concerning the Premises; to the End such Order may be made therein as to Justice doth appertain: And that you then and there certifie unto us what you have done in Execution of this Precept. Given under our Hands and Seals, &c.

An Order to the Mother and reputed Father of a Bastard Child.

WHereas due Proof hath been made before us P. L. *and* H. S. *Esquires, two of his Majesties Justices of the Peace* for the City and Liberty of *Westminster* (Quorum unus) *inhabiting in or near the Pariſh of,* &c. *upon the Oath of C. C. ſingle Woman Mother of a Femal Baſtard Child born the* 24*th Day of* April *laſt paſt, in the ſaid Pariſh, and there chriſtened S. That one G. C. did beget no the Body of the ſaid* C. C. *the ſaid Female Baſtard-Child, which ſaid Child is become chargeable to the ſaid Pariſh, of which the Church-wardens and Overſeers of the Poor thereof have complained.*

We the ſaid Juſtices, upon the Examination of the ſaid C. C. *the Mother upon her Oath touching the father of the ſaid Baſtard Child, and the Cauſe and Circumſtance thereof, do hereby adjudge and declare the ſaid* G. C. *to be the reputed Father of the ſaid Female Baſtard Child born of the Body of the ſaid* C. C. *in the Pariſh of* &c. *aforeſaid. And thereupon we do Order, as well for the Relieve, and to ſave harmleſs and keep indempnified the ſaid Pariſh, as for the keeping and maintaining and keeping the ſaid Female Baſtard Child; That the ſaid* G. C. *ſhall forthwith, upon ſight of this our Order (a true Copy hereof being firſt delievered unto him) pay or cauſe to be paid unto the Church-wardens or Overſeers of the Poor of the ſaid Pariſh, or to ſome or one of them, for and toward the Months lying in and laying of the ſaid* C. C. *the the Sum of* 11 s. 6 d. *for the firſt four Weeks from the Birth of the ſaid Child. And after the Expiration of the ſaid firſt four Weeks, the ſaid* G. C. *ſhall likewiſe pay or cauſe to be paid weekly and every Week the Sum of two Shillings and ſix Pence of lawful Money of* Great Britain, *for and towards the Reliefe and Maintainance of the ſaid Female Baſtard Child for ſo long Time as the ſaid Child ſhall be chargeable to the ſaid Pariſh.*

And laſtly, We do Order, That the ſaid G. C. *ſhall forthwith give ſufficient Security to the Church-wardens and Overſeers of the Poor of the ſaid Pariſh, for the true Performance of this our Order, otherwiſe to find Secureties for his perſonal Appearence at the next General Quater-Seſſions of the Peace to be holden for the ſaid City and Liberty; there to abide ſuch Order as the Juſtices, or the major Part of them then and there preſent ſhall think fit to make in that behalf.* Given *under our Hands and Seals,* &c.

A Warrant upon the foregoing Order.

To all Conſtables, &c.

THESE are in His Majeſty's Name to will and require you and every of you on Sight hereof, to take and bring before us, or either of us, or any other of His Majeſty's Juſtices of the Peace for the ſaid County, the Body of *R. P.* of *&c.* of whom you ſhall have Notice, to give ſufficient Security to the Churh-wardens and *Overſeers* of the Poor of the Pariſh of, *&c.* for the true Performance of an Order by us made for the indempnifying of the ſaid Pariſh from a female Baſtard-Child born of the Body of *S. C.* ſingle Woman, which Child is become chargeable to the ſaid Pariſh. And the ſaid *R. P.* upon the Oath and Examination of the ſaid *S. C.* is by us ajudged to be the reputed Father of the Child aforeſaid; otherwiſe to find Sufficient Sureties for his perſonal Appearanee at the next Seſſions of the Peace to be holden for the ſaid County, to anſwer his Contempt of our ſaid Order, and to abide ſuch further Order as that Court ſhall think fit to make therein. Hereof fail not at your Perils. *Given* under our Hands and Seals, *&c.*

A

A Release from the Overseers of the Poor to one that paid 7 l. 10 s. *to be freed from keeping a Bastard-Child.*

KNOW all Men by these Presents, That we *A. B. C. D.* and *E. F.* Overseers of the Poor of the Parish of St. *Martin in the Fields* in the County of *Middlesex*, do hereby acknowledge to have had and received of and from *G. H.* of the Parish of, *&c.* the Sum of *&c.* of lawful Money of *Great Britain*, to and for the Use of the Poor of the said Parish of. *&c* in full for the Education, Nourishing, Bringing up, and providing for *M. R.* a Female Bastard-Child born on the Body of *M. R.* Single Woman. And we the said Overseers of the poor, in Consideration of the Sum of Money aforesaid, have remised, released, and for ever quit-claimed, And by these Presents do for us and our Partners, and the rest of the present Overseers of the Poor of the said Parish, and their and our Successors, Remise, Release and for ever Quit-claim unto the said *G. H.* all and all manner of Costs, Charges, Sum and Sums of Money, Claims and Demand whatsoever, which we, our Partners, and the rest of the present Overseers of the Poor, and their and our Successors, any of them, shall or may at any Time or Times hereafter have, claim, challenge or demand of or from the said *G. H.* for or by Reason or Means of the Education, Nursing Bringing up, or Providing for *M. R.* aged about, *&c.* born of the Body of *M. R.* aforesaid· *In Witness*, &c.

A Commitment for refusing to obey an Order.

To the Keeper. &c.

WHEREAS *A. B*, stands charged before us *C. D.* and *E. F.* Esquires, Two of his Majesty's Justices of the Peace for the said County, upon the Oath of *G. H.* Single Woman, for being the reputed Father of a Female Bastard-Child lately born of her Body in the Parish of *&c.* where it is now chargable ; of which said Bastard Child the said *A. B.* is by Order, duly executed, adjudged the reputed Father.

And whereas the said *A. B.* being duly served with a Copy of the said Order, doth refuse to obey the same, or to find sufficient Sureties for his personal Appearance at the next Quarter-Sessions of the Peace holden for the said County, to abide such Order, or any other Order as the Justices there present shall in that behalf make : These are therefore to require you to keep the Body of the said *A. B.* in your safe Custody, until he shall find sufficient Sureties as aforesaid, or be discharged by due Course of Law Given under our Hands and Seals, *&c.*

A Bond to the Church wardens and Overseers before the Birth.

KNOW All Men by these Presents, That We *A. B.* and *C. D.* of *Amboy* in the County of *Middlesex* in the Province of *N. J.* Merchants, and *E. F.* of the same Place, Carpenter, are held and firmly bound unto *G. H.* and *I. K.* Church-wardens of Amboy aforesaid, for the Time being, and *L. M.* and *N. O.* Overseers of the Poor for the Time being, in the just and full Sum of Fifty Pounds, good and lawful Money of the Province of *N. J.* aforesaid, to be paid to the said Church-wardens and Overseers of the Poor, or to either of them or to either of their certain Attornies, Successors and Assigns. For the which Payment well and truly to be made or done, We do bind our selves, our Heirs, Executors and Administrators joyntly and severaly, for and in the whole, firmly by these Presents. Sealed with our Seals. Dated this 20*th* Day of *July*, in the 4th Year of the Reign of our Sovereign Lord *GEORGE*, by the Grace of God King of *Great Britain*, *France* and *Ireland*, Defender of the Faith, *&c. Annoq; Domini* 1718.

THE Condition of this Obligation is such, That if the above bounden *A. B. C. D* and *E. F.* or any of them, their or any of their Executors or Administrators do or shall from Time to Time, and at all times hereafter well and sufficiently save, defend, keep harmless and indempnifie the above-named *G. H.* and *J. K.* Church-wardens for the Time being, and *L. M.* and *N. O.* Overseers of the Poor for the time being of the Parish *&c.* abovesaid ; And also all and every other the Parishioners and Inhabitants which now are, or hereafter shall be of the same Parish, and every of them respectively of and from the finding, keeping, educating, instructing, bringing up and Providing for such Child or Children, as *S. H.* Single Woman late of the said Parish now goeth withal, whereof the said *A. B.* is the repnted Father and of and from the Charges of Lying in of the said *S. H.* of such Child or Children, and of and from all Actions, Suits, Costs, Charges, Troubles, Expences, Damages & Demands whatsoever, which they or any of them shall or may happen to incur, sustain or be put unto for or in Respect of such Child or Children, or the lying in of the said *S. H.* as aforesaid. That then this Obligation to be void, or else to remain in full Force and Virtue.

By the Statute of 7 *Jac.* the Justices of Peace may commit lewd Women to the House of Correction, who have Bastards that may be Chargeable to the Parish, there to be punished and set to Work for a Year ; and if they Offend a second Time, not to be enlarged without giving security to offend no more.

But if the Woman will discharge the Parish, she cannot be punished by this Act ; yet by Virtue of 18 *Eliz.* she may be punished by Whipping, as the Reputed Father may be.

The Constable having a Warrant to apprehend the Father, and willingly or negligently suffering him to escape, one Justice may bind him over to the Sessions, and there he may be ordered to contribute towards the Maintainance of the Child, or may be fined.

A Warrant for appprehending a Woman on Suspicion of having Murdered her Bastard Child.

To the Constable, &c.

WHereas Complaint upon Oath hath been made unto me by *C. D.* That *A. B.* hath had a Child born alive of her Body, and is suspected to have murdered, or else made away the said Child since the Birth thereof: **These are therefore**, in his Majesty's Name, to charge and command you, that immediately upon Sight hereof, you apprehend and bring the Body of the said *A. B.* before me, or some other of His Majesty's Justices of the Peace of the said County, to answer such Matters and Things as on His Majesty's behalf shall be Objected against her touching the Premisses; and also to make diligent Search, by all lawful Means, for the finding out of the Child aforesaid; and to bring before me or some other Justice of the Peace for for the said County, all such Persons as can give any Information on the behalf of His said Majesty touching the same. **And hereof** Fail not, as you will answer the contrary. **Given**, *&c.*

Bigamy.

THIS was prohibited by the Statute of 1 *Jac.* by which 'tis made Felony to Marry a second Husband or Wife, the first being living.

My Lord *Coke*, in his Exposition upon this Statute, hath made several Exceptions out of it: 3 *Inst.* 6: 27

That 1. This Law doth not extend to a Person whose Husband or Wife is beyond Sea, to to such who shall absent from one another in *England* for the Space of Seven Years: With this Difference, That if the Abode be beyond Sea, then, though either of them have Notice that the other is living, such notice is not material: But if in *England*, 'tis otherwise; for in such Case the Party is not exempted from the Penalty of the Statute. *Vide Bastardy p.* 27.

2. That it doth not Extend to Persons divorced *a Mensa & Toro.*

Nor to such whose former Marriage is by any Sentence in the Ecclesiastical Court declared void.

And therefore where a Man was divorsed *Causa Adulterii*, and married another Wife, the first being then alive, this was held to be within the Proviso of that Statute; for the first Marriage is severed by this Divorce: But if it had been *Causa Sevitia*, then he could not have married again; because that is only a Temporal Separation until the Anger is past.

4. Nor to thoſe who have been married within the Age of Conſent, *viz.* the Man under Fourteen, and the Wife under Twelve, who afterwards diſagree to that Marriage.

It has likewiſe been held, That if a Man marries a Woman beyond Sea, and is living, and his Wife marries another in *England*, this is not within the Statute; becauſe the firſt Marriage cannot be tried here,

The Offenders have Clergy.

Blaſphemy.

BLaſphemous Words are not only an Offence to God and Religion, but a Crime againſt the Laws, State and Government of this Kingdom.

Any Perſon bred in, or profeſſing the Chriſtian Religion, and who ſhall by Writing, Printing, Teaching, or adviſed Speaking, deny any one of the Perſons in the Trinity; or aſſert, That there are more Gods than one; or deny the Chriſtian Religion to be true, or the Holy Scripture to be of Divine Authority; and be convicted thereof by Indictment or Infformation at *Weſtminſter*, or at the Aſſizes, he ſhall be diſabled to have any Office, and ſhall not enjoy that Office which he hath, but the ſame is made void. 9 *&* 10 *W.* 3.

If convicted a ſecond Time, he ſhall be diſabled to ſue in any Court, or to be a Guardin, or Executor, or Adminiſtrator, and be incapable of any Legaey or Gift, or of any Office, and ſhall be committed for Three Years without Bail.

Conviction muſt be by Oath of two credible Witneſſes; the Information for *Words ſpoken*, muſt be by Oath before a Juſtice of Peace within Four Days after ſpoken: And the Proſecution of ſuch Offence muſt be within Three Months after the Information. But if the convicted Perſon, for the firſt Offence. ſhall within Four Months after his Conviction, acknowledge and renounce the ſame in that Court where he was convicted, he ſhall be diſcharged from the ſaid Penalties.

Bugery.

THIS is an Offence againſt the Order of Nature, committed by mankind with Mankind or Beaſts, or by Women with Beaſts.

The

The Words of the Statute which makes this Offence Felony, are, *viz.* If *any Person* shall commit the detestable Sin of *Buggery* with Mankind or Beast, *&c.* which Word [*Person*] extends as well to a Woman as to a Man; and as my Lord *Coke* tells us, that Word might be used by the Law-makers, because, a little before that Act was made, a great Lady had committed Buggery with a Baboon, and conceiv'd by it. 25. *H.* 8. c. 6. 3 Inst. 59.

There must be *Penetratio & Emissio Seminis*; for the one without the other will not make the Sin; and therefore the Indictment must be, *Quod carnaliter cognovit, &c.*

In my Lord *Audley's* Case, which happened *Anno* 6 *Car.* 1. and who was tryed by his Peers; the Fact was *Pollution, and using a Man upon his Belly Sodomitically,* without Peneration; and the Lords demanded of the Judges, Whether this was Buggery by the Statute 25 *H.* 8? The Lord Chief Justice *Hide* told them it was; but *Richardson*, the Chief Justice of the *Common-Pleas*, was of another Opinion: And this might create different Opinions amongst the Peers at that Triall, who were 27 in Number; whereof 12 acquitted him of the Buggery, and 15 found him Guilty,

It was anciently Punished by Death: But the old Writers differ in the Manner; for some say, the Offender must be burnt; others, that he shall be buried alive; and some say, the Man was to be hanged, and the Woman drowned; but now by the Statute of 25 *H.* 8. *cap.* 6 'tis made Feloney without Benefit of Clergy.

'Tis True, this Statute was repealed 1 *Mar.* but 'tis revived by 5 *Eliz.* *cap.* 17.

Agens & consentiens pari pena Plectantur, *viz.* by hanging till they are Dead, unless the Party consenting is within the Age of Discretion, and then 'tis not Felony.

And this may be the Reason why the Age of the Party is expressed in the Indictment, though I find it omitted in my Lord *Audley's* Case for this very Offence; and probably his Indictment was drawn by that of Mr. *Stafford*, for they vary only in this Particular and the Word *motus* is left out of one, but 'tis *motus & seductus* in the other. *Hutt.* 115

In *Easter*-Term 5 *Jac.* one Mr. *Stafford* was Indicted, and found Guilty of this Offence for which he was Executed.

Burglary.

IS Breaking and Entring a Mansion-house in the *Night-time*, with an Intent to commit Felony, whether such felonious Intent be Executed or not. *Moor* 660.

But an Infant under 14, a natural Fool, or a very Poor Person, who shall enter a House, being compelled by Hunger, are not Burglars.

Upon this Definition these Things may be observed:

1. What is a *Breaking*, &c. and where Burglary may be committed without an actual Breaking.
2. What is an Entry, and where Burglary may be done without an actual Entry by the Person himself:
3. What shall be esteemed a *Mansion-House*, and what Place make the Offence Burglary, and what not.
4. The Intention of the Person is to be considered.
5. *Clergy*, &c.

1. As to the first, The *Entring of an House* with the Doors open, is a Breaking in Law; yet tis not Burglary, unless the Door, Window or Wall are broken, or the Latch drawn, or the Door unlock'd.

If a Man comes into an House, and enters into a Chamber, and there breaks open a Trunk, and steals Money or other Goods; this is no *Burglary*, because the Trunk was no part of the Dwelling-house: But in such Case, if he breaks open the Chamber-door, or any Door of a Cupboard which is fixed to the Freehold, this is an actual breaking the House *Keeling* 58, 59.

2. But Burglary may be committed *without* an actual *Breaking*, as by those who watch to prevent a Discovery, whilst their Companions break the House.

By coming down a Chimney.

By entring with the Help of a Key.

By entring, the Door being open, and the Owner of the House retiring to a Chamber, which the Offender breaks open.

By breaking Glass in a Window, and hooking out Goods. *Anderson* 114. *Moor* 660. *Poph.* 42. *H. P. C.* 81.

By Pretending themselves to be robbed, and raising Hue-and-Cry, and with a Constable demanding Entry, the owner opens his Doors, then they bind the Constable, and rob the House, for this is in *Fraudem Legis*.

By the Help of a Servant within opening the Door or Window, and the Thief entring, 'tis Burglary in him, and Robbery in the Servant

The Master lyes in one part of the House, and the Servant in another Part, who in the Night draws a Latch, and enters the Chamber of his Master with an Intent to murder him, 'tis Burglary. *Hutt.* 26.

Anno 27. *Car.* 2. one *Far* a Sollicitor, had obtained Judgment against the casual Ejector, and the Sheriff delievered Possession of the House, which he entred, and sent the Defendant to *Newgate* for want of Bail, and carried away Goods to a Considerable Value; but having no Colour of any Title to the House, he was found guilty of Felony; and tho' a Solicitor, he could not read, and was Hang'd. 2. *Jnd.* 294

By

By putting the Hand or a Hook in the Window, and taking out Goods.
By turning the Key when the Door is lock'd on the Inside.

3. **The Church is a Mansion-House**, within the Meaning of the Law

And therefore an Indictment against the Offender, for that he, *Burglariter fregit* (without saying, *intravit*) *Ecclesiam in nocte ad spoliand' & depredand' bona Parochianorum in eadem existen*, but took nothing: This was held good. *Dyer* 99.

Where a Man hath two Dwelling Houses, and dwells in each by Turns, and one is broken, though no Person in it, 'tis Burglary.

A Man had a Lease of a Shop, which was in the Dwelling-House of another, and the Lessee worked there in the Day-time, but lay in another House, the Shop was broke open in the Night, and the Goods stole: This is not Burglary, because it was not a Mansion or Dwelling-House, for it was severed from the House by the Lease. *Hutt.* 33.

A Chamber in a Colledge or Inns of Court, though no Body therein; or the Chamber of a Guest, broken by the Innkeeper, with an Intent to rob.

Now the Reason why 'tis Burglary to break open a Chamber in the Inns of Court, is because every Gentleman hath a several Property in his Chamber: But *Somerset House*, or *Whitehall* are *Domus Mansionales* of the Queen; and if a Chamber is broke open there, it must be so alledged in the Indictment, and not *Domus Mansionalis* of the Person who lodged in it. *Keeling* 27.

A Barn or Stable contiguous to a Dwelling-House: But a Shop, distinct from the House, is not.

Nor a Booth; but yet, by a particular Statute, 'tis made Burglary to break it open.

And by a late Statute to break open a Shop or Ware-House belonging or used with the Dwelling-House, in the Day time, and taking Money or Goods to the Value of 5 *s*. tho' no Person is therein is *Burglary*: Which see *Postea*.

4. The *Intent* must be to common Felony; if it be to do a Trespass, 'tis not Burglary for breaking and entring: But going away may be Felony, but 'tis not Burglary.

If Thieves in the Night come to a Dwelling-House, and a Person within opens the Door to resist them, and one of the Rogues shoots into the House the Door being open, and missing the Person, breaks the Wall on the other Side with the Bullet; this is not Burglary, because the breaking the Wall with the Bullet was not a breaking the House with *Intent* to commit Felony. *Savile* 59.

But yet, where one *Intended* to commit Murder, and for that Purpose broke a Hole in the Wall in the Night, and perceiving where the Person was, shot at him thro' the Hole, but missed him; this was held Burglary. 1 *And* 114. 115.

And so are all the late Authorities, &c. That breaking a Dwelling-House in the Night-time, with an *Intent* to kill or rob, though there is not *any Person in the House*, yet 'tis Burglary. *Moor* 660. *Poph*. 52.

'Tis true, all the ancient Precedents were only, that the Criminal *noctanter & felonice fregit*; but in the latter Indictments 'tis usually inserted, that Some body is in the House, and put in Fear, because by the Statute 23 *H.* 8. Clergy is taken away from those who rob a House, the Owner or Dweller, his Wife, Children or Servants, then being within, and put in Fear. *Moor* 660, 661. *Poph.* 43.

Entring in the Day-time, and lying privately till Night, then robs and departs, 'tis not Burglary; but if he breaks open any Door to get out, 'tis Burglary.

5. **Clergy.** If an House was broke open, with an *Intent* to commit *Felony*, and no Body therein, in former Times the Offender had his Clergy; but if the Dweller had been within, and put in Fear, then by the Statute of 23 *H.* 8. *cap.* 1. Clergy was taken away, as 'tis now, for this was esteemed an Aggravation of the Offence and therefore the Precedents in those days were, *viz. Quod Domum Mansionalem noctanter Felonice & Burglariter fregit & intravit*, some Person being therein, &c.

Afterwards, 18 *Eliz. cap.* 6 Clergy was taken away in all Cases of Burglary; and *Anno* 39 *Eliz.* a Law was made, That if a House was broke open in the Day-time, and Money and Goods to the Value of 5 *s.* taken away out of the House, or Out-house thereunto belonging, tho' no Person therein, yet 'tis Felony without Benefit of Clergy.

But because Goods were often stolen in a Dwelling-House without an actual Breaking, a Law was made, That if any Person feloniously take away Goods, being in a Dwelling-House, the Owner, or other Person being therein, and put in Fear; or shall rob any Dwelling-House in the Day-time, any Person being therein. or shall be accessary to the same; or shall break any Dwelling-House, Shop, or Ware-House thereunto belonging, in the Day-time, and feloniously take away Goods to the Value of 5 *s.* tho' no Person therein; or shall counsel, hire, or command another to commit Burglary, shall not have Clergy. 3. & 4. *Will.*

If two are indicted for Burglary, and one is found guilty of Felony, and the other of Burglary, 'tis not a good Verdict as to the Felony, because the Jury might have found both guilty of Felony; but they cannot find one guilty of Burglary, and the other of Felony, upon the same Indictment and Evidence. *Syd.* 171.

This was the Case of a Father and his Son; the Father, being found guilty of Burglary, was hang'd; and the Son, though found guilty of Felony, was discharg'd.

If two are indicted for the same Burglary, and one convicted and the other acquitted, he who was acquitted shall never again be tried for that Fact; but if he took any Goods out of the House which were not mention'd in the Indictment, as Money of any Servant, &c. he may be indicted for that Felony, because the Facts are several Felonies. *Keeling* 30.

A Warrant

A Warrant.

To all Constables, and others His Majesty's Officers of the Peace whom these may concern.

WHereas Complaint upon Oath hath been made before me by *A. B.* That last Night her House was broken open by Thieves, who feloniously stole and carried away thereout a Silver Bowl, *&c.* and hath in Suspicion one *C. D.* and others, to have committed the said Burglary: *These* are in His Majesty's Name to require you to bring the said *C. D.* (of whom you shall have Notice) before me, or some other of His Majesty's *Justices* of the Peace, to be examined and dealt with according to Law: *Hereof* you are not to fail. *Given* under my Hand and Seal the Day of *Anno* 1719.

If any Person commits Burglary, House-breaking, Felony, in stealing Horses, Money, Wares or Goods, from whom the Benefit of Clergy is taken away by the Act of 11 *Will*, and being out of Prison, shall discover two more Offenders and convict them, he shall have a Pardon, which shall be a good Bar to an Appeal. 11 *Will cap.*

Burning of Houses. See *Fire.*

'TIS Felony at Common Law, maliciously and voluntarily to burn the House of another.

Whether,
1. There must be an actual Burning, and what that is.
2. It must be maliciously and voluntarily.
3. It must be the House of another.

1. 'Tis not necessary that the whole House should be burnt, for 'tis Felony to set on Fire and burn Part of it.

2. It must be done maliciously and voluntarily, and so is the Indictment, *Quod voluntarie & ex malitia sua praecogitata, &c.* for if 'tis done by Mischance or by Negligence, 'tis not Felony.

Sometimes

Sometimes the Law implies Malice, as if the Offender intends to burn the House of *A.* only, and by this Means the House of *B.* is set on fire; this is Felony, for the Event shall be coupled to the Cause, which was malicious.

3. The House of another: Formerly it was Felony to burn the Frame of an House, or the bare attempting to set on fire a Stack of Corn; and 'tis still Felony to set on fire a Stack of Corn in *Northumberland*, *Cumberland*, *Westmorland*, or *Durham*. 43 *Eliz. cap*, 31. 22. & 23. *Car.* 2. *cap.* 7.

And even now, 'tis Felony in the Night-time to burn Barns, Stables, Ricks of Corn. Hays, &c. or any of the Out-Houses which are contiguous to the Dwelling-House, and the Offender is not to have Clergy.

But if a Barn stand remote, and is not Parcel of the Mansion-House, then 'tis not Felony, unless it hath Hay or Corn in it,

He who is in Possession of a House by Lease sets it on fire, with an Intention to burn his Neighbour's House; this was held to be no Felony by the Opinion of three Judges, because the Offender being in Possession, it cannot be said to be done *vi & armis:* But Justice *Crook* was of a contrary Opinion, because the Offence falls under the Definition of Felony, which is a capital Crime, committed *felleo animo*, and here the Fact (though in his own House) was done maliciously, and so found by the Jury, and the Intention shall be coupled to it, which was *Nequiter factum & mala conscientia. Cro. Car.* 376. *Holmes's Case Jones* 351.

A Captain, Master, or Mariner, or other Officer belonging to a Ship, and burning or destroying it, or procuring the same to be done, to the Prejudice of the Owner or Merchant, must suffer Death as a Felon; and if committed where the Admiralty hath Jurisdiction, it shall be tried by Vertue of a Commission under the Great Seal, in such Places in the Realm as shall be therein limited; and such Offender standing mute, or challenging above the Number of 20 Persons, shall suffer Death without Benefit of Clergy.

Certiorari.

THIS is a Writ directed to the Justices of the Peace, issuing out of the *Chancery*, and then tis returnable in *Cancellaria Nostra*; or out of the *Kings Bench*, and then 'tis *coram Justiciariis nostris de Banco*; and the Justices must make a Return accordingly.

It was formerly held, That if delivered after the Return-Day, yet the Justices ought not to Proceed, because the Words of the Writt are *coram nobis*, &c. & *non alibi*. And 'tis still held, That 'tis a *Supersedeas* by Reason of those Words, *non alibi*. *Telv.* 32.

This

This Writ may be either to remove an Indictment, or the Tenour thereof, or a Recognizance, *&c* And it removes the whole Record; and therefore no *alias Certiorari* is to be allowed. *Stiles* 359.

But tis not to be allowed, unless the Party indicted will be bound with Sureties (such as the Justices shall approve) to pay the Prosecutor such Costs and Damages as the Justices shall assess within a Month after Conviction. 21 *Jac. c.* 18

And by a later Statute, 'tis not to be granted in Term-time, but upon Motion in Court; and the Party who desires it, must find Bail. (*Viz*)

Two Manucaptors before one or more Justices of the Peace in 20 *l.* to plead to the Indictment, and at his own Charge to procure the Issue to be joyned, and to be tryed at the next Assizes in that County where the Indictment was found after the Return of the *Certiorari*, if not in *London*, *Westminster* or *Middlesex*; and if in either of those Places, then the next Term after the *Certiorari* granted and if such recognizance is not given before the *Certiorari* is allowed they may proceed, tho' delivered. 5 & 6 *W. & M. c.* 5.

If the Party desiring the *Certiorari* be convicted, then *B. R.* may give Costs; and if not paid within ten Days after Demand, then upon Affidavit made of the Refusal, an Attachment goes, *&c.* and the Recognizance not to be discharged till Costs paid

In Vacation, any Judge of *B. R.* may grant it. He must endorse his Name, and the Name of the Party desiring it, and before the Allowance the Party must find such Sureties as aforesaid.

And by a subsequent Statute a Recognizance taken before a Judge of *B. R.* with like Condition, as in the former Act, which the Judge must mention on the Back of the Writ, and subscribe his Name, shall be as good as if taken before a Justice of Peace in the proper County 8 *&* 9 *W. cap.* 33.

The Condition of the Recognizance where the Certiorari *is brought to a Justice of the Peace, and not to a Judge of* B. R.

THE *Condition* of this Recognizance is such, That whereas the above-bounden *R. O.* hath prosecuted a *Certiorari* returnable, *&c.* too remove into the *Queen's Bench* an Indictment found against him at, *&c.* for, *&c.* If therefore the said *R. O.* shall plead to the said Indictment so removed as aforesaid, so as Issue may be joined upon the same; and shall likewise at his own Charge procure the said Issue to be tried at the next Assizes after the Return of the said *Certiorari*, to be held for the said County of, *&c.* where the said Indictment was found; Then this Recognizance to be void, *&c.*

Champerty.

T IS an Offence, viz. where any Person expecting Part of the Thing in Variance, doth by himself, or any other, move or prosecute the Suit at his own Costs and Charges: The Punishment is a Fine, and Imprisonment for Three Years.

My Lord Coke tells us, that Champerty is Maintenance, but not e converso; so that the Difference between these Offences seems to be thus: Champerty is where the Party prosecuting is to have Part of the Lands or Goods, &c. 2 Inst. 208. 1 Inst. 368. B.

Maintenance, is where the Prosecutor is to have no Part in the Thing in Variance.

Chance-medley, See Homicide.

Church, Divine-Service, Dissenters, &c.

BEfore I mention any Thing under this Title, relating to the Office of a Justice of Peace, I think it may not be Improper to give a short Account of the Rise and Continuance of the Divisions amongst us, &c.

Some certain Ceremonies which had been used in time of Popery, were thought fit to be continued by our Reformers, as useful to beget some Reverence in holy Exercises, but chiefly in hopes to bring those of the Roman Communion more easily to comply with that Reformation.

There were some Divines in the beginning of the Reign of Queen Elizabeth, who fled from Persecution in the Reign of Queen Mary, and had by that Means seen the Methods and Use of Foreign Churches, particularly that of Geneva, complained of this as a Complyance with Popery; and therefore since we had reformed from the Errors of that Church, would have none of their Ceremonies continued in ours.

The Queen was perswaded by some Persons of Power then at Court, to take the Revenues of the Bishopricks and Cathedrals into her own Hands, which would not only enrich the Crown, but it would likewise be an Expedient to unite all the Reformed Churches, and to bring the English Church to the Model of that of Geneva.

This was opposed by some Wise Ministers at that Time; who told the Queen, That If Matters of Religion came to be thus regulated here by popular Persons, they would quickly set up a Power distinct from hers, in Church-Matters, which by Consequence would entrench upon her Prerogative.

This

This seemed so reasonable to Her, that she resolved to maintain the ancient Government in the Church, and continued their Ceremonies; which the other Party did not dislike as unlawful, but for the Reasons aforesaid.

And now these Differences which were small in the beginning, became fixed and settled into Factions, and those who were against the Ceremonies, reproached the Church-men with *Non-Residence*, *Pluralities*, and many Abuses in the Spiritual Courts; and thus Matters stood for many Years in her Reign.

Afterwards, Lectures were set up in most Cities and Market Towns: I will not examine whether this was done purely in Opposition to the Church, or whether it was upon any Dislike of the mean Performances of those Persons who served the Cure of those Places; it may be the latter.

For in Ancient Times the Settled Allowance for the Secular Clergy in great Towns, *&c.* was very small, because the Perquisits were considerable by Oblations and otherwise; and even in the latter Ages of Popery, the Churchmen of these Places lived plentifully, tho' their Stipends were small, for the Superstition of these Times provided Fees for them by *Obits*, *Exequies*, and *Masses*, and they were obliged to live singly.

But these Things being disused after the Reformation, and the Allowances of the Clergy in great Cities and Towns being still very small, might be the Occasion for the richer sort of People in these Places to maintain Men of greater Abilities than the Incumbents, by a Voluntary Contribution.

These Men, by their Zeal in Preaching, gained a Party to themselves; who depending upon the Bounty of the People, were generally inclined to submit to the Humours of the Chief Contributors, and by this Means the Divisions was still increased.

In the succeeding Reigns, the People were not only settled into Parties, but were distinguished by Names, *viz.* The *Court* and *Country* Parties.

The Clergy stood firm to the Interests of the Court; and those who opposed that Interest in Civil Affairs, always cherished the other Party, commending them for good Protestants, and that it was the Interest of all Parties to unite.

But instead of that, the Breach was made wider by the Civil Wars, and both then and afterwards some designing Persons have, by sly Insinuations and other Methods, laboured to make both Parties Tools by Turns, to break in upon and crush one another, that they might make a Way for the common Enemies to enter.

But the Nation being come to a better Temper, a Law was made, *Anno* 1 *Guil. &* *Mary*, That neither the Statutes of 1 *Eliz. cap.* 2. 23 *Eliz. cap.* 1. 3 *Jac. cap* 4. shall extend to Persons dissenting from the Church.

They must likewise subscribe the Declaration mentioned in the Statute of 30 *Car.* 2. *cap.* 1.

These Oaths and Subscriptions the Justices in Sessions have Power to administer and take; and thoſe who do take the Oaths, muſt pay 6 *d.* for Regiſtering, and 6 *d.* for a Certificate.

They ſhall not be lyable to the Penalties in 35 *Eliz.* & 22 *Car.* 2. nor be proſecuted in any Eccleſiaſtical Court for Nonconformity.

But they muſt not aſſemble in Places with Doors locked, barred or Bolted, nor until the Place is Certified to the Biſhop of the Dioceſe, or to the Archdeacon, or to the Juſtices at Quarter-Seſſions, and Regiſtered there, and they have a Certificate thereof.

If Choſen to any pariſh Office, they may execute it by Deputy.

Then as to their Preachers, if they take the Oaths, and ſubſcribe the Declaration at the Quarter-Seſſions where they live, ſhall not be lyable to the Penalties in the Statute of 17 *Car.* 2. *cap.* 2. Which is not to come within Five Miles of any Town that ſends Burgeſſes to Parliament, if he hath not declared his Aſſent and Conſent to the Book of *Common-Prayer*, &c. under the Penalty of 40 *l.* nor to the Penalties in 22 *Car.* 2. *cap.* 1. which in being convicted of Preaching at a Conventicle, he forfeits, 20 *l.* nor to the Penalty of 100. *l.* mentioned in 13 & 14 *Car.* 2.

But then theſe Preachers muſt declare their Approbation, and ſubſcribe the Articles of Religion, except theſe Words in the 20*th* Article, *viz. The Church has Power to decree Rights and Ceremonies, and Authority in Matters of Faith:* And except the 34*th* Article; which is, *That the Church has Power to appoint Rights and Ceremonies which are not contrary to the Word of God, and that private Perſons are bound to conform to ſuch Ceremonies:* And except the 35*th* Article, which concerns the reading Homilies in Churches: And the 36*th* Ariticle, which relates to the Conſecration of Biſhops, &c.

Preachers thus ſubſcribing, &c. ſhall not ſerve on Juries, and ſhall be exempt from Pariſh-Offices.

And if any Perſon diſturb them in Preaching, he ſhall find Sureties to be bound with himſelf in a Recognizance of 50 *l.* to appear at the Seſſions; and being convicted there ſhall forfeit 20 *l.* to the King.

If he will not find Sureties, he ſhall be committed to Priſon till next Seſſions.

The Proof muſt be by two Witneſſes on Oath, before one Juſtice.

There is a Clauſe in this Act which concerns the Preachers in *Anabaptiſt's* Congregations, *viz.* That if they ſubſcribe the Articles of Religion, excepting in that Part of the 27th Article, which relates to Infant Baptiſm, and ſhall take the Oaths, and make and Subſcribe the Declaration, That they ſhall enjoy the ſame Advantages which Diſſenting Miniſters have by that Law.

Any Juſtice of Peace may require a Diſſenter to make and ſubſcribe the ſaid Declaration, and to take the aforeſaid Oaths; but becauſe there are ſome Perſons [Quakers] who ſcruple to take any Oath, therefore Proviſion is made to exempt them from the Penalties aforeſaid, if they make and ſubſcribe the ſaid Declaration, and likewiſe the Declaration of Fidelity; (which ſee in Title Oaths.)

They muſt likewiſe ſubſcribe a Profeſſion of their Chriſtian Belief, in theſe Words:

I A. B. *profess Faith in God the Father; and in Jesus Christ his Eternal Son, the true God; and in the Holy Spirit, One God Blessed for evermore. and do Acknowledge the Holy Scriptures of the* Old *and* New Testament *to be given by Divine Inspiration.*

These Declarations and Subscriptions must be recorded at the Quarter Sessions.

And if any Person refuse the Oaths when tendred, he shall not be admitted to make and subscribe the Declarations, tho required by a Justice of Peace at the Sessions; if he cannot, within 31 Days after such Tender, produce two Protestant Witnesses to testify on Oath, that they believe him to be a Protestant Dissenter, or produce a Certificate under the Hands of four Protestants conformable to the Church, or who have taken the Oaths, *&c.* and he must likewise have a Certificate under the Hands and Seals of six or more of the Congregation to which he belongs, owning him to be one of them.

And until such Witnesses and Certificate are produced, the Justice must take a Recognizance, with two Sureties of 50 *l.* for producing the same, or otherwise shall be committed till that time.

But by this Act 'tis declared, *That all the Laws made for frequenting Divine-Service on the Lord's Day, are in force against all Persons except they come to some Religious Assembly allowed by Law.*

The Precedents upon the Statute of 1 *Will.* are as follow.

The Form of the Certificate by four Protestants *conformable within* 31 *Days after the* Tender, &c.

We *whose Names are hereunto subscribed, being all conformable to the Church of* England, *do hereby certify whom it doth concern,* That *we do verily believe That* A. B. *of* &c. *is a Protestant Dissenter.* Given *under our Hands,* &c.

The form of a Certificate by four Protestants *not conformable, &c.*

WE *whose Names are hereunto subscribed, having all taken the Oaths and subscribed the Declaration enjoyned by a Statute made in the first Year of the Reign of the late King* William *and Queen* Mary, *Intituled,* An Act for exempting Their Majesties Protestant Subjects dissenting from the Church of *England*, from the Penalties of certain Laws; *do hereby Certify*, That *we do verily believe* A. B. *of* &c. *is a Protestant Dissenter.* Given *under our Hands*, &c.

The Form of a Certificate from six of the Congregation.

WE *whose Names are hereunto subscribed, being Members of the Congregation of*, &c. *do hereby Certify whom it may concern*, That *we do own* A. B. *of*, &c. *to be one of our said Congregation*, Given *under our Hands and Seals*, &c.

A Recognizance with two Sureties, &c.

Pensil, ss. BE *it remembered*, That *on the* 11 *Day of* ——— &c. *came before me* P. L. Esq; *one of the Justices of the Peace of our Lord the King, for the County aforesaid*, A. B. *of* C. *in the said County, Husbandman*, E. F. *and* G. H. *of the same Place, in the County aforesaid, Yeomen, and acknowledge themselves Indebted unto our said Lord the King*, (viz.) *each of the Sureties aforesaid, in* 40 l. *and the aforesaid* A. B. *in* 100 l. *of good and lawful Money of* Great Britain, *To be Levyed of their Goods and Chattles, Lands and Tenements, for the Use of our said Lord the King, His Heirs and Successors, if the aforesaid* A. B. *shall fail in the Performance of the Condition hereunder written.*

The Condition of this Recognizance is such, That whereas the Oaths enjoyned to be taken by an Act made in the First Year of the Reign of the late King *William* and Queen *Mary*, Intituled, *An Act*, &c. were on the first Day of *August* last past tendred to the above-bounden *A. B.* by the aforesaid *P. L.* which he the said *A. B.* did then refuse to take; and whereas also he was on the Third Day of the said Month of *August* required by the said *P. L.* to make and subscribe the Declarations injoyned likewise by the said Act: Now if the said *A. B.* shall within Thirty one Days after such Tender of the said Declarations as aforesaid, produce a certificate under the Hands of four Protestants who are conformable to the Church of *England*, or of four others who have taken the Oaths, and subscribed the Declaration in the said Act mentioned, attesting him the said *A. B.* to be a Protestant Dissenter; and shall likewise produce within the Time aforesaid, another Certificate under the Hands and Seals of six or more sufficient Men of the Congregation to which he the said *A. B.* doth belong, owning him thereby to be one of them; That then this Recognizance shall be void, &c.

Benefit of Clergy. See *Felony.*

AS to the Benefit of Clergy, it was introduced here by the Common Law, exempting their Persons from any Temporal Jurisdiction. 'Tis a Privilege, on purpose to save the Life of a Criminal in certain Cases, if he was a Man of Learning, as accounted in those Days; for as such he might be useful to the Publick. And as its Original was by the Law of the Church, so was for some Time only allowed to Clerks in Orders.

But lately the Law is such, That if any Criminal within the Benefit of Clergy, shall demand his Clergy, it shall be granted to him without Reading, except in the Case of Man-slaughter, or a Man marrying two Wives, or a Woman two Husbands.

I admit, that in the Reign of *Jac.* 2. it was resolved in the Case of *Goring* and *Deering*, upon an Appeal, that the Court might delay to call a Criminal to Judgment after a Conviction for Man-slaughter, on purpose to make him liable to an Appeal.

But this was since denied to be Law in the Case of *Armstrong* and *Lisle*, *Mich.* 8 *Will.* (*viz.*) That since several Statutes have been made to extend the Benefit of Clergy to Persons in particular Cases, that the Court ought, *ex Officio*, to call the Party to Judgment upon a Conviction of Man-slaughter, and to allow him the Benefit of Clergy, if he prays it.

That to suspend or delay such Allowance, is to deprive him of that Defence by which he might prevent a Conviction of Murder upon an Appeal, and that 'tis a manifest Injury to the publick Justice, unless there is some legal Reason appearing out of the Record it self to justifie such Delay; for since he may be found guilty either of Murder or Man-slaughter upon the same Indictment, it would be unjust to hang him upon one Verdict, and not to allow him that Benefit which the Law hath given him to save his Life upon the other, which will be not only to put it twice in Danger, but to subject it to the Opinion of a Court, though he might be saved by Law.

'Tis both for the Benefit of the King and the Party, not to have the Allowance of the Clergy till after a Tryal: Because, if convicted, the King may be entituled to the Forfeitures; and if acquitted then he stands not in Need of this Priviledge.

Now if a Man cannot read where Clergy is allowable, and 'tis recorded by the Court, *Quod non legit*; if the Offender should be reprieved till the next Assizes, the Book may be tendered to him again, because 'tis *in favorem vitæ*, for which Reason he may have it under the Gallows. *Dyer.* 205. *b.*

Anne

Anno 4 *Eliz*. One *Stone* committed two Felonies in the same Day, and Clergy was allowable for one, but not for the other: He was first Indicted for that Felony for which he might have Clergy, and was found Guilty, but could not read, so the Court recorded, *Quod non Legit*, but he was reprieved till the next Assizes; then he was indicted for the other Feloney, and found Guilty; but before Judgment prayed that the Book might be tendered to him again for the first Offence, and had it, and could then read, and the Entry was then contrary to what it was before, *viz. Quod legit ut Clericus*, but there was an Ommission of these Words, *Qoud crematur & tradatur Ordinario*; and the Question was whether he should have Judgment of Death upon the last Indictment? And held he should not, because if the Entry had been *Quod legit*, &c. *& tradatur Ordinario*, he ought not to be arraigned on the last Indictment, for by the former Conviction and Clergy allowed, and the party reading, he is discharged from all Felonies done before that Time, and is afterwards the Prisoner of the Ordinary, and 'tis the fault of the Officer for not making the Entry as he ought. If they had a Mind to hang the Man, he ought to be indicted for that Offence first for which he could not have Clergy. *Dyer* 214 *b*.

But by a late Statute we are told, That the tendring the Book to Read, is found by Experience to be of no Use; therefore the Offender is not required now to read, but he is to be punished as a Clerk convict without Reading. 5 *Anna*.

Clerk of the Peace.

HE is in Officer at the common Law, for he is Clerk to the Conservators of Justices of the Peace and tis very Probable he was first instituted by them to make Entries, and to record their Proceedings.

In former times the *Custos Rotulorum* had the keeping of those Records; but afterwards when that became an Office of Honour and Dignity then he appointed a Clerk of the Peace.

Thus it stood till 37 *H*. 8. and then a Law was made, reciting That the Chancellor had taken upon him an Authority to make a *Custos* for Life, and he to appoint a Clerk of the Peace for Life, which was a Grievance; and therefore from thenceforth the *Custos* was to be appointed by the King during Pleasure, and the Clerk of the Peace was to continue in his Office no longer than the *Custos*.

Afterwards by 4 *Ed*. 6. this Statute, as to the appointing of a *Custos*, was repealed, and the Chancelour had Power again to appoint a *Custos*; but the Office of the Clerk of the Peace remained as before.

And thus it continued till 1 *W*, *& M*. and then the Appointment of a *Custos* was enacted

enacted to be as by the Statute of 37 *H.* 8. and he is to appoint a Clerk of the Peace to enjoy the Office so long as he shall behave himself well.

This was introductive of a new Law, for before he was removeable with the *Custos*, but now he hath an Estate for Life, determinable upon his Misbehaviour.

So that by this Act, the Power of the *Custos* is abridged; for before he might appoint any Person at large, but now the Person appointed must reside in the County. Formerly the *Custos* might remove the Clerk, *&c.* and the Sessions could not, for they had only Power to suspend him for any Misbehaviour; but now the Justices may remove him upon a Complaint exhibited in Writing, and due Proof thereof, and the *Custos* cannot; and if he appoint not another before the next Sessions, the Justices may do it.

He is to be present at the Sessions, and to draw up the Process of the Court; he is to read Indictments, and to record the proceedings of the Justices.

He must record the Rates of the Servants Wages, and inroll the Discharge of Apprentices. 5 *Eliz. cap.* 4.

He is to certify into *B. R.* the Transcripts of Indictments, Outlawries and Convictions, before the Justices within 40 Days next after the Conviction, *&c.* or within 20 Days after the beginning of the Term next ensuing, or forfeits 40. *s.* to the King and Prosecutor. 34 *&* 35 *H.* 8. *c.* 14.

In an Indictment for Murder, the Fact was laid to be committed, 31 *Junii*, and the *Deputy*, in the Presence and Hearing of the *Clerk of the Assize*, did read the Indictment as it was: The Offender was tried, and then the *Clerk of the Assize* informed the Court of the Mistake in the Indictment, *(viz.)* That there were not 31 Days in *June*; but because he did not inform them before the Tryal, he was fined 40 *l.* and committed. *Moor* 555.

He must take nothing of any Witness who shall give Evidence against a Felon, nor take more than Two Shillings for drawing any Bill of Indictment against a Felon; the Forfeiture is 5 *l.* with full Costs. 10 *&* 11 *Will.*

And if he draw a defective Bill, he shall draw a new one without any Fee, under the Penalty of the like forfeiture, to be recovered by him who shall sue for the same in any Court of Record.

Conjuration.

ANY Person convicted to have used Invocation or Conjuration of any evil Spirit, or to have consulted, *&c.* any such Spirit, to kill, consume, or lam any

any Perſon; they, with their Acceſſaries, are Fellons without Benefit of Clergy.

So likewiſe any Perſon convicted to have, by Witchcraft, Charm, *&c.* undertaken to tell where Goods loſt or ſtolen, may be found, or where they are, ſhall be committed for a Year without Bail, and ſhall once in every Quarter of that Year ſtand in the Pillory.

Conſpiracy.

THIS is an agreement between two or more, falſly and maliciouſly to indict an innocent Man; who, after Acquittal by Verdict, hath two Remedies to puniſh the Offenders.

(1.) By a Writ of Conſpiracy, which is a civil Action, in which Damages are to be recovered.

(2.) By an Indictment at the Suit of the King.

The Action will not lie, unleſs the Party is *legitimo modo acquitatus.* *Noy* 116.

And as to this Matter, there is a very nice Caſe, *viz.* Conſpiracy, *&c.* for that they falſly procured him to be indicted, and to be impriſoned, *quouſque* before ſuch Judges, *legitimo modo fuit acquittatus*, and did not ſay, *inde acquittatus:* The Court was in ſome Doubt, becauſe that Word was ommitted, but certainly it could not be material; for having ſet forth that they procured him falſely to be indicted, *&c.* *quouſque* he was acquitted; this could not be intended of any other Matter but that for which he was indicted.

There are four incidents to this Action.

The Conſpiracy muſt be {
- Malicious;
- Falſe,
- Declared by ſome Proſecution;
- Voluntary.

The ſecond Remedy againſt Offenders of this Nature, is by indictment at the Suit of the King; and upon Conviction the Judgment is,

That they ſhall looſe their Free-Law, that is, they ſhall never be of a Jury nor Witneſſes in any Caſe; ſhall never appear but by Attorney; their Lands, Chattles and Goods ſhall be ſeized into the Kings Hands, their Trees cut down, and their Bodies impriſoned. *Stamf. placit. Coron.* 175. *b.* 3 *Inſt.* 143.

The Reaſon of this Judgment is, becauſe the Offenders have conſpired the ſhedding innocent Blood, and that under a Pretence of Juſtice, by a Courſe of Law, which is made for the Protection of the Innocent.

But

But there have been other Judgments given against these Offenders: as for Instance.

An Information was brought by one Miller *of* Kent, *against an Attorney and another, for a Conspiracy, maliciously to take away his Life, by accusing him for breaking open a Trunk, and taking out Money and a Lease, for which they indicted Mr.* Miller *at the Assizes; it was found* Ignoramus, *the Conspiracy was proved, and the Sentence was, That the Attorney should be degraded, and cast over the Bar; That both should loose their Ears, and be marked in the Face with the Letter C. to stand on the Pillory with Papers of their Offences, to be whipped, and each fined* 500 l. *This Sentence was Executed on them,* Anno 11 Jac. Godb. 205.

So where two conspired to accuse Sir *Anthony Ashley* for a Murder done 16 Years before. *Cantrell* was to be the Accuser, and Sir *James Creighton* articled with him That he should have a Sixth Part of Sir *Anthony*'s Estate, and that he would beg the Whole of the King. *Cantrell* agreed, and procured one *Smith*, who was Servant to Sir *Anthony*, to accuse both his Master and himself for putting Poison into Drink, which his Master commanded him to carry to one *Rice*, which he did and so poisoned him. For this Fact he caused his Master and himself to be indicted, but afterwards discovered the Conspiracy, and *Creighton* was fined 1000 *l.* and committed; another of the Defendants was fined 300 *l.* and to stand in the Pillory, and was burnt with a hot Iron on both Cheeks with the Letters F. and C.

Constable.

'TIS not material in this Place to enquire, whether the Word or the Office is of *Saxon* or *Norman* Original. 2 *Inst.* 123.

Some are of Opinion, That upon the Increase of the People, the Sheriff alone could not take Sufficient Care of the Peace of the County, but that it was divided into Hundreds, and a High-Constable was appointed, over each Hundred to preserve the Peace; but 'tis uncertain when this Division began, for Mr. *Selden* differs from the common Opinion of other Writers, who affirm it to be in the Reign of King *Alfred*, and he tells us it was before that Time.

But notwithstanding this Division (be it when it will) neither the Sheriff together with the High Constables, could in After-times take due Care of the Peace in the County and Hundreds over which they presided; and therefore Petty Constables were appointed for that Purpose in each Town, Village and Parish of every Hundred, to be Assisting to the High Constables.

'Tis also incertain when this Division began; it seems to me to be very ancient, and that both High and Petty-Conſtable are Officers at Common Law; that the one was long before the Statute of *Winton*, and the other before the beginning of the Reign of *Ed.* 3. ſo that ſuch old Statutes which firſt mention this Officer, do only recite the Common Law.

How and where choſen. It may be at the Leet, either by the Steward himſelf, or by Preſentment of the Grand Jury there; but this muſt be warranted by Cuſtom, and where a Court-Leet is uſually kept, and in ſuch Caſe the Juſtices of the Peace cannot interpoſe.

But where Neglects and Miſcarriages are, either in keeping of ſuch Courts, or chuſing them, the Juſtices at their Quarter-Seſſions may appoint and ſwear a High Conſtable, and this is the uſual Courſe at this time; but in Caſe of Refuſal, Death or the Removal, one Juſtice of the Peace may chuſe and ſwear another.

'Tis true, they may be ſworn at any other Time by a Warrant from the Seſſions, and they may alſo be choſen out of the Seſſions by the greater Number of Juſtices of a Diviſion: But this is not uſual.

He who is choſen Conſtable muſt be an honeſt, underſtanding and able Man, both in Body and Eſtate, and not of the meaner Sort; and therefore it has been held, That he is not to be choſen by Houſe or by Cuſtom, if not fit to execute the Office.

He is likewiſe to be reſident where choſen, and if he is not thus qualified two Juſtices upon Complaint, may appoint another.

But now tis ruled, that a Cuſtom for every Inhabitant to ſerve by Turns is good; for if it happen on a Woman, ſhe may hire one to ſerve. *Sid.* 355.

Attornies, Clergy-men, Juſtices of the Peace, Infants, Lawyers, Madmen, Phyſicians, Poor, Old and Sick perſons are exempted from being choſen Conſtables.

Formerly it has been doubted whether he might make a Deputy, but now 'tis allowed; but *reſpondeat ſuperior* for his Miſcarriage, unleſs the Deputy is ſworn and allowed by the Court. *Sid.* 355. *Moor* 1453. *Bulſt.* 77. 1 *Roll. Rep.* 274.

Diſſenters choſen Conſtables, may make a Deputy, *per* Statute 1 *Will. & Mar.* 7 *Jac. cap.* 5.

If any Perſon refuſe to ſerve, the Juſtices may bind him over to the Aſſizes or Seſſions, and there he may be indicted and fined; but you muſt alledge the Place where he was required to take the Oath, and before whom he refuſed to be ſworn, and not *ad Seſſionem* generally, otherwiſe it may be quaſhed.

1 *Keb.* 4 8. 1 *Mod.* 24. 13. *Allen* 78. 2 *Roll. Rep.* 78. 2 *Sand.* 29. *Sid.* 272. *Stiles* 394.

If an Action be brought againſt a Conſtable, it muſt be laid in the proper County where the Fact is ſuppoſed to be done, if 'tis brought againſt him for any Thing in the Executing his Office, he may plead the General Iſſue and give the ſpecial Matter in Evidence; and if the Plaintiff is Non-ſuited, or diſcontinue, or a Verdict

dict for the Defendant, he ſhall have double Coſts. 7 *Jac. cap.* 5. 21 *Jac. cap.* 12.

If a Conſtable dye, or remove out of the Pariſh, two Juſtices may chuſe and ſwear another, and he is to continue in the Office till next Seſſions, and then the Juſtice may either approve him, or appoint another and ſwear him. This Office is to continue for one Year; and if longer, Juſtices in their Seſſions may diſcharge him.

His Duty is to be conſidered under theſe ſeveral Heads following, *viz.*

Affrays,	Exciſe,	Hue-and-Cry,	Peace,	Rogues,
Ale-houſes,	Felons,	Juries,	Phyſicians,	Superſedeas,
Arms,	Forcible Entry,	Lords, Day,	Plague,	Swearing,
Bridges,	Gaming-houſes,	Meaſures,	Priſoners,	Vagabounds,
Cuſtoms,	High-ways,	Militia,	Rent,	Warrants,
Eſcapes,	Horſe ſtoned,	Miniſters Diſturbed	Riots,	Watches.

Affrays. *And firſt his Duty concerning* Affrays, *and therein what is to be done to thoſe who fight in his Preſence.*

Aſſaulting, threatning to kill or beat another in his Preſence, or whatever is a Breach of the Peace, he may carry the Offender before a Juſtice of Peace without a Warrant; but if the Fighting is over he muſt have a Warrant, and this is to find Sureties for his good behaviour.

If the Quarrelling or Fighting is not in his Sight and he is informed of it, and refuſes to go and keep the Peace, he may be preſented by the Grand Jury at Seſſions, and fined.

He may Command ſuch to depart; and if they refuſe or make any Reſiſtance, he may juſtifie the beating of them, and call others to his Aſſiſtance, and if either he or they happen to be killed, 'tis Murder.

He may break open the Doors to ſee Peace kept.

If any Perſon ſhall be wounded in fighting, he may carry the Offender before a Juſtice of Peace, who may bail or commit, &c.

Moſt of the Things above-mentioned the Conſtable may do by Virtue of his Office; for before Juſtices of the Peace were made, he was *Conſervator Pacis*, but he could not take Security by Recognizance or Bail, becauſe he was not an Officer on Record: He might put a Man in the *Stocks* who broke the Peace in his View but he could not arreſt a Man to find Sureties of the Peace upon any Complaint made to him, unleſs he did actually ſee the Peace broken. *Owen* 105

A Man brought a Child about two Months old to the Church, and left it there, deſigning it ſhould Periſh, the Conſtable put him into the Stocks, and kept him there till he he agreed to take the Child; and this was held Juſtifiable, it being to prevent a Felony. Moor 284.

The Puniſhment of a Conſtable for Neglecting to obey a Warrant from a Juſtice of Peace, conſiſts in the Forfeitures following, *viz.*

Ale-houſe unlicenſed. If he doth not levy 20 *s.* to the Uſe of the Poor upon ſuch who keep unlicenſed Ale-Houſes, which he may ſell after three Days; and if no Diſtreſs, then if he doth not whip the Offender, one Juſtice may commit the Conſtable without Bail, until the Ale-houſe-keeper is puniſhed, or until the Conſtable pay 40 *s.* to the Uſe of the Poor.

If an Ale-houſe-keeper ſells leſs than Meaſure, *viz.* full Quarts; then if the Conſtable doth not levy 20 *s,* he is to forfeit 40 *s.* to be levied by Warrant from one Juſtice; and if no Diſtreſs to be committed.

If an *Ale*-houſe-keeper ſuffer Townſmen to be Tippling, and the Conſtable having a warrant, doth not levy the 10 *s.* ſhall forfeit *ut prius*, &c. if no Diſtreſs can be had, he muſt certifie that default within Twenty Days, or forfeits 40 *Shillings*, *ut prius.*

Upon thoſe Convicted of Tippling, he muſt levy the Penalty of 3 *s.* 4 *d.* or if he Neglect, having a Warrant for ſo doing, forfeits 10. *s.*

Upon thoſe Convicted of Drunkenneſs, he muſt levy 5 *s.* for the Poor; if the Party is not able to pay it; he muſt ſit in the *S*tocks ſix Hours, *&c.*

If a Traveller pay, or offer to pay ready Money for Lodging, and is refuſed; a Conſtable may cauſe the Ale-houſe-keeper to be indicted next Seſſions, and there he may be fined and Committed.

Arms. He may take Arms from them that ride or go armed in Terrour of the People, and may carry ſuch Perſons before a Juſtice of Peace to find Sureties.

They muſt aſſiſt ſuch Perſons who have a Warrant from the Lord Lieutenant or his Deputy to ſearch for Arms, *&c.* which muſt be in the Day-time, unleſs in Towns; and if reſiſted, may enter with Force.

Bridges. Where a common Bridge is in Decay, and it cannot be known who or what Lands are to repair it, the Conſtable and Two of the moſt able Inhabitants in the Pariſh muſt aſſeſs, and Four Juſtices muſt allow ſuch Aſſeſſment.

Cuſtom. A Conſtable muſt, upon Requeſt, aſſiſt ſuch Perſons who have a Warrant from the chief Magiſtrate to ſearch for Goods which have not paid Cuſtom; and he may (if within a Month after the Offence) enter into any Houſe in the Day-time, and, if reſiſted, break it open.

He muſt be aſſiſting to all Perſons appointed by the King to collect or manage his Cuſtoms.

Eſcapes. If he ſuffer a Felon to eſcape before he is actually in Cuſtody, 'tis a Miſdemeanor, for which he may be indicted and fined; but if he was actually taken, and then he voluntarily ſuffer him to eſcape, or to deſtroy himſelf, 'tis Felony in the Conſtable, but if the Eſcape is by Negligence, or involuntary, 'tis only

only finable; but the Place where the Party was taken, and where he eſcaped, muſt be alledged in the Indictment. *Cro. Eliz.* 752. *Cro. Eliz.* 200.

If he diſcharges any Perſon taken upon Suſpicion of Felony, 'tis juſtifiable' if no Felony was committed, but otherwiſe he muſt not diſcharge him, tho' he knoweth that the Party is innocent; but it muſt be done by due Courſe of Law.

He may put a Felon into the Stocks, and lock him in, or put Irons upon him, or pinnion him to prevent Eſcapes when he is about to carry him before a Juſtice of Peace, or to Gaol.

Exciſe. Officer of Exciſe muſt have a Conſtable when he enters into a Brewhouſe by Night to gauge Fats or Veſſels.

A Conſtable, by Warrant from Juſtices, is to levy the Penalties on the Offenders againſt any Law of Exciſe, by Diſtreſs, *&c.* and if none, *&c.* may carry him to Gaol.

Maker or Retailer of Vinegar, Cyder, *&c.* for Sale, refuſing a Gauger to enter in the Night-time with a Conſtable, forfeits 15 *l.*

Brewer ſo refuſing, forfeits 20 *l.*

Exciſeman ſuſpecting ſecret Conveyance of Worts, may upon Requeſt, and in Preſence of a Conſtable, break open a Door in the Day-time, and if oppoſed, forfeits 20 *l.* by the 7 & 8 *Will. cap.* 30.

Felons. A Conſtable is bound, *ex Officio*, to endeavour the taking of Felons, and may raiſe Men to aſſiſt him; he may likewiſe apprehend upon Suſpicion; and upon Complaint or common Fame, may ſearch ſuſpicious Houſes.

If a Felon fly, the Conſtable may ſeize, and make an Inventory of his Goods, and ſend Hue-and-Cry after him; that is, he may raiſe the Town at any Time, and give the next Conſtable Notice: The Neglect is finable by the Juſtices.

If upon ſuch Flight he is apprehended in another County, the Felon muſt be committed where taken, and not where the Fact was done.

Two Juſtices, *Quorum unus*, are to ſet a Tax upon every Pariſh in a Hundred, where Damages are recovered againſt any one or more Inhabitants of that Hundred, upon the Statute of *Winton*; and the Conſtables of every Pariſh are to ſet a Tax upon every Inhabitant of theſe Pariſhes where they refuſe to contribute, and may levy the ſame by Diſtreſs, *&c.*

Forcible Entry. If he refuſe to aſſiſt the Juſtice in removing the Force, or carrying the Offender to Gaol, he may be committed himſelf, and fined.

Games. He muſt once a Month ſearch Houſes where unlawful Games are kept, as Tables, Tennis, Bowles, *&c.* and may commit the Maſter of the Houſe, and the Gameſters, till they give Sureties not to do the like again; if the Conſtable neglects, he forfeits 40 *s.* for every Default.

He may, by Warrant from one Juſtice of Peace, enter and ſearch the ſuſpected Houſes of any Perſon not qualified, and if he find any Game there, ſhall carry the Offender before a Juſtice of Peace. 4 & 5 *W. & M. cap.* 23.

Horſes

Horſes ſtoned. A Conſtable muſt aſſiſt ſuch who call him to ſeize ſtoned Horſes put into Commons where Mares are uſually kept; which Horſes are not (at the Age of two Years) fifteen Hands high, the Horſes muſt be brought to the next Pound and meaſured by a Conſtable in the Preſence of three Men; if he refuſe to meaſure, forfeits 40 *s.*

In Fenn Grounds the Horſes may be but 13 Hands high.

Hue-and-Cry. A Conſtable is to raiſe Hue-and-Cry upon Notice, and deſcribing the Felon, and telling him which Way he is gone; and for this Purpoſe he may call upon the Pariſhioners to aſſiſt him in the Purſuit of the Felon to the next Conſtable, and he to the next, *&c.* and in the mean Time to make an Inventory of his Goods in the Preſence of his Neighbours: If he refuſe to purſue the Offender, he may be indicted, *&c.* but the Place where he gave Notice muſt be ſet forth in the Indictment. 10 *Eliz.* 655.

He was indicted, for that a Burglary was committed by Perſons unknown, and that *J. S.* gave him Notice thereof, and required him to make Hue-and Cry, which he refuſed: Exception was taken to the Indictment, becauſe the Proſecutor did not alledge where he gave him Notice; and this was held a material Exception. *Cro. Eliz.* 654.

Juries. Conſtables, *&c.* muſt every Year at *Michaelmas* Seſſions give in a Liſt of their Names and Places of Habitation within their reſpective Limits, of all Perſons qualified to ſerve on Juries between the Age of 21 and 70 Years; and if he neglects, forfeits 5 *l.* to the King

The Qualifications are 80 *l. per Ann.* for a Grand Jury-man, and 10 *l. per Ann.* for a Petty Jury-man. 7 *&* 8 *W. cap.* 32.

Labourers. A Conſtable, *ex Officio,* may in Hay or Corn-Harveſt ſet any ordinary Tradeſman on Work by the Day, being required by thoſe who want Labourers, and put them into Stocks for two Days and a Night if they refuſe; and the Conſtable neglecting his Duty herein, forfeits 40 *s.*

Militia. They are to levy the Money charged upon any Perſon by the Lord Lieutenant or his Deputies, for the providing Arms for Horſe and Foot Soldiers; and if no Diſtreſs is to be found, may by Warrant from the Lord Lieutenant, *&c.* commit the Offender until he make Satisfaction.

Miniſter diſturbed. A Conſtable, *ex Officio,* may apprehend the Offender, and carry him before a Juſtice of Peace.

Plague. He may command any Perſon infected to keep within his Houſe; and if after ſuch Command he wilfully go Abroad, having a Sore upon him, 'tis Felony; and if no Sore, he may be puniſhed as a Vagabond, and bound to his Good Behaviour for a Year.

If he neglects to levy the Money appointed by Juſtices to relieve poor People infected, forfeits 10 *s.* for every Offence.

Carrying Priſoners to Gaol, He, by Warrant from a Juſtice of Peace, may

may ſell the Offender's Goods to defray his Charges, and of thoſe who carry him to Gaol; but ſuch Goods muſt be appraiſed by ſome Inhabitants of the Place.

If the Offender hath no Goods, then the Town where he was apprehended muſt be at this Charge; and the Conſtable, *&c.* and three Inhabitants, may impoſe a Tax on every Inhabitant; which being allowed by a Juſtice of Peace, the Conſtable by Warrant may levy it on thoſe who refuſe; and being appraiſed by four Inhabitants there, may ſell it.

If a Conſtable be ſued, he may plead the General Iſſue, and ſhall have trebble Damages beſides Coſts, if he recover.

In conveying a Felon either before a Juſtice, or to Gaol, he may lock him in the Stocks, if unruly, to prevent his Eſcape.

Before I treat of this, I ſhall mention his Oath, *viz.*

The Conſtable's Oath.

YOu ſhall ſwear, That you ſhall well and truly execute the Office of a Conſtable or Head-borough, for the Town, or for the Pariſh of *H.* for the Year enſuing, and until another be ſworn in your Room, or until you ſhall be legally diſcharged thereof.

This Oath is now adminiſtred for the Shortneſs of it, but by the other Oath he was uſually ſworn to theſe particulars, *Viz.*

Affrays to ſuppreſs and preſent. Armed Men to arreſt. Barretors to apprehend. Blood-ſhed to preſent. Drunkenneſs to preſent. Felons to apprehend. Gaming-houſes and Gameſters to preſent. Hue and Cry to ſee made. Idle Perſons puniſhed. Night-walkers to puniſh. Peace to keep, *&c.* Reſcues to preſent. Riot to ſuppreſs and apprehend. Rogues to puniſh. Vagabonds. Warrants to execute. Watch to keep. And all other Things relating to his Office, according to his Ability.

This he is bound to do, but few make true Preſentments of theſe Offences within their Liberties; they make Returns formally, and bring them to a Juſtice to ſign, and carry them to the High Conſtable, who makes Oath that he had them from the Petty Conſtable: And they are not altered when they ſignify nothing.

It hath been lately queſtion'd, Why a High Conſtable ſhould be ſworn by a Matter of Form, and not a Petty Conſtable to the Subſtance of Return? Which, as a late Author obſerv'd, ought to be carried to a Juſtice ſome Time before the Seſſions, to be examined to the Truth of every Article.

Few Pariſhes there are, but what have Inmates and unlawful Cottages; and this muſt unavoidably fall under their Obſervation.

Rent

Rent. A Conſtable muſt aſſiſt the Party diſtraining, and ſwear two Men to appraiſe the Goods, and the Overplus, after Debts ſatisfied, may be left in his Hands.

Riots. He is, *ex Officio*, to ſuppreſs all Riots, and to commit the Offenders, and all ſuch who break the Peace.

Lords-Day. He muſt levy the Penalty of 3 *s.* 4 *d.* by Warrant from one Juſtice, of ſuch who uſe unlawful Games; and if he cannot diſtrain, muſt put the Offender in the Stocks for three Hours.

Thoſe who on that Day keep or reſort to Bowling, Dancing, Ringing, or any Sport or Paſtime whatſoever, forfeits 5 *s.* if above 14 Years old; if under, 12 *d.* which the Conſtable muſt levy by Warrant of one Juſtice by Diſtreſs; and if no Diſtreſs can be taken, then to be put three Hours into the Stocks.

He muſt likewiſe levy 6 *s.* 8 *d.* by Warrant on a Butcher, who ſhall kill or ſell Fleſh on that Day.

Every Servant, Day-Labourer, Common Soldier, and Common Seaman, being convicted of **Swearing**, forfeits 1 *s.* to the Poor, and every other Perſon 2 *s.* and double for the ſecond Offence, and trebble for the third, to be levied by Warrant of one Juſtice. *6 & 7 W. & M. cap.* 11.

If a Conſtable have a Warrant to execute for Sureties of the Peace, and afterwards has a *Superſedeas* from a Juſtice, *&c.* yet if he will perſiſt to have the Party find Sureties, and he refuſe and is detain'd, 'tis falſe Impriſonment, *&c.*

Conſtables muſt cauſe Night Watches to be ſet from *Whitſuntide* till *Michaelmas*, *viz.* from Sun-ſet to Sun-riſing, with four Men or more, who muſt be able and Inhabitants of the Place, and watch by Turns; if they refuſe, the Conſtable may complain to the Juſtice of Peace, who may bind the Party refuſing to Good Behaviour, *&c.*

A Conſtable appointed a Man to watch, and becauſe he refuſed, he put him into the Stocks: In an Action of falſe Impriſonment, the Defendant juſtified as Conſtable, but did not ſhew that the Plaintiff was an Inhabitant of the Town; *for he might be a Stranger, and then he could not appoint him to wacth, nor put him in the Stocks for refuſing, but muſt complain to a Juſtice of Peace. Cro. Eliz.* 204

He muſt not diſpute, but execute *Warrants*; and if the Juſtices exceed their Authority, the Conſtable is excuſed.

But if the Juſtice of Peace ſends a Warant to execute where he hath no Authority, or where he is no proper Judge, a Conſtable may be puniſhed if he execute it.

So, if the Warrant is miſtaken in the Penalty, or if it command the Conſtable to do Things out of his Precinct.

He need not ſhew his Warrant, but may acquaint the Party with the Contens of it.

If he apprehend a Perſon without a Warrant and obtain one afterwards, 'tis falſe Impriſonment.

If

If he let the Person go upon his Promise to return and appear before a Justice of Peace, he cannot retake him by Vertue of his first Warrant; but if the Party escaped he may pursue him, though in another County, and bring him back to the Justice of Peace.

If there are two Persons of one Name, and the same Addition, and the Constable takes a wrong Person, 'tis no false Imprisonment.

But if the Warrant is against a particular Person by Name, and he apprehends another who is really the Offender, such taking is wrongful, and the Party may have his Action of false Imprisonment, but will recover but little Damages.

A Man may be bound to his Good behaviour for any Abuse or Contempt to the Justice's Warrant and may be indicted and fined for it.

In Cases of Treason, Felony, or Breach of the Peace, a Constable may by Warrant from a Justice of Peace break open an House to take the Criminal; but first he ought to require the opening of the Doors, and to acquaint the Persons for what Purpose he came thither.

If he is Indicted for not executing of a Warrant, you ought to shew some particular Act of Disobedience, and not generally, that he did not execute it *Trin.* 20. *Car. B. R.*

He may justify the Detaining an Offender for a Day, by the Command of a Justice of Peace without a Warrant, not having an Opportunity then to examine him. *Moor* 408.

A Warrant to remove a Constable, *continuing in his Office above a Year.*

To *A. B. of C. Yeoman.*

P. ss. WHereas *it appeareth upon Oath to us,* P. L. *and* J. M. *Two of his Majesty's Justices of the Peace for the County aforesaid, That* A. B. *hath lately executed the Office of a Head-borough in and for the Parish of* C. *aforesaid; during the Space of one whole Year, and doth still continue to* Execute *the said Office after the Expiration of the said Year contrary to the Form of the Statute in that Case made and provided: Now we do hereby, according to the Power and Authority given unto us concerning the Premises, discharge you the said* A. B. *from the Office of* Constable *in and for the said Parish of* C. *requiring you from henceforth to forbear the Execution thereof in any Matter or Thing whatsoever, until further Order shall be taken therein.* Given *under our Hands and Seals,* &c.

A Warrant for a New Constable to appear and be sworn.

To D. E. of &c. Yeoman.

Kent. ss. WHereas A. B. *hath lately been discharged by us, P. L. and J. M. two of his Majestie's Justices, for that he continued to Execute the Office of a Constable for the Parish of C. aforesaid, above the Space of one whole Year* : :: *Or whereas A. B. late Constable of the Parish of C. is departed this Life, (or) is removed with himself and Family out of the Parish of C. within the Year in which he should have served in the Office of Constable* ; *or is, by reason of his Age and Inability, not capable to execute,* &c. *the said Office* : These are therefore *to require you, and in his Majesty's Name to charge and command you, personally to come before us, or before some other of his Majesty's Justices of the Peace for the said County, to take the Oath of a Constable, to serve His Majesty within the Town or Parish of* C. And hereof *fail not.* Given *under our Hands and Seals,* &c.

By the Statute of 3 *Jac. cap.* 10. An Offender who is to be carried to Goal, must bear his own Charges, and of those who convey him ; if he refuse, then the Constable, by Warrant from one Justice may sell his Goods, &c.

A Warrant to levy upon the Offender's Goods the Charges of carrying him to Goal.

To the Constable of the Town of C.

K. ss. WHereas it appeareth to me, upon the Complaint of the Parishioners of, &c. in the County aforesaid, upon Oath, That the Charges of *S. P.* and of those who conveyed him to Gaol, being sent thither by my Warrant upon Suspicion of Felony, did amount to 11 *s.* and that the said *S. P.* hath Goods and Chattels within your Township sufficient to defray the said Expence : These are therefore, in His Majesty's Name, to command you to levy the said Sum of 11 *s.* by Distress and Sale of the Goods of the said *S. P.* within your Parish, causing the same before the Sale thereof to be appraised by some of the Neighbours there, and that you pay the said Sum unto the Parishioners of, &c. in your said County : And hereof fail not, &c.

If the Offender hath no Goods, &c. then the Constable and Church-wardens, and three of the Inhabitants, and if there are no such Officers, then four of the principal Inhabitants, may tax all the rest ; which Tax must be allowed by one Justice: And if they refuse, then by a Warrant from one Justice the Officer may levy it.

A Warrant

A Warrant to levy the Tax upon thoſe who refuſe to pay, &c.

To the Conſtable, &c.

Kent ſſ. WHereas the Perſons whoſe Names are under-written, have been lawfully taxed in the ſeveral Sums herein after-mentioned, and which are added to their reſpective Names, in order to ſatisfy the Charges expended by *T. M.* and thoſe whom he called to his Aſſiſtance to carry *S. P.* to Gaol; which ſaid Perſons, as Oath hath been made, have refuſed to pay the ſame, contrary to the Form of the Statute in that Caſe made and provided: Theſe are therefore to require you, or either of you, to levy the ſaid Sums upon the ſeveral Goods and Chattels of the reſpective Perſons ſo taxed as aforeſaid, and refuſing to pay the ſame, returning the Overplus to them reſpectively: Given under our Hands and Seals, *&c.*

By this Statute the Conſtables, and other Inhabitants of the Pariſh, may tax all Perſons chargeable, by the 43 *Eliz. cap.* 2. to reimburſe their Charges for conveying Vagabonds, *&c.* to the Houſe of Correction, and for other Pariſh-Charges.

Now the Perſons to be taxed by the Act are, every Inhabitant of the Pariſh, the Parſon or the Vicar, and every Occupier of Houſes, Lands, Tythes and Woods; but the Land-Lord is not to be taxed in reſpect of his Rent.

The Tax upon Lands is to be made according to the Yearly Rent, but no Man is to be taxed for the Stock he hath upon the Lands; but if a Clothier or Merchant, having a conſiderable Stock in Trade or Merchandize, and occupy Lands, they may be taxed for both.

The Taxation of Perſonal Eſtates muſt be in the Pariſh to which 'tis taxed, and after the Rate of 5 *l.* for every Hundred.

This Tax or Rate muſt be confirmed under the Hands and Seals of two Juſtices of the Peace; and then if the Perſons taxed refuſe to pay; the Conſtable, by Warrant from two Juſtices, may levy it.

Firſt, if the Inhabitants refuſe to make a Tax, two Juſtices may make a Warrant, requiring them to do it.

The Form of which Warrant may be thus:

A Warrant, enabling the Pariſhioners to make a Tax to reimburſe the Conſtable.

To A. B. D. E. G. H. K. L. *and other the Inhabitants of the Pariſh of* D. *in the County of* Kent.

Kent ſſ. WHereas we are inform'd by *T. M.* Conſtable of your ſaid Pariſh,

That he hath expended several Sums of Money in the necessary Execution of his Office, and that he hath not been reimbursed the same; but hath desired our Direction and Assistance for that purpose: These are therefore, in His Majesty's Name, to require and command you, or the greater Number of you, who shall be met together upon Notice of this Precept, to examine the Accompts of the said Constable relating to the Premisses; and that if you shall find his said Expences to be necessary in the Execution of his said Office, that then you forthwith do tax every Inhabitant within your Parish, in several and proportionable Sums, amounting to so much as will reimburse him. And we do likewise hereby give Authority to the said Constable to demand and collect the respective Sums so assessed; and that if any Person so taxed shall refuse to pay the same, that then the said Constable do return unto us, or to some other Justice of this County, the Names of the Persons refusing. Given under our Hands, &c.

The Names of the Persons refusing to pay the Tax being returned by the Constables to the Justices of the Peace, then they may issue forth this Warrant to appear, and shew Cause why they refuse to pay, &c.

To the Constable, &c. of the Parish of D. *in the County of* Kent.

Kent ss. THese are in His Majesty's Name, to command you, That you, or some or one of you, do give Notice unto *J. K. L. M. &c.* to appear before us at the House of, *&c.* called or known by the Sign of, *&c.* in *M.* in the said County, on *Thursday* the 8th Day of this Instant *August*, at 10 of the Clock in the Morning of the same Day, to shew Cause why they severally refuse to pay the respective Sums of Money assess'd upon them, for and towards the Reimbursement of the Charges which *T. M.* Constable of the Parish *D.* aforesaid, hath sustained in the necessary Execution of his said Office: And hereof fail not. Given under our Hands and Seals, *&c.*

If they appear, then the two Justices may bind them over to appear at the Sessions, if they think fit so to do. The Condition as follows.

THe Condition of this Recognizance is such, That whereas the above-bounden *A. B.* and *C. D.* have severally refused to pay to *T. M.* late Constable of the Parish of, *&c.* in the County aforesaid, such Sums which have been severally and respectively assessed upon them, in order to reimburse the said Constable what hath been necessarily expended by him in the Execution of his said Office: If therefore the said *A. B.* and *C. D.* shall Personally appear at the next General Quarter-Sessions of the Peace, to be held at *M.* for the County aforesaid, and shall then do and receive what shall be injoined by the said Court relating to the Premisses; then this Recognizance shall be void, or else to stand in full Force and Vertue.

Capt. & cogn. octavo die Augusti, *Anno supradicto coram nobis.* P. L. J. M.

When they appear at the Seſſions, they may be preſented and indicted there, ſetting forth, That the Aſſeſſment was reaſonable, and it muſt appear to be for a Conſtable's Rate, and conclude, *contra formam Statuti.*

If they refuſe to appear upon Notice, then the Juſtice may iſſue forth this Warrant:

To the Conſtable of, &c.

Kent ſſ. WHereas we are informed, That *A. B.* and *C. D.* of your Pariſh Yeomen, had Notice given unto them reſpectively to appear before us at a certain Time and Place mentioned in a former Warrant for that Purpoſe, to ſhew Cauſe why they did not pay unto *T. M.* late Conſtable of the Pariſh of *D.* aforeſaid, the reſpective Sums aſſeſſed upon them towards the Reimburſement of his neceſſary Charges in the Execution of his ſaid Office: And whereas they have refuſed or neglected to appear according to the Purport of the ſaid Warrant, or to pay the ſaid Money: **Theſe are therefore,** in His Majeſty's Name, to command you to bring the aforeſaid *A. B.* and *C. D.* before us, or ſome other Juſtice of the Peace for this County, at the Houſe of, *&c.* in *M.* upon *Thurſday* next, by Ten of the Clock in the Fore-noon of the ſame Day, to anſwer the Premiſſes **Given** under our Hands and Seals, *&c.*

If they appear before the Juſtices, and they do not think it expedient to bind them over to the Seſſions, then they may grant a Warrant to diſtrain, *&c.* for the Charges, as followeth:

To the Conſtable of the Pariſh of D. *in the County of* Kent.

Kent ſſ. WHereas it appeareth unto us, upon the Oath of *T. M.* late Conſtable of the ſaid Pariſh, That *A. B.* and *C. D.* Inhabitants of the aforeſaid Pariſh, have refuſed to pay the Sums herein after written; that is to ſay, The ſaid *A. B.* hath refuſed to pay 1 *s.* and the ſaid *C. D.* 1 *s.* 6*d.* being ſeverally aſſeſſed upon them towards the reimburſing ſuch Charges which the ſaid *T. M.* hath neceſſarily expended in the Execution of his ſaid Office: **Theſe are therefore** to require you to levy the ſaid reſpective Sums ſo aſſeſſed upon the ſaid Perſons by Diſtreſs and Sale of their reſpective Goods, rendring to them the Overplus, if any ſhall be. **Given** under our Hands and Seals, *&c.*

On his ſerving of Warrants.

THIS is a Precept in Writing under the Hand and Seal of the Juſtice of the Peace.

It ought to contain the Cauſe, and therefore a Warrant to anſwer ſuch Things as ſhall be objected, without mentioning any Thing in particular, is not good

good. This is the Opinion of my Lord *Coke*, 2 *Inſt.* 591.

If any Perſon *abuſes* the Warrant, as by throwing it in the Dirt, or treading it under Foot, or not executing it, 'tis a *Contempt* of the King's Proceſs, and he ſhall be indicted and fined.

The Juſtice ought not to grant a *Blank Warrant*, for this is finable; nor a Warrant for Felony, without examining the Perſon who required it, upon Oath, and binding him over to give Evidence.

The Officer. The Conſtable being a Perſon to whom it is directed, he ought to execute it with all convenient Speed; and if 'tis a Warrant for the Peace or Good Behaviour, he may break open Doors.

Upon arreſting the Party, he need not ſhew his Warrant, but he ought to declare the Contents of it.

If he is *reſiſted* or *aſſaulted*, he may juſtifie the beating and wounding, &c.

If after the Arreſt the Officer lets his Priſoner go, upon his Promiſe to return to appear, he cannot retake him upon the firſt Warrant, becauſe it was executed; but if the Priſoner eſcape, he may take him upon a freſh Purſuit without another Warrant.

If a Juſtice grants a Warrant in Caſes beyond his Authority, the Officer muſt *obey*: but if it be where he hath no Juriſdiction, or in a Cauſe where he is not properly a Judge, if the Officer executes ſuch Warrants, he is puniſhable.

As if a *Poor's Rate* is illegally aſſeſſed, and afterwards levied by a Warrant from the Juſtice, &c. this will not excuſe the Church-wardens. *Cro. Car.* 394.

Where a particular Perſon who hath an Authority to act, commits a *Miſtake* in any Thing which is in his Power or Juriſdiction, in ſuch Caſe the Officer will be excuſed for executing it; but where he exceeds his Authority, all is void, becauſe 'tis limited.

Where the Party is to be brought. If the Warrant is General, *viz.* to be brought before the Juſtice who grants it, or any other Juſtice, &c. the Conſtable, who is the Officer and Miniſter of Juſtice, may carry the Party before any Magiſtrate, becauſe he is preſumed to be an indifferent Perſon, and ſworn to execute his Office duly; and therefore 'tis reaſonable that the Election ſhould be in him. 5 *Rep. Forſter's Caſe.*

It was the Opinion of my Lord Chief Juſtice *Wray*, That the Juſtice, &c. may grant a Warrant to bring the Perſon before himſelf, becauſe he who hath taken the Examination is moſt fit to do Juſtice.

Where the Officer is liable to falſe Impriſonment. If the Warrant is to apprehend *A. B.* and there are ſeveral of that Name, and the wrong Perſon is arreſted, an Action of falſe Impriſonment lies.

If after the Arreſt the Officer procures a Warrant, having none before, this is a wrongful Taking, and the Officer is liable to the like Action. *Dyer.* 244.

If a Warrant is granted to take *A. B.* the Son of *C. B.* and the Officer arreſts *A. B.* the Son of *D. B.* though he is the Offender, yet 'tis falſe Impriſonment, becauſe

because he had no Warrant against such a Person.' *Quare.*

If an Action of false Imprisonment be brought against an Officer arresting another upon Suspicion of Felony, the Constable may plead the General Issue, and give the Special Matter in Evidence; which, together with the Warrant, will be a sufficient Excuse for him. 7 *Jac. c.* 5.

Coroners.

THE Office of a Coroner is very Ancient, and has been, and yet it is held in high Esteem: For the Lord Major of *London*, is held to be Coroner there, 2 *Cro.* 531. And the Chief Justice of the King's bench is Soveraign Coroner of all *England*, 4 *Co.* 57. *b.* And he upon view of the Body of one killed in open view, as a Coroner, may make a Record returnable into the Kings bench, *ibid.*

But to come nearer to the intended Purpose, amongst other Matters, It is the Coroner's Business to view the Bodies of such as come to Casual Deaths, make away themselves, or are made away by others, or suspected to be put out of the World by a violent Death, or Dying Languishing in Prison, where there may be any Suspicion the Party Dyed not Naturally, but by hard Usage, Starving, or that the Imprisonment causeth his Death, *&c.* For he is to know, and certifie how the King came to loose a Subject.

He is, says 3*d Institute*, Fol. 129. to have *Visum Corporis* of a Prisoner Dying in a Goal, by reason of Duress. And the Jury or Inquest, before the Coroner, is to be of persons within the four next adjacent Vills, made by the Constables, and no Challenge lies to any of them so legally Summoned on the Inquest, 2 *Cro.* 135. And upon a View of the Body, and a strict Examination how the Party came by his Death, they must give in their Verdict to the best of their Judgment, according to the Evidence, or other Matters appearing to them, whether it be *Felo de se*, he Killed or Drowned himself, *&c.* or Died by the Hand of other Person or Persons, or by the Fall of a House, Wall, Timber, Kick of a Horse. or any other Matter or Thing that brought the Party to an untimely End; and the Coroner being so satisfied, he is to give his Warrant for the Burial of the Party, according as it shall be found upon Verdict, and an Indictment may be grounded thereon against such Party or Parties as shall be found concerned And in this Case he has Power to Commit and Bind over Persons accused before him of Murther, or the like, as he sees Cause. And for doing his Office of one Slain or Murthered, he may lawfully take 13 *s.* 4 *d.* of the Slayer or Murtherer, and if he have none, then of the Town where the Murther was committed, or the Murtherer suffered to Escape, 3. *Hen.* 7. *Chap.* 1. *Lamp.* 454.

By

Who ought to be a Coroner, and who not. By the Statute of *W.* 1 *cap.* 10. they were to be Knights; that is, they were to be Free-holders, and Men of Estates sufficient to qualifie them for this Office; for being chosen by the Free-holders of the County, 'tis they must answer the Fines, and other Duties imposed on the Coroners in Matters relating to their Office, if they are not of Ability to do it themselves.

And therefore if he hath not sufficient Lands within the Hundred, a Writ may issue to chuse another; for in such Cases he ceases to be a Coroner, and need not be discharged formally by a Writ. *Godb.* 105. *F, N. B.* 163. *contra.*

They must be Men who *melius sciant, ac possunt Officio intendere*; and therefore a blind, deaf, lame or sick Man, or who is *perpetuo languidus*, is not fit for this Office, and may be removed if chosen.

How chosen, and how many in a County. By Vertue of a Writ *de Coronatore eligendo*, directed to the Sheriff, he is to be chosen by the Freeholders of the County, and the Sheriff after the Day of Election is to certifie it, and the Name of the Person chosen, *&c.* *F. N. B.* 1633.

He is likewise to administer the Oath of his Office to him; as to the Number 'tis uncertain, but in most Counties there are generally Four Coroners

And because he is elected by the Freeholders, his Office is not to determine by the Demise of the King. 1 *Levinz.* 120.

His Office in relation to the Dead, and the Witnesses: He is to enquire *super visum Corporis*, How the Person was killed, and by whom, and what Goods and Chattels he had at the Time of the Fact committed.

If the Body cannot be found, then he has no Authority; but in such Case the Matter may be presented to the Justices in the Quarter-Sessions, and there found by the Jury; and this will entitle the King to a Forfeiture of the Goods. 1 *Roll. Rep.* 216, *Noy* 87. *Poph.* 209. *Livinz.* 141. *'tis traversable.*

He must take the Deposition of Witnesses in Writing attested under their Hands, and may bind them over to the next Sessions, Assizes, or Gaol-Delivery to give Evidence, *&c.*

If the Jury impannelled by him is sworn, and the Witnesses not ready, he may then adjourn them, and bind them by Recognizance to appear again.

When he hath Notice given to view the Body, he must make a Precept directed to the Constable where it lieth, to summon Twenty-four Men (who are to be of the Jury) to appear before him at a certain Day and Place, to execute such Things as shall be given to them in Charge.

If the Body is buried before he comes, the Vill, *&c.* must be amerced, and he may dig it up again; the Vill may be also amerced for neglecting to send for him, so that the Body is putrified to the Annoyance of the People.

He may find any Nusance which occasioneth the Death of a Man; as that a Bridge is in Decay, and by Reason of a Breach the Person fell in and was drowned, and the Town shall be amerced. *Allen* 51.

Deputy.

Deputy. He is a judicial Officer, and therefore cannot make a Deputy: besides, by the Statute called *Officium Coronatoris*, he is enjoined *Statim accedere ad occisos*, which implies, That he ought to execute his Office in Person; and therefore he ought to see the dead Body; and an Inquisition otherwise taken is void. *Stamf. Pl. Coron.* 51. 3 *Ed.* 1.

His Fees. He being an Officer at the Common Law for the Administration of Justice, was to have no Fee for executing his Office; but by the Statute of 3 *H.* 7. he is impowered upon View of the Body to take 13 *s.* 4 *d.* of the Goods of the Slayer; if he has none, and is fled, then he may amerce the Town for suffering the Criminal to escape, and take that Fee out of the Amercement, but he cannot demand any Fee upon the View of a Person killed by Misfortune. 2 *Inst.* 176.

If he doth not come, having Notice of the Death of any Person, he may be fined and imprisoned by the Justices.

He may be punished. For not binding over Witnesses to the next Gaol-Delivery, *&c.* for not certifying his Recognizances, and the Evidence and Inquisition taken before him, the Justices may fine him.

Inquisition, and Matters relating to it. He is to take an Inquisition upon Flight of the Felon, to intitle the King to a Forfeiture. 5 *Rep.* 109. *B.*

But this must be within his proper Jurisdiction in the County; for if any Person be killed within the Verge of the King's Houshold, the Coroner there hath an exempt Power 4. *Rep.* 45.

If there is any Practice with him to suppress the Evidence for the King, *B. R.* may set aside the Inquisition upon a *male se gessit*; and if he omit or neglect to enquire, *B. R.* as Supreme Coroner, may do it, or appoint Commissioners; but then it must be *super visum Corporis*, if done by Commissioners. 1 *Vent.* 182.

He ought to deliver his Inquisition at the next Gaol-Delivery, or to certifie it to *B. R.* where the Chief Justice is the Supreme Coroner: if he refuseth, he may be discharged of this Office, and fined by the Justices.

And therefore, where a Coroner did not return his Inquisition, it being found Murder, and the same Person being indicted at the next Gaol-Delivery, and the Jury found the Bill for Manslaughter, the Party came in and confessed the Indictment, and was bailed, and afterwards pleaded his Pardon, which was allowed; yet the Court made him plead to an Indictment upon the Coroner's Inquest, which he did, *viz. Auterfoit Convict*, and for this Neglect the Coroner was fined.

He may find any *Nusance* which occasioned the Death, *&c.* As if one riding over a Bridge, fell into the River, and was drowned, the Bridge being broken, or out of Repair, the Coroner may fine it, and in such Case the Town shall be amerced; but it must likewise be found, that the Town is bound to repair it. *Allen* 51.

The Vill, *&c.* shall be amerced, if the Coroner doth not take an Inquisition *super visum Corporis*, because it shall be intended they did not give him Notice.

An Information was brought by the Master of the Crown-Office against the Debtor of a *Felo de se* the Money being by that Means forfeited to the King; if the

Substance of the Inquisition be not set forth in the Information, 'tis void. 1. *Saund.* 275.

Melius Inquirend'. A *Melius inquirend'* is never granted after an Inquisition *super visum Corporis* is filed, unless it is quashed upon Oath made of a Misdemeanor in the Coroner or the Jury, as that they did not go according to their Evidence. 1 *Mod.* 82. 3 *Mod.* 80. 238.

And in some Cases it may go to the Sheriff, as if the Coroner *super visum Corporis* find that a Man *fortuito* fell into a Pit, *&c.* yet there may go a *Melius inquirend'* to the Sheriff, to enquire of the Death, *&c.* and what Goods and Chattels he had at that Time.

By the Statute of 4 *Ed.* 1. the Inquisition should be taken *super sacrum*, &c. *hominum Villarum prox' adjacen'*, but it was *per sacrum*, &c. *proborum & legalium hominum de Parochia*, &c. yet it was held good. *Sid.* 204. *Latch.* 166. 1 *Vent.* 182. *Cro. Eliz.* 371.

Matters of Form may be amended, as *seipsum felonice submersus fuit*; and it should be *jecit seipsum in aquam, & ibidem seipsum mersit. Sid.* 259.

Returning of a Process. If he return *fugam fecit*, 'tis not traversable; but if he find the Person *Felo de se*, it may be traversed. 2 *Levinz* 152. 1 *Vent.* 178. 352.

He is a Ministerial as well as a Judicial Officer; and therefore where an Exception is to the Sheriff, *viz.* That he is of Kin, or Tenant to the Party, or where 'tis at his own Suit, or if any Default is in him by Partiality or otherwise, in making the Pannel; in either of these or like Cases, the Coroner shall return the Process.

But then if the Original Process is directed to him, all other Process in the same Suit must be so likewise, tho' another and more indifferent Sheriff be appointed whilst that Suit is depending.

And if such Process is directed *Coronatoribus*, it hath been held, Two may return it, tho' there are more in the County, but one cannot, for in this Case they are but as one Officer; and therefore if one arrest a Debtor, and he escapes, the Action shall be brought against both. 3 *Levinz* 399.

Relating to the Coroners Office. &c.

IF any Man or Woman, *&c.* be Wounded, and thereby, in Peril of Death, the Party that did it, or was helping in doing it, being apprehended, may be Committed and kept in Custody, till it be perfectly known by the Testimony of skilful Persons whether the Wounded Party will Live or die of those Wounds or Blows given; and if he dye, the Coroner, upon view of the Dead Body, shall enquire of him,

him, or them that have done the Fact, whether Man or Woman, and take the Names of them that were present as Witnesses, or any otherways knowing of it. Also he shall take especial notice of the Abettors and Concealers in, or towards the Fact, or any way therein concerned, and so found to Enroll and Certifie the same.

The Coroner, according to his Inquest, shall give in their Verdict, if there be Cause; for he is to take care to Prosecute the Offender or Offenders, if the Relations of the Deceased or others refuse, or are slack in so doing; so that if any Man, *&c.* be Slain or Murthered, and thereof the Slayers, Murtherers, Abettors, Maintainers and Comforters may be Indicted, and brought to Arraignment and Tryal of the Issue, whether they are Guilty of the Murther, Manslaughter, *&c.* or not Guilty, which may be done any time in a Year and a Day after the same Felony and Murther Committed, which must be Dated from the Time of the Wounding, or Beating, not from the Time of the Dying, if the Party Languish, and live any Time after, tho' some what considerable, as a Week, a Month, or more.

And the Wife, or Heir of the Person so Slain, or Murthered, as the Case requires, may Commence his or her Appeal in proper Person any time within the Year after the said Felony done, before the Sheriff and Coroner of the County where the said Felony and Murther was done, or before the King in his Bench or Justices of Goal delivery. And the Appellant in any Appeals of Murther, or Death of a Man, *&c.* where Battle by the Course of Common law lieth not, may make their Attorneys, and Appear by the same.

And the said Appeals after they be Commenced, may be proceeded into the end of the Suit and Execution.

If a Murtherer or Man-slayer escape, the Justices of the Peace have Power to enquire of such Escapes, and to certifie them in the King's-Bench; and that after the Felony found, the Coroners deliver their Inquisitions before the Justices the next Goal delivery in the County where the Inquisition is taken: and they are to proceed against such Murtherers, if they be in Goal, or else certifie the Inquisition in the King's-Bench, or as it's worded, put the said Inquisition before the King in his Bench.

All such Coroners as are Remiss in their Office, or Duty of their Place, and make not their Respective Inquisitions upon the view of the dead Body and certifie not according as aforesaid, or ordained, every Coroner for such Offence Forfeits to the King, 5 *l.* by 3 *Hen.* 7 *Chap.* 1.

And now that the Coroner may not be ignorant what Murther is,

Counterfeits.

IS an Offence at Common Law, and 'tis likewise enacted, That getting Money or Goods falsely or deceitfully by Counterfeit-Letters, &c. and being convicted thereof at Quarter-Sessions, shall suffer any corporal Punishment, except Death.

Two Justices (*Quorum unus*) may bind the suspected Person to appear at the next Sessions, or bail them till that Time, &c. or may commit him at their Discretions. 33. *H. 8. cap.* 1.

Anno 15 *Car.* one *Terry* got a Wedge of Silver, Value 200 *l.* by a false Note, in the Name of another, and being convicted, he had Sentence to stand in the Pillory, and was fined 500 *l.* and committed during Pleasure; tho' my Lord *Coke* tells us, That a Man cannot be *fined* upon the Statute for this Offence, because the Law directs only a corporal Punishment. *Cro. Car.* 564. 3 *Inst.* 133.

At another Time, one *Hubort* of *Norfolk* procured *Webster* to *personate* A. B. who was then beyond Sea, and in his Name to acknowledge a *Fine* of his Lands, for which he was fined and imprisoned, and the *Fine levied* was made void. But now by 21 *Jac. cap.* 26, this is made Felony. *Cro. Eliz.* 530. 12 *Rep.* 123 *Moor.* 630.

A Warrant against one for getting Money, &c. by Counterfeit Letters.

To all Constables, &c.

Kent ss. WHereas Information upon Oath hath been made before me *E. F.* one of his Majesty's Justices of the Peace for the said County, by *C. D.* That *A. B.* hath falsely and deceitfully, by Counterfeit-Letters, cheated and defrauded him of Money and Goods to the Value of, &c. These are therefore in his Majesty's Name, to charge and command you, on Sight hereof, to apprehend and seize the Body of the said *A. B.* and bring him before me or some other of his Majesty's Justices of the Peace for the said County, there to be examined and dealt with according to Law. Hereof you are not to fail, as you will answer the contrary. Given under my Hand and Seal, &c.

Custom, and Custom-house Officers.

REsisting, hindring, affronting, or abusing or wounding Officers or Deputies, shall be committed by the next Justice till next Quarter-Sessions, to be fined, not exceeding 100 *l.* and to remain in Prison till discharged by Order of the *Exchequer*, or till he discover who set him on Work. 13 and 14 *Car.* 2. *cap.* 11.

One Justice, by Oath of two Witnesses, may commit any Person assisting in the Landing or Shipping prohibited Goods, or for which any Duty is payable, if such Person have no Warrant; or if no Officer be present, there to remain till he find Sureties for his Good Behaviour, and till he be discharged by the Lord Treasurer, *&c.*

For second Offence, Commitment for two Months, or till he pay 5 *l.* to the Sheriff, for the use of the King; or till he be discharged by the Lord Treasurer, Chancellor, Under-Treasurer, or Barons of the *Exchequer*.

A Warrant against those who abuse or resist a Custom-house Officer, and a *Mittimus* to send the Offender to Gaol.

To the Constable, &c. of M. *in the said County of* Kent, *and to the Keeper of the Common Gaol there.*

Kent *ss.* WHereas Complaint hath been made unto me upon the Oath of *A. B.* of *M. &c.* an Officer of his Majesty's Customs, That *C. D.* and *E. F.* of *M.* aforesaid, Yeomen, did lately, whith Force and Arms, resist the said *A. B.* at K. in your County, being then in the Execution of his said Office: These are therefore in His Majesty's Name, to command you the Constable of, &c. to apprehend the said *C. D.* and *E. F.* and to deliver them to the Keeper of the Common Gaol in the said County, together with this Precept, hereby also commanding you the said Keeper to take into your Custody the said *C. D.* and *E. F.* and them safely to keep until the next Quarter-Sessions which shall be held for the same County, there to be punished according to the Statute in that Case made and provided. And hereof fail not at your Perils. Given under my Hand and Seal, *&c.*

R. B.

A Warrant

A Warrrant against an Offender assisting in the Landing Goods, and carrying them away without paying Custom.

To the Constable of, &c. *in the said County.*

Kent *ss.* WHereas Complaint hath been made unto me upon Oath, That *A. B.* of, *&c.* hath lately assisted in the landing and carrying away several Goods at *M.* in the said County, for which a certain Duty was due and payable to his Majesty, which was not paid; and whereas it appeareth to me, upon the Examination of, *&c.* and others. That he the said *A. B.* had not a Warrant for his so doing, and that he had not given Notice thereof to any Officer of the Customs, and that no such Officer was there present: **These are therefore** in his Majesty's Name to command you to apprehend the said, *A. B.* and to bring him before me, or some other Justice of the Peace for their County, to answer the Premisses: And hereof fail not. **Given** under my Hand and Seal, *&c.*

Commitment for the first Offence.

To the Constable of, &c. *and to the Keeper of the Common Gaol of the County of* **Kent.**

Kent *ss.* WHereas *it hath been duly proved upon Oath before me, That* A. B. *of,* &c. *hath* (as in the former Warrant) **These are therefore** *in His Majesty's Name to command you the said Constable to convey the said* A. B. *to the Common Gaol, and to deliver him to the Keeper thereof, together with this Warrant, hereby also requiring you the said Keeper to take the said* A. B. *into your Custody, and him safely to keep, until he shall find Sureties for his Good Behaviour, and until he shall be discharged from the same by the Lord Treasurer, Chancellor, Under-Treasurer, or Barons of the Exchequer: And hereof fail not at your Perils,* **Given**, *&c.* 13 and 14 Car. 2. *cap.* 1.

Cutting out Tongues, &c.

BEfore the Statue of 5 *H.* 4. it was not Felony to cut out the Tongue, or put out

out the Eyes of any one; and therefore when Men were beaten, wounded and robbed, it was usual to put out their Eyes, or cut out their Tongue, that the Offenders might not be accused.

This Mischief is prevented by that Statute, by making it Felony: And my Lord *Coke* tells us, That from the Time of the making of this Law, for above the Space of two hundred Years, he could not find more than one Person indicted upon this Act. 5 *H.* 4. *c.* 5.

But notwithstanding this Law, cutting off Ears was not Felony; for by the Statute of 37 *H.* 8. it was no greater Offence to cut off the Ear of a Man than to cut out the Tongue of any living Beast; for in both Cases the Offender is to forfeit 10 *l.* to the King, and treble Damages to the Person grieved. 37 *H.* 8. *cap.* 6.

It was a Question after these Laws, and before the Statute of 22 *Car.* 2. Whether cutting off the Privy Members, tho' the Man should be taken in Adultery, was Felony or not? For by *Bracton* 'tis said, That in such Case, *Sequitur pœna aliquando capitalis*; and yet I find, that *Anno* 13 *H.* 3. one *John*, a Monk, was taken by *Henry Hull* in the Act with his Wife, and he cut off the Privy Members of the Monk, and was only indicted for a Mayhem. 3 *Inst.* 118.

But now by the Statute of 22 *Car.* 2. cutting out an Eye, slitting of the Nose, or cutting it off, or the Lip, or cutting off or disabling any Limb or Member, with an Intention to maim or disfigure the Person, is made Felony without Benefit of Clergy, in the Actor, Counsellor, Aider or Abettor, being privy to the Offence. 22 *and* 23. *Car.* 2.

One *Stapleton* was lately convicted at the Sessions in the *Old Baily* upon this Act, for putting out the Eye of one *Russel*, by flinging *Mercury* in his Face; afterwards in *Hillary*, 1 *Jac.* he pleaded his Pardon.

Drunkenness.

BY the Statutes of King *James*, 'tis enacted, That any Justice of Peace upon his own View, Confession of the Party, or Proof of one Witness upon Oath, may convict any Person for Drunkenness. 4 *Jac.* 1. c. 5. 21 *Jac.* 1. *cap.* 7.

Being convicted, he is to pay 5 *s* for every Offence to the Church-wardens of the Parish where the Offence is committed, within one Week after Conviction; which if he neglects or refuse, the same may be levied upon his Goods by Warrant from one Justice, before whom he was convicted; and if not able to pay it, then he is to be put into the Stocks six Hours for every Offence.

If

If he is convicted the ſecond time, then to be bound with Two Sureties in 10 *l.* to be of the Good Behaviour, or be committed.

The Proſecution muſt be within Six Months after the Offence.

The Inferiour Officer neglecting to levy the Penalty, forfeits 10 *s.* to be levied and diſpoſed as the Penalty it ſelf.

This is the Subſtance of the Statutes, 4 *Jac. cap.* 5. and 21 *Jac. cap.* 7. the former Statute being made Perpetual by the latter.

An Ale-houſe-keeper convicted of Drunkenneſs, is diſabled to keep an Ale-houſe for 3 Years. 21 *Jac.* 3.

A Warrant on the firſt Conviction within Six Months after the Offence.

To the Conſtable of, &c. *and to the Church-wardens of,* &c. *in the ſaid County.*

Kent ſſ. WHereas *A. B.* of the Pariſh of, *&c.* in the ſaid County, Taylor was on this preſent Day, upon due Proof upon Oath, convicted before me for being drunk on the 11*th* Day of *Auguſt* laſt paſt, in the ſaid Pariſh: Theſe are therefore to require you to demand the Sum of 5 *s.* of the ſaid *A. B.* for the Uſe of the Poor of the ſaid Pariſh; which, if not paid into the Hands of the Church-wardens of the Pariſh aforeſaid, within one Week next enſuing, that then you levy the ſame upon the Goods and Chattels of the ſaid *A. B.* by Diſtreſs and Sale thereof, rendring unto him the Overplus: And if the ſaid *A. B.* ſhall not be able to pay the ſaid Sum, and if no Diſtreſs can be taken, that then you ſet him in the Stocks, there to remain for the Space of Six Hours. Given under my Hand and Seal, *&c.*

Eſcape.

THIS is where one is arreſted, and afterwards is at Liberty, not being delivered by due Courſe of Law; and 'tis either Negligent or Voluntary: but in Treſpaſſes, or any Offence not Treaſon or Felony, there is no Difference whether the ſame is voluntary or not, for in both Caſes the Officer is finable.

By

By a Stranger.

If a Stranger apprehend a Felon, or one suspected, and delivers him to another who suffers him to go at large, 'tis an Escape in both; for the first Man ought to have delivered him to the Constable.

For Murder, the Township shall be amerced if the Murderer escape *tempore Diurno*, though it was committed in the Town, Field, or in a Lane, but then there should be Complaint made to a Justice of Peace.

By Negligence in Officers.

To bail one not bailable by Law *pro defectu Scientia*, is a negligent Escape.

A Gaoler suffering a Prisoner to go Abroad, though he return, 'tis a negligent Escape, and finable, for he ought to keep him in *arcta Custodia*; yet *per Hale*, Chief Just. If after a negligent Escape, and before the Gaoler is punished, he take the Prisoner upon fresh Suit, he is excused. 3 *Rep. Rigeway's* Case.

If the Gaoler is insufficient, the Sheriff must answer for these Escapes, because 'tis in a Civil Action; but 'tis otherwise where the Offence is Criminal.

The Punishment is aggravated by the Proceeding against the Party escaping; for if attainted, and afterwards he escapes, 'tis 100 *l.* Fine; if indicted, 5 *l.* Fine if not, then 'tis finable at Discretion.

1. The Act must be Felony at the Time of the Escape, otherwise 'tis but finable.
2. There must be a legal Commitment.

After a Pardon for Murder, but pending an Appeal, the Prisoner was suffered to escape, 'tis Felony in the Gaoler. *Plowd.* 476. *B.* So it is likewise to suffer a Felon willfully to escape, or to bail him, for he hath no Power to take Bail.

'Tis the same Crime in a Justice to take a Felon out of Gaol without Bail, or to suffer him to go at large without Bail or Commitment who confesses a Felony before him.

'Tis Felony likewise in a Constable to suffer a Felon to destroy himself.

He who suffers the Escape, must be punish'd for the same Crime for which the Party escaping stood committed.

A Man was put in the Stocks upon Suspicion of a Felony, and another lets him go; this was held to be Felony at Common Law, although the Party was never indicted. *Dyer* 99.

As to the Amercement of a Vill where a Felony is done, and the Offender escapes, if it is in the *Day-time*, the Vill is answerable; but if in the *Night*, 'tis otherwise. 1 *Leon.* 107.

If a Felon escapeth after Condemnation, and is retaken, upon Confession or Proof that he is the same Person, he shall be executed. *Poph.* 131.

He who wounded another is taken by a Constable, and suffered to escape, the wounded Man dies within a Year and a Day, 'tis only finable, 3 *Leon.* 207.

A Man is taken for Manslaughter *per infortunium*, or *se defendendo*, and suffered to escape, 'tis not Felony in the Officer, but finable.

These Escapes must be presented before the Offender shall be compelled to answer.

Justices of the Peace have Power in Sessions to enquire of Escapes of Felons. 1. *R.* 3. 3.

By a late Statute, the Sheriff may commit his Prisoner to the Gaol where he keeps Prisoners for Debt, and not to the Common Gaol of that County where the Offender was taken; but subject to the same Restrictions, Regulations and Penalties, as if he had been committed to the Common Gaol; and if the Party escape out of such Place, the Sheriff shall be answerable as in other Escapes. 5. *Annæ*.

But the Offender may be retaken, even upon the Lord's Day, by Vertue of a Warrant from a Judge, upon Oath made before any Person commissioned under Seal of the same Court; and the Oath duly filed, as if such Oath had been made before the Judge himself.

My Lord *Coke*, in his Exposition upon the Statute *de Frangentibus Prisonam*, is of Opinion, That the Gaoler shall not answer for a Voluntary Escape until the Prisoner be attainted. 2 *Inst.* 592.

Estreats.

These are the Extracts of Fines, Forfeitures and Amercements, taken out of the Rolls of the Clerk of the Peace; of which he makes Two Parts, and delivers one to the Sheriff, the other to the Barons of the *Exchequer*.

Estreats of the Penalties for shooting in Guns, must be sent into the *Exchequer* by the Justice who examined the Matter.

The Sheriff levying the King's Debt, without shewing the Party the Estreats under the Seal of the *Exchequer*, must be fined, and pay treble Damages to the Party.

Issues estreated shall not be levied upon any other Person than upon him who by the Estreat ought of Right to be charged, upon Pain that every Clerk writing

writing such Estreat, and causing it to be executed, and the Officer, shall forfeit five Marks to the King, and as much to the Party grieved, to be recovered by Action of Debt, *&c.* 27 *Eliz. cap.* 7.

By the Statute of 2 *and* 3 *Phil. & Mar. cap.* 8. Stewards of Leets have Power to fine those who do not work on the Highways; and within six Weeks after *Michaelmas* they must deliver Indentures of those Fines estreated, one to the Bailiff or High-Constable of the Liberty, the other to the Constable or Church-warden of the Parish where the Offence was committed.

In Default of Presentment at Leets, the Justices, in their Session, shall fine these Defaulters; and then the Clerk of the Peace must deliver indented Estreats under his Hand and Seal as aforesaid, which shall be a Warrant to levy, *&c.*

Evidence. See Felonies.

THE Witnesses, *&c.* must be bound in a Recognizance to appear and give Evidence at the next General Gaol-Delivery; if they refuse, they may be committed, or bound to Good Behaviour.

The Wife can be no Witness against her Husband, unless she is the Party grieved; in such Case it hath been allowed.

In my Lord *Audley's* Case, which was for being Accessary to a Rape of his Wife, she was admitted as Evidence against him; and then a Distinction was made between the Case of a common Person between Party and Party, and the Case between the King and the Party upon *an Indictment*; in the first of which Cases she may not be a Witness, and in the last she may: But my Lord *Hales* was of another Opinion, *viz.* That in Felonies neither the Wife, nor her Examination, shall be used for or against her Husband; and that Distinction in my Lord *Audley's* Case hath since been denied to be Law. *Hutt.* 116. *H. P. C.* 253. *Raym.* 1.

But yet a Wife *de facto*, as an Heiress taken away, and by Threats prevailed on to marry the Man, shall be a good Witness against him, and if convicted upon her Evidence, shall be hang'd. 1 *Vent.* 243.

An Infant may be a Witness even against his Parents indicted for Witchcraft. *Dalt.* 366.

One attainted of Perjury, though pardoned, or of Forgery or Conspiracy, is not to be a Witness; yet the Justice may bind such Witnesses to give Evidence, but he is to inform the Judge of their Credit. Yet one convicted of Felony, and pardoned, is a Witness, for the Pardon takes away both *pœnam & reatum*; *Godb.* 288. *Raym.* 369. 1 *Vent.* 349. So likewise if burnt in the Hand *Stiles.* 388.

 A Person

A Person convicted for publishing a Libel, and another for singing a Ballad against the Government, and both sentenced to the Pillory, were Witnesses to a Will; and upon an Appeal to the Delegates they were allowed to be good Witnesses, because the Infamy arises from the Nature of the Crime, and not from the Judgment; but in this Case neither of the Offences are infamous, either by the Canon of Civil Law; (and 'tis upon those Laws that they were now to judge) tho' 'tis otherwise by the Common Law. *Levin.* 3 *Part* 426.

But a Person duly set in the Pillory, is not allowed by our Law to be a Witness. *H. P. C.* 263.

If a Witness is not able to travel, the Justice may excuse his Personal Appearance, and certify his Examination at the next Assizes.

If a Felon confess the Fact, he may give Evidence against another, as well to the Jurors who shall then inquire thereof on the Behalf of the King, as also to those who shall pass upon the Trial of the said *T. P.* for the same.

In the Case of the Regicides, it was resolved, That any of the King's Councel might privately manage the Evidence for the King before the Grand Jury, in order to the finding the Bill, because the King's Councel are the only Prosecutors in his Cases.

In Treason working Corruption of Blood, or in Misprision of such Treason, the Party accused is not to have a Note of the Witnesses Names against him; but they must be two lawful Persons, and both to the same Overt-Act of the same Treason: And therefore, if two or more distinct Treasons are alledged in one Indictment, one Witness to one, and another to another Treason, they shall not be esteemed two Witnesses. 7. *W.* 3. *cap.* 3.

And no Evidence shall be admitted to an Overt-Act which is not expresly laid in the Indictment.

The Accused may make his Defence by Witnesses upon Oath, and may have the same Process to compel them to appear, as is usually granted for Witnesses against him.

By the Statute of 4 *Jac.* 1. *cap.* 1. Felonies committed by *Englishmen* in *Scotland*, are to be tried by a Jury in *Cumberland*, *Westmorland*, or *Northumberland*, and the Felon shall be admitted to have his Witnesses examined upon Oath, *&c.* which my Lord *Coke* tells us is a good Precedent for the Discovery of Truth, and to inform the Consciences of the Judge and Jury, for *Jurato creditur in judicio*, and that there is not so much as *Scintilla juris* against the Examination of such Witnesses upon Oath. But notwithstanding his Opinion, it was never allowed in Treason before the Statute of 7 *Willi.* and the Practice was still otherwise in all other Felonies.

But now by another Statuted, 1. *Anna*, any Person produced as a Witness on the Behalf of a Prisoner upon Trial for *Treason or Felony*, must be upon Oath. **To speak the Truth, the whole Truth, and nothing but the Truth;** and if convicted of wilful Perjury, shall suffer such Punishment as by the Law may be inflicted on such an Offender.

As

As to what Evidence shall maintain the Indictment, these Things are to be observed.

1. If the Felony is laid to be committed one *Day*, the Jury may find the true Day, and the Forfeiture shall relate to that Day.

2. If 'tis laid to be done in a certain *Place*, the Evidence may be of the Fact in another Place, but then it must be in the same County.

3. If the Indictment and Evidence differ in the *Manner* of the Death, then it doth not maintain it; as if a Man is indicted for Poisoning, and the Evidence is of Stabbing: But where they agree in Substance, 'tis otherwise as if the Indictment is for Poisoning with one sort of Poison and the Evidence is of another.

4. Indictment, that *A.* gave the mortal Wound, and that *B.* and *C.* were *present and abetting*; the Evidence was, That *B.* gave the Wound, and the other were abetting.

5. So on Indictment against *B.* as Accessary to *D.* and *R.* and the Evidence is only, That he was Accessary to *one* of them:

6. So for Murder of *Malice fore-thought*, and the Evidence is of Malice only *in Law*; as killing an Officer, or without Provocation.

In all these Cases, the Evidence maintains the Indictment.

A Warrant to Summon a Witness concerning a Felon.

To the Constable, &c.

Sussex *ss.* WHereas I have been informed, That *A. B.* of, *&c.* was lately robbed at, *&c.* and that *C. D.* of, *&c.* is a material Witness to prove by whom the said Robbery was committed: These are therefore to require you to cause the said *C. D.* forthwith to come before me, or some other Justice of the Peace for this County, to give such Information and Evidence as he knoweth concerning the said Offence, that such further Proceedings may be had therein as to Justice doth appertain. Given, &c.

Indictment of a Felony 30 *November* and the Evidence is of another Day; the Jury may find the true Day, and the Forfeiture shall relate to it.

The Felony is laid to be committed at such a Place, and the Evidence proves the Fact at another Place in the same County, 'tis well enough.

Of poisoning with one Kind of Poison, and the Evidence is of another; or killing with one Weapon and the Evidence is of another; this maintains the Indictment, for it agrees in Substance.

That *P.* gave the Wound, and that *J.* and *R.* were abetting; and the Evidence. That *O.* gave the Wound, and that *J.* and *R.* were present with another and abetting *&c.* 'tis sufficient Indictment as accessary to two, and the Evidence prove him accessary to one 'tis sufficient.

For Murder, *Ex Malitia præcogitata*, the Evidence was of Malice implied, as killing an Officer in Execution of Justice, &c. it maintains the Indictment.

Upon the Statute of Stabbing, the Evidence was, That the Deceased gave the first Stroke, 'tis sufficient to maintain the Indictment for Manslaughter.

But if the Indictment and Evidence differ in the Manner of the Death; as if it be for Poisoning, and the Evidence is of Stabbing; that will not maintain the Indictment.

A *Feme-Covert* or Infant being a Witness, cannot be bound in a Recognizance to appear at Sessions; and if she is bound with her Husband, 'tis void as to her; but they may be bound by Sureties, and if a *Feme-Covert* cannot find Sureties, she shall be committed.

Examination.

THE Justices may examine Witnesses upon Oath; and by Virtue of the Statute of 2 & 3 *Phil. & Mar.* they may examine the Felon likewise, but not on Oath. *H. P. C.* 262.

This Examination must be in Writing, and it must be certified to the next Assizes, or else the Justice may be fined by the Judge.

It may be given in Evidence at the Trial, but 'tis not sufficient to convict, unless the Accused confess at the Trial; yet Mr. *Dalton* mentions a Conviction upon it without any further Evidence.

And yet in the Case of *Tongy*, *Phillips* and *Stubbs* who were indicted for High Treason, it was resolved by all the Judges, That if a Traitor is examined before a Justice of Peace, or Privy-Councellor, and confesseth the Treason, and should afterwards deny it at his Trial; yet two Witnesses, who can prove such Confession, are good Evidence against the Party himself, who made it at his Examination, but not against any other Person whom he then accused; and that in such Case there needs not two Witnesses to prove the Criminal guilty of Treason.

So in my Lord *Morley's* Case it was held, That if Witnesses examined before the Coroner were dead, or unable to Travel and Oath made thereof such Examination might be Read, the Coroner making Oath that they are the same and not altered.

Several Persons conspired, &c, to pull down Inclosures, and to provide Armour, &c and to go to *London* and join with more; and this they confessed on Examination: The Question was, Whether they should be arraigned for this Offence, because they had confessed it already? And it was held they should, and that their Confession before the Arraignment might be given in Evidence against them. 2. *And* 67.

If

If upon Examination the Felon confesseth the Fact, the Justice should take his Name subscribed to his Confession.

And such Confession may be given in Evidence with an Oath, before whom it was made. *H. P. C.* 264.

Examination taken in one County, may be certified in another

The Felon may be examined before he is committed, but not upon Oath, because *Nemo debet seipsum accusare.*

His Examination, as well as that of the Witnesses, must be certified by the Justice to the next Assizes.

The Form of the Examination of the Felon.

THE Examination of *A. B. &c.* taken before me, *P. L.* Esq; one of His Majesty's Justices of the Peace for the County of *K.* on the 10 Day of *August.* &c,

This Examinant saith, *&c.*

The Examination of Witnesses must be taken severally and upon Oath thus:

The Examination of *C. D.* of, *&c.* taken upon Oath before me, *P. L.* Esq; *ut prius.*

Extortion.

IS an Offence, where an Officer by Colour of his Office takes Money, or any other Thing of Value not due, or more than is due, or before 'tis due: And in a large Sense, 'tis where any Person is oppressed by an extorting Power, or under a Pretence of Right. 1. *Inst.* 368. *b.*

An Attorney taking 1 *l.* 3 *s.* of his Client, *Extorsive contra formam Statuti*, which must be the Stat. of 3 *Jac. cap.* 7. which gives the Client Costs and treble Damages, where an Attorney demands by his Bill more than his due Fees and Disbursements; the Question was, Whether this is to be recover'd by Action or Information? And by some Opinions an Information will lie. *Sid.* 434.

A Bailiff of a Hundred, taking 50 *s. colore Officii*, without expressing particularly for what: After Verdict this was held sufficient, by reason of the Words *colore Officii*; but it had been otherwise upon Demurrer. *Sid.* 91.

A Bailiff to a Sheriff, indicted at Sessions for taking 20 *s.* of *T. P. Extorsive colore Officii*, was committed, and pleaded, and was tried the same Day in Sessions and convicted, and upon a Writ of Error the Judgment was reversed, because

because a Man cannot be indicted and tried at the same Sessions. *Cro. Car.* 438. *Jones* 379. 280. But the Damages are to be recover'd by Action.

Taking more than *Four Pence* for an Arrest, forfeits treble Damages to the Party grieved, and besides 40 *l.* between King and Prosecutor, *per* 23 *H.* 6. *cap.* 10. But the Jury must find the single Damages, and then the Justices may treble them. *Sid.* 91.

An Information against a Clerk of Assize, for taking more than his Fees, was ordered to be tried at Bar. *Sid.* 420.

A Coroner taking more than his Fees, or refusing to view the Body before he had 6 *s.* 8 *d.* for himself, and 2 *s.* for his Clerk; he was committed, *&c.* 3 *Inst.* 149.

A Gaoler taking more than his Fees.

He was convicted of Extortion, fined 1000 Marks, committed during the King's Pleasure, bound to his good Behaviour for a Year, and Ordered to acknowledg his Offence publickly at the next Assizes and turned out of Commission.

A Sheriff taking more than his Fees, or any Thing of a Constable for bringing a Felon to Gaol.

'Tis Extortion in him to take 60 *l.* to execute a Judgment in Dower, 1 *Keb.* 743. but if he is acquitted, no new Trial shall be had. 2 *Keb.* 404.

By stat. of 12 *Q. Annæ*, 'tis enacted, that no Person after 29 *September*, 1714. take for Interest above 5 *l. per Cent. per Annum.* on the Forfeiture of treble the Value of the Money lent, and the Bonds, *&c.* to be void. *vid.* 12 *Annæ*.

Scriveners, Brokers, *&c.* taking above 5 *l. per Cent. per Annum* for Brokage, Soliciting, or Procuring the Loan, or Forbearance; or above 12 *d.* besides the Stamp-Duties, for making or renewing the Bond, *&c.* forfeit 20 *l.* with Costs of Suit, and half a Year's Imprisonment; One Moiety to the King, the other to the Informer. To be recovered by Bill, Plaint, *&c.* in any of His Majesty's Courts at *Westminster*, *&c.*

Felo de se,

IS one who committeth Felony, by murdering himself voluntarily.

It has been the Opinion of learned Men, That a Person who is *Compos Mentis*, cannot be guilty of so much Malice towards his Person, which may occasion him wilfully to kill himself; because naturally the Intention of Men aim at what

is

is good for themselves, and at what conduceth to their own Preservation; and therefore 'tis to be presumed, that where a Man killeth himself, he is not *Compos Mentis*.

The Person who is guilty of this Offence, must be,

1. Of the Age of Discretion. 2. *Compos Mentis*. 3. The Act must be voluntary. 4. Death must ensue within a Year and a Day after the Stroke or Wound; otherwise no Forfeiture of Goods, *&c.* incurreth.

But in some Cases the Act may be involuntary: As, if I am assaulted, and draw my Sword to defend my self, and happen to fall down, and the other pursuing his wicked Intentions to destroy me, falls upon my Sword and kills himself, he is *Felo de se*.

But if I stand upon my Defence without being assaulted, and am only in Danger thereof, and another runs upon my Sword and kills himself, he is not *Felo de se*.

Conviction. This must be by the Oath of Twelve Men before the Coroner *super visum Corporis*; and when his Inquisition is returned and filed, 'tis not traversable. *Sid.* 90. 1 *Vent.* 278. *contra*.

If the Body cannot be found, *&c.* then the Inquiry may be before the Justices in Sessions; and this is traversable. 3 *Inst.* 55.

So if the Inquiry be in *B. R.* in the same County, 'tis traversable by Executor or Administrator.

And till Conviction, no Goods are forfeited.

The Coroner's Inquest found, That *seipsum felonice submersus fuit*, he was ordered to attend *B. R.* to amend it; for it should be *jecit seipsum in aquam*, &c. *Sid.* 259.

If a Presentment is made before a Coroner, that a Man was *Felo de se*, and that he had Goods in the Possession of *S.* this Presentment, must be certified into *B. R.* upon which, Process out of the Crown-Office issues against *S.* and 'tis continued till he is outlawed. 2 *Leon.* 200.

This is Forfeiture of all the Goods and Chattels which the Party had at the Time of the Stroke given, or at any Time since; for it relates to that Time, and not to the Death.

And yet there is an Opinion in my Lord *Dyer*, That if Money is owing to one, who is *Felo de se*, upon simple Contract, and not on *Specialty*, the Debt is not forfeited; because such Debtor may wage his Law with the King *Dyer* 262.

A Debtor was bound with Sureties to pay the Money, and made a Bargain and Sale to the Sureties of Goods, to the Value of the Debt, to indemnifie them; in which Deed there was a Covenant, That if the Debtor saved them harmless, that the Bargain should be void, and that in the mean Time he should have the Use of the Cattle: Before the Debt became due, the Debtor killed himself, and the Sureties seized the Cattle; but it was held, the Lord Almoner should have them, or the Money for which they were sold, tho' the Property was in the Vendees; but then he ought to discharge them from the Debt. *Dyer.* 160.

Melius Inquirendo. Not granted but where a Misdemeanour in the Coroner. *Vent.* 182, 352.

Of all Offences, *&c.* except Murder, a *Felo de se* is not under this Exception, (Pardon) because there is a Difference between Killing ones self and another; for the first is against the Law of Nature, the other against the *Mosaical* Law, by which Vengeance is to be taken against the Man-slayer; but no Vengeance can be had against one who is *Felo de se*; therefore his Goods, *&c.* are forfeited to the King for depriving him of the Benefit of a Subject. *Levinz.* 1 *Part* 8.

Felonies. Vide *Benefit of Clergy, Evidence, Larceny and Outlawry.*

MY Lord *Coke* tells us, this Word is derived from the *Latin* Word *Fel*, or from the old *Saxon* Word *Fell*; the one signifying *Gall*, and the other *Fierce*; and his Reason is, because either of those Words are suitable to the Crime, which is always intended to be done with a *bitter or fierce* Mind.

This makes me reflect on what my Lord *Verulam* wrote to that Great Lawyer, *viz.* That when he spoke in the Law, (which he calls his own Element) he had no Equal; but when he wandered (as he tells us he often did) he was very much out of the Way: And this appears by his Derivation of this Word, and in many more Instances which I could mention.

The learned Sir *Henry Spelman* gives us a different but a true Account of this World (*viz.*) That 'tis derived from the *Saxon* Word *Feah*, which we now call *Fee*, and which then Signified a Reward or Estate; and from the *Germain* Word *Lon*.

Which in *English* is *Price*; so that this was a Crime which was punished with the Price (that is the Loss) of his Estate.

For in those Days there was a Pecuniary Punishment for all Crimes, which was abolished by *Hen.* 1. and instead thereof he appointed Hanging for Felony.

What Felonies are *by Common or statute Law.*

Felonies at Common Law are, (1) Against the Life of a Man, as Chance medley, *Deodand*, *Felo-de-se*, Manslaughter, Manslaughter, *ex necessitate* & *Se defendendo*, Murder.

(2) Against the Goods, as Larceny, Robbery, Piracy,.

(3) Against the Habitation, as Burglary,

(4) Against publick Justice, as Burning his House, Breack of Prison, *&c.*

Felonies

Felonies by Statute Law are,

Stealing of Goods which by Agreement he is to use, or shall be let to them in Lodgings. 4 *W. & M.*

Delivering Silk by a Throwster to a Man to work, and he steals it, this was Felony before that Statute: So the Delivery of Plate to a Butler, or Sheep to a Shepherd, and they steal it; because the Property was still in the Owner. *Keelling* 35.

Imploying the King's Armour, Munition, or Ordinance, to the Value of 20 s. Prosecution must be within a Year, loseth Lands but during Life, no Corruption of Blood, the Wife shall have Dower. 31 *Eliz. cap.* 4.

This cannot be determined in Sessions.

Bail acknowledged in the Name of another not privy or consenting. 21 *Jac. cap.* 26. But if taken *de bene esse* at a Judge's Chamber, and not filed, no Felony. *Sid.* 90.

Concealing the Death of a Bastard, unless the Mother proves by one Witness it was dead-born. 21 *Jac. cap.* 27.

Buggery, With Man or Beast, there must be *Penetratio & Emissio, &c.* 25 *H.* 8. *cap.* 6. revived by 5 *Eliz. cap.* 7. No Clergy.

Burglary, *Vid.* Robbery.

Burning, a Rack or Stack of Corn, Hay or Grain in the Night-time, or Barns or Out-houses. 21 & 22 *Car.* 2.

But where a Man was indicted, for that he being possessed of an House, did *felonice* set in on Fire, with an Intent to burn his Neighbours Houses: This was adjudged no Felony, but a Trespass. *Keeling* 29.

Cloth stolen from the Tenters in the Night. 22 *Car.* 2.

Stealing Good. out of a Coach-House, to the Value of 5 s. tho' not broke open, or assisting any Person to do it either by Day or Night. 10 & 11 *W.* 3 *H.* 5. *cap.* 1. 2 *H.* 6. *cap.* 9. Clergy.

Blanching Copper or Silver for Sale, or mixing blanched Copper with Silver, or knowingly buying or selling it, or offering it to Sale, or any maleable Composition of Minerals, or Metals heavier than Silver, and looking like Standard-Gold; paying or putting off counterfeited Mill'd Money, or unlawfully diminish'd (and not cut in Pieces) at a lower Rate than its Denomination doth import.

No Corruption of Blood, Loss of Dower: Prosecution must be within three Months, *&c.* continue till next Sessions of Parliament. 8 & 9 *Will.*

Enrolled in the Name of another not privy or consenting. 21 *Jac. cap.* 26.

Egyptians above Fourteen Years of Age remaining here a Month. 1 & 2 *Phil. & Mar. cap.* 4. 5 *Eliz. cap.* 20. No Clergy.

Prisoner suffered voluntarily to escape being under an Arrest for Felony, 'tis Felony in the Officer.

To counterfeit or forge Exchequer-Bills or to demand Money on them, knowing them to be counterfeit. 8 & 9 *Will.*

 Acknowledg-

Acknowledging a Fine in the Name of another not privy or consenting. 21 *Jac.c.* 26. Sessions have no Jurisdiction of this Offence. See *Counterfeits*.

Forging a Deed; after a former Conviction for the like Offence. 5 *Eliz. c.* 14 No Clergy.

Hunting] in a Forrest, unlawfully by Night with painted Faces. 1 *H.* 7. *cap.* 1.

Destroying or killing Horses in the Night-time; but wounding them only, forfeits treble Damages.

Receiving, Retaining or maintaining a Jesuit knowingly. 27 *Eliz.* c. 2. No Clergy.

Imagining or conspiring to kill the King, or any of his Council 3 *H.* 7. *cap.* 14. No Clergy.

A Limb cut off or disabled, with an Intention to maim or disfigure the Person. 22 & 23 *Car.* 2. No Clergy.

Marrying (1.) A second Husband or Wife, the first living, but then the Man must be above 14, and the Woman above 12; if under that Age, and marry, and disagreeing afterwards, may marry again.

(2.) Either of them being absent above seven Years beyond Sea, tho' Notice; but if in *England*, must not have Notice that the Party is living.

(3.) Divorce *a mensa & thoro* may marry: As *Causa Adulterii*, which was *Middleton's* Case; or *causa Sævitiæ*, which was *Rook's* Case.

(4) After a Sentence of nullity in the Ecclesiastical Court, in these three last Cases may Marry again 1 *Jac.* 11. Clergy.

A Rape was Felony at Common-Law; but by the Statute of *W.* 1, *cap.* 13 made a Misdemeanour only, Punishable by Fine and Imprisonment: But 10 Years afterwards, by the Statute of *W.* 2. *cap.* 34 it was made Felony again.

And it is a Rape if the Woman is under 10 Years, tho she consent, *per* 18 *Eliz. cap.* 6 If above 10 Years, and not consenting to do the Act, tho' she doth consent after 'tis done.

But in this subsequent Consent the Husband may appeal, 6 *Rich.* 2 *cap.* 6. no Clergy, 18. *Eliz.Cap.* 7. upon Conviction, Confession or Outlawry.

In *Michaelmas*-Term, 14 *Eliz.* a *Scotchman* was indicted for a Rape upon a Girl seven Years old, and no more, and upon the Evidence of credible Witnesses was found guilty; but the Court very much doubted whether the Fact could be committed upon such a young Girl: And this was the Reason of making that Statute 18. *Eliz.* declaring it Felony to ravish a Girl under 10 Years of Age, tho' consenting to the Act. *Vide*, *Rape*. *Dyer.* 304.

Stealing of Records 8 *H.* 6. *cap.* 12. Clergy.

Robbing a House, Barn or Stable in the Day-time, and taking in Value 5 *s.* tho' no Body within, and breaking in the Night-time, and putting the Owner &c. in Fear. 39 *Eliz. cap.* 15.

Subjects in Passing over the Sea to a Foreign Prince in order to serve him 3 *Jac. cap.* 4.

Servants above Eighteen Years old, Other than Apprentice, going away with or imbezelling the Goods of his Master, in Value 40 *s.* delivered to him, &c.

21 *H.*

21 *H.* 8. *cap.* 7. After Deceafe of his Mafter, fpoiling Goods, *&c.* 33. *H.* 6. *cap.* 1. and not appearing in *B. R.* upon Proclamation, he hath Clergy by the Statute of 1. *Ed.* 6. *cap.* 12. See the Act 12. *Annæ. pag.*

If I deliver a Bond to my Servant to receive 20 *l.* which he receives, and goes away with the Money, this is not within the Statute, becaufe a Bond is not properly Goods, but a Chofe in Action: So if I deliver Goods to my Servant to fell in a Market; which he doth, and runs away with the Money; 'tis not within this Law, becaufe he had not the Money by my Delivery: But if one Servant delivers Goods to another Servant, and he runneth away with them, this is Felony, becaufe the Delivery of the Servant is the Delivery of the Mafter. *Dyer.* 6. *b.*

Breaking a Warehoufe, Shop, or Stable in the Day-time, and taking to the Value of 5 *s.* 3 *&* 4 *W. & M.* Tho' he doth not break it in the Day-time, yet if he take the Value of 5 *s.* 10 *&* 11 *W.*

Stealing any Goods, which by Contact or Agrement the Party was to ufe; Felony 3 *&* 4 *W. & M.* now made perpetual *per* 6 *&* 7 *W.*

Acknowledging a Statute in the Name of another, not privy or confenting. 21 *Jac. cap.* 26.

Transporting a Rogue, and he returning without Licence. 39 *Eliz. cap.* 4. 1 *Jac.* 1 *cap.* 7. 25. Clergy. If burnt no Clergy.

Witchcraft In the firft Degree.

1. By Invocation or Conjuration of Evil Spirits.
2. Confulting, entertaining or employing them.
3. Taking up a dead Perfon to be employed, not actually ufed in Charm or or Witchcraft.
4. Doing any Witchcraft Inchantment or Charm *&c.* whereby any Perfon is killed, deftroyed, confumed, or lamed; no Clergy, 1 *Jac. cap.* 12.

Witchcraft In the Second Degree.

By taking upon them by Inchantment, Charm, *&c.* to tell where Treafure is, or where Goods loft, *&c.* may be found, or to provoke unlawful Love, or by deftroying Goods or Cattle, or ufing witchcraft to hurt any perfon, tho' not done, The firft Offence is Imprifonment for a Year, and Pillory; and being Convicted thereof, and receiving Judgment, and offending again, 'tis Felony. 1. *Jac. cap.* 12.

Dr. *Lamb* was indicted, for that he ufed *quafdam malas & execrabiles & diabolicas Artes*; and the Indictment was quafhed, becaufe there was not a Word in it wich fignified Witchcraft: It may be expreffed by the Word *Incantatio. Latch.* 156.

A Woman Taken away againft her Will and marrying her; but then fhe muft have lands or goods, *&c.* or be an Heir Apparent, and muft be married or defiled. 3, *H.* 7. *cap.* 2.

A Woman

A Woman Taken in one County and marrying in another, Trial must be where married; it cannot be in Sessions Felony.

A Woman Privy to Marriage, and not to the Force, not Guilty; marrying with Consent, but under the Force, Felony. 39 *Eliz. cap.* 2. no Clergy.

The Indictment for a Felony in Stealing Goods must be, *quod Felonice cepit & asportavit*. Now if Goods are delivered to a Carrier to carry to *D.* and he carrieth them to another Place, and there converteth them to his own Use, this is Felony; for tho' it cannot strictly be said, that he *Felonice cepit* those Goods, yet the carrying them to another Place, and there disposing of them to his own Use, sheweth that he always intended to Steal them, and not to take them upon the Contract or Agreement of the Owner.

So if one come to a Market pretending to buy a Horse, and the Owner giveth Leave to ride the Horse to try his paces, and he rideth away, this is Felony: So if I deliver Goods to a Porter to carry to such a place, and he carrieth them to another Place, and there Openeth and disposeth of them; this is Felony.

The Law is the same if the Goods were carried to the place appointed, and then embezell'd; because when they are brought to that Place the Contract is determined, and the Possession is revested in the Owner, and so being taken away afterwards, 'tis Felony. *Keeling* 82, 83.

By the Statute 10 & 11 *William* 3. 'tis enacted, That he who buys stolen Goods, knowing the same to be stole, or who shall receive or conceal any Burglar, Felon or Thief, knowing them to be so, shall be adjudged Accessary to the Fact, and being convicted, shall suffer Death. But if the principal Felon cannot be taken, then the Buyer or Receiver of the Goods which he stole shall be prosecuted only for a Misdemeanour, and fined and imprisoned, or suffer any other Corporal Punishment as the Court shall inflict, though the principal Felon is not convicted; and this shall exempt the Accessary from any farther Punishment, if it shall happen that the Principal should afterwards be convicted.

By the Statute 7 *Annæ* 'tis made Felony to forge or counterfeit any *Exchequer* Bill, or any Indorsement thereon, or to tender any such Bill in Payment, or demand to have the same exchanged for ready Money by the Governour of the Company of the Bank of *England*, or by any Receiver or Collector, knowing the same to be forged or counterfeited, with an Intent to deceive any Person; and 'tis Felony without Benefit of Clergy.

And by another Statute made 12 *Annæ*, For the more effectual preventing and punishing Robberies that shall be committed in Houses, as well in the Day as in the Night, it is Enacted, That whoever should steal Money or Goods to the Value of 40 *s.* being in any Dwelling-house or Out-house thereunto belonging, although such House or Out-house be not actually broken by such Offender; and altho' the Owner of such Goods, or any other, be or be not in such House or Out-house, or shall assist, or aid any Person to commit any such Offence, being thereof convict-

ed;

ed, ſhall be abſolutely debarred from the Benefit of Clergy.

Provided, it do not extend to Apprentices under the Age of 15 Years, who ſhall rob their Maſters as aforeſaid.

And there having been ſome Doubt, Whether the entring into the Manſion-houſe of another, without breaking the ſame, with an Intent to commit ſome Felony and breaking the ſaid Houſe in the Night-time to get out, be Burglary. It is Enact, That if any Perſon ſhall enter into the Manſion-houſe or Dwelling-houſe of anothe, by Day or by Night, without breaking the ſame, with an Intent to commit Felony; or being in ſuch Houſe ſhall commit any Felony, and ſhall in the Night-time break the ſaid Houſe to get out of the ſame, ſuch Perſon ſhall be adjudged and taken to be guilty of Burglary, and the Offender ouſted of the Benefit of his Clergy in the ſame Manner as if he had entred the ſaid Houſe in the Night-time with an Intent to commit Felony.

And by another Statute, 12 *Annæ*, the Counterfeiting or Forging of Lottery Orders; or to ſell the ſaid Orders, knowing them to be counterfeited or forged, is made Felony without the Benefit of Clergy.

No Clerk of Aſſize or Peace ſhall take any Thing of a Witneſs for giving Evidence againſt a Felon. Which ſee under Title, Clerk of the Peace.

Felonies committed in the Reign of one King, the Proſecution may be in the Reign of another.

Felonies committed in one County, and the Offender taken in another, may be impriſon'd where taken, and remov'd to be proſecuted where the Fact was done.

But if he carry the Goods with him, tis Felony in every County where they are carried.

By the Statute of 23 *H.* 8. *cap.* 1. Clergy is taken away from Principals and Acceſſaries in Robbery: And becauſe Men robbed in one County, and fled into another, and ſo were indicted only for Felony, and had their Clergy; therefore by the Statute of 25 *H.* 8. *c.* 3. Clergy was taken away from thoſe who were found guilty in *any County* for ſtealing Goods, if it appear to the Judge that he ought not to have Clergy if he had been tried in the County where the Fact was committed. *Anno* 13 *Eliz.* a Man committed a *Robbery* in *Wilts*, and fled into *Berks*, where the Goods were taken upon him, and there he was indicted only for Felony, and found guilty to the Value of 10 *d*. And it appearing to the Court that he had robbed the Perſon in the *High-way*, the Queſtion was, Whether he ſhould be hang'd by the Statute of 25 *H.* 8. or only whipp'd for Petty Larceny? And reſolv'd by all the Judges, That he ſhall be only whipp'd, becauſe the Statute extends only to ſuch who ſhall *demand their Clergy*, and ſays it ſhall be *denied*, if upon Examination it ſhall appear there was a *Robbery done*: But here is found guilty of *Larcony* only, and ſo need not *demand* his Clergy. Moor. 550.

Officers may break open an Houſe to take a Felon, or any one ſuſpected thereof.

And

And if such Officer hath a Warrant to take a Felon, who is killed in resisting, 'tis no Felony in the Officer; but if the Officer, is killed, *contra.*

If a Felon escape from an Officer by Force, and he cannot otherwise retake him, he may be killed, for the Officer will be justified by his Authority.

Cutting Corn, and carrying it away at the same Time, no Felony; but if he lay it aside, and afterwards carries it away, Felony.

A Felon brought before a Justice upon Suspicion, tho' it appear he is not guilty, yet he is not to be discharged without a Trial.

A Warrant to search for a Felon, and to raise Hue-and Cry, &c.

To all Constables and other Officers in the County of K. *&c.*

Kent ss. WHereas A. B. *of* &c. *hath this present Day upon Oath complained unto me* P. L. *Esq; one of His Majesty's Justices of the Peace for the county aforesaid,* That *upon* Tuesday *the second day of* September *last at* &c. *he was robbed of* &c. *and other things, and that he hath great Cause to suspect* C. D. *an idle person,* [here describe his Person Cloathes and Age.] These are therefore *to require you, and each of you, to search diligently within your several precincts for the said* C. D. *and likewise to make Hue-and Cry after him from Town to Town, and from one County to another, as well by Horse-men as Foot-men; and if you should find the said* C. D. *that then you apprehend him, and carry him before some Justice of Peace where he shall be taken, to the end he may be examined touching the Premices: And hereof fail not.* Given, *&c.*

A Warrant to apprehend a Felon.

To the Constable.

Kent ss. WHereas A. B. *of* &c. *hath this present Day made Oath before me,* P. L. *Esq; one of His Majesties Justices of the Peace for the said County, and thereby charged* C. D. *of* &c. *with the felonious taking,* &c. *from him the said* A. B. *on,* &c. These are therefore *to Command you to apprehend the said* C. D. *and to bring him before me, or some other of His Majesty's Justices of the Peace for this County, to be examined concerning the Premisses with which he is charged: And hereof fail not.* Given, &c.

Another Warrant to search for suspected Persons, &c. and to apprehend &c.

To the Constables, of M. *in the County of* K. *and to all the other Constables within the said County.*

Kent ss. WHereas Complaint upon Oath hath been made unto me by *A. B.* of, &c. That certain Sheep &c. and other Goods, were lately feloniously taken from him, and that he hath just Reason to suspect several idle and disorderly Persons within your Parish to have unlawfully taken the same: These are therefore to command you, that immeadiately upon Receipt hereof, you diligently search every suspected House and place within your Parish, which you and the said *A. B.* shall think convenient (to search; and if you shall find any of the said Goods in the Possession of any such suspected Person or Persons, or shall have any just Cause to suspect any Person, that then you bring such Person or Persons before me, or some other Justice of the Peace for the County aforesaid, to answer the Premisses, and to be examined concerning the same: And hereof fail not. Given. &c.

If he confesseth the *Felony*, then you may take his Examination subscribed by him thus, *viz.*

The Examination of a Felon.

Kent ss. THE Examination of *C. D.* of &c. taken before me *P. L.* Esq; one of His Majesty's Justices of Peace for the said County, the second Day of *September* 1719.

The said *C. D.* being charged before me by *A. B.* of &c. That the said *C. D.* did lately feloniously steal out of the House of the said *A. B.* in the Parish of, &c. Woollen, &c. and other Goods of the said *A. B.* to the Value of, &c. He the said *C. D.* did upon his Examination by me, the said second Day of *September* confess that he stole the said Goods, and sold them to *E. F.* of, &c. for 15 l. And further saith not.

P. L. *C. D.*

A Mittimus.

To the Keeper of the Common Gaol of the County of K. *or to his Deputy.*

Kent ss. THese are to charge and command you to receive into your Gaol the Body of *C. D.* late of *&c.* taken by *J. O.* and *J. P.* Constables of *&c.* and brought by them before me for Suspicion of Felony; and that you safely keep him in your said Gaol and Custody until he shall be from thence discharged by due Course of Law. Given under, *&c.*

A Warrant to cause witnesses to appear and give Evidence.

To the Constable, &c.

Kent ss. YOU are hereby required forthwith to warn *W. S.* of, *&c.* and *R. M.* of, *&c.* to be at my House in *O, &c.* upon *Tuesday* the second Day of, *&c.* by Nine of the Clock, *&c.* to testifie their Knowledge concerning a certain Felony suspected to be done by *C. D.* of, *&c.* And hereof fail not. And that you be there likewise with this Precept, to shew how you have executed the same. Given under my hand, *&c.*

To give Evidence at Sessions.

To the Constable, &c.

Kent ss. WHereas I am inform'd, That *W. S.* of, *&c.* is a material Witness to be examined on His Majesty's Behalf, concerning a felonious Act suspected lately to be done by *C. D.* &c. These are therefore to command you to warn the said *W. S.* personally to appear at the nex Genreal Quarter-Sessions of the Peace, to be held for the said County at *M* then and there to give Evidence upon such Matters as he shall be examined· Given under my Hand, &c.

Condition of a Recognizance to appear and give Evidence against a Felon.

THE Condition of this Recognizance is such, that if the said *W. S.* shall personally appear at the next Generall Sessions of the Peace, to be held at *M.* for the said County of *Kent,* and then and there to give such Evidence as you know against, *&c.* of and concerning his felonious stealing of two Sil-

ver,

ver Spoons, the Goods of *A. B.* and do not depart thence without Leave of that Court, that then, *&c.*

If there be no direct Charge against the Person, but only Suspicion, then you bind the Person in a Recognizance, with a Condition to appear at the Assizes or Sessions, as followeth.

The Condition for a suspected Person to appear, &c.

THE Condition of this Recognizance is such, That if the above-bound *A. B.* shall personally appear, *&c.* and do then and there answer all such matters and Things which shall be objected against him being suspected to have feloniously taken the Goods of, *&c.* and do not depart without Leave of the Court, That then this Recognizance to be void, &c.

This Statute is but an Affirmance of the Common Law; for there is a Writ to deliver the Goods upon Security given, and 'tis grounded upon this Reason, That the Felon may have something to support himself in *Prison*; but the Statute doth not extend to a Person *at large*, for in such Case the Officer may seize them by the Statute, 25 Ed. 3. *cap.* 14. *Raym.* 414.

So that at Common Law such Goods are not forfeited till Conviction, and till then the Party ought to have the Benefit of them to maintain himself; 'tis true they may be put in *salva Custodia*, but cannot be seized for the Use of the King till the Party is convicted.

If the Felon doth not fly, but is apprehended with the Goods, the Owner shall have them; if he flies, and fresh Pursuit is made, and he waives the Goods and they are *taken up and carried away* before the Owner comes, the *property* is altered by the *Seizure*, and vested in the Lord; but if the Pursuit was always in View of the Felon, 'tis otherwise. *Het.* 65.

Felony; Pleas thereunto.

THese are of three Sorts, *viz.* 1. Demurrer. 2. In Abatement or Barr 3. The General Issue.

1. If the Defendant demur, he ought to be very certain that the Indictment is faulty; for if it be adjudged good, he shall have Judgment and Execution, because by the Demurrer the Fact is confessed as laid in the Indictment.

2. In Abatement, 1. *Misnosmer* in the Sir-name. 2. *Misnosmer* in the Christian Name.

If in the Sir-name, 'tis a good Plea in Abatement unto an Appeal, but not to an Indictment; but in the Christian Name; tis a good Plea to an Indictment; and if 'tis found or confessed by the Attorney-General, 'tis naught; but then the Party must confess his true Name, that he may instantly be Indicted.

In Bar, *Auterfoitz* Acquit. 1. This must always be intended of a lawful Acquittal; for if the Indictment or Appeal is insufficient and faulty, and the Defendant is acquitted thereon, he may be indicted again for the same Felony, unless Judgment is given upon such Indictment, for that must stand till reversed by Error.

2. This must be always of the same Felony, and therefore 'tis no good Plea to an Indictment or Appeal for another Felony.

3. An Acquittal upon an Indictment of Death; is no Plea to an Appeal brought for the same Death; but an Acquittal upon an Indictment or an Appeal, in Cases of Felony, is a good Plea to any other Indictment for the same Felony, though 'tis not so in the Case of Death. But then the Appeal must not be erroneous in Substance nor be brought by a wrong Person.

Auterfoitz Convict, Of Manslaughter, either upon an Indictment or an Appeal is a good Plea to any other Indictment for the same Death.

Feme-Covert

THE Peace may be granted against her, or against an Infant, tho' under 14 Years of Age; but then she must not be bound, tho' with her Husband, for the Recognizance will be void as to her, but she must find Sureties; Which, if she cannot do, she must be committed.

If she commit a Riot or Trespass without her Husband, she may be indicted and fined, but the Fine shall not be levied on her Husband, but on her after his Death, and she shall be committed till 'tis paid, 9 *Rep.* 72. Dr. *Hussey's* Case; 11 *Rep.* Dr. *Foster's* Case.

If She steal Goods by Compulsion of her Husband, 'tis not Felony in her, because of the Necessity of Obedience; but if it was at his Perswation without any Constraint, she is then guilty of Felony, and her Husband is Accessary.

But this Priviledge doth not prevail in Cases of Treason and Murder, because of the Greatness of those Offences.

It hath been held, That if both steal together, this shall be taken to be the Act of the Husband alone, and that she cannot be so much as Accessary to it, it, because of the Neceſſity of Obedience, as aforeſaid; but I think Obedience ſhould only extenuate the Crime, for ſuch it is, and ſhe ought not to conſent to it, if ſhe doth, ſhe may be indicted.

She cannot ſteal her Huſband's Goods; but if ſhe is taken away with them againſt his Conſent, 'tis Felony in him that takes her: ſo 'tis if ſhe deliver her Husbands Goods to an Adulterer, this is Felony in him.

In an Indictment for her ſelling Ale without Licence, the Husband muſt be joyn'd, becauſe he is to pay the Fine.

She may be committed for a Force or Riot, as aforeſaid, but an Infant cannot; yet if ſhe be asked to find Sureties of the Peace, and cannot, ſhe may be committed.

Force Lawful.

IN this Caſe Doors may be broke open, 1. To apprehend, For Treaſon, Felony, or Suſpicion thereof, Any Perſon, who hath wounded another very dangerouſly, and flieth for the ſame to a Houſe, Or a popiſh Recuſant Excommunicate.

2. An Affray in the Houſe, and the Doors ſhut.

3. Upon a Warrant for the Peace or Good Behaviour, *quære*.

4. Upon a *Capias Utlegatum* in a Perſonal Action, and upon a *Capias pro fine* directed to the Sheriff.

A Man was outlawed for want of an Appearance: The Sheriff came to his Houſe with a *Latitat* and with a *Capias Utlegatum*, without the Privity of the Plaintiff, and the outward Door being open, he entred; then he and his company ſhut the Door and drew their Swords, and went up to the Chamber where the Man was in Bed, and knocked gently at the Door, which was lock'd, but did not tell who they were, or for what they came; but the Door not being immediately opened, they broke it open, and arreſted the Perſon upon the *Latitat*. and took Bond for his Appearance, and 40 *s*. for ſuing out a *Superſedeas* to the Outlawry; but the Sheriff was fined 200 *l*. for this Outrage and Terror, and for not telling who he was, that the Door might be opened without Violence.

So where a Sheriff had *meſne Proceſs* againſt one, and came to his Houſe and knock'd gently at the Door, the Wife opened it a little to ſee who it was, and he forced in with his Sword drawn, and broke open the Door where the Defendant lay: This was unlawful, becauſe the firſt Entry was ſo, for the opening

opening the Door by Craft and Violence, which was intended.

But if upon such *Process* a Bailiff catch the Defendant by the Hand, as he held it out of the Window; this is such a Taking, that he may justify the breaking open the House.

5. Upon a Forcible Entry or Detainer, found by Inquisition before the Justices, or upon their own View,

6. Upon a Judgment in Ejectment, but then the Officer must signify the Cause of his Coming. 5 *Rep.* 91.

7. In all Cases where the King is Party, or hath any Intrest, *&c.*

But you cannot break open a Door upon an Execution at the Suit of a Common Person, for 'tis illegal; and if the Officer is Kill'd in doing it, 'tis only Manslaughter. *Jones* 592.

Forcible Entry.

AT Common Law, where a Man had a Title to Lands, he might not only enter, but detain by Force; and tho' it was done in the Presence of an Officer, yet he had no Power to Interpose, unless some great Mischief (as Murder *&c.*) was committed.

And this was the Occasion of making the Statute of 5 *R.* 2. *c.* 7. which prohibits the Force, tho' the Person had a Title, and appoints that the Justices shall inquire into it, and not otherwise, that is, in their Sessions.

This being for that very Reason found to be inconvenient, a quicker Remedy was provided to remove the Force, by the Statute of 15 R. 2 which gives one or more Justices Authority to take sufficient Power with them, and to view the Place where the *Entry* and Detainer is, by Force, and to commit the Offenders, there to remain till they have made Fine and Ransom to the King.

By this Statute likewise, the Sheriff and all others are to be Assistant to the Justices, upon Pain of Fine and Imprisonment.

But still there remained some Inconveniencies which this Law did not remedy:

1. As if the Entry was peaceable, and the Detainer by Force.

2. If the Persons were gone before the Justices came, they could proceed no farther.

3. They had not Power to give Restitution to the Party grieved,

All these Matters were remedied by the Statute of 8 *H.* 6. which gives Power to one or more Justices, by Warrant, to command the Sheriff to summon a Jury to inquire of the Force, and to seize the Tenements as well in the Absence as Presence of the Offender.

It

It likewise appoints the Statute of 15 *R.* 2. to be put in Execution, altho, the Detainer by Force was after a peaceable Entry; and all at the Costs of the Party grieved.

It likewise inflicts the Penalty of 20 *l.* upon the Sheriff neglecting his Duty, to be recovered by Indictment at Sessions, and divided between King and prosecutor.

But the Justices cannot make Inquiry into a Force, after a peaceable Possession for three Years. 2 *Cro.* 199.

And by the Statute 31 *Eliz.* no Restitution can be made upon Indictment of Force *&c.* where the Party had such a quiet Possession for three Years, as aforesaid.

Afterwards some Doubts arising, whether the Justices had any Power but only in Cases of Freehold; this was the Occasion of making the Statute of 21. *Jac. cap.* 15. by which they have Power to give Restitution to Tenants for Years, Tenants by *Elegit*, Statute, *&c.* Copyholders *&c.* as well as to Freeholders, put out or detained by Force; So that now a compleat Remedy is given.

1. Against those who enter with Force, and continue the Possession peaceably.
2. Against those who enter peaceably, and hold out with Force.
3. Against those who both enter and hold out with Force.

What is a Forcible Entry. It must be *manu-forti*, and 'tis Force if he enter to commit a Trespass tho' the Party doth not quit the Possession; but if the Entry is peaceable, then 'tis Disseisin, not Force; being provided with Weapons, threatning Life or Loss of Limbs, breaking open Doors, or entring, the Doors being open with unusual Armour or Weapons, ejecting or distraining for Rent with Force.

The Reason why it must be set forth to be done *manu forti*, is to distinguish it from all other Trespasses; those are peculiar Words adapted to an Indictment for this Offence; And therefore *vi & armis*, or *fortitudine & potentia magna*, or such like words, tho' they may signify the same Thing, yet will not make the Indictment good. *Stiles.* 135. *Cro. Eliz.* 461. 2 *Bulst.* 258. *Noy* 155.

Forcible Detainer, Is Denying Entrance to the Justice, though by one Person. By keeping Cattle in another Mans Ground, claiming any Right of Common *&c.* Menacing to keep the Possession, though no Force used.
Resisting, threatning, or rescuing in Cases of Distress for Rent or Common, one Justice may remove the Force, record it upon View, but cannot make Restitution.
One alone, without the Help of another.

What Persons may be guilty of Both. Indictment for a *Forcible Entry* and *Detainer*, the Jury find the *Entry with Force*, but the *Detainer Peaceable*; and this was held insufficient to grant Restitution upon it.

So where the Jury found *quoad* the *Entry ignoramus*, and *quoad* the *Detainer* *Billa*

Billa vera, and upon Restitution awarded by the Justice of Peace, *B. R.* set it aside, and granted a Restitution; because the Indictment being entire for the Entry as well as the Detainer, and the Jury having found but one, 'tis therefore void. *Yelv.* 99. 100. 2. *Cro.* 151. *Sid.* 97. 414 *contra.*

Indictment *quare in medietatem intravit* is void, for the Entry must be into the whole. *Palm.* 419.

An Infant above 14, *&* *Feme-Covert*, for which they may be committed and fined, tho' 'tis Prudence not to commit the Infant, and the Husband shall not be charged with the Fine of his Wife.

If several come with an Intention to enter, and one commit the Force, all are guilty, tho' the other are peaceable.

If more then three, 'tis a Riot, and then the two next Justices may inquire within a Month by a Jury.

The Power of the Justices upon the Statute of. 15 *R.* 2. *c.* 2.

One Justice may go to the Place and take the Assistance of the Sheriff if he thinks fit, may break open the Door if resisted, and may arrest and commit the Offenders; he may command any one to assist him, and commit and fine those who refuse.

If he sees the Force, he may Record it, and commit the Offenders, for his View is a Conviction, and this Record being certified in *B. R.* the Court will grant Restitution, and assess a Fine. 8. *Rep.* 120.

If the Offenders are gone before the Justices come, then they may direct their Precept to the Sheriff, to impanel 24 Men of 40 *s. per Annum* Freehold each of them; and 12 must be sworn to inquire of the force, and when found the Justices may either themselves put the Party in Possession, or make a Precept to the Sheriff for that Purpose: And this must be done, tho' they view the Force, if they intend to put the Party into Possession. *Upon the Statute of* 8. *H.* 6. *two Justices.*

The same Justices, before whome the Force, was found, having made a Precept to the Sheriff to restore the Party, may grant a *Supersedeas* to stay Restitution if he see Cause.

But if the Party doth not think fit to apply himself to the Justices, then he may have an Action of Trespass against the Defendant (who had no Title of Entry) and entring with Force, and may recover treble Costs and Damages: but if his Entry was upon good, title tho' with Force, then you must proceed by Indictment.

Continuing in Possession Three Years peaceably, he may justifie the Detainer by Force.

But must not resist the Justice when he comes to view.

This possession may be pleaded to an Indictment for a Force, which will not only excuse the Fine and Commitment, but prevent the Restitution.

The Entry must be *vi & armis*, or peaceably and detaining with Force, according

ing to the Words of the Statute of 8 *H*, 6. *Roll. Abr.* 2. *pag.* 80.

The Quality of the Thing upon which the Entry is made, must also be set forth, as into a Messuage, Meadow, Wood, *&c.* for entrnig *in Tenementa* generally is not good, because of the Incertainty, for it may extend to a House or Cottage, 2 *Roll. Rep.* 46. So an Entry into two Closes, *Prati-sive Pasturæ* is not good. *Roll Abr.* 2. *pag.* 81.

It must be either *manu Forti*, or *multitudine Gentium*, and it must conclude *adhuc extratenet*, for without those Words there cannot be any Restitution; and likewise *contra formam Statut. Roll. Abr.* 2. *pag.* 82.

It must be certain, therefore an Entry into *Messuagium*, or *Cottagium sive Tenementum*, is void. *Roll. Abr.* 2. *pag.* 80.

But *in Clausum* is good, for that is certain enough.

And as to the *Certiorari*, that must be delivered in open Sessions, which is a *Supersedeas*.

But the Traverse is no *Supersedeas*, because the Force being found upon the Indictment, the Justice may restore the Party grieved, or otherwise may certify the Indictment to *B. R.* but he that tendereth the Traverse, must bear all the Charges of the prosecution, both before the Justice and in *B. R.*

If the Justice will try the Traverse presently, it must not be by the Jury who found the Force, but by a new Jury, to be returned by the Sheriff the next Day, and this Traverse must be in Writing,

The Justice may direct his precept to the Sheriff to impannel a Jury *ut prius*, and upon Default of their Appearance, may award an *alias & pluries*, and return 40 *s.* Issues upon the second Precept on each of the Jury, and 5 *l.* Issues on the third Precept, aud at every Time afterwards double.

The Expulsion must be out of House or Lands, and so set forth in the Indictment.

In the Indictment, the Estate must be set forth, for 'tis not enough to alledge generally that *Possessionatus fuit*, because a Tenant at Will may be so possess'd, and he is not within either of the Statutes. *Sid.* 102. 1 *Mod.* 73.

But since I have mentioned the Statutes, I must likewise take Notice, that 'tis not the best Way to recite them in the Indictment; for if misrecited in any Particular, it will be quashed. *Cro. Eliz.* 93, 96, 106, 307, 697. 1 *Bulst.* 218.

The Indictment was for a Forcible Entry into a *Copyhold*, *viz.* That the Defendant *ejecit & disseisivit*, for which Reason it was quash'd, because *Disseisin* is applicable only to a *Freehold*; and therefore in all Cases, except for a *Freehold*, it ought to be *ejecit expulit & amovit Raym.* 67. 4 *Inst.* 176.

And even in the Case of a Freehold *expulit seu disseisivit* is void, because 'tis in the Disjunctive; for there must be an actual Expulsion and Disseisin. 1 *Roll. Rep.* 406.

And so is *disseisivit*, without shewing what Estate he had. 1 *Vent.* 306.

If it is for *disseising* the Landlord, and *expelling* the Tenant, tho' the Entry was made by Command of the Landlord, and he opposed Restitution; yet it was granted by *B. R.*

for they may reform the several Degrees of Wrongs; but if it had been only for expelling the Tenant, he could not have Restitution. *Yelv.* 81.

It must be *adhuc existens liberum Tenementum*, as well as *adtunc.* 2 Cro. 214. 639. *Levinz.* 1 p. 90.

Pleas to an Inditment.

1. Quiet Possession for Three Years before the Inquisition found. 31. *Eliz. Cap.* 11. *Raym.* 84.

This must be understood of a Term of Years; but if it had been a Freehold, then he must set forth that he was seized, *&c.* and was in Possession for three Years, *&c.* and 'tis not material to shew how seised, because 'tis not the Title, but the Possession which is requisite to be alledged. *Sid.* 156.

2. The Defendant may tender a Traverse.

3. He may demur to the Insufficiency of the Indictment.

4. And plead to Insufficiency of Jurors, not having 40 *s.* Freehold.

5. May bring a *Certiorary*, which is a *Supersedeas*, for Tythes, Rents, &c. 1 *Cor.* 146.

To remove a Force out of a Parish-Church or Personage-House, tho' there is another Remedy by *vi Laica removenda.* Sid. 101.

After Enquiry the Justice may break open the House and restore the Party himself, for none but he who is actually put out of Possession can be restored.

Where they find a Force, and make a Record of it on their own View, they may commit the Offenders, but cannot grant Restitution. 1 *Vent.* 308. *Sid.* 156.

It must be of House or Land, it cannot be of Rent, Common Advowson, *&c. Quære.*

If the Defendant traverse the Indictment, the best Way for the Justice is to certifie it into *B. R.* Sid. 287

But after a Traverse, the Court cannot grant Restitution. 1 *Vent.* 165. But in Dyer there is a contrary Opinion. *Dyer.* 122.

If the Justices certifie, That Complaint was made to them of a Forcible Entry into an House, and thereupon they went thither and found it true, and removed the Force, and fined the Defendant 20 *l.* This Certificate is not good, because they do not shew the *Time* when the Complaint was made, which they ought to do, because such Certificate is in Nature of an Inditment, and traversable, 2 *Roll. Rep.* 39

No other Justice or Justices (except *B. R.*) but he or they before whom the Force is found can award Restitution.

But then the Force must be found by an Inquisition of Twelve Men, or otherwise the Justice may be punish'd; but the Entry and Holding with Force being found, the Justice may re-seize by Virtue of the Statute of 8 *H.* 6. *cap.* 9. and restore the Party to his Possession.

Or

Or he may direct his Precept to the Sheriff for that Purpose, *Teste* by himself. *Dyer* 187

And if the Sheriff return, that he cannot make Restitution because he was resisted, he shall be fined; for he may raise the *Posse Com.*

The Justices, upon an Indictment found, may give Restitution to a Freeholder, to to a Tenant for Years, or by Copy of Court-Roll; to Tenant by *Elegit*, Statute-Merchant or Staple. 21 *Jac. cap.* 15.

One Joint-tenant or Tenant in common putteth out the other, *Quere* what the Justice can do there, because his Entry and Possession was lawful.

If an Indictment be removed, and no Prosecution the next Term, the Court may award Restitution.

A Man cannot justifie the breaking open an House, by Vertue of a Warrant from a Secretary of State; and no House can be broke open, unless there is a Civil Officer present.

But if a Man hath a Warrant to apprehend another, and he break open a Door to execute it, and so mistakes the Law, he is not guilty of Felony, for that was not his Design. Now since there must be a felonious Intent to make a Man guilty of Felony, and there being no such Intention appearing, the Party is only a Trespasser.

If after a Door is broke open, one of the Company steals any Thing, 'tis Felony only in him, and not in the rest, unless they were assenting to it.

The Record of a Forcible Entry upon the View of a Justice, upon the Statute of 15 R. 2

Kent ss. I P. S. *Esquire one of the Justices assign'd to keep the peace in the County aforesaid, Do Certify that on the 9 day of June, in the year of the Reign &c.* A. B. *of* M. *in the County aforesaid, Yeoman hath Complained to me that* C. D. *of &c. and others disturbers of the peace of our said Lord the King to me unknown, the day of in the year aforesaid into One Messuage with the appurtenances then and hitherto being the free Tenement of* E. F. *Gentleman and in the possession of the aforesaid* A. B. *for the Term of 7 years yet to come Situate in* M. *aforesaid, in the County aforesaid, peaceably and Quietly have Entered And afterwards (viz) the aforesaid 9 day of June in the year aforesaid at* M. *aforesaid, in the County aforesaid, the aforesaid* A. B. *from the aforesaid Messuage with force and Arms, (viz) with staves, Swords, &c. unlawfully and with a strong hand, did Expell, Eject, and remove and the aforesaid* A. B. *being so Expelled Ejected and removed from the Messuage aforesaid, with the appurtenances as aforesaid with force and Arms unlawfully and with*

 a strong

strong hand then and there did keep out and detain to the great Damage of the said A. B. *and against the peace of our said Lord the King, and Contrary to the form of the Satute in such Case made and provided, and whereupon the aforesaid* A. B. *hath required of me a Remedy and in that behalf to be Reliev'd. Therefore I the aforesaid* P. S. *immediately in my proper person came to the Messuage aforesaid with the appurtenances, and then and there found the aforesaid* A, B. *of the aforesaid Messuage with the appurtenances by the aforesaid* C. D. *with force and Arms unlawfully and with a strong hand kept out and detain'd against the form of the Statute aforesaid, upon which I the aforesaid* P. S. *then and there Caused the aforesaid* C. D. *to be taken and arrested and to the Gaol of* M *in the County aforesaid to be sent there to remain under safe Custody untill he should find, before me or some other Justice of our said Lord the King, assign'd to keep the peace in the County aforesaid, Sufficient Security that he should personally appear at the next General Sessions of the peace of our said Lord the King in the County aforesaid to be held to answer the trespass and Contempt aforesaid: And that in the mean time he should well behave himself, In Testimony whereof I the aforesaid* P. S. *to this Certificate have put my hand and Seal the* 11 *day of* June. *&c.*

A Precept to the Sheriff in the Name of a *Venite Facias*, to summon a Jury.

Kent *ss.* P L *Esquire one of the Justices of our Lord the King assign'd to preserve the peace in the County aforesaid, To the Sheriff of the same County Greeting; On the behalf of our said Lord the King, I Command thee that thou Cause to come before me at* M. *in the County aforesaid, the first day of July next, Twenty Four honest and careful men of the Vicinage of* M. *aforesaid, Every one of them having* 40 *s. of Lands and Tenements or Rent at least by the Year, beyond reprizes, to inquire upon their Oaths for our said Lord the King of a certain Ingress with strong hand made into the Messuage of one* A. C. *at* M. *aforesaid against the form of the Statute in such Case made and provided, and see that upon every one of the Jurors by himself in this behalf to be impanell'd Twenty Shillings as Issues at the Day aforesaid thou dost return: And this thou art by no means to Omit, under Penalty of Twenty Pounds, and have thou then there this Precept Witness the said* P, L. 13 *July.* Anno *&c.*

An Inquisition upon the Force.

AN Inquisition taken for his Majesty at M. *in the County of Kent, on the first day of July and in the Year of his Majesty's Reign* &c. *upon Oath of* A. B. C. D. E. F. G. H. &c. *before* P. S. *appointed one of his Majesty's Justices for preserving the Peace of the Said County, as also for trying and Judging all felonies, tresspasses, and other crimes committed in the said County; who upon Oath declare that* I. K, *of* M. *Yeoman in the said County was legally and peaceablely seised in his Demeasne as of Fee, and in one Messuage with it's appurtenances in* M, *aforesaid, and did peaceably continue his said possession, untill* R. S. *of &c. an* R. W. *of &c. and other Malefactors not Known, on the thirtieth of June last past, did by force and Armes viz. Battoons, Swords, and Guns, enter into the said Messuage with it's appurtenances, and disseised, and with a strong hand expelled the said* I. K. *and thus disseised and expelled from the aforesaid Messuage on the thirtieth of June, untill the day of the taking this Inquisition they have with a Strong hand, and armed power kept him out, and do as yet keep him out, to the great disturbance of the peace of his said Majesty and against the form of the Statute in that Case made and provided where none of them nor any other Person whom he or they might represent, either held or did hold any part in the aforesaid Messuage with its appurtenances, or any parcel thereof for three years immediatly preceeding his aforesaid entry, nor any other time avoiding to the knowleg of the aforesaid Deponents.*

The Entry and Expulsion being thus found by the Jury, the Justice may make a Precept to the Sheriff for Restitution thus:

Kent ss. P L. Esquire, one of his Majesty's Justices of the Peace for the said County to the Sheriff thereof, Greeting: Whereas by a certain Inqusitiou taken before me the first Day of *July* last past, at M. in the County aforesaid, upon the Oath of *A. B. C.* D. &c. according to the Form of the Statute in that Case made and provided: It was found, That *R. W. R. S.* and others, (*prout in the Inquisition*) as by the said Inquisition of Record doth more fully appear: These are therefore in His Majesty's Name to require you to go to the said Messuage and other the Premises, and cause the same with the Appurtenances to be reseised, and the aforesaid *J. K.* to be be reftored thereunto, and to his full Poffeffion thereof, in as large and ample Manner as he was before the faid Entry was made: And hereof fail not, Given under my Hand and Seal, &c.

A Mittimus *of fuch who hold Lands*, &c. *by Force.*

Kent ʃʃ. P L. Efquire, one of His Majefty's Juftices of the Peace for the County aforefaid: To the Keeper of the Common Gaol at M. in the faid County, or to his Deputy there Whereas on this prefent Day of *September*, in the Year 1719. Complaint hath been made unto me by *A. B.* of, &c. of a Forcible Entry made by feveral Perfons into his Lands at, &c. I went immediately to the faid Lands, where I found *C. D. E. F. G, H.* &c. of &c. Labourers, forcibly and with ftrong Hands holding the Premifes, againft the Form of the Statute in that Cafe made and Provided: Therefore I fend you herewithal the Bodies of the faid *C. D. E. F.* &c. being convicted of the faid forcible Holding by my own View, commanding you in His Majefty's Name to receive them into your Gaol and Cuftody, and there fafely to keep them until they fhall be from thence delivered by due Courfe of Law. Given under my Hand and Seal the Day and Year firft above-written.

Forfeiture.

THIS is occafioned by the Tranfgreffion of fome Penal Law, whereby the Offender lofeth his Lands and Goods.

But this Difference is to be obferv'd That where Lands are forfeited, it fhall relate to the Time of the Offence committed; but in cafe where Goods and Chattels are forfeited, there fhall be no Relation, for the Goods of the Felon are his own till Conviction or Attainder; and the Sheriff or other Officer ought not to remove them, becaufe the Property is not alter'd till Conviction; but ufually they fecure the Goods of the Felon as foon as he is apprehended; but this is exprefly againft the Statute of 1 *R.* 3. *cap.* 3 by which 'tis enacted, That none fhall feife the Goods of any arrefted for Sufpicion of Felony, before he is convicted or attainted thereof, upon Pain to forfeit double the Value of the Goods, &c. to be recovered by the Party grieved, in an Action of Debt, &c.

If it is found by the Coroner's Inqueft, that the Party *fugam focit*, he forfeits his Goods

Goods notwithstanding he should be afterwards acquitted of the Felony by the Petty-Jury, and they should find that he did not fly for the same: So where a true Man is pursued as a Felon, and he fleeth and waiveth his *own Goods*, those are forfeited as if they had been stolen; for *fatetur facinus qui judicium fugit.*

Now the Reason of the Forfeiture in the first Case, is because the King hath a Prerogative to take the Advantage of that Record which is most for his Interest, and that is the Record of the Coroner. *Stamf. Pl. Coron.* 183. B.

If a Man is acquitted of the Felony, but the Jury find *quod fugam fecit*, he shall lose his Goods which he had at the Time of the Acquittal, and not at the Time of the Flight. *Goulds.* 135.

In Treason, Lands in Fee or in Tail, or for Life or Years, after Conviction or Attainder All the Goods and Chattels of what Kind soever. In Petit-Treason Lands In Fee, for a Year and a Day. Lands in Tail, during Life of the Offender.

In Felony, Lands in Fee-Simple, for a Year and a Day from the Time of the Felony committed, and the Profits during Life of the Offender, Goods and Chattels from the Time of the Attainder or Conviction.

In Man-slaughter and *Felo de se*, Petit-Larceny. Offenders in these Cases, forfeit Goods and Chattels.

In Chance medly, and *Se defendendo*, Offenders forfiet Goods and Chattels, but they may have Pardon of Course.

Forgery.

THIS is an Offence at the Common Law, and likewise punishable by a particular Statute. 5 *Eliz. c.* 14.

If the Indictment is at Common Law, the Offender convicted must stand in the Pillory, be fined and imprisoned during the Pleasure of the Court. *Ray.* 81.

Mr. *Dalton* is of Opinion, That Justices of Peace cannot meddle with these Offenders, because they cannot take Notice of the first Conviction.

Besides, by the express Words of the Statute of 5 *Eliz.* Justices of Assize, and of Oyer and Terminer are to hear and determine this Offence. *Cro. Eliz.* 87, 601, 697.

Since the making this Statute, few Indictments have been brought for Forgeries at Common Law; some there are, *viz.* One *Howell Gwynn* cut off a dead Man's Hand, and put a Pen and Ink in it, and signed and sealed a Deed with the Hand, and made Oath that it was the Hand-writing of *B.* and that he sealed and delivered the Deed; he was convicted and fined 100 *l.* and was to stand in the Pillory two Hours at the Hall-Gate. Stiles. 363.

So one *Farmer* was indicted for a Forgery; he demurred to the Inidctment, and it was found against him, and had Judgment to stand in the Pillory, was fined 100 *l.* and imprisoned during Pleasure. *Raim.* 81.

But since the Statute many Indictments have been brought to punish an Offender

of

of this Nature, who for the firſt Offence That is for forging 1. Falſe Deeds 2. Writing ſealed. 3. Court-Roll. 4. Will: To the Intent that the Freehold of the Lands on the Right or Title thereof, may be troubled or charged he is to be *ſet in the Pillory in ſome Market-Town, to have his Ears cut off there, and his Noſtrils ſlit. and ſhall forfeit the Profits of his Land to the King during his Life, and ſhall be committed alſo for Life.*

Every Indictment brought upon the Statute muſt purſue ſome of the Words of it; as if a Man is indicted for forging a Will, by which a Leaſe for Years is conveyed; this is not within the Statute under the Word *Will*, becauſe it doth not charge the Freehold, or diſturb the Right thereof; and the Word *Will* in the Statute, relates only to ſuch Wills which convey a *Freehold*; but it comes under the Words *Writing ſealed*, and therefore ſhall be puniſhed by that Law. *Dyer* 302.

Four Years after the making of this Statute, one *Taverner* was convicted for forging a Cuſtomary of a Manor, in which he had inſerted ſeveral falſe Cuſtoms. and had put the Hands and Seals of Eleven Tenants to it; and it was proved that he did it wittingly, ſubtilly, and falſly; and this was held Forgery within the Statute. *Dyer* 322 *B*.

In the next Paragraph, there are other Offences mentioned as Forging a Leaſe for Years, Annuity, Obligation, Bill, Acquittance, Releaſe, or other Diſcharge of a Perſonal Thing.

And there is ſome Variation in the Puniſhment of theſe Offences, *viz. Pillory*; but the Offender loſes but *one* of his Ears, and is to ſuffer but a Year's Impriſonment without Bail.

The ſecond Offence in all the Caſes above-mentioned, is Felony; but this ſeldom or never happens.

Now forging a Deed, by which Goods and Chattels are conveyed, are within neither of theſe Paragraphs; firſt, becauſe it doth not concern a *Freehold*, and 'tis neither a Bill, Bond, Acquittance or Diſcharge of a Perſonal Thing, and ſo not within the Words of the Statute.

The Father bound his Son Apprentice, and gave Bond of 100 *l.* for his Good Behaviour; the Maſter raiſed out *Libris*, and put in *Marcis*, and this was held not within the Statute, becauſe he did a Prejudice to none but himſelf; that is by making the Bond void, or at leaſt by putting in a leſſer Sum for a greater; but if he had increaſed the Sum, it had been otherwiſe. *Moor* 619.

Forging an *Aſſignment* of a Leaſe is not within the Statute, becauſe it doth not charge the Lands, but only tranfers an Intereſt which was in being before. *Noy* 42.

But making a Foeffment, tho' Livery and Seiſin was not indorſed when the Deed was delivered, and afterwards ſelling the Land for a valuable Conſideration to another, and

and the endorsing Livery on the first Deed; this was held Forgery both in the Feoffor and Feoffee, because it was to deceive an honest Purchaser. Moor 655.

The Testator appointed a Man to write his Will, and to insert such a Clause, which he omitted, this is not Forgery; so if he write a Will without any Direction, and bring it to the Testator, who is not of perfect Memory, and he signs it: But if the Devisor directs a Gift to one for Life, Remainder to another in Fee, and the Writer omits the Estate for Life, so that the Remainder vests immediately upon the Death of the Devisor; this is Forgery. Noy 18. Moor 760.

Games, unlawful, and Gaming-Houses.

BY the Statute of 33 *H.* 8. One Justice may commit those who keep unlawful Gaming-Houses, till they find Sureties by Recognizance not to keep such Houses any more; they likewise forfeit 40 *s.* a Day, to be divided between the King and Prosecutor. 33 H. 8. c. 9.

He also may commit, without Bail, any Person resorting to, or playing there, till he be bound in such Sum as the Justice shall think reasonable, not to offend again; and besides, he forfeits for every Offence 6 *s.* 8 *d.*

And in order to apprehend such Persons, the Statute giveth the Justice Authority to enter into any common Place where unlawful Games are suspected to be used: As Bear-baiting, Cock fighting, Football, Bull-baiting, Coits, Nine-Pins, Bowling, Dice, Tennis; Cards, are unlawful Games.

Persons prohibited by this Law, are Apprentices, Husbandmen, Servants of all Kinds, Artificers, Labourers, Fisher-men. Mariners, Watermen.

They must not play at any of these Games except at *Christmas*; nor then, but in their own Houses, and Servants in their Masters Houses, and by their Leave.

The Forfeture is 20 *s.* for every Offence, to be devided as aforesaid.

But a Man of 100 *l. per Annum* may licence his Servant to play at Bowls or Tennis.

One Justice may commit for Cheating at Play. *Cro. Car.* 235.

And *Anno* 9 *Annæ*, For the better preventing Excessive and Deceitful Gaming, a Law was made, That all Notes, Bonds, Securities, *&c.* whatsoever, entred into on account of Gaming or Playing at Cards, Dice, Tables, Tennis, Bowls, or other Game whatsoever; or on Betting, or lending Money thereon, shall be void.

And where the Securities, *&c.* shall be on Lands, *&c.* such Mortgage, *&c.* shall be for the sole Benefit of the next in Remainder, as if the Grantor had been actually dead. 9 Annæ.

If any Person lose 10 *l.* in Money or Goods, to one or more Person or Persons,

 he

he may within three Months sue for the same by Action of Debt: Or, if the Loser do not sue for the same, any other Person may, and recover treble the Value, with Costs, against the Winners: One Moiety to the Person who sues for the same, the other to the Poor where the Offences committed.

Any Persons cheating at Play, or winning above 10 *l.* and being convicted by Indictment or Information, shall forfeit Five times the Value: And in case of such ill Practice, the Offenders shall be deemed infamous, and suffer corporal Punishment as in Cases of wilful Perjury. The Penalty to be recovered by Action as aforesaid.

And that such dissolute Persons as support their extravagant Expences by Gaming, may be brought before Two or more Justices to find Sureties for the Good behaviour for 12 Months, or be committed to the common Gaol.

If after finding Sureties he shall play again to the Value of 20 *s.* durcing the Time he shall be so bound, the Recognizance to be forfeited.

And any Person challenging or fighting another on Account of Gaming or Betting, forfeits to His Majesty all his Goods and Chattels, and shall suffer two Years Imprisonment without Bail.

Playing within any of His Majesty's Palaces, where His Majesty, *&c.* shall be actually resident, is excepted; so as such Playing be not in any House, the Freehold whereof shall be out of the Crown, *&c.* and so as such Playing be for ready Money only.

A Warrant upon 33 H 8. against Gaming-Houses.

To all Constables, &c. *and other His Majesty's Officers whom these may concern.*

Kent *ss.* WHereas Complaint upon Oath hath been made unto us, whose Hands and Seals are hereunto set, His Majesty's Justices of the Peace of the County of *Kent*, That there are many unlawful Gaming-Houses set up within the said County, which has and now does prove ruinous and destructive to His Majesty's Liege Subjects, and tends to the Ruin and Debauchery of Youth; and the Cause of many heinous Murders, Robberies, Felonies, Outrages and Riots, to be done and committed; and the Divine Service, by such Misdoers, on Holy and Festival Days, not heard or solemnized, to the high Displeasure of Almighty God, and contrary to the Laws and Statutes of this Realm: These are therefore, in His Majesty's Name, to charge and command you, and every of you, to whom these Presents shall come, to make due Search within the said County of *K.* And to come, enter and resort into all

all and every the Houses and Places where such Games shall be suspected to be holden exercised, used or occupied; and as well the Servants, Agents, and Keepers of the same, as also the Persons there haunting, resorting and playing, to take, arrest and imprison; and them so taken and arrested, to bring before us, and other His Majesty's Justices of the Peace, which will be assembled at a Petty-Sessions held for that Purpose at the Vestry-Room of *&c.* in the said County, the next Morning by Ten of the Clock, after such their being taken as aforesaid, to the end they may be examined and dealt with according to Law; Hereof you are not to fail. Given under our Hands and Seals, *&c.*

Recognizance thiron.

A. B. of, *&c.*---40 *l.* *C.* D. of, *&c.*---20 *l.* *E. F.* of, *&c.*---20 *l.*

Upon Condition, That the above-bound *A. B.* shall no longer use, keep or occupy any Common House, Alley or Place (where any unlawful Game shall be held or exercised;) nor any unlawful Game whatsoever: That then, *&c.*

Gaoler and Gaol, Prisoner and Prison.

A Prison is a Place where a Man is restrained of his Liberty, to answer an Offence done against the Law.

The Commitment must be by a Judge of Record, and by a lawful Warrant.

There are several Sorts of Prisons, *viz.* 1. The Common Gaol, and to this Place Justices must commit Murderers and Felons, and not elsewhere.

2. The Stocks.

3. The Prison of a Lord of a Franchise.

4. The Custody by any who hath lawfully taken the Offender, or the House of a Constable, or other Person, where a Prisoner is lawfully detained.

A Felon escaping from any of these Places, makes it a Breach of Prison.

To break a Prison there must be an actual Force; for if he go out, the Doors being open, 'tis not Felony; neither is it material that 'tis the King's Prison, for if 'tis the Constable's House 'tis sufficient.

Rescuing him to bring him away, is Felony in the Rescuer. If the Gaoler permits a voluntary Escape, 'tis Felony in him: But if the Escape is negligent, and not voluntary 'tis

tis Felony in the Prisoner, and a Misdemeanor only in the Gaoler.

If the Gaoler permits a Felon to escape, 'tis Felony; but if he kill an unruly Prisoner, 'tis not Felony; if by hard Usage, 'tis Murder.

If he refuse to receive a Felon, being sent to him by Warrant, *&c.* he is finable, and the Township must keep him till the Gaol-delivery.

Justices in Sessions have Power to tax every Parish in the County, not exceeding 8 *d. per* Week, towards the Relief of the Prisoners in Gaol. This Tax is to be levied every *Sunday* by the Church-wardens, and by them to be paid Quarterly to the Constables; but if in a Corporation, then to the chief Officer, and the Constables; and such chief Officer is to pay the same every Quarter-Sessions to the Collector, who is to distribute it Weekly to the Prisoners. 10 & 11 *W.* 3.

And if those Officers neglect their Duty, forfeits 5 *l.* between King and Prisoners.

The Majority of Justices in Sessions, upon Presentment of the Grand Jury of the Insufficiency or Inconveniency of the Goal, may agree upon a Sum, as upon Examination of able Workmen shall be thought necessary, for building, finishing, or repairing thereof.

This Sum, by Warrant under their Hands and Seals, may be levied upon the several Hundreds and Divisions by equal Portions.

This Warrant is to be directed by the Justices in Sessions to the High Constables, Petty Constables, Bailiffs, or other Officers, as they shall think fit for levying the same.

Persons refusing or neglecting to pay the Assessment four Days after Demand by the proper Officer who is to collect it, or conveying away their Goods or Estate, *&c.* one Justice present at that Sessions may make a Warrant to the Collector to levy the Sum assess'd by Distress and Sale, *&c.* and keep the same four Days before Sale at the Charge of the Owner; and if he doth not pay the Money within the four Days, then the Goods must be appraised by Two Inhabitants where they were taken, or by other sufficient Persons, and sold by the Collector returuing the Overplus, but deducting the Charge of taking and keeping the Distress.

Justices in Sessions are to appoint one or more Receivers, giving Security to be accountable for the Money received and disbursed in Pursuance of such Order as he shall have under the Hands anh Seals of the Justices.

Officers refusing to account for four Days after Demand, the Justices may commit them without Bail.

The Receipt of the Receiver shall be a Discharge to the other Officers paying the Proportion of their Assessment.

Discharge of Justices under Hand and Seal in Sessions to the Receivers, shall be be allowed as sufficient Release in any Court of Law or Equity.

Justices may covenant with Persons for building, finishing, or repairing, &c.

Murderers and Felons shall be imprisoned in the Common Gaol and not elsewhere.

Justices, in the County have no Power to meddle in Corporations, but Head Officers only. 14 *Eliz. cap.* 5.

Prisoner in carrying to Gaol is to bear his own Charges, and the Charge of those who attend him; if he refuse, one Justice may send a Warrant to the Constable of the Place where the Prisoner hath any Goods, to sell as much as by the Appraisement of the Neighbours may be sufficient to satisfie the Charge; and if he hath no Goods, then the Constable and Church-wardens, and two or three of the Parish, or if there are no such Officers, then four of the chief Men of the Parish where the Felon was taken, may make a Rate, which one Justice may allow, and then 'tis to be paid; and if any Person refuse to pay it, the Justice may send his Warrant to levy it by Distress, &c. and Sale after Appraisement. 3. *Jac. cap.* 10.

A warrant for false Imprisonment.

To all Constables, &c.

Kent ss. THese are in His Mafesty's Name to command you, and every of you, upon Sight hereof, to take and bring before me, or some other of His Majesty's Justices of the Peace for the said County, the Body of *A. B.* and *C. D.* of whom you shall have Notice, to answer to all such Matters and Things as on His Majesty's Behalf shall be objected against them by *E. F.* for falsly and unlawfully imprisoning her by the Space of Six Hours, and untill she did give unto the said *A. B.* and *C. D.* the Sum of Fifteen Shillings for her Discharge, for which they stand Indicted; to which Indictment they the said *A. B.* and *C. D.* have not yet appeared, as appears under the Hand of *S. H.* Esquire Clerk of the Peace of the County of *Kent*, and to find sufficient Sureties for their several Appearances to plead to and and answer the said Indictment: Hereof fail not at your Peril. Given under my Hand and Seal, &c.

Good

Good Behaviour.

THOSE who are of ill Fame, or common Disturbers of the Peace; or accused or Guilty of any of the Offences herein-after specified, may be required by one Justice to enter into a Recognizance, with Sureties or without, according to the Discretion of the Justice, to be of the Good Behaviour; and upon Refusal, may be committed.

Offences for which Persons may be bound to Good Behaviour, are.

Those who Tipple frequently in Ale-Houses or Taverns.

Persons going or Riding armed offensively before the King's Justices, or other his Officers or Ministers, or elswhere, by Night or Day, or be committed, and the Arms taken away. 2 *Ed.* 3. *cap.* 3. 7 *R.* 2, *c.* 13. 20 *R.* 2. c. 1.

Those who are reputed to be the Fathers of Bastard Children, and likewise the Mother of such Child, if chargeable to the Parish; but it must be for her second Offence:

Those that are instrumental in sending away a Putative Father. *Dalt. c.* 11. *p.* 39.

Common Barretors.

Those who Frequent Bawdy-houses, and the People who keep such Houses; likewise Whoremongers and Common Whores; for 'tis a Temporal Offence, and against the Peace of the Kingdom.

Cheaters and Cozeners by Cards, Dice, false Letters, or any other Game or Games whatsoever.

A Drunkard Convicted by one Justice of Peace, or Head Officer, or by Proof of one Witness upon Oath.

Felons Acquitted of Felony, or Convicted and pardoned, if the Person be of ill Fame; but this is Discretionary.

Those who steal Fish, or destroy the Pond, the Person must be Convicted.

Such Who frequent Gaming-houses, and those who Game and have no Estates to support themselves.

Hue-and-Cry, Raising it without a Cause.

Idle Persons, Living well, and having no Estates, Trades or Employment, to support themselves.

Those who misbehave themselves before a Justice of Peace, or before any other Officer, in the Execution of Justice: Those who speak contemptible words of him, or abuse his Warrants; those who delude his Authority by Complaints without Prosecution.

Those

Those who contrive, procure or publish Libels, Whether true or false, either against Persons living or dead, by Writing, Words, Pictures, or any other Signs of Reproach.

Misbehaviour of any Kind whatsoever; this must be left to the Discretion of the Justice, it being a general Word.

Murderers and Man-slayers, Such who are likely to commit either of these Offences.

Those who are suspected to steal any Thing in the Night, or to commit any Misdemeanor against the Person and Goods of another.

Those who break the Peace, in any Manner whatsoever.

Disturbing Preachers in their Duty; but now they must enter into a Recognizance with two Sureties in 50 *l.* to appear at the next *Sessions*; and upon Conviction there, must forfeit 20 *l.*

Mingling Poison with Corn, and giving in to poultry.

Those who are guilty of Quarrels or breaking the Peace.

Those of a bad Report or Name.

Those who continue in the very Act of a Riot, but if the Riot is over, then the Inquiry must be by Jury.

Those who lay in wait, or attempt to rob another, or suspected to lie in wait to rob, *&c.*

A Warrant for the Good Behaviour.

To the Constables, &c.

Kent *ss.* WHereas Information hath been given unto me upon Oath, That *A. B.* of *&c.* is a Person of a lewd Life and Conversation, and common Disturber of the Peace: **These are therefore** to command you forthwith to bring the aforesaid *A. B.* before me, or some other Justice of the Peace for this County, to answer unto such Matters as shall be objected against him by C. D. of, *&c.* and also, That you require him the said *A. B.* to bring sufficienr Sureties for his Good Behaviour until the next General Quarter-Sessions of the Peace, to be held *&c.* **And hereof** fail not. **Given** under my Hand and Seal *&c.*

Upon this Warrant, the Officer may break open an House to take the Party *Moor's Rep. 606.*

The Form of a Recognizance for the Peace.

BE it Remembered, That on the day of -- and in the Year of the -- Reign of our Soveraign Lord *George*, by the Grace of God *&c.* P. P. of *S*, in the County aforesaid, Gold Smith, came in his proper person before me *T. L.* Esquire, one of the Justices for preserving the Peace of our said Lord the King, in the said County and assigned and assumed upon himself, under the Penalty of Fifty Pounds; and *W. I.* of *M.* in the County aforesaid Yeman; and *D.N.* of *&c.* Husband-man, then and there likewise came in their proper Persons and under took for the aforesaid *P. P.* to wit, every of them severally, under the Penalty of Twenty five Pounds, that the same *P. P.* shall personally appear before the Justices of our Lord the King for the Peace, at the next General Sessions of the Peace in the County aforesaid to be holden, to do and receive what to him shall then and there by the Court be enjoined, and that he shall in the mean time keep the Peace of our said Lord the King, and all his People, especialy towards *N. M.* of - Yeoman; and what Damage or Mischief any what corporal, and a Greviance to the aforesaid *N. M.* or to any of the People of said Lord the King, which may fall out to the hurt and Disturbance of the Peace of him our Lord the King or of the aforesaid *N. M.* shall not in any wise do, neither procure to be done. Which certain Sum of Fifty Pounds, the aforesaid *P. P.* and every the aforesaid undertakers, the aforesaid several Sums of Twenty five Pounds, they Do owe to the said Lord the King to be Levied out of their Lands and Tenements, Goods and Chattels of any and every of them, to the use of our said Lord the King, his Heirs and Successors, to be done and paid of the hands of whomsoever might come, If it should happen that *P. P.* himself, the premisses, or any of them in any thing to break, and afterwards in Legal manner to be convicted. *In Testymony whereof* I the aforesaid *G. T.* have put my Seal, Dated at &c.

Note here, if the Justice only subscribe his Name to the Recognizance without putting his Seal, it may be well enough, And further, that all Bonds, Obligations, and Recognizances that shall be taken by any Justice of the Peace, or any other Person, for any cause touching the *King must be* made and be taken in his Name, and by these words, and under a Penalty to him that takes them, as I have elsewhere said, Our Lord the King.

The Condition of this Recognizance is such, that if the within bounden *P. P.* shall personally appear before the Justices of our said Sovereign Lord the King, at the next General Sessions for the Peace, to be held in the said County of *Kent*, to answer to such matters as shall be objected against him, by *N. M.* within named, to do and receive what the Court shall then and there enjoyn; and that he do in the mean time keep the Peace of our said Soveraign Lord the King, towards the King's Majesty, and all,

all his Liege People, and eſpecially towards the ſaid *N. M.* of *E.* aforeſaid, Yeoman; that then this Recognizance to be void and of none effect, or elſe to be and remain in full Force and Virtue. Acknowledged before me, the day and Year above *T. L.*

A Condition for one to appear before the Juſtices of the peace at their next Seſſions.

THE Condition of this Recognizance is ſuch that if the within Bounden *W. A.* ſhall make his Perſonal Appearance before the Kings Majeſties Juſtices of the Peace at the next Quarter-Seſſions of the Peace, to be holden for the ſaid County of S. then and there to make Anſwer unto ſuch Matters, as on His Majeſty's behalf ſhall be objected againſt him (by *W. A.* or concerning, *&c.*) [and there ſhew the Matter ſhortly] and ſhall alſo ſtand and abide ſuch further Order as the ſaid Court ſhall award, or ſet down therein, that then and from thenceforth this preſent Recognizance ſhall be fruſtrate and void, or elſe to remain in full Force and Virtue.

A Condition for one that hath dangerouſly hurt another.

THE Condition of this Recognizance is ſuch, that whereas the within bound K. *R.* hath now dangerouſly Hurt, Wounded *L. G.* of *R.* within the ſaid County of S. Butcher, giving him divers Blows, or Cuts on the Head, Face, *&c.* with a Chopper made of Iron and Steel, ſo as the ſaid *L. G.* is in danger of Death thereby. If therfore the ſaid *K. R.* ſhall make his Perſonal Appearance before the King's Majeſty's Juſtices at the next General Gaol delivery to be held in the ſaid County of *S.* then and there to make Anſwer to the Premiſes, and to receive that which then ſhall be by the Court injoyned him, and that he the ſaid K. *R.* in the mean time do keep the Peace of our ſaid Sovereign Lord the King towards the King's Majeſty, and all his Liege people, that then, *&c.* as before.

The Juſtices muſt certify the Recognizance at the next *Seſſions*, or forfeits 10 *l.* and if the Party doth not appear, the Recognizance it ſelf, with the Cauſe of the Forfeiture, muſt be certified in the *Exchequer*, that Proceſs may be awarded againſt the Offenders. *Dalt.* 190.

This Mr. *Dalton* ſays, is very near of Kin to the Good Behaviour, and therefore I have placed it under this Head ; for the Good Behaviour includeth the Peace.

It may be demanded by the Juſtice, of Perſons guilty of anywiſe breaking the

Peace, as Affrays, Assaults, Battery, Fighting, Quarrelling, Riot, Suspected to break the Peace. Threatning to kill, *&c.* Wounding another.

But 'tis generally demanded of the Justice at the Instance of the Party; and before he grants it, he is to administer the following Oath to him or her who requires it.

The Oath.

YOU shall swear, That you are in Fear of your Life, to of some Bodily Hurt to be done, or to be procured to be done, to you by J. O. &c. and that you do not require the Peace of him for any Malice, Vexation or Revenge, but for the Causes aforesaid.

The Warrant.

To the Constable of, &c. *and to the Keeper of,* &c.

Kent *ss.* WHereas *A. B.* of, *&c.* hath this present Day made Oath before me, That he is afraid that *C. D.* of, *&c.* will beat, wound, maim or kill him, and hath therefore prayed Surety of the Peace against him: These are therefore to command you to cause the said *C. D.* to come before me, or some other Justice of the Peace for this County, to find sufficient Security, as well for his Personal Appearance at the next General Quarter-Sessions of the Peace, to be holden for, *&c.* then and there to abide and do what shall be injoin'd him by the said Court; as also in the mean time to keep the Peace, and especially towards the said *A. B.* and if the said *C. D.* shall refuse so to do, that then you convey him to the Gaol aforesaid, and deliver him safely to the Keeper thereof: Commanding you also the aforesaid Keeper to receive the said *C. D.* into your Custody, and him there to keep until he shall find such Security as aforesaid, or otherwise to be discharged by Law. Given, &c.

If this Warrant is directed to a sworn Officer, he need not shew it to the Party; but he ought to tell him the Contents, and may break open the Doors to take him. *Dalt.* 404.

A Warrant to find Sureties for the Peace, where an assault is made upon an Officer in discharge of his Office.

To all Constables, &c.

Kent ss. These are in His Majesty's Name, to command you and every of you, upon Sight hereof, to take and bring before me, or some other of His Majesty's Justices of the Peace for the said County, the Body of *A. B.* (of whom you shall have Notice) to answer all such Matters and Things as on His Majesty's Behalf shall be objected against him by *C. D.* one of the Constables of &c. for assaulting, beating and bruising him in the Execution of his Office, as Oath hath been made: Hereof you are not to fail at your Peril. Given, &c.

A *Mittimus*.

To the Keeper, &c.

Kent ss. Receive into your Custody the Body of *A. B.* this day brought before me, and accused upon the Oath of *C. D.* one of the Constables of, &c. for assaulting, beating and bruising him in the Execution of his Office; and for refusing to find sufficient Sureties for his Personal Appearance at the next General Quarter Sessions of the Peace to be holden for the said County of *K.* There to answer the said complaint: Him in your Custody safely keep until he find Sureties as aforesaid, or otherwise be discharg'd by due Course of Law. Given, &c.

A *Liberate*.

To the Keeper of, &c.

Kent ss. Whereas *A. B.* hath before me found sufficient Sureties for his Personal Appearance at the next General Quarter-Sessions of the Peace to be holden for the said County, there to answer what shall be objected against him by *C. D.* Constable of &c. for assaulting, beating and bruising him in the Execution of his Office: These are therefore to will and require you upon Sight hereof, to set at Liberty the Body of the said *A. B.* if detain'd for the Cause aforesaid and no other: And for your so doing this shall be your Warrant. Given, &c.

The Recognizance.

E. F. of *&c.* Blackſmith. —— 20 *l.* *G. H.* of *&c.* Taylor —— 20 *l.*

Upon Condition, That *A. B.* ſhall perſonally appear at the next General Quarter-Seſſions of the Peace to be held for the ſaid County, there to anſwer what ſhall be objected againſt him by *C. D.* Conſtable of *&c.* for aſſaulting beating and bruiſing the ſaid *C. D.* in the Execution of his Office; and in the mean time to be of his Good Behaviour; That then, *&c.*

Capt' & Recogn' 5 *die Auguſti Anno* 1719 *Coram me,*

P. L

Harveſt-Time.

Artificers and Perſons fit to Labour, may in Harveſt-time be compelled by one Juſtice or Conſtable, and upon Refuſal may be put into the Stocks two Days and one Night; and the Conſtable and other Head Officer is to do it, under Penalty of 40 *s.* 5. *Eliz. cap* 4.

Hawkers and Pedlars.

By the Statute of 8 & 9 *W.* 'tis enacted, That every Hawker, Pedlar, or Petty-Chapman, or other Trading Perſon, going from Town to Town, *&c.* muſt take a Licence;

And if on Foot he muſt pay four Pounds. If with Horſe Aſs or Mule, Eight Pounds.

And if he travels without a Licence, or contrary thereto, he forfeits for every Offence to the Informer and poor of the Pariſh where diſcovered, 12 *l.*

Refuſing to ſhew his Licence, being demanded by any Officer of the Peace, he forfeits to the Poor where the Demand ſhall be made, 5 *l.*

And for Non-payment of the ſame, muſt ſuffer as a Common Vagrant, and be ſent to the Houſe of Correction.

Travelling with forged Licences, forfeits to the King and Proſecutor, to be recovered in the Courts at *Weſtminſter*, 50 *l.* and to be ſubject to the Penalties for Forgery.

A

A Conſtable neglecting or refuſing to aſſiſt in the Execution of this Act, being Convicted on Oath before a Juſtice of the Peace, forfeits for every offence to the Poor and Proſecutor, to be levied by Diſtreſs, *&c.* 2 *l.*

Any Perſon may ſeize and detain ſuch Hawker till he produce a Licence, or If Trading without a Licence, till Notice be given to a Pariſh-Officer, who is to carry him before a Juſtice of the Peace; who upon Confeſſion of the Party, or Oath of one Witneſs, That the Offender had traded without a Licence produſed, ſhall by Warrant levy. 12 *l.*

And becauſe ſome Abuſes were afterwards committed by Perſons letting out to Hire the Licences by them taken to trade as Hawkers; therefore another Law was made 3 *&* 4. *Ann. cap.* 4.

That every Perſon trading as an Hawker, *&c.* ſhall produce his Licence on Demand, or otherwiſe he ſhall incur the ſame Forfeiture as if he had Traded without a Licence; aud if any Perſon lend a Licence to Hire, either the Lender or the Trader ſhall forfeit 40 *l.* and the Lender ſhall forfeit the Licence; One Moiety of the 40 *l,* to the King, and other to the Informer, by action of Debt, Bill, Plaint or Information, *&c.*

And in the ſame Act 'tis declared, That traders in the Wollen and Linnen Manufactures, ſending their Goods to Markets and Fairs on Horſes, and ſelling the ſame by Wholeſale, neither they, or thoſe imployed under them, ſhall be taken to be Hawkers.

The Officer muſt render the Overplus after Deduction for the Charge of Diſtraining, and out of the Sale of the Goods diſtrained, pay the Penalties and Forfeiture.

A Warrant to levy 12 *l.* for Hawking without Licence.

To the Conſtables, &c.

Kent *ſſ.* WHereas Information hath been given unto me, one of His Majeſty's Juſtices of the Peace for the ſaid County, upon the Oath of *A. B.* of *&c.* That *C. D.* of, *&c.* Labourer, did on the 24th Day of *Auguſt* Inſtant, trade without Licence in, &c. and carried about and expoſed to Sale three Pieces of Silks called *Ruſhy James*, he not being the Worker or Maker of ſuch Silks, nor Apprentice, Agent or Servant to ſuch real Workers or Makers of ſuch Silks he ſo carried Abroad, and expoſed to Sale as aforeſaid, which the ſaid C. D. hath confeſs'd before me upon his Examination, contrary to a late Act of Parliament for Licenſing Hawkers and Pedlars, *&c.* For which ſaid Offence he the ſaid *C. D.* hath forfeited the Sum of 12 *l.* the one Moiety thereof to the Informer, and the other Moiety to the

the poor of the Parish, &c. where the said Offence was comitted: These are therefore to authorize and require you, or any of you, upon Sight hereof, to demand of the said *C. D.* the said Sum of 12 *l.* and in case he refuse to pay the same, that then you levy the said Sum of 12 *l.* by Distress and Sale of the Goods, Wares and Merchandizes of the said *C. D.* rendring to him the Overplus (if any be, resonable Charges for taking the said Distress being first deducted) to be imployed to the Use above-mentioned; and in case of his Inability for Non-payment thereof, that then you forthwith bring the said *C. D.* before me, or any other of His Majesty's Justices of the Peace of the County aforesaid, to be further dealt with as the Act directs: And hereof fail not. Given, &c.

High-Ways

PRivate Ways are to be required by the Village, and some times by a particular Person; but Publick Ways by the Parish, unless a particular Person was obliged by Custom or Prescription; and Clergy-men are liable to all Charges imposed by Act of Parliament, and in particular to repair High-ways. 1 *Vent.* 273.

On the 26th Day of *December* every Year, unless that happen on the *Sunday*, and then on the Day following, after this Manner: *Viz.*

The Parishioners being met, are to make a List of a competent Number of Names of Men thus qualified:

1. They must have an Estate of 10 *l.* *per Ann.* either in their own Right, or in the Right of their Wives.
2. Or they must be worth 100 *l.* in Personal Estate.
3. Or rent 30 *l.* *per Annum.*

If there are not any such Persons in the Parish, then a List must be made of the most sufficient Persons.

The List must be returned to two or more Justices of the Peace near the Division in which the Parish lieth, at a Special Sessions to be held on the Third Day of *January*, or within 15 Days afterwards.

The Constables neglecting to return such List, do each of them forfeit 20 *s*

Out of this List so returned, the Justices at that Sessions do appoint one or more to be Surveyors, &c. by an Order under their Hands and Seals.

The Person thus appointed, must within six Days afterwards have Notice thereof given unto him by the Constable, leaving a Copy of the Justice's Order at the House of the Party, and then he must take upon him the Office.

But

But if he refuse, being so nominated and appointed, and served with the Order then he forfeits 5 *l.* to be levied by Warrant from a Justice of the same Division; or in Default thereof, from the Neighbouring Justices upon Oath made, *&c.*

The Forfeiture being levied one Moiety is to go to the Informer, and the other to repair the High-ways; and the Justices may appoint one or more Surveyors again, who upon Notice, must take upon him or them the Office, *&c.* under the same Penalty.

He must, within 14 Days after the Acceptance of his Office, and so from Time to Time every four Months, view the Roads and Bridges, *&c.*

He must present upon Oath before some Justice, *&c.* such Ways which are not in Repair, or he forfets 5 *l*, unless two Justices shall allow his Excuse.

He must give publick Notice from Time to Time every four Months, what Default he finds: This Notice must be given in the Parish Church the next *Sunday* after Sermon ended; and if not amended within 30 Days afterwards by those who ought to repair, *&c.* then the Surveyor must within other 30 Days next following amend the same.

He must give an Account upon Oath at a Special Sessions, of all Money that comes to his Hands, and how dispos'd, *&c.* and if any remains, he must deliver it to the next Surveyor, or forfeits double the Value of what the Justices shall judge in his Hands; to be levied by Warrant of two Justices, one Part to the Informer, *&c.*

If he neglects his Duty in any Thing, he is to forfeit 40 *s.* one Moiety to the Informer, the other to amend the High-ways; and this Forfeiture may be levied by a Warrant from one Justice: And by 6 *Anne*, c. 29. the Penalty is increased to 5 *l.* 22 *Car.* c. 12. 1 *Justice*, 1 *Witness.*

He is to appoint 6 Days for providing Materials to amend the Ways, giving Notice of the several Days by him appointed; at which Time all Persons liable must work, and the Ways must be amended before the Feast of St. *Luke*

Every Man keeping a Horse-Teem must send out a Cart and two able Men; and if he keeps Oxen, then he must send them out, and a Wain with two Men, every Day so appointed by the Surveyor; and if he keeps both, then he must send that which will do best Service, or forfeits 10 *s.* for every Day wherein he makes Default.

If all the Carriages in the Parish shall not be thought necessary by the Surveyors, then the Person whose Carriage is spared must send out two able Men, or forfeits 10 *s.* for every Man not sent.

Every Housholder, Cottager and Labourer, must either work themselves, or hire one to work each of these 6 Days, or forfeits *per* Day; and all of them must work eight Hour every Day. *Per Stat.* 22 *Car.* 2. *cap.* 2. *'tir* 1 *s.* 6*d.*

If any Man hath a Plow-Land or Pasture in several Parishes, he shall be chargeable only in the Parish where he lives; but if he keeps in his Occupation several Plow Land-

Lands or Pastures, &c. in several Parishes, he shall be chargeable in every Parish.

In such Place where Carts are not used, the Inhabitants must send Horses, according to the Custom of the Place, with able Persons, &c. under the like Penalty.

A Parson is not chargeable for his Glebe; but if they use other Land, 'tis otherwise.

The Surveyor may complain to the next Justice, &c. who upon Oath made of the Default, may send his Warrant to levy the Forfeitures by Distress and Sale of Goods; *Viz.*

	l.	s.	d
On a Labourer neglecting	0	2	6
For every Man and Horse, &c.	0	4	0
For every Cart with two Men	0	14	0

for every Day they shall neglect; which Penalties, when levied, must be imployed towards the amending of the Ways.

Bushes in High-ways. These must be cut down by the Owners of the Soil within 10 Days after Notice given by the Surveyors, on Pain of 5 *s.* to be levied for every Neglect on the Goods of the Offender by Distress, &c. on Warrant of two Justices of the same Division, or in Default thereof by any Neighbouring Justices; but there must be Oath made by one Witness; one Moiety of the Forfeiture is to the Informer, the other towards repairing of the Ways. 3 & 4 *W.* & *M.* *cap.* 12.

No Bushes, Trees or Shrubs, shall grow or stand, or Bough or Branch over-hang a High-way not 20 Foot broad. Offender forfeits 5 *s.* to be levied and imployed as aforesaid.

Those who pull up, cut or remove, any Post, Block, great Stone, Bank of Earth or other Security of a Horse-way or Causway from Waggons, Carts, &c. forfeit for every Offence 20 *s.* 7 & 8 *Will.*

The Conviction is to be by Oath of one Witness, before one Justice of the Division, or upon his own View, and 'tis to be levied by his Warrant by Distress and Sale, &c. one Moiety to the Surveyors to repair the Ways, the other to the Informer.

Of Annoyances in the High-ways by Ditches, &c.

By the Statute of 5 *Eliz.* those who have Lands adjoyning to the High-way, in which Ditches ought to be, must scour them as often as there is Occasion and lay Trunks or Bridges where there are Cart-ways into any Ground, that the Water may have free Passage, upon pain to forfeit 12 *d. per* Rod; but by the Statute of 3 & 4 *W.* & *M.* if they neglect 10 Days after Notice, the Forfeiture is 5 *s.* which is to be levied by Warrant of two Justices of the same Division, &c. upon Oath made, &c. one Moiety to the Informer, the other to amend the ways.

If

If in scouring the Ditches they lay the Soil in the High-way, and suffer it to lay there 6 Months, they forfeit 12 *d. per* Load; but by the Statute of 3 & 4 *W.* & *M,* if not carried away within 10 Days after Notice, to be levied and imployed as aforesaid.

The Surveyors have Power to turn any Spring or Water-Course out of the High-ways into those Ditches; and where the Ditches already made are not sufficient to carry away the Water, they have Power by 3 & 4 *W. & M.* to make new Ditches and Drains in and through the Lands adjoining, which they must keep scour'd; and for that Purpose, may with Workmen come upon the said Lands, without being Trespassers,

Persons laying any Thing in the High-way not 20 Foot broad, forfeits 5 *s.* to be levieb and imployed as aforesaid; and if Timber, Stone, Hay, Straw, or Stubble, or other Matter for making Dung, or any othe Pretence, shall be laid in any High-way, those who possess Lands next adjoyning may remove and dispose thereof to their own Use.

Cannot lay Logs or Timber in the High-way, tho' there is a sufficient Room for Travellers left.

All Matters concerning the High-Ways, must be determined in the County where they lie, and not elsewhere; and none shall be punish'd, unless prosecuted within six Months after the Offence is committed. The Party grieved may appeal from any Act done by the Jusiices to the Quarter-Sessions, whose Order shall conclude all Parties, and on Presentment, Indictment or Order, shall be removed by *Certiorari.* If any Action should be commenced against those who put that Act in Execution, they may plead the General Issue, and give the Act it self and the Special Matter in Evidence; and if the Plaintiff be nonsuited, discontinue, or a Verdict against him, the Defendant shall have double Costs.

A Warrant against a Surveyor, for not putting the Laws in Execution.

To the Constable, &c.

Kent *ss.* WHereas it hath been duly proved before me, *P. L.* Esquire &c. That *E. F.* Surveyor of the High-ways of the Parish of *M.* in the said County, did on the 15th Day of *August* last, wilfully suffer a Waggon loaded with Goods and Wares, and not imploy'd in and about Husbandry, (*ut prius*) to be in the

the common High-way, in the said Parish of *M.* with seven Horses, and hath hitherto neglected to put the Laws in Execution made for Repairing the High-ways; by Reason whereof he hath forfeited 5 *l.* These are therefore, &c.

Concerning Indictments about High-ways.

WHere a Person by any Inclosure streightens a High-way on both Sides, tho' the Parish repaired it before, yet now he is obliged to maintainit at his own Charge; but if he abates the Inclosure, and leaves the Way open as it was before, then the Parish to repair it again. *Cro. Car.* 366. *Sand.* 160.

If Lands are exempted from repairing *&c.* by a Grant of the King, made before the Statute of 2 & 3 *Phil.* & *Mar.* yet that shall not be a good Discharge upon the Land. 5 *Mod.* 96.

A High.way is that which leads from one Market-Town to another, and is to be repaired by common Right by the Parish where the Decay is, unless some other Person is bound by Prescription or Custom; and therefore *reparare debet* generally, without shewing how, is not good.

But if the Defendant pleads *Reparare non debet*, and 'tis so found, he shall be acquitted. tho' it doth not appear who should repair; and the Reason may be, because *de communi jure* the Parish is bound to repair their own High-ways, and therefore they are never allowed to plead Not guilty, and give in Evidence that another ought to repair by Prescription or Tenure. for if they would discharge themselves, they must plead it *Sid.* 140. 1 *Vent.* 256.

A Common Way is that which leads from a Village or Town to the Parish-Church, or Fields; 'tis also called a Private Way; and is to be repaired by the Village or Hamlet, and sometimes by a Private Person: If such a Way be out of Repair, every Inhabitant may have an Action, but an Idnictment will not lie. 1 *Vent.* 208,

But a Hamlet within a Parish cannot be charged generally to repair without Prescription, *&c.* *Stiles.* 163.

All Nusances must be set forth to be in a *High.way*, for if 'tis alledged to be in a Horse-way, the Indictment will be quash'd; and tho' a Nusance may be alledged *in via Regia*, yet 'tis not good if the Indictment doth not express where, or in what County.

A Warrant to levy the Five Pounds for not taking upon him the Office of Surveyor.

Kent ß. WHereas it appeareth unto us, *&c.* That *A. B.* of *M.* in the said County, was on the Fifteenth Day of *August* last past, lawfully Nominated and appointed to be Surveyor of the High-ways, in and for the said Parish, for the Year next ensuing; and that within six Days after the said Nomination and Appointment, he had due Notice thereof: And whereas *C. D.* of *M.* aforesaid hath now made Oath before us, that the said *A. B.* hath refused to take upon him the said Office, by reason whereof he hath forfeited the Sum of Five Pounds; One Moiety thereof to the said *C. D.* the Informer, and the other Moiety to go towards the Repairing the said High-ways: These are therfore in His Majesty's Name to command you forthwith to levy the said Forfeiture of Five Pounds, by Distress and Sale of the Goods of the said *A. B.* rendring to him the Overplus, if any be, (necessary Charges of Destraining being first Deducted;) And hereof fail not, Given under our Hands and Seals the 20th Day of *August, &c.*

A Warrant against a Surveyor neglecting to View the Ways, and not present to a Justice in what Condition they are in.

To the Constable, &c.

Kent ß, WHereas it appeareth unto us, *P. L.* and *J. M.* Esquires, two of His Majesty's Justices *&c.* upon Oath, That *A. B.* of *&c.* being lawfully nominated and appointed Surveyor of the High-ways in the Parish of, *&c*, for this Present Year, hath neglected within Fourteen Days after his Acceptance of the said Office, to View the Ways, Water-courses, Bridges and Causways, which are to be repaired by the said Parish, and to Present upon Oath to some Justice of the Peace in what Condition he found them, having for such his Neglect no reasonable Excuse allowed by Two Justices of the Peace; so that he hath forfeited the Sum of Five Pounds, according to the *Statute* in that Case made and provided. These are therefore, &c.

A Warrant against a Surveyor not Presenting the State of the Ways at a Special Sessions.

Kent ss. WHereas a Special Sessions was held by the Justices of the Peace for the said County at, *&c.* on *Monday* the 25th Day of *July* last past, to which Sessions *E. F.* and *G. H.* Surveyors of the High-ways belonging to the Parish of, &c. were duly summoned: and whereas it hath been duly proved before us P. *L.* and *J. M.* Esquires, Two of his Majesty's Justices of the Peace of the County aforesaid, that the said *E. F.* and *G. H.* did neglect to appear at the said Sessions, and to present upon Oath the State of the High-ways belonging to the said Parish, of which they were Surveyors, or what Offences and Neglects any Persons were guilty of relating to the same, by reason whereof he hath Forfeited Forty Shillings. These are therefore, &c.

Against a Surveyor refusing to Accompt.

To the Constable of, &c.

Kent ss. WHereas it hath been duly proved upon Oath before us, *P. L.* and *J. M.* Two of His Majesty's Justices of the Peace for the said County, That *E. F.* and *G. H.* of, *&c.* Surveyors of the High-ways in and for the Parish aforesaid, hath neglected to give an Accompt upon Oath at any Special Sessions, of all Money which hath come to his Hands, and which ought to be imployed in amending the High-ways, and how he hath disposed thereof, so that for such his Neglect he hath forfeited the Sum of 40 *s.* One Moiety to the Informer, and the other to repair the High-ways in the said Parish. These are therefore, &c.

A Warrant against a Person for laying Timber, Stones, *&c.* in the High-way.

To the Constable, &c.

Kent ss. WHereas *A. B.* hath this Day made Oath before us, *P. L.* and *J. M.* Esquires, Two of His Majesty's Justices, *&c.* That *C. D.* of of &c. did within Six Months last past, lay Timber and Logs in the High-way leading from, &c. in the Parish of, &c. the said Way not being Twenty Foot broad, so that the same was much obstructed, by reason whereof he hath forfeited Five Shillings; One Moiety to the said *A. B.* who hath informed us of the said Offence, the other Moiety towards amending the said High-ways. These are therefore, &c.

The like Warrant against any Owner of Land, who doth not cut down a Tree, Bush or Shrub in the High-way not Twenty Foot broad, within Ten Days after Notice given by the Surveyor.

A Warrant of Distress for refusing to pay the Surveyor's Rate.

To the Surveyors of the High-ways of the Parish of, &c. *in the said County, and to all other Person or Persons whom these may concern.*

Kent ss. WHereas Complaint upon Oath hath been made unto us by *A. B.* and *C. D.* Surveyors of the High-ways of the Parish of, &c. in the said County, That the several Persons hereafter named, to wit, *J. K.* for refusing to pay the Sum of Six Shillings of lawful Money of *Great Britain*; *L. M.* also for refusing to pay the Sum of Eight Shillings of lawful Money; and *N. O.* for refusing likewise to pay the Sum of Ten Shillings, being assessed upon them severally for and towards the Repairing, Amending, and Inlarging the High-ways of and belonging to the said Parish, to repair and amend according to the Statute in that Case made and provided; which said Sums of Money, being legally demanded, the said Persons above-named, and every of them have, and do refuse and neglect to pay the same, These are therefore, in His Majesty's Name, to command you, some or one of you, to demand again of the several and respective Persons above-named, the several Sums following their several and respective Names; and in case he, she or they shall refuse or neglect to pay the same, That then you forthwith levy the same by Distress and Sale of the several and respective Goods of the several and respective Persons so refusing to pay the same, as aforesaid, rendring to the Parties the Overplus, (if any) and in Default of such Distress, that you certify the same to us, to the end there may be such further Proceeding touching the Premisses as to Justice doth appertain. Hereof you are not to fail. Given, &c.

Homicide.

Homicide.

MAnſlaughter or *Homicide*, is the killing a Man upon a ſudden Provocation without any Malice, and in the Heat of Blood.

By this Definition it appeareth, that in Manſlaughter.

1. There muſt be no deliberate Act, but the falling out muſt be ſudden.

2. The Act muſt be unlawful; for if lawful, then 'tis Chance-medly; and it muſt be without an Intention of any perſonal Wrong; for if the Intent is ill, tis Murder.

A ſudden falling out is, *viz*. If two Men fight, and one of them breaks his Sword, and a Stranger lends him another, with which he kills his Adverſary; 'tis Manſlaughter in both.

To fight, and part preſently; meet, and one killed; this is a continued Affray and therefore Manſlaughter.

Malice between two; the Deceaſed challenges the other, who refuſed to meet but ſaid he ſhould go to ſuch a Place; the Deceaſed meets him, and was killed; Manſlaughter *H. P. C.* 48.

Entring a Houſe with Force; thoſe who are turned out of Poſſeſſion come to ſet it on Fire, and one within ſhoots and kills another without Doors; 'tis Manſlaughter, becauſe the Entry was unlawful. *H. P. C.* 56.

A Servant draws his Sword in Defence of his Maſter, and in the Affray the Maſter is killed; 'tis Manſlaughter in the Servant. *Sid.* 254.

A ſudden Provocation, and Death enſuing, doth ſo far extenuate the Crime as to make it Manſlaughter.

As an Husband killing another committing, Adultery with his Wife. *Raym.* 212.

A Priſoner in Execution for Debt eſcaping and the Keeper coming to the Place where he is, kills him either in Purſuit or Reſiſting; 'tis Manſlaughter. 1 *Roll. Rep.* 189. 2 *Cro.* 296.

Unlawful Acts where Death enſues, are, *viz*. Playing at Foils, throwing Stones, ſhooting at Deer in another Man's Parks, Forcible Entry, and ejecting another, and ſuch-like, are unlawful, but without any malicious Intention to kill, and therefore Manſlaughter. *Allen, Rep.* 12.

Bailiffs coming to ſerve an Execution, and the Debtor ſhuts his Door, which they break open, and one is killed, 'tis Manſlaughter, becauſe the breaking of the Door was unlawful.

The Offender has the Benefit of the Clergy the firſt Time, and forfeits his Goods

Goods and Chattels.

If a Man is in Execution for Debt, and *escapes*, and the Gaoler hearing where he is, attempts to take him, and he resisting is killed by the Gaoler; 'tis Manslaughter. 1 *Roll. Rep.* 189.

My Lord *Rolls* distinguishes where a Man is in Execution for Debt, and where he is only committed for Felony, and *escapes*; for in the first Case he says, the Gaoler must go back as far as he can before he attempt any Violence upon the Person, otherwise, if he kill him, it may amount to more than Manslaughter; But I think 'tis his Business to press forward, for otherwise he shall never retake his Prisoner.

Chance-medley, or per Infortunium.

THIS is where a Man is killed by another casually, when he is doing any Thing which is lawful, and without any Intent to hurt:

As shooting at a Bird, which is a lawful Act, and killing a Man; the Father or Master correcting a Son or Servant, and Death ensuing.

A House was building Thirty Foot from any common High-way, and one of the Workmen being about to throw a Piece of Timber out of the House, called aloud, *Stand clear*; the Timber fell upon one of the Labourers, and killed him: This was held to be *per Infortunium*, for he was doing nothing but what was lawful and usual to be done; and he could have no ill Intention, because he gave Notice what he was about to do: But if this had been in the Streets in *London*, it had been Manslaughter, because of the continual Passing of the People; for in such Case it shall be presumed, that his Intention was to do some Mischief.

In this Case the Special Matter must be found, that the Court may judge whether the killing was *per Infortunium*; and therefore 'tis not sufficient to find it generally.

My Lord *Coke* tells us, there is no express Judgment in Chance-medley; but the Offender forfeits his Goods, and hath a Pardon of Course.

This was anciently by *Certiorari* out of *Chancery* to remove the Record; which being certified, the Lord Chancellor issues forth a Pardon; But now 'tis done by Certificate of the Judge or Justices, *&c.*

The

The Form of which Writ is thus:

BECAUSE we have understood by the Record of our welbeloved and faithful T. P. *Knt. and* L. P. *Knt. Our Justices for the Gaol delivery for the County of* S. *Assign'd That* A. B. *taken and detain'd in the Gaol aforesaid for the death of* C. D. *whereupon he was indicted and found that he hath Slain* C. D. *by missfortune, By which the said* A. *to our Gaol aforesaid is sent there to Expect our Grace, We being with piety mov'd have pardon'd the said* A. *the Suit of our peace which to us appertaineth for the Death aforesaid, and him to our firm peace thereof have restored, So Nevertheless that he stands right in our Court If any against him will Speak of the death abovesaid In Testimony.* &c.

Homicide ex Necessitate.

IN the Execution of the Offenders, It must be by a proper and lawful Officer, as the Sheriff, and not by a Stranger, for then 'tis Felony.

2. The Judgment must be given by one who had a proper Jurisdiction to try the Cause; for if a Justice of Peace give Judgment in Treason, the Execution is Murder, both in him and in the Officer; if in Trespass he give Judgment of Death, 'tis Felony in him, but not in the Officer.

3. The Execution must be pursuant to the Judgment: See *postea* in Judgment.

In Advancement of Justice, in Cases Criminal; As if a Man indicted for Felony is killed by an Officer, whom he resists, having a Warrant to apprehend him.

Or if a Prisoner is killed by an Officer, carrying him to Gaol, and endeavouring to escape after a Felony actually committed.

Or if a Prisoner is killed by a Gaoler, the Prisoner assaulting him.

For if a Felon by Resistance or Flight cannot be taken without killing, he who kills him must be acquitted without Forfeiture of Goods, because every Man is warranted by Law to apprehend him, but then there must be a Felony actually done; which Circumstance is not required where a Man hath a Warrant to take a Felon. 3 *Inst.* 221.

In Cases Civil.

Resisting an Officer, who hath any legal Process, and killed by him.

Upon Not Guilty pleaded, the Special Matter must be given in Evidence; and it being found for him, he is to be acquitted without Forfeiture or Pardon.

But in all these Cases the Necessity must be unavoidable, and there must not be any Colour of Malice.

Homicide is justifiable, and no Forfeiture.

In Defence of House or Goods. As if I kill a Man who sets my House on Fire; or a Thief who steals my Goods, or comes to Rob me.

If a Woman kill a Man that endeavoureth to ravish her: But if I kill a Man claiming a Title to my House, and endeavouring to enter, 'tis Manslaughter.

Se defendendo, This *Homicide* is excusable, but the Goods are Forfeited.

But then it must be done only upon an inevitable Necessity, and he must give back as far as he can without endangering his own Life.

And the mortal Wound must be given after the Party retires to the Wall; for if before 'tis Manslaughter.

Casual Death.

THis is when a Man is slain otherwise than by the Hands of another; as by a Fall by a Horse or Carr, *&c.*

'Tis the proper Office of a Coroner to enquire of such Death, which he is to do by Jury, *&c.*

Any Thing which is the Cause of such Death, is forfeited to the King, but not till found by Matter of Record; and this Forfeiture shall have Relation from the Time of the Stroke given; so that if the Owner sell the Goods after that Time, and before the Inquisition taken, the Property is not bound, but the King shall be entitled to it.

Deodand.

MY Lord *Coke* defines this to be when any moveable Thing which is inanimate or a Beast animate, causeth the untimely Death of *a Reasonable Creature*, without the *Will*, Offence, or Fault *of himselfe*; but it must be on the Land, and not on the Sea.

This being found by Inquisition, is forfeited to the King, as being *pretium Sanguinis*, to be distributed in Works af Charity to appease the Wrath of God.

If the Party slain *by a Fall* is under 14 Years of Age, then no *Deodand* is due; but if he be kill'd *by an Ox or Horse*, &c. that is a *Deodand*.

A Man ringing a Bell, was strangled with the Rope; it was a Question, Whether the Bell should be a *Deodand* or not, because, as 'twas objected, it was fastened to the Freehold, and given to God before? There was no Judgment given; but two Judges were of Opinion, That it was not a *Deodand*, 1 *Levinz* 136. Two Men riding over the *Trent*, were drowned by the Violence of the Water; their Horses were not *Deodands*, because the Men were drowned by the Violence of the Stream, and not carried by their Horses out of Depth. 2 *Roll. Rep.* 23. 2 *Cro.* 483. *Poph.* 136.

Horses

IN order to preserve the Breeding of strong Horses, a Law was made, 32 *H.* 8. *cap.* 13, prohibiting Persons to put Stone-horses above Two Years old, and under Fifteen Hands high (every Hand being four Inches) into Forests or Commons where Mares are kept, upon Pain of forfeiting the Horse: After this Manner;

Viz. The Horse must be brought to the next Pound by the Keeper of the Ground, by the Constable, or Headborough of the next Parish, and must be measured by him in the Presence of three other sufficient Men, and if found under the Statute, he who seized him, may take him to his own Use.

Refusing to measure, or to be present at the Measuring, Forfeiture is 40 *s.* apiece for each Offence; one Moiety to the King, the other to the Prosecutor.

Justices in Sessions may hear and determine Offences against this Act, and Stewards in Leets may take Presentments only, but must certify them to the next Sessions,

upon

upon Pain of 40 *s.*

Scabbed or infected Horſes ſhall not be put in common Fields. on Pain to forfeit 10 *s.* to the Lord of the Leet.

But now by 22 *Car.* 2. *cap.* 13. any Horſe may be exported, paying 5 *s.* at the *Cuſtom Houſe.*

The Property of ſtolen Horſes ſhall now be altered,

1. If not rid, or ſtand open in the Fair One Hour. This my Lord *Coke* tells us is in Affirmance of the Common Law.

2. All Parties to the Contract muſt be preſent with the Horſe, and before the Book keeper.

3. Their Names muſt be enter'd in the Book, and their Dwellings, and the Colour and Mark of the Horſe.

Juſtices in Seſſions have Power to here and determine Offences againſt this Law.

But Horſe-ſtealing ſtill increaſing, by reaſon the Thief could ſell them in Fairs and Markets, purſuant to the aforeſaid Act, to Horſe-Courſers, and at a great Diſtance from the Owners; therefore, to Preſerve the Property ſtill in them, another Law was made. 31 *Eliz*; *cap.* 12.

1. That no Sale ſhall be made in Fairs, unleſs the Toll-taker or Keeper know the Seller, or unleſs he bring ſome credible Perſon who knoweth him. 13 *Eliz. cap.* 12.

2. The Names, Sirnames, Myſtery and Dwelling, of both of them, and the Price of the Horſe ſold, muſt be enter'd in the Book.

3. The Book keeper muſt give the Buyer a Note of theſe Particulars ſubſcribed by him, if required, paying 8 *d.* for the ſame.

4. He who ſells without being known to the Book-keeper, or without bringing a Voucher; and he who voucheth without knowing the Seller, and the Book-keeper making Entry without knowing either, forfeits each of them 5 *l.* One Moiety to the King, the other to the Proſecutor, and the Sale is void. 1 *Lut.*

Now though the Sale be in all Circumſtances purſuant to this Act yet, the Property is not bound, if the right Owner claim within ſix Months after 'tis Stolen: Which he muſt do in this Manner;

If the Horſe is found in a Town Corporate, then he muſt claim him before the Mayor, or Chief Officer; if in the County at large, then before a Juſtice of Peace.

The Proof muſt be by Two Witneſſes upon Oath, who muſt depoſe before ſuch Mayor, Chief Officer or Juſtice, within 40 Days after the Horſe is found, that the

S Pro-

Property is in the Person claiming, &c. and that the Horse was stole from him within six Months before the Claim.

Upon this Proof, the Party shall have his Horse, paying the Buyer what he shall depose he gave for the same.

Clergy taken away from Accessaries before and after the Fact.

Selling a House by a false Name, maketh the Sale void.

Houses where they may be broke open. See Arrests, and Doors.

Houses of Habitation.

THese are privileged by the Law in several Respects, *viz.*

They are Castles for the Defence of the Inhabitants.

They protect the Persons of Men from any Arrests on *Mesne* Process at the Suit of any Subject.

A House may be defended by Force against Thieves or Robbers; and if killed 'tis not Felony.

But notwithstanding these Priveledges, it may be broke open in these Cases following; the Person first signifying the Occasion of his coming, and requiring the opening of the Doors, and being refused:

1. In Treason, Felony, or Suspicion thereof.
2. To apprehend any Person who hath dangerously wounded another, being freshly pursued.
3. An Affray being in a House, the Constable may break it open to keep the Peace.
4. Upon a Forcible Entry or Detainer found by an Inquisition,
5. To apprehend any Person upon a *Capias Utlegatum* on *Fine* or upon Process of Excomunication, or upon a Warrant of the Peace, or Good Behaviour.
6. Upon a Recovery in a Real Action, the Sheriff may break it open to deliver Possession.
7. And generally in any Case where the King is Party, or hath any Interest, for no Man's House shall Protect him against the King.

Houf

House of Correction.

MAny Laws have been made for Punishing Beggars and idle Persons, but none to set them on Work before 39 *Eliz. cap.* 4. which gives the Justices in Sessions Authority in three things:

1. To appoint that Houses of Correction be built.
2. To make Orders for Maintaining and Governing them when built.
3. To see that the Offender sent thither be set to Work, or punish'd.

My Lord *Coke* tells us, That for some Time after this Law was made, and untill the Justices became remiss in their Duty, there was not a Rogue to be found in the Kingdom.

But the Justices taking no Care for the Building or Providing such Houses, and neglecting to put the Law in Execution; another Statute was made, 7 *Jac. cap.* 4.

That a House of Correction shall be built or provided in every County within a Time therein Limited, with all Conveniencies to set Rogues and idle People to work, or every Justice, shall forfeit 5 l. one Moiety to the prosecutor, the other towards building the House.

Which House, when built or Purchased, shall be conveyed to Persons appointed by Justices in Sessions in Trust, to be imployed for the Keeping, Correcting, and Setting to work, Persons sent thither.

Master of a House of Correction is to be appointed by the Justices in their Sessions; he is to set on Work, and moderately to correct Persons, by Whipping or Fettering them if unruly.

He is Yearly to have such an Allowance as Justices in Sessions shall think fit; which is to be paid Quarterly, by the Treasurer of the County-Stock; and in Default of such Payment, he may levy it upon the Treasurer by Distress aud Sale of his Goods.

He is to give an Account Quarterly, at the Sessions, of all Persons who have been committed to his Custody; and if any Escape without being discharged by due Course, the Justices in Sessions may fine him at Discretion; the Fine is to be paid to the Treasurer of the County-Stock.

Hue-and-Cry.

THIS is a Pursuit of any Person after a Felony committed, and flying for the same.

'Tis

'Tis to be made from Town to Town, and from County to County, by Horſ-men and Foot-men; and of this, there are two Sorts:

1. *Hue-and-Cry* by the Common Law which is, where a Felony is committed, or any Perſon wounded, the Party grieved, or any other in his Behalf may reſort to the Conſtable of the next Town and acquaint him therewithall, deſcribing the Party, and telling him the Way he is gone; who thereupon is to raiſe the Town, and to give the next Conſtable Notice, and he the next, and ſo on to the Sea ſide: And this my Lord *Coke* ſays, was the Law before the Conqueſt.

And thoſe who neglect to make Hue-and-Cry, or do not purſue it when made, ſhall be fined and Impriſoned.

2. *Hue-and Cry* by Force of Statutes are many, but chiefly upon the Statutes of Robberies:

As by the Statute of *Winton*, the whole Hundred is made liable in which a Robbery is committed; but now by 27 *Eliz. c.* 13. the Inhabitants of any Hundred where Hue-and-Cry is made; and if they ſhall neglect to purſue, muſt anſwer one Moiety of ſuch Damages which ſhall be recovered againſt the other Hundred.

This Statute of *Ed.* 1. extends only to Robberies done *to the Perſon*, for it was made for the Safety of *Travellers*; aud therefore if a Houſe ſhould be Robbed in the Day-time, and the Felons eſcape, and Hue-and-Cry is made, and they are not taken, the Hundred ſhall not be anſwerable for the Reaſon above-mentioned.

The Perſon robbed ſhould give Notice as ſoon as he can. *Noy.* 155.

He uſually goes to a Juſtice of Peace, and is examined after this Manner.

The Examination of A. B. *of* &c. *taken upon Oath before* P. L. *Eſquire one of his Majeſty's Juſtices of the Peace for the County of* &c. *the* 14*th Day of* January. 1720.

THis Examinant depoſeth, That on *Tueſday* the Day of this Inſtant *June*, he was aſſaulted in the High-way leading from, *&c.* at or near a Place called, *&c.* about Ten of the Clock in the Morning the ſame Day, by three Men on Horſe-back, who ſeized this Examinant and carried him out of the Road to a By-place adjoyning, and Robbed of *&c.* And farther ſaith, That he is ſince Informed that the ſaid High-way and By-place are both in the Pariſh of *M.* and within the Hundred of, *&c.* in the ſaid County, and that he did not then, or yet doth know either of the Perſons who committed the ſaid Robbery.

A

A Warrant for a Hue-and-Cry.

To all Constables, and other Officers, as well in the said County of Kent, *as others to whom the Execution shall belong.*

Kent ss. WHereas Complaint hath been made unto me upon Oath, That Three Persons (here describe their Age, Colour, Apparrel, Horses, &c.) did on the Day of this Instant *August*, assault and take from *A. B.* of, &c. Fifty Pounds, &c. and that they are since fled for the same, and not yet apprehended: These are therefore to command you forthwith to make diligent Search within your Precincts for the said Persons, and to make Hue-and-Cry after them from Town to Town, and from County to County, and that as well by Horse-men as Foot-men, according to Law; and that if you shall find them, or either of them, that then you bring them before some one of His Majesty's Justices of the Peace for the County where he or they shall be taken, to be dealt withal according to Law, And hereof fail not, &c.

Hue-and-Cry raised without a Cause, is a Breach of the Peace.

And if it be made falsly, and the Person enter into a House, though with a Constable, and bind and Rob the Master in the Night, tis Burglary.

To charge the Hundred with a Robbery, these Things must be done:

1. The Person robbed must with all convenient Speed, give Notice of the Robbery to some Inhabitant near the Place where he was robbed.

2. He must be examined upon Oath within Twenty Days next before he brings his Action, by one Justice dwelling near the Hundred where the Robbery was done, whether he knew the Robbers, or either of them; and if he did know them, then he shall be bound before the Justice to prosecute them

3. The Hundred is not chargeable if any of the Offenders are taken, tho' after the Twenty Days limited by the Statute of 28 *Ed.* 3 *cap.* 11. for the taking them. *Sid* 12.

4 The Action must be brought within a Year after the Robbery done.

After Recovery and Execution of Damages it may be levied on one Person; but then upon Complaint, &c. two Justices of the Hundred, *Quorum unus*, &c. may take in Proportion the Towns, Villages, Parishes and Hamlets of the said Hundred to make an equal Contribution to relieve the Persons against whom Execution was taken.

After such Taxation, the Constables and Headboroughs of every Parish in the said Hundred shall assess the Inhabitants according to their Abilities, to pay the Sum taxed or laid by the Justices upon their respective Parishes.

Constables, upon Refusal of any Inhabitant to pay the Assessment, may distrain and

and sell, rendring the Overplus, and after it is levied, shall within Ten Days deliver it to the Justices, or one of them, and the Justices must pay it to the proper Persons.

Like Taxation for a Contribution of a Moiety out of a Hundred where any Default was in Pursuit, &c. to reimburse the Hundred where the Robbery was done.

Indictment.

IS the Verdict of a Jury charged to enquire into the Offence, &c.

This being in the Nature of a Declaration for the King, ought to be certain, and must not be supplyed by Implication or Intendment; and if 'tis upon a Penal Statute, never recite it because a small Misrecital makes it vicious. 3 *Bulst.* 22.

In every Indictment, these Things are requisite.

1. The *Name*, *Sur-name*, and *Addition* of the Party indicted.

Therefore *Misnosmer* shall not be made good by an *Alias dictus*.

But where the Name of the Offender cannot be known, it may be *cujusdam ignoti*, because the King is entitled to the Forfeiture; and if 'tis for Goods stoln, they may be carried into another County, and so the true Owner not known. *Dyer* 99. *Moor* 466.

Treasons, Felonies, Robberies, Murder, &c. done on the Seas, or beyond Seas, may be tried in any Place appointed for that Purpose by the King's Commission. *H. P. C.* 204. 35 *H.* 8. *cap.* 2.

A Robbery in *Middlesex*, and the Thief is taken with the Goods in *Sussex*, he may be indicted for the Felony there; but for the Robbery, it must be in *Middlesex*.

For an Offence at Common Law which is *contra Pacem*, an indictment will lie at Sessions; so for Fraud or Deceit, as for, selling deceitful Goods, or by false Weights and Measures; and tho' there are particular Statutes relating to this Matter, yet that doth not alter the Case, for the Difference is this; That where an Offence at Common Law is made, so likewise by any Statute, and a Punishment appointed by that Statute, yet the Offender is indictable as it is an Offence at Common Law; but where a Statute creates a new Offence, and inflicts a Punishment, that must be pursued, and no other.

And therefore where one was indicted for Usury, in taking more than 6 *l.* for the Lone of 100 *l.* and concluded *contra formam Statuti*, tho' it appeared plainly to be corrupt; yet because it was not expresly set forth that it was by corrupt Lending, the Indictment was quashed. 11 *Rep.* 58.

Traverse

Traverse.

THis is the most antient way of Trying the Fact; all Indictments may be Traversed, that is, you may take Issue upon the matter, or deny the chief Point in the Indictment.

This Traverse is to be tryed by a Jury at a General Quarter-Sessions, except in Riots and Forcible Entries.

By the Statute of 11 *Will.* the Clerk of the Peace shall have no more than 2 *s.* for drawing an Indictment, upon pain to forfeit 5 *l.* to the Party grieved; if he draw it defective, shall make a new one without fee, under the same Penalty.

Judgment: In High-Treason.

IN all cases (except Counterfeiting of Coin) that the Offender shall be drawn to the Gallows, and there hanged by the Neck and cut down alive, his Entrails taken out and burnt, his Head cut off, his Body quartered, and his Head and Quarters hanged up. So 'tis for uttering such Money, knowing it to be so. *Cro. Car.* 383. So 'tis for Clipping. *Dyer* 230. B. But for Counterfeiting Money, 'tis to be Drawn and Hanged. In both Cases the Judgment for a Woman is to be drawn and burnt.

Counterfeiting in this case, is meant Counterfeiting by Coining, for that is esteemed an inferior sort of Treason, in respect to such which concerned the King; and i *Drawing* and *Hanging*, but without *Quartering*, is the Judgment for Coyning, then by the same Reason it must be so for Clipping, for that seems a lesse degree of the same species of Treason.

In *Petty Treason*, For a Man, 'tis to be Drawn and Hanged For a Woman Drawn and burned.

In *Felony*; The Offender is to be Hanged till Dead; and 'tis commonly said this cannot be altered to Beheading.

In *Petty-Larceny*; To be Whipt, and Forfeiture of Goods.

In *Death, se Defendendo*, or by *Chance-medly*; There is no express Judgment, but the Goods are forfeited.

In *Misprison of Treason*; Forfeiture of Lands during Life, of Goods, and perpetual Imprisonment.

But the Goods of these Offenders are not to be seized before an *Indictment* found, or removed before Attainder.

Peculiar Punishments are appointed by divers Statutes for several Offences, and in such Cases the Justices cannot mitigate; and therefore 'tis not warrantable to admit an Offender indicted on a Penal Law, to submit with a *Protestation* of *Not Guilty*.

As to what relates to Executions, 'tis usually said, That in Treason the King may Remit all other parts of the Sentence, except Cuting off the Head; but in *Felonies*, the Judgment must be executed in the Method prescribed by Law; and therefore, if in such case the King should order a Criminal to be Beheaded, when Judgment is to be Hanged, it would be Murder in the Sheriff and his Officers, and they must suffer for it, without Pardon.

Jurors and Juries.

ALL Aliens, Apothecaries, Physitians, Clergy-Men, persons Indicted or attainted for any Crime, Conspirators, non Compos mentis, Infants under 14 years of Age, are excepted from serving on Juries, by 6 and 7 *William* 3. 1 *Anne*.

By the Statute of 2. *W. cap.* 28. by which they were ordered to summon in one Assize Four and Twenty, and no more,

But it hath been adjudged, That this Statute extends only to Jurors returned in Civil Cases, and not for Trials of Criminals, for in such Cases the Sheriff might be commanded by the Court to return as many as they please; and 'tis usual to return Sixty, because of the Challenges. *Keil.* 16.

If there are not enough of the principal Pannel, the Sheriff must return the *Tales* out of some other Pannel of Jurors then attending; and if such *Tales-men* withdraw, the Judge may fine them. 7 and 8 *Will.* 3.

Any Freeholder or Copyholder who is the Kings' Leige Subject, and returned by the proper Officer, *May be a Juror*.

In *Michaelmas* Sessions, the Constable shall return to the Justices a List of the Names and Abodes of Persons who are qualified to serve, between 21 and 70 years of Age, a Duplicate of which List the Justices shall order the Clerk of the Peace to deliver to the Sheriff before *January* following.

This List must be entred in a Book, and kept amongst the Records of the Sessions, and none to be impannelled whose Name is not entred in the List. 7 and 8 *W. cap.* 32.

And because the Constables, Headboroughs and Tything-men were negligent in returning such Lists; therefore by another Act, the Justices every year at *Midsummer* Sessions shall issue out their Warrants, at least under the Hands of Two of them, directed to the High-Constables of each Hundred, requiring them to issue out their Precepts to their respective Constables Headboroughs, &c. That they should meet the High-Constable within 14 Days

Days afetr the Date of such Precept at some convenient Place within the Hundred, there to prepare a List as aforesaid; which List they must sign, and at the *Michaelmas* Sessions following deliver it into Court. 3 *and* 4 *Anne*.

The High-Constable not issuing out such Precept to his Petty-Constable, or Headborough, forfeits 10 *l.*

The Petty-Constable or Headborough not meeting according to the Precept, and failing to prepare a List, and to return it as aforesaid, forfeits 5 *l.*

The petty-Constable or Headborough not meeting according to the Precept, and failing to prepare a List, and to return it as aforesaid, forfeits 5 *l.*

The Offenders are to be prosecuted at the Sessions, but there is no Direction how, or to whom the Forfeitures shall be applied.

Jurors must be summoned at least Six Days before the Sessions, by shewing a Warrant under the Seal of the Sheriff's Office. But if not at Home, then a Note left by the Officer at the Dwelling-house with any Person inhabiting there, is sufficient.

If summoned otherwise than as aforesaid, the Sheriff forfeits 20 *l.* to the Party grieved, to be recovered in the Courts at *Westminster*.

None shall be returned but once in Four years, the City of *York*, and Town of *Kingston upon Hull*, excepted.

Inhabitants of *Westminster* shall not serve in a *Jury* at the Sessions in *Middlesex*.

The *Grand-Inquest* must consist of Forty eight Freeholders and no more, each having 80 *l. per Annum*.

There shall not be above Forty Persons returned at the Sessions of the Peace for *Yorkshire*. 7 and 8 *W. cap.* 32.

They may be more than Twelve, and 'tis best to have an odd Number; and if Twelve agree, 'tis conclusive to the rest.

They ought not to have a Keeper, nor to be without Victuals, but may be adjourned to give their Verdict.

If they discover their Secrets, they must be fined; and if they make a favourable Presentment, they may be committed, and fined.

Justices of Peace may make an Alteration in the Pannel after 'tis returned, if they see Cause, and may remove a *Juror* after he is sworn. 3 *H.* 8. *cap.* 12.

Regularly they cannot inquire into any Thing but what ariseth in the County for which they are returned; and therefore if a Stroke be given in one County, and the Death happen in another, the party could not be indicted where the Person died; But this is now remedied by the Statute of 2 and 3 *Ed.* 6. *cap.* 24.

So likewise the Law in Criminal Cases is now altered by other Statutes, as in Confederacies, Felonies, Murders, Robberies and Treasons done on the Sea; the Offender shall be tried where the King, by His Commission, shall appoint. 28 *H.* 8. *cap.* 15.

So in Treasons and Misprisions of Treasons done *out of the Land*, the Offenders shall be tried in the *King's Bench* by a *Middlesex* Jury, or by the King's Commission in any County by a *Jury* of that County. 35 *H.* 8. *cap.* 2.

If the Grand-Inquest *conceal* any Thing which they ought to present, the *Justices* of Peace my impannel an Inquest to inquire of such Concealment, and fine them. 3 *H.* 7, *cap*, 1.

If a *Jury*-man will keep his Fellows without giving any Reason, or will withdraw from them, he may be committed and fined, because he is sworn well and truly to try the Issue; and therefore to be obstinate without Cause, or do art, is a Misdemeanor.

But if he differs in *Judgment* from the rest, tho' his Dissent be not as reasonable as the Opinion of those who agree, yet he cannot be fined, tho' he keep the rest for a Time from giving their Verdict.

For Misdemeanors they may be fined, but not barely for going against the Direction of the Court,

In Cases of Life or Member, if they cannot agree of their Verdict at the Assizes, they must be carried the Circuit, till they do agree, 1 *Vent* 97.

If they eat and drink before or after they are agreed of their Verdict, they are to be fined; only with this Difference, That if they eat at their own Charge, the Verdict shall stand; but if at the Charge of the party, it shall be set aside 1 *Leon*. 133. *Dyer* 137.

Some of them have been fined for having Pigs and Pippins in their pockets, though they did not eat them. 1 *Leon*. 133. *Moor* 599.

If after they are gone from the Bar, one of the *Jury* calls a Witness, who was sworn, and had given his Evidence in Court, and desires him to repeat it again, which he did; this is a Misdemeanor, and the Verdict shall be set aside. *Cro. Eliz* 189.

An Attorney was turned over the Bar, for giving Direction to the Sheriff what Persons he would have returned of a *Jury* *Moor* 88.

Act 10 *Anne* reviv'd for exempting Apothecaries from serving the Offices of Constable, Scavenger, and other Parish and Ward-Offices, and from serving upon *Juries*.

Justice of Peace.

JUstices of the Peace were created 36 *Ed.* 3. *cap.* 12. But in the Space of Threescore years their Number so increased, that *Anno* 12 *R.* 2 *cap.* 10, a Law was made prohibiting, that there should be no more than Six in every County, as at the Beginning of their Constitution; and their Number Two years afterward increased to Eight.

They

They are now Judges of Record, and have a larger Power than the Conservators had, because they could not commit the Offenders for a Breach of the Peace; but the Justices may send Warrants to bring Delinquents before them to be examined, and may also commit where they see Cause.

This Law, is not abrogated at this Day, but the Number of Justices is greatly increased in every County, which made Mr, *Lambard*, above One hundred Years since, complain of the excessive Number; and after him Sir *Henry Spelman* takes Notice, that there are above Threescore in each County.

'Tis true, in *Wales* there were but Eight in a County; they were confined to that Number by a Clause in the Statute of 34 and 35 *H.* 8, but by a late Act of 5 *Will.* and *M.* that Clause is repealed.

Therefore this Author would have the Number reduced to the old Standard, *viz.* That in each County there should be Eight Honorary Justices constituted of Men of the best Quality therein, who should not be obliged constantly to attend the Service any farther than their Zeal for Justice, and Love for their Country, shall incline them; and Eight acting Justices who should be fit for Business, who should constantly apply themselves to this Attendance, but be intitled to a Reward for their Pains, and be subject to penalties upon any Neglect, without a reasonable Excuse; and that without Five, no Sessions should be held.

Among the Petitions made at a Parliament held at *York*, 8 *Ed.* 3. this was one, (*viz.*) That all *Justices* of the Peace were to have certain Fees for their Attendance; the Petition was again renewed 36 *Ed.* 3. and the King answered, He would provide therefore: But what that Fee was, doth not appear. *Hill* 12 *C.* 2. it was enacted, That they should have 4 *s. per Diem* for every Day they sate in Quarter-Sessions; and since, by particular Statutes, they are to have also Part of the Forfeitures upon Conviction of Offenders against these Laws; and by the Statute of Labourers, they are to have 5 *s. per Diem* for every May they shall sit in Execution of that Act above three Days. *Cett. Abr. fol.* 15, 93. *Wages.* 12. *R.* 2. *cap.* 10, 19. *H.* 7. 5 *Eliz. cap.* 4.

And such Care was then taken to reward those Magistrates, that it was provided by a Statute, *Anno* 14 *R.* 2. that the Names of the *Justices*, and the Days of their Sitting, should be written in the Indentures of Estreats of every Sessions; one Part whereof was to remain with the Sheriff, that he might know to whom the Wages should be paid; and the other with the Barons of the *Exchequer*, that the Sheriff might have Allowance made, &c. in passing the Accompts; and if he neglected or refused to pay the Wages allowed by Law, an Action of Debt would lie against him.

Their Qualifications are described by several Statutes, *viz.*

They must be Men of the best Reputation, the most prevalent Men in the County, as they were formerly called, together with some Lawyers; they

U must

must be substantial Persons, dwelling also in the County; they must be Men of good Governance, and must not be Steward to any Lord, or desire this Office; and they are not qualified unless they have 20 *l. per Annum*, except Men of the Law. 18 *Ed.* 3. 2. 34 *Ed.* 3. 1. 2. H. 5. 4. 18 H. 6. 11. 12 R. 2. 10.

And therefore an Indictment was brought against One, because he acted as a Justice of Peace, not having 20 *l. per Annum, contra Pacem* &c. but the Indictment was quashed, because the Time of his Acting was not laid, &c. for he might have 20 *l. per Annum* then, though not afterwards. *Roll. Rep.* 2 *Part.* 247.

In some Cases Justices Power is Ministerial, (*viz.*) On a *Supplicavit* out of *B. R.* for taking Surety of the Peace, on the Statute of *Northampton* for a Forcible Entry, and on a *Certiorari.*

But in most other Cases relating to his Offices, he is a Judge of Record, for none but such can take a Recognizance for the Peace.

By the Statute of 18 *Ed.* 3. *cap.* 2. he hath Power to hear and determine *Felonies* and Trespasses, and to inflict Punishment, &c. He hath the like Power by 34 *Ed.* 3. *cap.* 1. and likewise by *R.* 2. *cap.* 10. he hath Power to proceed to the Deliverance of Thieves and Felons.

Now tho' these Statutes do inlarge their Power, yet because by a subsequent Law, (*viz.*) 1 and 2 *Phil. and Mar. cap.* 13. they are to certify the Examinations in *Homicide* and Felony to the Justices of Gaol-delivery, therefore the Sessions do not proceed to determine great Felonies; but for Petit-Larceny, and other small Felonies, they usually try Offenders, or they may proceed in any Case where a Felony is by any Statute limited to be heard before them.

And generally in all Cases they may take the Examinations, and commit the Offenders, and bind over the Prosecutors to the Assizes, and certify their Proceedings.

Where he hath a Jurisdiction, his Warrant is not to be disputed by any Constable, who may be indicted for not executing it. 2 *Roll. Rep.* 78.

In some Cases, as in *Force, Riots, Presentments of High-ways*, his single Testimony is of greater Authority than an Indictment of a Jury.

But in his own Case he is not Judge, and ought not to execute his Office, unless he is assaulted, and then he may commit the Offender: He may likewise record a Forcible Entry upon his own Possession.

He shall not be punished for any Thing done by him in Sessions. When he justifieth the Fact done by him as a Justice of Peace, he need not set forth his Commission, because he is a Judge of Record, and his Commission remaineth with the *Custos Rotulorum.*

If any Man abuseth him, an Indictment will lie against the Offender. That is, if the Abuse be in any Thing relating to his Office; as where an Order was affirmed

affirmed upon an Appeal, and the Party in Anger said, *If I cannot have Justice here, I will have it elsewhere*; he was indicted for this Contempt, and fined by the *Justices* 5 *l.* and committed for Non-payment; and this was held lawful. 'Tis true, *Justice Twisden* was of a contrary Opinion, *viz.* That the Words were not spoken in Contempt, but by way of Appeal to another Court, and did not accuse the Sessions of Injustice; but this is a strained Construction of a plain Sentence.

And as they are favoured by the Law in Execution of their Office, so they are punished for any Irregularities.

As for Instance: An Information was brought against a *Justice* of Peace for compounding Recognizances, and not returning them to the Sessions; and for taking 20 *s.* for every unlicensed Ale-house, and converting it to his own Use, he was fined 1000 Marks, and imprisoned during the King's Pleasure, was to find Sureties for his Good Behaviour for a Year, and to acknowledge his Offence at the next Assizes. *Sid.* 192.

But he may perswade an Agreement between the Parties for small Trespasses, but not where the King is to have a Fine. *Nov.* 103.

He may send his Warrant to apprehend any Person *accused* of Felony, though the *Accusation* should be false, but not unless accused, 1 *Leon*, 187. *Cro. Eliz.* 130.

One Justice, *&c* cannot commit another for a Breach of the Peace; the Sessions may.

They cannot hold Cognizance of Pleas upon Penal Statutes without an express Power given to them by those Acts; and without such Authority, the Indictment, if taken, will be void.

But his Power is determined by the Death of the King, by a Discharge under the Great Seal, by a *Supersedeas*, by granting a new Commission; by Accession of another Office, as being made Sheriff or Coroner.

Larceny Petty.

'TIs a Felonious Taking and Carrying away the Personal Goods of another, not from his Person, nor out of his House, and not exceeding the Value of 12 *d.*

In this Definition, these Things are to be considered, 1 *Who may be guilty of this Offence.* 2, *What shall be accounted a Felonious Taking, and where.* 3. *What shall be a Carrying away,* 4, *What are the Personal Goods, of another, and what not.* 5. *The Value.*

As to the *First*, Infants under Fourteen, and married Women, may be guilty

guilty, *&c.* but i a *Feme Covert* taketh the Goods of the Husband, and delivereth them to another, 'tis not Felony in the Receiver.

'Tis likewise an Excuse to her, if she commit Felony by the Command of her Husband, if both are in the same Felonious Act; but 'tis no Excuse in a Servant by the Order of the Master.

To make it Felony, There must be an actual Taking, and therefore the Indictment is always *quod Felonice cepit & asportavit* or *abduxit*; for if it be *quod abduxit* only, 'tis naught; and therefore if Goods are found, and afterwards converted *animo furandi.* 'tis not Felony.

If a Man hath the Possession of Goods by Delivery, as a Carrier, who imbezels them, 'tis no Felony, unless the Privity be determined; that is, if by Agreement the Goods were to be carried to such a place, which he doth not; or if they are brought thither, and afterwards the Carrier takes them, *animo furandi.*

But in some Cases, tho' the party hath the Goods by Delivery, yet 'tis Felony to go away with them; as if a Shopkeeper delivers Goods to a person pretending to buy them, and he runneth away with them, 'tis Felony, for the Goods were not properly out of the possession of the Owner by his Delivery, but by compleating the Contract which was then began; and the running away shews the Intention of the party, by coming into the Shop (*viz.*) to get the Goods into his possession, *animo furandi.*

But Felony may be committed by a person who hath the Charge or Use of a Thing, as a Shepherd of his Sheep; or a Guest, of plate brought for his Use in an Inn.

It may be committed by making use of the *Process* of the Law to obtain Goods, *viz.* By obtaining a *Replevin* where a Man hath no Property, and by that Means get a Horse delivered to him, this is a Felonious Taking; so by getting Goods out of an House upon an Ejectment, where he hath no Title. *Sid.* 254.

A Guest removes Goods out of his Chamber, and is taken before he gets out of the Inn; or taking an Horse with an Intent to steal, but is apprehended before he can get out of the Ground where he was departing. *This is a Carrying a way.*

A Man who hath a Property only *pro tempore*, as a Bailiff, if Goods are taken away from him, 'tis Felony.

Stealing a Bond is Felony, because 'tis a Thing in Action.

Taking Fish in a Trunk or Pond, is Felony, because they are deprived in these Places of their natural Liberty; so taking Swans kept in a Pound or private River.

Things which have been *feræ Naturæ*, if made tame, are Personal Goods; as Conies, Deer, Partridges, Pheasants, and 'tis Felony to steal them, knowing them to be the same.

So

So where a Man hath a Property, *rations impotentiæ*, in Things which are wild in their Nature, as young Hawks, or Pidgoons in their Nests, 'tis Felony to steal the same.

So 'tis to take Things which are *dom tæ Naturæ*; as Ducks, Hens, Turkeys, &c. Horses, Colts, &c.

To steal the Shrowd of a Person buried is Felony, for 'tis *bona Executorum: Quære.*

Wrecks, Waifs, and Estrays before Seizure, Fish in a River, Conies in a Warren, for a Man hath no Property in them but *ratione loci.*

Corn or Grass growing, Apples growing, taking Lead off a Church.

Things of a base Nature, as Dogs, Foxes, Monkeys, Parrots, Ferrets; these and such like are not Personal Goods, and so no Felony to take them.

If the Indictment be for taking Goods to the Value of 10 *s.* and the Jury, find only to the Value of 10 *d.* 'tis Petty-Larceny.

If several small Matrers are taken from the same Person at several Times, and all amounting to more than 12 *d.* they may be put into one Indictment and the Offender, being found guilty, shall have Judgment of Death.

The Judgment in this Offence is to be whipped, and forfeits his Goods.

Who are not Felons. A Wife stealing by Compulsion of her Husband; otherwise if not constrained; but if she commit Murder by her Husband's Consent, 'tis Felony.

They steal Goods together, 'tis Felony in the Husband alone; but if she steal her Husband s Goods, or receive him, being a Felon, she is not guilty as a Felon in the one Case, or as Accessary in the other.

Leather.

PErsons exercising the Mystery of a Tanner, not having served 7 Years as an Apprentice, or Hired Servant, except the Widow or Children of a Tanner, and having been brought up in that Profession 4 Years, Cutters or Workers of Leather-Tanning; forfeit all the Leather they Tan, or the Value.

Over-liming his Hides, or using any Thing but the Bark of Ash or Oak, Tap-Wort, Malt-Meal, Lime, Culver-Dung or Hen-Dung; or suffers 'em to be frozen, or parched with Fire or Sun, or tans rotten Hides; forfeits every Hide so tann'd and put to Sale, or the full Value.

Raising Hide for Sole Leather by any Mixtures, forfeits the same.

Hastening the Tanning of Leather by unkind Heats with hot Wooze, or otherwise, forfeits 10 *l.* and to stand in the Pillory three Days in the next Market-Town.

Currying Hide or Skin insufficiently tann'd and dried, or out of his own House in some Market-Town, or gashing or spoiling them, forfeits 6 *s.* 8 *d.*

each, besides the Value, and double Damage to the Party grieved.

Using the Art of a Tanner, Shoemaker or Butcher, or other who useth Cutting of Leather, forfeits for every Hide or Skin he cutteth, 6 *s.* 8 *d.*

Refusing to curry Leather within 8 Days in Summer, and 16 in Winter after he takes it in Hand, forfeits for every Hide not curried 10 *s.*

Not currying his Leather sufficiently, forfeits the Value.

For every Hide not sealed and searched, forfeits 6. *s.* 8 *d.*

Leather tann'd and curried. Putting to Sale tanned Leather red and unwrought, but in Fair or Market, unless searched and sealed before; or offering to sell any such Leather, forfeits for every Dozen of Calf or Sheep Skins, 3 *s.* 4 *d.* and for every Hide 6 *s.* 8 *d.* besides the Hides, &c. or the full Value.

Insufficiently tann'd or dried, and put to Sale, forfeit the Whole.

Selling tann'd Leather in *London* before it is searched and sealed; or selling tann'd Leather (red or unwrought) before it be registred; buying any tann'd Leather before it be searched and sealed, or carrying it out of the Fair or Market before it be registred, forfeit the same, or the Value.

Opposing Searchers and Sealers, Forfeiture 5 *l.*

Artificers (using tann'd and curried Leather) putting into his Wares Leather insufficiently tann'd or curried, forfeit the Wares or Value.

And such Artificers selling any where but in open Shop, Fair or Market, where due Search may be made, forfeit Wares, and 10 *s.* for every Offence.

And buying forfeited Wares to sell them again, forfeit 3 *s.* 4 *d.* for every Parcel.

Persons in *London* or three Miles, putting Leather to be curried to any but Freemen of the Curriers Company, forfeits the same.

In *London*, putting into made Wares any curried Leather before it be searched and sealed, forfeits 6 *s.* 8 *d.* a Hide or Skin, and the Value of the same.

Shoemakers, not making their Boots and Shoes of good Leather, nor sewing them well: and selling them on *Sunday*, forfeit for every Offence, 3 *s.* 4 *d* and the Value of the Wares sold.

All the above Forfeitures to be divided; one Third to the *King*, one to the *Prosecutor*, and the other to the City, Borough, or Lord of the Liberty where the Offence is.

By 9 *Anne* All Mayors, &c. and other Persons whatsoever are duly to execute and comply with the said Statute:

And by the same Statute any Butcher or other Person wilfully or negligently gashing Hides or Calve Skins, and offering the same to Sale, forfeits 2 *s.* 6. *d.* *per* Hide, and 1 *s.* *per* Skin; one Moiety to the Poor, the other to the Informer.

2 Justices to summon the Party accused, and the Witnesses on either Side; and the Party appearing or not, to examine Witnesses upon Oath, and determine.

All

All Collar-makers, Glovers, Bridle-cutters and others who taw, or make Leather in Oil, Allom or Salt or Meal, or cut and make the same into Wares, are Tawers and Dressers within the Act, and subject to the Forfeitures

Lodgers. *See* Cottages, Inmates.

TAking away with an Intent to steal or imbezel any Bedding, Furniture or Chattels, which by Agreement they are to use with their Lodging, 'tis Felony. 3 and 4 *W.* and *M.* continued by 4 and 5 *W.* & *M. cap.* 24.

Lord's Day

THE Observation of this Day is not only a Divine Command, but a very wise and politick Constitution; for it gives Countenance to Christianity, and keeps bad Men from growing worse.

The Prophanation of this Day doth generally arise from, 1. Covetousness: Or, 2. Licentiousness.

Shoemakers. *First*, From a covetous Desire of Gain, as *per* Stat. 1 *Jac.* 1. *cap.* 11. Shoemaker putting Boots or Shoes to Sale, forfeits 3 *s.* 4 *d.* and the Goods: Then by the Statute of 3 *Car.* 1. *cap.* 1. Carriers, Drovers, Waggoners travelling on that Day, such are prohibited under the Penalty of 20 *s.* for every Offence.

The Proof must be before one Justice by two Witnesses upon Oath, or by Confession of the Party, unless the Fact was done in view of the *Justice*.

Prosecution within six Months after the Offence.

These Forfeitures are recoverable by Distress on a Warrant, or by Bill or Information in Sessions, to the Use of the Poor where taken.

Carriers. But though the Carriers, &c, Driving is through several Parishes, yet there shall be but one Forfeiture for one Day.

By 29 *Car.* 2. *cap.* 7. the Conviction is made more easie; and by this Statnte, publick and private Duties of Piety are enjoyned, all worldly Business is prohibited (except Works of Necessity and Charity) and all above the Age of 14 Years offending in the Premisses, forfeits 5 *s.* to the Use of the Poor; but the Justice may reward the Informer out of the Penalties, so that it doth not exceed the third Part,

Drovers, or their Servants coming to their Inns on that Day, forfeit 20 *s.*

for every Offance, The Prosecution must be within Ten Days after the Offence. The proof by one Witness upon Oath before one Justice, and if the Offender is not able to pay the Forfeiture, he must be put in the Stocks for Two Hours.

Secondly, Irreligious Licentiousness, *per* 1 *Car.* 1. *cap.* 1.

Meeting together out of their own Parish for any Sports or Pastimes, they forfeit 3 *s*, 4 *d*. each. Prosecution must be within a Month, &c. Proof by one Witness before one Justice, or Confession of the Party. Forfeiture is for the Poor of the Parish where the Offence is committed, and to be levied by Distress on a Warrant, &c. and in Default thereof the Offender is to be put in the Stocks for three Hours,

¶ Any Process served on this Day, except for Breach of the Peace, Felony or Treason, is void, and the Person serving the same must answer Damages, as if he had done it without a Warrant, 29 *Car.* 2. *cap.* 7.

But this Statute doth not extend to dressing of Meat in Inns, Cooks Shops or Victualling Houses.

All the Laws for frequenting of Divine Service on this Day, are still in Force, notwithstanding the Statute of 1 *W.* & *M*, *cap.* 18. unless Persons go to some Congregation tolerated by that Act.

A Warrant to levy the Forfeitures on such who use Sports on that Day.

To the Constable, &c.

Kent ss. WHereas *A. B*, of, &c. *C. D.* of, &c, and *E. F.* of, &c, have been lawfully convicted before me upon Oath, That they, and each of them, did on the 18*th* Day of *November* last past, being the Lord's Day, meet and were present with a Concourse of other People out of their own parishes, for Sports and pastimes, *viz*, to play at Foot-ball *(or as the Case is)* contrary to the Laws in that Case made and provided, by Reason whereof each of the persons before-mentioned have forfeited 3 *s*, 4 *d*. for the Use of the poor of your parish: *These are therefore* in His Majesty's Name to command you forth-with to levy the respective Sums of 3 *s*. 4 *d*. on the respective Goods and Chattels of the several Offenders before-mentioned, by Distress and Sale thereof, rendring to them the Overplus, if any; and in case no such Distress can be had, that then you cause the said person or persons, wanting such Distress, to be set publickly in the Stocks for the Space of Three Hours. *Given* under my Hand and Seal, &c.

To

To levy the Penalty on Persons travelling on that Day, &c.

To the Constable, &c.

Kent ss. WHereas it hath been duly proved before me, That *A. B.* of, &c. being a common Carrier, did on the 8*th* Day of *November* last past, being the Lord's-Day, travel with his Horses into, and through your said Parish of, &c. contrary to the Statute in that Case made and provided, by Reason whereof he hath forfeited 20 *s.* to the Use of the Poor of the said Parish, *These are therefore*, &c. to command you forthwith to levy the said Sum of 20 *s.* on the Goods and Chattels of the said *A. B.* by Distress and Sale thereof, rendring to him the Overplus; and that you see it employ'd to the Use of your said Parish, as by Law it ought. *Given* under, &c.

3 Car. 1. *cap* 1. One Justice *ut prius*, but by the Oath of Two Witnesses. Prosecution must be within six Months; but *per* 29 Car. 2. c. 7. Ten Days.

To levy Five Shillings on those that use a Trade on that Day.

To the Constables and Churchwardens of, &c.

Kent ss. WHereas *A. B.* of the Parish of, &c. Barber, standeth convicted before me *P. L.* Esq; one of His Majesty's *Justices* of the Peace for the said County, upon the Oath of *C. D.* of, &c. Labourer, for Exercising his Trade or ordinary Calling upon *Sunday* the 29*th* Day of *August* Instant, in his House situate in, &c. For which said Offence he hath forfeited the Sum of 5 *s.* to the Use of the Poor of the said Parish, according to the Form of the Statute in that Case made and provided. *These are therefore*, in His Majesty's Name, to command you upon Sight hereof, to demand of the said *A. B.* the said Sum of 5 *s.* And if he shall refuse to pay the same, that then you forthwith levy the same by Distress and Sale of his Goods for the Use aforesaid, rendring to him the Overplus (if any be.) And in Default of such Distress, That then you set him publickly in the Stocks by the Space of Two whole Hours. Hereof fail not at your Peril. *Given* under my Hand and Seal this 31*th* Day of *August* 1714.

To levy the Penalty for exposing Goods to Sale, &c.

To the Constable,

Kent ss. WHereas it hath been duly proved upon Oath before me, That *A. E.* of, &c. did on *Sunday* the 29th Day of *August* last past, expose Apples, &c. to Sale at, &c. contrary to the Law in that Case made and provided, whereby he hath forfeited the said Goods to the Use of the Poor of the said Parish, &c. *These are therefore*, &c. to require you forthwith to seize the said Goods so put to Sale as aforesaid, and that you sell the same, and imploy the Money arising by such Sale to the Use of the Poor of your said Parish, as by Law it ought: *And hereof* fail not at your Peril. *Given*, &c.

But crying and selling of Milk, and Works of Necessity and Charity, are excepted.

A Lisence to go by Water.

Kent ss. WHereas *A. B. C. D. E. F.* the Bearers hereof, have made it appear before me, that they have urgent Occasions to pass on the next *Lord's-Day* from *A.* to *B.* by Water, and to return again the same Day: All Constables, Church-wardens, and other His Majesty's Officers, are therefore required to permit the said Gentlemen to pass without Interruption. *Given* under my Hand and Seal, &c.

J. C.

A Lisence to Travel on the *Lords-Day.*

Kent ss. WHereas *A. B.* of *C.* &c. where he now dwelleth, having informed me that he hath a Brother living at *C.* in the County of *H.* where he lieth now very sick, and he hath a Desire to see him: *Know ye* that for this Cause I do hereby lisence him to Travel upon the next *Lord's Day* the direct Way to his Brother: Willing and requiring you not to molest or hinder him for the same, so that he behave himself orderly in his Travel: *Given* under my Hand, &c.

Markets

Markets and Fairs.

THese are either by Grant or Prefcription; and if held otherwife, they are unlawful. 2 *Sand* 74.

Now becaufe it may be neceffary to know how far the Property of a Thing is diveftred by Sale in Market Overt; therefore 'tis to be confidered, that in *London* every Day, except *Sunday*, is a Market Overt, and the Sale in Shops there for a valuable Confideration is good. But then it muft be fuch Goods which are proper to the Trade of him in whofe Shop 'tis fold, as Plate to a Goldfmith, &c. And it muft be fold openly in the Shop, and not in a fecret Manner; and the Buyer muft not know that the Goods are ftolen,

In the Country, where Things are fold in diftinct Places in a Market or Fair, the Goods *muft* be fold in the ufual Place appointed for the Sale thereof, otherwife the Property is not altered, *Moor* 300.

If I deliver Goods to another to keep for me, or if I pawn them, and he fells them in a Market, the Property is ftill in me. *Hob.* 79.

Sale upon a *Sunday*, tho' in Market or Fair, fhall not alter the Property,

A Fair muft be kept no longer than the Grant or Ufe by Cuftom will Warrant for what is Warrantable; and Goods fo Sold after the Expiration of the Time, as Merchandize, &c. the Seller fhall forfeit to the *King* double the Value of what is Sold, and the profecutor fhall have the fourth part. The Fair muft be duly Proclaimed by the Sheriff, or Lord of the Fair, and the Time it is to continue mentioned, the place or ground appointed, fet out, and care taken that there be no Riots or Difturbance, but an orderly keeping of it during the time it lafts.

Where there is a Beaft fair for Horfes, Mares, Geldings, and other Cattle, they muft have their appointed places, that thofe that refort thither may have a Certainty where to find them. And one fufficient perfon, or more muft be appointed to take Toll, and keep the fame place from Ten in the Forenoon, every Day till Sunfet, during the Time of the Fair or Market, upon pain to forfeit for every Default 40 *s.* And in Tolling, the party thereto appointed muft have before him the parties Bargaining, upon his Tolling any Horfe, Mare, &c, And muft Write in his Book the Chriftian Names, and Sir Names of all the Parties; alfo their Dwelling Places, with the Colours and fome particular Marks of the Horfe or Mare, &c, fo Sold or Bargained for, on Penalty to forfeit for every Default 40 *s.* and he is to have one credible Perfon known to him to Vouch the Horfe or Mare, &c, and teftifie his knowledge of the Seller, and his Name and place of aboad must be entred with the others in the Book, with the Colour, Mark, or Price of the Horse or Mare, Sold or Exchanged, and the Buyer requiring it, may have a Note in Writing out of the Book, Reciting the Contract, and Toll-man's Hand thereto, for which he may take Two pence.

If any Toll-keeper suffer a Sale to pass without a Voucher, unless he well know the party, and every Party making a false Testimony, or Avouchment, or every Seller unknown, not bringing a Voucher, and causing the same to be entred, forfeits Five Pounds, one Moiety to the *King* and the other to the Prosecutor, and the Sale of the said Horse, &c. to be void. Yet notwithstanding such Vouching, the Owner of a Stollen Horse, &c. so Sold, his Executors or Administrators, claiming him within six Months after the Stealing, may Redeem at the price he was Sold for, making proof that it is his, and that it was Stollen, by two sufficient Witnesses before a *Justice* of the County where he is found, or the Head Officer or Magistrate of a Corporation, and the price to be such, as the Buyer upon Oath shall testifie before the *Justice*, he paid for him; and if the Stollen Horse be not Sold in open Fair or Market, and lawfully Toll'd, the Right is in the Owner from whom he was Stole, and he may Seize or Replevy him in any place where he finds him.

If any person Buy Oxen, Goats, Sheep, Calves, Heifers, Lambs, &c, alive, he shall not Sell them again alive till he has kept them in his pasture by the space of five Weeks.

As for Measure, there shall be only the *Winchester* Bushel, and no other Bushel, and that to contain 8 Gallons; and who so Sells by any other, according to t e 22*d*. *Car*. 2. *Chap*. 8. forfeits 40 s. And upon the Clerk of the Market's refusing to Seal such Measure as shall be full Gauged, he forfeits for the first Offence 5 *l*. for the second 10 *l*. Or if the *Ki gs* Clerk of his Market of his House exact, or take more Fees than his due, that is, above one penny for Sealing a Bushel, a Half-penny for half a Bushel, and one Farthing for Measures of less proportion, he incurs, and shall undergo the penalty in the Statute, *Caroli* 1.

A Brass Bushel is to be chained to a post, or publick place in the Market-place, at the Charge of the person taking Toll for the publick Use of Measuring, upon penalty of forfeiting of five pounds, 22 *Caroli* 2 *Chap*. 8.

Whosoever shall Sell or Buy Corn without Measuring, being thereunto required, so Selling or Buying it in Sacks, or Bags, or in any other thing, shall forfeit the said Corn, or the value thereof to the party making his Complaint of this Offence against the Statute, 22 and 23 *Caroli* 2 *Chap*. 12. And upon Complaint the Defendant by the Oath of one or more Witnesses before a Justice of the peace, must prove that he or they did Buy or Sell according to the Statute of 22 and 23 *Car*. 2, or else pay the Forfeitures by the

the latter directed, which upon Warrant may be Levied by Distress and Sale of Goods; the Warrant to be given under the Hand and Seal of one or more Justices, before whom such Conviction shall be, one half to the poor of the parish where the Offence is committed, and the other to the Informer, *Ibid.*

Misdemeanors. *See* Good Behaviour.

A general Warrant for the same, returnable before a particular Justice.

To the Constable, &c.

1 *Justice.* These are (in His Majesty's Name) to command you, That you, do cause *A. B*, of *C.* to come before me, to answer unto such Matters of Misdemeanor as (on His Majesty's Behalf) shall be objected against him by *D. E.* for assaulting, beating and bruising him without Provocation, as he hath made Oath; and farther to do and receive as to Justice doth appertain. *Hereof* fail not at your Perils. *Given* under my Hand and Seal, *&c.*

Or Thus.

These are to will and require you, and (in His Majesty's Name) straightly to charge and command you, and either of you, that immediately upon the sight hereof (or upon *Thursday* next at Two of the Clock in the Afternoon) you bring *A. B* of your said Town, *Barber* before me, to answer to such Matters of Misdemeanor as (on His Majesty's Behalf) shall be objected against him by *D. B.* for assaulting and beating him, as he hath made Oath: *And hereof* fail not at your Perils. *Given* under, *&c.*

One sent a Challenge by another to fight; they were both indicted for a Misdemeanor, and fined 100 *l*, apiece, and committed for a Month without Bail, and were to make a publick Recantation as the Court should direct, and to be of the Good Behaviour for 7 Years. *Sid.* 186.

A Man and his Wife disagreeing, she applied her self to one *Golding* a Parson, and offered him 40 *s* to whip her Husband. The Parson undertook it, and came to the House in Woman's Cloaths, and to the Chamber where her Husband was, and endeavoured to whip him wit a Rod; in striving they

Z were

were both hurt; and the Parson run away from the Husband, who died a little time after this Scuffle: And this being proved, the Wife and the Parson were each of them fined 500 *l.* *Poph.* 129.

Sir *C. S.* was indicted at Common Law for a Misdemeanor, *viz*, For shewing himself naked in a Balcony in *Covent-Garden*: He confess'd the Indictment, was fined 2000 Marks, and to be committed for a Week without Bail, and to be of the Good Behaviour for 3 Years, *Sid.* 168.

Another was indicted for Seducing an Apprentice to a Bawdy-house, and causing him to spend his Master's Money, *Sid.* 208.

Another for intending to Kill the Master of the *Rolls*, and offering a Person 100 *l.* to do it: He was fined 1000 Marks, to be imprisoned three Months without Bail, and to be of Good Behaviour during Life. *Sid.* 231.

Another for Reading a Release to an illiterate Man in other Words than it was written; which he sealed.

Misprision of Treason. *See* Treason.

Misprision of Treason, is, where one knoweth that another hath committed Treason or Felony, but was not consenting to it, and yet conceals the Offender.

If he knoweth of the Treason *before* 'tis committed, and assents to it, then he is a principal Traitor.

So if he receive and comfort a Traitor, knowing him to be so.

Concealing Treason, was Treason by the Common Law; but now by the Statute of 1 & 2 *Mar. cap.* 10. 'tis declared to be Misprision.

Forging Foreign Money, is Misprision of Treason, *per* 14 *Eliz. cap.* 3.

The Judgment in Misprision of Treason, is Forfeiture of Goods forever; Forfeiture of Profits of Land during Life, and Imprisonment during Life.

By the Common Law, concealing a Felony, or procuring the Concealment, or compounding it, was Misprision of Felony.

But if a Man knows that a Felony is committed, and taketh his Goods again, 'tis no Offence, unless he taketh them or other Amends not to prosecute; and then 'tis called *Theft-bote*, which is an Offence more than a Misprision of Felony, because 'tis more than a Concealment of the Felon.

But the punishment is the same in both Cases, *viz.* Fine and Imprisonment, if in a common Person; if in an *Officer*, Fine; and tho'paid, Commitment for a Year.

Other Misprisions, *viz.* A Grand Juror, discovering the Persons indicted, or Evidence; punishable by Fine and Imprisonment.

Any

Any Person assaulting a Judge, the like Punishment.

Abusing a *Juror* for giving a Verdict against the Offender, the like Punishment.

Rescuing a Prisoner from the Bar of *B. R.* loses his Right Hand, Goods, *&c.* Profits of Lands during Life, and perpetual Imprisonment.

Striking, during the Sitting the Courts at *Westminster* in Presence of the Court, or drawing a Weapon, the like Punishment

Drawing a Weapon in Presence of those Courts, or before the Judge of Assize, upon any Judge or Justice, tho' no Stroke given, the like Punishment.

Striking in the Presence of the King, if Blood is drawn, Loss of Right Hand, and perpetual Imprisonment, *per* 33. *H.* 8. *cap.* 12.

Tho' Justices of Peace are not impower'd by their Commission, or by any Statutes, to hear and determine these Offences; yet since 'tis against the Peace, they may cause the Offenders to be taken, and two *Justices* may take Informations upon Oath against such Persons, and put it into Writing, and bind the Witnesses in a Recognizance to prosecute and give Evidence at the Assizes, *&c.*

Money.

IF any refuse lawful Money in Payment, he may be compelled by the Officer of the Place to receive it, and be committed or punished as he thinks fit; and if an Officer refuse it, a *Justice* may punish him at Discretion. 19 *H.* 7. *cap.* 5.

Mittimus.

MUst be to the Common Gaol, by 23 *H.* 8. *cap.* 2. It must be under Seal. It must contain the Cause of Commitment. It must have an apt Conclusion, (*viz.* There to remain till delivered by due Course of Law;) or else the Warrant is void.

Murder,

IS the Killing a Perſon within the Realm upon *Malice Fore-thought*, the Death enſuing within a Year and a Day. *H. P. C. Fol.* 53.

But this Crime is aggravated by the Quality and Condition of the Perſon who commits it; as where a *Maid-Servant* and a *Stranger* conſpired to rob the *Miſtreſs*, and in the Night-time the Servant let the other into the Houſe, and lighted him to her Miſtreſes Bed, where he killed her, the Servant neither doing or ſaying any Thing, but only held the Candle: This is Murder in the *Stranger*, and Petty-Treaſon in the *Servant*. *Moor* 91. *Dyer* 128.

So where the *Wife and her Servant* conſpired to kill the *Husband*, and appointed both Time and Place, and the *Servant* alone in the *Abſence of the Wife*, killed him; this is Petit-Treaſon in both: But if he had been killed by a *Stranger*, the Wife ſhould be hanged, and not burnt, becauſe ſhe cannot be guilty of Petit-Treaſon where the Principal is only guilty of Murder.

This Offence was always puniſhed with the Death of the Offender.

The *Place* where the *Stroke was given* muſt be ſet forth in the Indictment; and therefore it is not ſufficient to ſay, That he aſſaulted the Perſon, and that he gave him a mortal Wound, without ſhewing *in what Place*. 1 *Bulſt.* 203.

Two of my Lord *Dorſet's* Servants quarrelling at the Fire, went out and fought in the Park, *juxta Knowl*, and one was killed; for which the other was indicted, but it did not ſet forth in what *Place* or County the Park was, neither was the Word *percuſſit* in the Indictment, but *dedid vulnus*; and for theſe Reaſons it was quaſhed. 1 *Bulſt* 12.

So when it was *percuſsit cum gladio*, but did not ſay *Felonice*. *Cro. Eliz.* 193.

The Stroke was laid to be *ſuper ſiniſtram partem Lateris*, and did not ſhew in what Part; and this was held certain enough, becauſe 'tis well underſtood what is meant by the Word *Latus*; but where it was *cum pugione in ſiniſtra parte collis percuſſit*, this was held ill, for it ſhould have been *Colli*.

So where the Stroke was alledged to be given at *D.* whereof the plaintiff died at *S*, & *ſic apud D.* he killed him; this is impoſſible. *Noy* 45.

Then as to the *Day* the Indictment was, That the Defendant aſſaulted the perſon on the 12*th* Day of *February* at *Oxford*, *adtunc & ibid. dans ei* a mortal Wound, &c. and that he languiſhed from the 12*th uſque ad.* 13 *Feb*, on which 13*th Day* he died; and ſo the ſaid *R. C.* on the 13*th Day* did kill him; This is impoſſible, becauſe the Word *uſque* excludes the 13*th* Day. 1 *Bulſt.* 203.

But

But where it was, That on the 22 *Januarii, &c. percussit* the Person at *B. dans ei plagam mortalem, &c.* of which he died the 23th of *Feb.* following, and so he murdered him, *die &c. præd'* that must refer to the Day last mentioned; for otherwise there being Two Days mentioned, it would be incertain to which it should relate, *viz.* either to the Day of the Stroke, or Death. *Cro. Eliz.* 739.

But to return to the Word *(Murder)* as above defined, we may examine, *viz.* 1. What is a Killing.

And this may be by several Means, as by laying a Sick Man in the Cold, hiding an Infant under Leaves of Trees, which is afterwards destroyed by Vermin; stirring up a Dog, or any other Beast accustomed to bite or do Mischief, knowing it to be such.

The Person killed, must be *in Rerum Natura*; for if a Woman take Poison to destroy the Child within her, being Quick, 'tis not Felony, but a great Misprision, unless born, and afterwards dies through this Occasion.

Advising to destroy it before born, and afterwards 'tis born and destroyed, the Adviser is Accessary.

3. If a Person be Wounded, and dye beyond Sea, the Offender cannot be punished at Common Law, but may before the Constable and Marshal.

Wounded, and dying upon the Sea, before the Admiral of *England*, by Virtue of the Statute of 22 *H.* 8. *cap.* 13.

Striking on the Sea and dying, *infra Corpus Comitatus*, is an Offence, which my Lord *Hales* tells us is not punishable, *H. P. C. fol.* 54. and yet 'tis not denied but that the Killing shall have Relation to the Death, and not to the Stroke. 4 *Rep.* 41.

Striking in one County, and the Person dieth in another, the Trial shall be where he died.

But Accessary in one County to a Murder done in another, when the Principal is convicted, and that is certified, may be tried in the County where Accessary. *H. P. C.* 54.

Malice Implied, may be collected several Ways, *viz.* by wilful Poisoning; by riding into a Fair with an unruly Horse, knowing him to be so, on purpose to do Mischief, and Death ensues. *Moor* 754. Throwing a Stone over an House amongst a Multitude of People.

These and such like are unlawful Acts; and it appears plainly, that the Person had an Evil Intention of doing Hurt to somy Body, though not against any Person in particular; and this implies Malice.

A Smith struck his Servant with an Iron Bar, and killed him: So if a Father correct his Son, or a School-Master his Scholar, with such Instruments as may probably kill them, and Death ensues, 'tis Murder.

So if a Smith runs a hot Iron into his Servants Belly, or a Mother kicks and

 stamps

ſtamps on her Childs Belly, and Death enſues: In all theſe Caſes 'tis Murder, and the Law ſupplieth the Malice in Perſons who are guilty.

But in a late Caſe, we are told, This is Expreſs Malice, (*viz.*) If a Man aſſaults another with a dangerous Weapon, but without any Provocation, 'tis expreſs Malice from the Nature of the Fact, which is Cruel.

Killing without a Provocation, is ſuch a Provocation as muſt extenuate the Killing from Murder to Manſlaughter, muſt be where there is ſome actual Violence or Striking; for Words alone are no Manner of Provocation, though they are never ſo opprobrious, nor any affronting Geſtures, though never ſo reproachful.

But if angry Words paſs between two Perſons, and then one pulls the other by the Noſe, or fillips him with his Finger, and the Perſon thus aſſaulted kills the other with a Sword, this is but Manſlaughter, becauſe the Peace was broken by the Deceaſed, and with a great Affront to him upon whom he made the Aſſault.

And here it may not be improper to mention *Mawgridge's* Caſe:

He threw a Bottle at Mr. *Cope*, which ſtruck him on the Head, and immediately drew his Sword and gave him a mortal Wound; but between the Time of drawing the Sword and giving the Wound, Mr. *Cope* threw another Bottle at *Mawgridge*, with which he broke his Head, but Mr. *Cope* had no Sword drawn, and never ſpoke a Word afterwards: This was adjudged Murder, for it was out of Malice prepenſed; for the throwing the firſt Bottle was with Deſign to do Miſchief and the drawing his Sword was to proſecute that Deſign; and though Mr. *Cope* threw another Bottle at *Mawgridge* before the Wound was given, that will not alter the Caſe, for it was juſtifiable in him, and in his own Defence.

If two Men fall out, and give each foul Words, and a third Perſon ſtrikes one of them and kills him, this is Murder.

But if *A.* aſſaults *B.* without any Provocation, and draws his Sword and runs at him, and then *B.* draw his Sword in his own Defence, and is killed by *A.* 'tis Murder.

But if two Men fight, and another Perſon coming to aſſiſt one of them, killeth the other, this is *Manſlaughter*, becauſe there was an actual Fighting and ſtriving with Violence between the other two.

Yet if a Man is unduly arreſted or deprived of his Liberty, and makes no Reſiſtance, and another reſcuing him, kills a Man, this is *Murder*, for Injuries muſt not be redreſſed by Force. *Keeling* 60, 61.

If one who is wounded neglects his Cure, or lives diſorderly; yet if he die of thoſe Wounds, 'tis *Murder* or *Manſlaughter*, as the Caſe ſhall appear upon the Evidence againſt the Criminal, becauſe the Wounds were the principal Cauſe of the Death which enſued. *Keeling*, 26.

Stabbed without Weapon drawn. 1 *Jac. cap.* 8.

Give

Five Years after the making this Statute it was held, That if the Person killed had a *Stick* in his Hand, it shall be accounted *a Weapon drawn.*

And since that Time there have been many nice Expositions of this Law; the Words are, *viz*, Stabbing another that hath not *then* any Weapon drawn, or that hath not *then first stricken* the Party which stabs, and the Person dying within 6 Months then next following, this is Murder, and without Clergy. There is a *Proviso*, That the Act shall not extend to one who kills another *Se Defendendo*, or by Misfortune; nor to one who in keeping the Peace, or chastizing his Servant or Child, shall unwillingly commit Manslaughter.

Anno 9 *Car.* 1. One *Byard* struck *Ward*, who struck again, and then *Byard* stabbed the other with a Knife; the Question was, Whether he should have his *Clergy*, because he was struck by the other before he stabbed him? And adjudged he should not, because the Words *first stricken* in the Statute shall be construed the very first Stroke given by the Party slain at the Beginning of the Quarrel, and not any Stroke before the Stab.

So where two quarrel, one throws a Pot at the other, which missing him, the other drew his Sword and killed him; and being indicted on the Statute of Stabbing, the Matter was found specially, and the Doubt did arise upon the Words of the Statute, *viz.* He that stabs another, not having a Weapon *then drawn*, *&c.* whether the Particle *then* should relate to the beginning of the Quarrel, or to the Time of the Stroke given? And by the better Opinion, it was held to extend to the Quarrel; for if in fighting one lets his Sword fall, or throws it at another, and is *then* killed, 'tis plain he had not *then* a Weapon, *viz.* at the Time of the Wound given; but yet, because it was once drawn during the Quarrel, the Prisoner shall not be excluded his Clergy. 3 *Leviniz* 255. 4 *Rep.* 51. 9 *Rep.* 66.

Anno 15 *Car.* One *David Wiliams*, walking on St. *David*'s Day with a Leek in his Hat, was jeered by a Porter, and thereupon *Williams* threw a Hammer out of *Marbury*'s Shop at the Porter, with an Intention to hit him; but he missed the Porter and struck *Marbury*, of which he died; The Question was, Whether this was within the Statute of Stabbing, for *Marbury* had no *Weapon drawn?* And adjudged, that it was not. There is no Reason given for this Judgment by Justice *Jones*, who reports the Case; but I suppose it might be, because *Williams* had no Anger or Displeasure against *Marbury*, and so was within the *Proviso* of the Statute, which exempts any killing by *Misfortune*, as this seemed to be. *Jones* 432.

But it seems *Williams* was not indicted for Murder, but for Manslaughter, on the Statute of Stabbing; if he had been indicted for Murder, he ought to have been found guilty, for the Provocation was not so great as to excite him to kill another. *Keeling* 133.

If the Indictment is, That *R.* stabbed the Person, and that *P.* and *H.*

were present and abetting, and they are all found guilty, R. shall be hanged, but the other Persons shall have their Clergy, for if it can be known who gave the Stab, then tho' in Judgment of Law all those who were present and abetting are Principals, yet the Statute being penal, ought to be extended only to him *who actually stabbed* the other. *Allen* 44.

A Constable killed, or any assisting him in Execution of his Office, the like of any other Magistrate.

This is Murder, but then they must know he was Constable, and coming to keep the Peace, and for that Purpose he ought to command them in the King's Name to keep the peace, otherwise 'tis but Manslaughter in him that kills him.

Officer killed in the Execution of a lawful Warrant, tho' he doth not shew it, being demanded, and though there is a Mistake or Error in the process, but then he must be doing what is warranted by Law, for if he open a Window to arrest, &c. and is killed, 'tis only Manslaughter. *Match.* 3. 1 *Cro.* 132, 183. 4 *Rep.* 91. *Cro. Car.* 386, 537.

An Officer had a Warrant to arrest Sir *H. Ferrers*, Knight, but he was a *Baronet*, and never Knighted, and the Officer was killed in executing his Warrant; This was held to be Manslaughter, because he had no Authority to arrest the *Baronet*, and so his Warrant was illegal. *Cro. Car.* 378.

All who are present and assisting a person arrested, knowing of the Arrest, are principal Murderers if the Officer is killed. *Sid.* 160.

A Collector of the Chimney-Money distrained a Silver Cup; the Maid-Servant, in the Absence of the Master, hinder'd him from going out, for which he beat her against the post and killed her; this was held to be *Manslaughter.* 1 *Vent.* 216.

Several come to rob a park, one kills the Keeper, 'tis Murder in the other, if in the same park, tho' at a Distance when the Fact was done, because their Entry was unlawful, and from thence Malice may be implied. *Palm.* 35. *Jones* 429. 2 *Roll. Rep.* 120. *Moor.* 86.

Several Owlers had loaded Wooll to transport it, the King's Officers opposed them in the Night, one of the Owlers shot out of a Fuzee and killed one of his own Company; this was held by all the Judges to be no Murder.

For it was not found that he discharged the Gun against the King's Officers, tho' it might be reasonably intended he did, because he was armed, and in prosecution of an unlawful Act in which he was obstructed; and in such Case, if he had killed one of his own party, though by Accident, it had been Murder in him, but not in the rest, unless they knew his Design was to kill the Man.

One assaults another with an Intention to rob him, and being resisted, kills the person he assaulted, it's Murder.

If a

If a Goaler, by hard Usage, kills a Prisoner, the like Offence. And executing Martial Law in time of Peace, its Murder. *Malice* may be collected out of Circumstances, shewing the Temper of the person killing.

As if two fight in a Tavern, and are parted, and one of them alledgeth the Inconveniency of the place to fight in, and they appoint another Place to fight presently, where one is kill'd; its *Murder*, because Reason had so far the Mastery of his Passion, as to judge of the Conveniency of the place. *Sid.* 277. 1 *Bulst.* 86 2 *Bulst.* 171.

If two fall out in the Morning, and fight in the After-noon, and one is killed 'tis *Murder*; for there being Time to allay the sudden heat, the second Meeting must be *Malice*.

But some Provocations are so violent, that they mittigate the Crime; As where two Boys fought near their Fathers House, and one being bloody, complained to his Father, who was then a mile off, but he went and beat the Boy, so that he dyed; It is not Murder. *Godb.* 182. 2 *Cro.* 296.

So where the Husband found another in the Act of Adultery with his Wife, 1 *Vent* 158.

Malice Express may appear in the Principal, As, if a man commits a Resolution to do an Unlawful Act, as to Rob an Orchard, and Death ensueth, 'tis *Murder*.

Malice between two, they fight, tho' the Deceased give the first Stroke, 'tis Murder in the other. 1 *Bulst.* 86. 3 *Bulst.* 171. 172. 1 *Roll. Rep.* 360.

If the Deceased challengeth another, who refuseth to fight, but afterwards upon Importunity meeteth and kills him, 'tis Murder.

All who are Present and assisting are Principals. *Sid.* 160.

If they are not present, yet if they come to do an unlawful Act, and are in the same House or Place, though at a distance, 'tis Murder in them.

Tho' Death not intended, if the Act be deliberate and malicious, and Death ensueth, 'tis Murder: As the Keeper of a Park finding a Boy stealing of Wood, tied him to a Horses Tail, which in runing away killed the Boy; this was Murder, because a deliberate Act. *Cro. Car. Holloway*'s Case, 131. *Jones* 198. *Palm.* 547.

Malice between two, the one striketh at the other, and killeth a third Person, 'tis Murder; but if no Malice between them. 'tis Manslaughter.

Malice between two, and the one assaulting the other, kills his Servant coming to his Defence, Murder. *Dyer* 128. *b.*

One buys Poison to kill another, and a third Person eats it and dies, Murder. *Plowd. Com.* 473. 476.

Two or more come to do an unlawful Act, one of them kills a Man, 'tis Murder in both, if abetting or ready to abet, tho' but looking on.

But then the Abettor must know the malicious Design of the other, and the

the Killing must be in Pursuance of that unlawful Act, and not collateral to it.

And not only so, but it must be done deliberately; for if 'tis upon a sudden Affray, and Death ensues, 'tis but Manslaughter.

Besides, the unlawful Act ought to be such which tends to the Hurt of another, either immediately, or by Consequence: as if Persons assemble in a Riotous Manner with offensive Weapons, and one is killed, 'tis Murder.

Two having Malice, fight, the Servant of one of them not knowing the Malice, &c. killeth the other: this is Murder in the Master, and Manslaughter in the Servant.

One commands another to kill a third Person with a Gun, he kills him, not by shooting, but with a Sword; tis Murder in the Person commanding.

But if by Mistake he kills another Person, 'tis Murder in him killing, and the Person commanding is not so much as Accessary to it.

If one command another only to beat a third Person, and upon this Beating, Death ensueth, 'tis *Murder* in the Person commanded, to which he who commands is likewise Accessary, because Death ensued upon that unlawful Act of Beating.

In the War with *France*, Mr. *Mansell* seized some *French* Goods at Sea, and brought them Home; and one *Herbert* pretending to be Deputy Admiral, came with Force to Mr. *Mansell*'s House, and assaulted those who kept Possession of the Goods; a Gentlewoman came to the Door without any Weapon, and was killed with a Stone, which was thrown by Mr. *Herbert*'s Servant at another; and it was held, That this was *Murder* in Mr. *Herbert* and all his Company, for the Person was killed in Defence of the Possession of the House and that made it *Murder*, tho' there was no Malice prepensed. Serjeant *Moor*, who reports this Case, says, That the Person killed was Aunt to both the Gentlemen, and perswaded them to be Friends. *Moor* 87. *Dyer* 128. *b*.

The Judgment in *Murder* must be the common and ordinary Judgment allowed by Law; and it cannot be, that the Offender shall be hanged in Chains, tho' for a notorious Murder, as for stabbing the Duke of *Buckingham* by *E.* but when he is dead, the Body is at the King's Dispofal. *Het* 126.

By the Statute of 24 *H.* 8. *cap.* 5. 'tis enacted, That if any Person should be indicted for the Death of another attempting to Murder, Rob, or commit Burglary, and 'tis so found by Verdict, he shall forfeit no Lands or Goods, but shall be acquitted.

A Man in the Night-time *attempted* to break open the Door of a Dwelling-House, and one who was only a Lodger would have diswaded him from it; who thereupon broke the Windows, and thrust his Rapier at the Lodger, who with a Spit wounded the *Rogue* in the Eye, of which Wound he died: This was held not to Felony, but excusable by this Statute, though it was done by a Lodger, a Lodger, and not by the Master of the House in Defence of his Possession *Cro. Car.* 544.

I shall add but one Case more to this Title, because 'tis a very strange one, *viz.* Husband and Wife had lived many Years together, and became very poor; the Man told his Wife, he was weary of living, and that he would kill himself; the Woman replied, She would die with him: Thereupon he desired her to buy Rats-bane, and they would put it into Ale, and drink it together; she bought it and put it into the Cup, and both drank. The Wife considering what she had done, took Sallet-Oyl and expelled the Poison by vomiting, and recovered, and the Man died. The Question was, Whether this was Murder in the Wife? I do not find it was resolved. *Moor* 754.

By a Statute made in the Reign of King *James* 'tis declared, That where a Bastard-Child shall be *concealed*, it shall be taken to be murdered; so that by this Statute, *Concealment* of the Birth of a Bastard is made the Crime. Now if a Woman is with Child of a Bastard, and going well to Bed is taken with Travelling-pains in the Night, and knocks for some Body to assist her, but is delivered without any Help, and then puts the Child in a Trunk, and conceals it for a Day; if there was no Sign of any Hurt upon the Body of the Child, 'tis not Murder within that Statute, because at first there was no Intent to *conceal* it; and there being no visible Sign of Hurt, it shall be intended the Child was dead-born; but if there had been an Intent to conceal it, then 'tis Murder, tho' the Child was not born alive.

A Condition of a Recognizance to prefer a Bill of Indictment, and to give Evidence at the next General Goal-Delivery, alias *Assizes, to both Juries in case of Murder.*

Vide Title Recognizance.

THE *Condition* of this Recognizance is such, That if the above-bound *W. B.* do personally appear before His Majesty's *Justices* of Gaol-delivery, at the next General Goal-delivery to be holden for the within-named County of *Kent*, and do then and there prefer, or cause to be preferred, a Bill of Indictment against *A. B. C. D. E. F. G. H.* and *J. K.* for the Murder of *L. M.* Gent. deceased, wherewith the said *A. B.* and *C. D.* are chargeable before the within-named *Justice*, and with Suspicion whereof the said *E. F. G. H. J. K.* are also charged before the Justice aforesaid, and do also then and there give such Evidence as he knoweth concerning the Murder aforesaid, as well to the Jurors as shall inquire thereof for our Sovereign Lord the King, as also to the Jurors that shall pass upon the Trial of the said *A. B. C. D. E. F. G. H. J. K.* or any of them for the same, then this Recognizance shall be void, or else it shall stand in full Force and Virtue.

A Condition to prefer a Bill, and give Evidence at Assizes.

THE *Condition* of this Recognizance is such, That if the above-bound *A. B.* do personally appear before His Majesty's Justices assigned to keep the Peace in the above-named County of *C.* at the next General Sessions of the Peace to be holden for the said County at the Castle of *C.* in the County aforesaid, and do then and there prefer, or cause to be preferred, one or more Bill or Bills of Indictment, against *M. W.* of, &c. and do then and there also give such Evidence as he knoweth concerning the same against the said *M. W.* to the Jurors that shall inquire thereof on the behalf of our Lord the King that now is; That then this Recognizance shall be void, and of no effect, or else it shall stand in full force.

Night Walkers. *See* Watch.

IF suspected to be of ill Fame, may be apprehended, (*viz.*) Such who sleep by Day, and haunt Bawdy-houses at Night, or keep suspicious Company, these may be compelled to find Sureties for Good Behaviour. 13 *H.* 7. *cap.* 10. *Popham* 208, *Latch.* 199.

They may be indicted at the Sessions. *Poph.* 208. *Bendl*, 199.

Nusance.

MEN may meet in a peaceable Manner, and with proper Instruments, to remove a *Nusance*, but not in greater Numbers than are needful for that Purpose.

Upon an Indictment for a Nusance, the Court never admits the Person to a small Fine till 'tis removed, and *Affidavit* made thereof, or else certified by Two Justices.

Neither ought the Defendant to take any Exceptions to the Indictment till he hath pleaded to it.

Oaths.

AN Oath is an Affirmation or Denial of any Thing before one or more, who have Authority to give the same for the Advancement of Truth and Right, calling God to Witness that the Testimony is true; and 'tis called a Corporal Oath, because he toucheth the Scripture with his Hand.

There were Four Sorts of Oaths required of Subjects, to testify their Allegiance to the King.

The First was an Oath at Common Law, taken in the Court-Leet.

The Second was by Act of Parliament, 28 *H.* 8. *cap.* 7. which concerned the Supremacy.

The Third was *per* Stat. 1 *Eliz. cap.* 1. which altered the Oath of Supremacy.

The Fourth was the Oath of Allegiance, *per* Stat. 6 and 7. *Jac.* and upon this last Act the Lord *Vaux* was indicted, he refusing to take the Oath, and being convicted on his own Conviction, had Judgment of *Præmunire.*

If an Oath be taken before a Magistrate who hath no Authority to administer, 'tis void; but if 'tis voluntary and false, the Offender was punished formerly in the *Star-Chamber*; and if 'tis in a Spiritual Matter, *viz.* If a Woman swear to marry a Man, and doth not; she may be punished in the Ecclesiastical Court *pro lesione Fidei. Cro. Eliz.* 469. *Knight* vers. *Rushworth.*

Peers are sworn as Witnesses, *in Juramentum probationis*: But when they are Defendants, they answer upon their Honour. *Jones* 154. the Earl of *Lincoln's* Case.

The Oaths of Allegiance and Supremacy were injoined by 1 *Eliz.* and 3 *Jac.* but are now abrogated by the Statute of 1 *Will.* & *Mar. cap.* 8. and these following Oaths injoined, *viz.*

I *A. B.* do sincerely Promise and Swear, That I will be Faithful, and bear true Allegiance to his Majesty King *George. So help me God.*

I *A. B.* do Swear, That I do from my heart abhor, detest and abjure as Impious and Heretical, that damnable Doctrine and Position, That Princes Excommunicated or deprived by the Pope, or any Authority of the See of *Rome*, may be deposed or Murdered by their Subjects, or any other whatsoever: And I do declare, That no Foreign

reign Prince, Person, Prelate, State or Potentate, hath or ought to have any Jurisdiction, Power, Superiority, Pre-eminence or Authority, Ecclesiastical or Spirital, within this Realm. *So help me God.*

Two or more Justices, (*Quorum unus.*) may send Warrants to Constables to summon any above Eighteen Years to take the said Oath; which being lawfully tendred, and refused, the Offender may be committed to Goal, for Three Months without Bail, unless he pay 40 *s.* or any lesser Sum the Person tendring shall think fit, to the Use of the Poor where the Offender did last reside.

If after the End of Three Months he still refuse, he shall be committed for Six Months, unless he pay 5 *l.* and under 10 *l.* and must be bound with Two Sureties to be of the Good Behaviour, and to appear at next Assizes, and there the Oath shall be tendred again in open Court, and if he refuse, &c. shall be incapable of any Office, and be of Good Behaviour till he take the Oaths.

And if he refuse to subscribe the Declaration mentioned in the Statute of 30 *Car.* 2. *cap.* 1. shall be taken to be a Popish Recusant.

The Declaration in the Statute of 30 Car. 2. cap. 1.

I *A. B.* do solemnly and sincerely, in the Presence of God, profess, testify and declare, That I do believe, that in the Sacrament of the Lords Supper there is not any Transubstatiation of the Elements of Bread and Wine into the Body and Blood of Christ, at, or after the Consecration thereof, by any Person whatsoever: And that the Invocation or Adoration of the Virgin *Mary*, or any other Saint, and the Sacrifice of the Mass, as they are now used in the Church of *Rome*, are Superstitions and Idolatrous. And I do solemnly, in the Presence of God, profess, testify and declare, That I do make this Declaration, and every part thereof, in the plain and ordinary Sense of the words read unto me, as they are commonly understood by *English Protestants*, without any Evasion, Equivocation or mental Reservation whatsoever, and without any Dispensation already granted me for this purpose by the Pope, or any other Authority or Person whatsoever, or without any hope of any such Dispensation from any Person or Authority whatsoever, or without thinking that I am, or can

can be acquitted before God or Man, or absolved of this Declaration, or any part thereof, altho' the Pope, or any other Person or Persons, or Power whatsoever, should dispence with, or annul the same, or declare that it was Null and Void from the beginning.

[*Note*, That before a Magistrate, or other Officer, enters upon his Office, he first takes the Oaths of the *1st of Wm.* & *Mary*, *cap.* 8. as before set down, and then he subscribes this Declaration, 30 *Car.* 2. *cap.* 1.

By 7 *and* 8 *Will. cap.* 27. If after 1 *May* 1696. any refuse to take the said Oaths when rendred, or to appear when summoned, shall be liable to the Penalties of Popish Recusants Convict.

Shall not give a Vote at the Election of Members for Parliament.

The Person tendring, may mitigate the Penalty of 40 *s. per* 1 *Will.*

By 7 *and* 8 *Will.* upon Refusal to swear, or to appear upon Summons, the Justice must enter in Parchment the Names and Abode of the Persons, &c. with the Time of the Tender, and certify it to Assizes or Sessions, who may certify it to the *Exchequer*, who may issue Process against Goods and Lands of the Offender.

By the same Statute, 'tis a *Præmunire* for any Lawyer to practise after 25 *May* 1696. not having before taken the Oaths, and made and subscribed the Declaration. 25 *Car.* 2. *cap.* 2.

I *A. B.* do declare, That I do believe that there is not any Transubstantiation in the Sacrament of the Lords Supper, or in the Elements of Bread and Wine, at or after the Consecration thereof, by any Person whatsoever.

Lords Spiritual and Temporal must not Sit or Vote before they take the said Oaths, and make and subscribe the Declaration mentioned, 30 *Car.* 2. *cap.* 1. 1 *W.* & *M.*

Two Justices out of the Sessions may tender those Oaths to any Person of 18 Years of Age or upwards, which stands convicted or indicted of *Recusancy*, or to those who have not received the Sacrament twice in the Year before, &c. 3. *Jac. cap.* 4.

And now by a late Statute 'tis provided, That any Two Justices of the Peace (*Quorum unus*) may summon before them such Persons whom they shall suspect to be disaffected to the Government, and may tender the following Oath to him; and if he refuse to take it, then he must certify his Christian and Sir-

Name, and Place of Abode, to the next Quarter-Sessions, there to be recorded; which Record the Clerk of the Peace shall certify, either to the Court of *Chancery* or *Queen's Bench*, and there likewise to be recorded; and if the Person so refusing shall not at the next Term or Sessions, after such Refusal, appear in that Court where the Certificate shall be returned, and take and subscribe the said Oath, he shall be adjudged a Popish Recusant Convict, and shall forfeit such Penalties as such a Recusant ought to do.

The Oath to be taken by every Person who shall be admitted to any Office, Civil or Military.

I *A. B.* do truly and sincerely acknowledge, profess, testifie and declare in my Conscience, before God and the World, That our Sovereign Lord King *George* is Lawful and Rightful King of this Realm, and of all other his Majesty's Dominions, and Countries thereunto belonging.

A Certificate for one who hath taken the Oaths, and subscribed the Declaration, 1 W. & M. cap. 8.

These are to Certifie, That *A. B.* of the Parish of, *&c.* in the County aforesaid, Esq; came before his Majesty's Justices of the Peace at the Sessions held at *M.* on Wednesday, *&c.* and then and there before the said Justices at the said Sessions, did take the Oaths mentioned in a Statute made in the first year of the Reign of the late K. *William* and Q. *Mary*, entit. *An Act for the abrogating the Oaths of Allegiance and Supremacy, and appointing other Oaths*; and did likewise then and there make and subscribe the Declaration mentioned in a Statute made in the 25 year of the Reign of the late K. *Charles* the second, entit. *An Act for preventing Dangers which may happen from Popish Recusants*; and that what he did then and there concerning the Premises is Registred according to the direction of the Act first above mentioned. Signed, —— Dated, &c.

A Mittimus,

A Mittimus for Refusing, &c. *and not paying the* 40 *s*.

To the Keeper, &c.

WE *H. P.* and *W. M.* two of his Majesty's Justices of the Peace for the County aforesaid, whereof one is of the *Quorum*, do by virtue of our Warrant, commit to your Custody the Body of *A. B.* of *C.* for refusing to take the Oaths mentioned in a Statute made in the first year of the Reign of the late K. *William* and Q. *Mary*, entit. *An Act for abrogating*, &c. which said Oaths were lawfully tendred to the said *A. B.* and for that he hath refused to pay the Sum of 40 *s* to the Poor of the Parish of *H.* where the said *A. B.* did last reside, according as appointed by the said Act, Requiring you the said Keeper to receive the said *A. B.* into your Custody, and him safely to keep without Bail or Mainprize for the space of three Months; and for your so doing this shall be your Warrant. Given under our Hands and Seals, &c.

Dissenters are bound to take the Oaths above-mentioned, and to subscribe the Declaration mentioned 30 *Car.* 2.

Justices in Sessions are to tender and administer the Oaths to Persons who shall offer themselves.

Those Dissenters who scruple taking any Oaths, must make and subscribe a Declaration of Fidelity, and likewise a Profession of their Belief, 1 *Will.* &c. *cap.* 18.

The Declaration of Fidelity.

I *A. B.* do sincerely promise, and solemnly declare before God and the World, That I will be true and faithful to King *George*; and I do solemnly profess and declare, That I do from my heart abhor, detest and renounce, as Impious and Heretical, that damnable Doctrine and Position. That Princes excommunicated or deprived by the Pope, or any Authority of the See of *Rome*, may be deposed or murdered by their Subjects, or any other whatsoever. And I declare, That no Foreign Prince, Person, Prelate, State or Potentate, hath or ought to have any Power, Jurisdiction, Superiority, Pre-eminence or Authority, Ecclesiastical or Spiritual, within this Realm.

The

The Profession of Belief.

I *A. B.* do profess Faith in God the Father, and in Jesus Christ the Eternal Son, the true God, and the holy Spirit, one God blessed for evermore; & to acknowledge the holy Scriptures of the Old and New Testament to be given by Divine Inspiration.

They must likewise make and subscribe the Declaration mentioned in the Statute of 30 *Car.* 2. *cap.* 1.

Any Justice of Peace may at any Time require a Dissenter to make and subscribe Declarations, and to take the Oaths or Declarations, of Fidelity, (if he scruple the taking any Oath.)

Upon Refusal, may commit him to Prison, without Bail, and certify his Name in the next Sessions, where he resides.

If the Person committed shall, upon a second Tender at the Sessions, refuse, &c. it shall be recorded, and he shall be then taken for a Popish Recusant convict.

1. *The Oath of a Bailiff or Under-Sheriff.*

I *A. B.* do Swear, That I will not use or exercise the Office of a Bailiff or Under-Sheriff of *D.* Corruptly during the time I shall remain therein; Neither will I accept, receive, or take by any colour, means or device whatsoever, or consent to the taking any manner of Fee or Reward of any Person for Impannelling or Returning any Inquest, Jury or Tales, in any Court of Record for the King, or between Party and Party, above 2 *s.* or the value thereof, or such Fees as are allowed and appointed for the same by the Laws or Ordinances of —— But will, according to my Power, truly and indifferently, with convenient speed, impannel all Jurors, and return all such Writ or Writs touching the same, as shall appertain to be done by my Duty or Office, during the time I shall remain in the said Office. *So help me GOD.*

The Penalty is to be divided between the King and Prosecutor; and Justices in Sessions have Power to hear and determine, and to award Process.

2. *Oath of a Constable who attendeth on a Jury.*

YOu shall well and truly keep together every Person sworn of this Jury, in some convenient place, without Meat, Drink, Fire, Candl-

Candle or Lodging: You shall not suffer any person whatsoever to speak to them, or any of them; neither shall you your self speak to them until such time as they be agreed of their Verdict, unless it be to ask them if they be agreed of their Verdict. *So help you God.*

3. *Of a Clerk of the Peace in Sessions, before he enters upon his Office,* 1 W. & Mary, cap. 21.

I *A. B.* do Swear, That I have not, neither will I pay any Sum or Sums of Money, or other Reward whatsoever, or given any Bond or other Assurance to pay any Money, Fee or Profit, directly or indirectly, to any Person or Persons, for nominating or appointing me Clerk of the Peace of *Middlesex. So help me God.*

4. *The Oath of the Church-Warden.*

YOu shall execute the Office of a Church-warden in the Parish of *W.* where you are chosen for this ensuing year, according to your Skill and Discretion in his Majesty's Laws, *&c. So help you God.*

5. *The Oath of a High-Constable, when he delivers in his Presentments.*

YOu shall true Presentment make to the Grand Inquest, of all Offences and Misdemeanours done or committed within your Hundred, and which are in any wise come to your knowledge, and belonging to you to Present, without any Concealment. *So help you GOD.*

6. *The Oath of a Constable.*

YOu shall Swear well and truly to execute the Office of a Constable for the Parish of *M.* for the year next ensuing, and until another shall be Sworn in your Room, or until you shall be lawfully discharged from the said Office. *So help you God.*

7. *The Oath of a Coroner.*

YOu shall Swear, That you will truly serve the King and his People in the Office of a Coroner, and as one of his Majesty's Coroners

Coroners of this County of *H.* and therein you ſhall diligently and truly do all things appertaining to your ſaid Office, according to the beſt of your Knowledge and Power, both for the Kings Profit, and the good of the Inhabitants within the ſaid County, taking ſuch Fees as you ought by Law. *So help you GOD.*

8. *The Oath of a Juſtice of the Peace,* 13 *Edw.* 3. *cap.* 3.

YOu ſhall Swear, That as a Juſtice of Peace for the County of *L.* in all the Articles of the *Kings* Commiſſion to you directed, you ſhall do equal Right to the Poor and Rich, after your Cuning, Wit and Power, and after the Laws and Cuſtoms of this Realm, and Statutes thereof made. You ſhall not be of Council with any Perſon in Quarrel depending before you; and that you hold your Seſſions after the Form of the Statutes thereof made, and the Iſſues, Fines & Amerciaments that ſhall happen to be made, and all Forfeitures which ſhall fall before you, you ſhall cauſe to be entered, without Concealment or Imbezling, and truly ſend them to the *Kings* Exchequer. You ſhall not Let, for Gift or other Cauſe, but well and truly you shall do the Office of a Juſtice of the Peace in that behalf; and that you take nothing for your Office of Juſtice of the Peace to be done, but of the *King*, and Fees accuſtomed, and Coſts limited by the Statute. You ſhall not direct, nor cauſe to be directed, any Warrant (by you to be made) to the Parties, but to the Conſtables of the ſaid Counties, or other the *Kings* Officers or Miniſters, or other indifferent Perſons, to do Execution thereof. *So help you GOD.*

The Nomination of Officers by the Juſtices.

WE his Majeſty's Juſtices of the Peace of the ſaid County of *H.* whoſe Hands and Seals are hereunto ſet, do Nominate and Appoint *L. M.* of the Townſhip of *P.* in the ſaid County, *Aſſeſſor*, of of the Township aforesaid, and *M. N.* of the said Township to be *Collector* of the same, Commanding each of them to take upon him his respective Office aforesaid, until he shall be from thence lawfully Discharged, and forth-with to repair to one of his Majesty's Justices of the Peace of the County aforesaid, before him to take his Oath for the faithful Execution of the said respective Office. Given under our Hands and Seals at, *&c.*

Orchards.

A Warrant against Robbers of Orchards.

WHereas it hath been duly proved upon Oath before me, That *M. K.* of your Town of *S.* Weaver, hath within three Months last past, Robbed the Orchard or Garden of *G. K.* of your said Town, and carried away great Quantities of Apples, &c. (*Or digged up his fruit-trees, or cut Corn, Grass, or pulled up his Fence, &c.*) to the value of 50 *s.* And that *S. M.* of your Town, Baker, hath abetted him in so doing, and received and bought of him divers of the same things, to the great damage of the said *G. K.* contrary to the late Acts of Parliament in that case made and Provided. *I do Therefore* hereby Order and Require, That the said *M. K.* shall within *six* days after Notice to him given of this my Order, pay to the said *G. K.* 20 *s.* and that the said *S. M.* do within *six Days* after Notice to him given of this my order, pay likewise unto the said *G. K.* 30 *s.* more, in recompence to him for his Wrongs aforesaid; and that these payments be made in the presence of the said Constable hereby Commanded, upon Request, to see it done: And hereof you are forth-with to give them Notice; and if either of them shall not pay the same, that then you do give me Notice thereof, to the end that they may be farther proceeded against according to the said Statute (43 *Eliz. cap.* 7. 15 *Car.* 2. *cap.* 2.) And hereof fail not, *&c.* Given under my, *&c.*

Upon Non-payment of the of the aforesaid Sums.

WHereas it hath been duly proved upon Oath before me, That *M. K.* of your Town of *S.* Weaver, hath within *three Months* last past, Robbed, *&c.* (*as in the former, to the words (made and provided)* Wherefore, the Premises considered, and that I judge the said Offenders *M. K.* & *S. M.* unable to make Satisfaction for the said Wrong. I do hereby Order that they be forth-with committed to the said Constable of *S.* to be Whipt; the which you are hereby Required forth-with to do, as you will answer the contrary at your Peril. Given under, *&c.*

By the *Stat*. 43 *Eliz. cap.* 7. the Conviction is by one Witness before one Justice and to make Satisfaction, or be Whipt. The Officer neglecting his Duty, to be Imprisoned till the Offender be punished.

Barking Fruit-Trees, forfeits treble Damages to the party grieved, and 10 *l.* to the King; The Damages to be recovered by Action of Trespass. 37 *Hen.* 8 *cap.* 8.

Perjury,

IS an Offence, where a *Lawful Oath* is administred to a Witness by any who hath *Authority* so to do in any *Judicial* Proceeding, and the Person sweareth falsely, either himself, or by the Subornation of another, in a Matter *material* to the Issue or Cause.

'Tis punishable either at *Common Law*, or by the Statute 5 *Eliz. c.* 9. A false Oath in any *Court* of *Record*, or in any *Judicial* Proceeding, tho' not in a Court of Record, is *Perjury* at Common Law, tho' 'tis not in any Thing *material* to the Issue: *Stiles* 374. *Roll. Abr.* 2 *Part* 257, 258. *Sid.* 274.

And therefore Perjury in the *Spiritual Court*, or in a *Court Baron*, is punishable at *Common Law*: But where the Indictment is upon the *Statute*, it must appear to be committed in a *Court of Record*; as if the Defendant is indicted for *procuring* a Witness to take a false Oath before the Town-Clerk of *London*; this is not within the Statute, for 'tis *coram non Judice*, and the *Subornation* must be to give Evidence in a *Court of Record*. 3 *Leon.* 170.

So where a Man was prosecuted in the *Star-Chamber* for a Perjury in the *Court of Requests*, where the Freehold of the Land came in Question; it was resolved by all the *Judges*, That the Man was not punishable, because that Court had no Authority to examine Titles of Land, and therefore what he swore was no more than an idle Oath. *Yelv.* 3.

But if a Man swear in common Discourse, that he hath a Property in a Thing when really he hath not: or if a Constable is sworn to execute his Office truly, and doth not; these and such-like Oaths are called *Extrajudicial*, and are punishable either at Common Law, or by the Statute of Perjury.

If an Indictment is grounded upon the Common Law, there needs not so great a Certainty in it as if brought on the Statute, *Sid.* 100.

By the 5 *Eliz.* 'tis enacted, *That whosoever shall procure another to commit corrupt Perjury in any Court of Record, or* in perpetuam rei Memoriam, *the Suborner shall forfeit* 40 *l.* *being convicted; and if not worth it, then he shall be committed Six Months without Bail, and shall stand in the Pillory one Hour in some Market-Town adjoyning, or where the Offence was committed, and be never more a Witness till Judgment reversed.*

The

The Suborned, or he who by his own Act commits wilful Perjury, shall, upon Conviction, forfeit 20 l. *and be committed Six Months without Bail, and be disabled to be a Witness till Judgment is reversed; and if not worth* 20 l. *then to be set in the Pillory as aforesaid, and have both his Ears nailed.*

One Moiety of the Forfeitures to the King, *the other to the Party grieved who will sue for the same.*

Justices in Sessions have Power to hear and determine, &c. *the Offences against this Statute.*

My Lord *Coke*, in his Paraphrase upon this Statute, tells us, That the Indictment must set forth the *Judicial* Proceeding; it must also shew, that the Oath was taken in something material to the Issue, because the Act gives the Remedy to the Party grieved, and if the Deposition is not in the Thing which is conducing to the Issue, the Party is not grieved. *Cro. Car.* 152. 3 *Inst.* 165.

Perjury may be committed in an *Answer in Chancery*, tho' not in a matter charged in the Bill; but then the Indictment must be laid at *Common Law*, because 'tis in a Thing not *material* to the Issue: But if it had been in a Deposition, 'tis not Perjury, if not contrary in a Matter particularly charged in the Interrogatories, because the Commissioners, who administer the *Oath*, have not Power but only in Matters therein charged. *Sid.* 274.

The Reason why Perjury cannot be punished by the *Statute* for a false *Affidavit* taken before a Master in *Chancery*, or for a false *Answer*, is, because the Statute extended only to *Witnesses* in Causes between the *Parties*; but such false *Affidavit* may be punished as aforesaid, by an Indictment at Common Law; and in such Case the *Affidavit* must be filed, and after the Perjury is assigned, you must conclude *prout patet per Recordum. Stiles* 336.

But if it appears that the *Oath* was made in something *conducing to the Issue*, setting forth that the *Master* had Power to administer an Oath, the Indictment may be good upon *the Statute*.

If an Indictment is at *Common Law*, supposing the Perjury to be committed in a *Deposition* to Interrogatories in *Chancery*, you need not set forth to what Interrogatory; but if 'tis upon *the Statute*, then you must shew that the Commission was under the Great Seal of *England*, that it may appear to the Court that the Commissioners had Authority to administer the *Oath*, and you must assign the Perjury to be in a Point conducing to the *Issue* in *Chancery*, and shew how it concerned the same.

So likewise, if it be upon *the Statute*, it must appear to be *willful* Perjury; for if 'tis that the Defendant *falso & deceptive deposuit*, 'tis not good, tho' the Indictment includes *& sic commisit voluntarium Perjurium*, because the one is no positive Allegation that he did it *wilfully*; and the other is but a wrong Conclusion from the Premisses.

If Issue be joyned upon Indictments, and the Prosecutor will not try it, the

Defendant may bring it on by *Proviso*, tho' 'tis not in the Case of the *King*, because 'tis for the Benefit of the Subject not to lie under such an Imputation.

And because the Fact shall be tried, the Courts above do not grant *Certioraries* to remove these Indictments, nor quash them upon Motions before Trial.

Neither after Trial do they grant a *new one*, tho' there is apparent Cause; but this must be understood where the Defendant is acquitted, for 'tis otherwise where he is found guilty. *Sid.* 49. 1 *Lev.* 9.

R. was convicted of Perjury, upon the Evidence of *D.* and afterwards *R.* convicted *D.* of Perjury in the very same Matter; but before he can be restored to his Credit, he must bring a Writ of Error to reverse the Judgment upon the first Perjury. *Sid.* 217.

I shall mention a Case or two more, and conclude this Title.

B, a Midwife, was indicted for Perjury; the Case was thus, *viz.* One *Dormer* was Tenant for Life, with Remainder in Tail to his Son, and for want of such Issue to his Daughter, &c. he married and lodged with his Wife in *Chancery-Lane*, and in a short Time died; the Wife soon after his Death declared, That she was delivered of a Daughter; and upon a Trial in Ejectment between the Infant and him in Remainder, it was proved that she was delivered by Circumstances usual in such Cases; but the Midwife deposed, That this was the Child of a poor Woman in St. *Giles*'s *in the Fields*, which she bought of the Mother for Half a Crown, and that she conveyed it into the Bosom of Mrs. *Dormer* who cried out, and then the Midwife took the Child from her, and that there was a Bladder of Blood, and some other Things provided by her to shew the After-Birth. The Jury gave Credit to the Midwife, and acquitted her of the Perjury.

Moor. 657. A Bill in *Chancery* was filed against *B.* and *B.* put in his Answer, and made Affidavit, that *C.* was so ill that he could not travel; when the Cause came to be heard, *C.* came into Court, and affirmed, That he was not sick, but that it was a Contrivance of *B.* who desired him to feign himself sick in Bed, that he might depose he left him so. The Lord Keeper *Egerton* ordered both Parties to attend, and to be examined on Interrogatories, and *B.* denied the Practice; but *C.* affirm'd it, and produced some Witnesses, who proved it very plainly. Now this being double Perjury, for making a false Affidavit, and afterwards denying the Practice on Interrogatories, he was fined 20 *l.* to the *King*, and committed. This I have mentioned, because there have been some Doubts whether the *Chancery* could punish Perjury.

Price was *indicted* upon the Statute, for that he being produced a Witness for the *King* upon the Trial in an Information, he did forswear himself, and shewed wherein, and it was held, That a Witness for the King cannot be punished by an *Indictment On the Statute*. Which is meerly at the Suit of the *King*, for he cannot punish his own Witness, but he may be prosecuted upon the

the Statute by an *Information*, because one Moiety of the Penalty goes to the Informer.

Sir *John Jackson* obtained a Verdict against one *Primate*, in Trespass, who indicted the Witnesses for Perjury; and this coming to a Trial, Sir *John* ordered his Servants to beat the Witnesses who were to prove the Perjury; which was done, so as they could not appear that Day: And thereupon the Defendants were acquitted. And because after an Acquittal in a Criminal Case a new Trial cannot be granted, therefore the Court directed an Information against Sir *John Jackson* for this Offence, and he was convicted upon it, and fined 1000 *l.* and bound to his Good Behaviour for a Year. *Lev.* 124. *Sid.* 153.

Pick-Pocket.

THIS is called, by my Lord *Hales*, Larceny, from the Person, without putting him in Fear, for 'tis done *clam & secrete*, without his Knowledge; and in such Case, the Offender shall not have the Benefit of his Clergy, for 'tis taken away by 8 *Eliz. cap.* 4.

But 'tis not Capital, unless the Thing taken be of the Value of 12 *d.* or more; for though the Statute took away the Privilege of Clergy, it did not alter the Offence, but it remains still Petit-Larceny, if under that Value. Therefore,

1. It must be *clam & secrete.* 2. The Thief must have the actual Possession of the Thing taken. 3. It must be without putting in Fear.

Pillory.

THIS is an infamous Punishment used here in the *Saxon* Times, and since that appointed by several Statutes, as,

51 *H.* 3. On Bakers. 31 *Ed.* 1. On Fore-stallers. 11 *H.* 7. For false Weights. 33 *H.* 8. *cap.* 1. Getting Money by Counterfeit-Letters. 2 *Ed.* 6. *cap.* 15. Workmen conspiring about Wages, second Offence. 5 *Ed.* 6. *cap.* 6. Counterfeiting Seals of Cloath, or taking them off. 5 *Eliz. cap.* 9. Perjury.

Justices of Peace should be well advised before they give *Judgment* herein, and the safest Way is to follow the Acts of Parliament. 3 *Inst.* 219.

Poor.

IT was the Complaint of my Lord Chief, Justice *Hales*, That the Laws of this Kingdom are defective in the Provision for the Poor, and that (contrary to all other Nations) the more populous we are, still we are the poorer.

But as the Law now stands, which is chiefly that of 43 *Eliz. cap.* 2. the Fault seems wholly to be in the Overseers of the Poor, who have only got a Custom of taxing the Parish, and neglect their Duty in the most material Things relating to their Poor.

These Persons are usually nominated in the *Easter-Week*, or within a Month afterwards, and this by an Appointment under the Hands and Seals of two Justices dwelling in or near the Parish, or Division where the Parish lieth. The Form is thus:

WE whose Names are subscribed, being Justices of the Peace for the County of *K.* do appoint *A. B.* and *C. D.* of, *&c.* in the said County, to be Overseers of the Poor of the said Parish, for and during the Space of one whole Year next ensuing the Date hereof, according to the Form of the Statute in that Case made and provided. *Given* under our Hands and Seals, *&c.*

Justices Order to appoint an Overseer in the Place of one that has fined.

W*Hereas* We His Majesty's Justices of the Peace for the said County, (*Quorum unus*) have, out of the List of Names returned to us to nominate and appoint Overseers of the Poor of the Parish of, *&c.* for the Year One Thousand Seven Hundred and Fourteen, chosen *A. B.* of, *&c.* in the Room and Place of *C. D.* (who was lately chosen, and fined for the same;) And he the said *A. B.* together with *E. F.* before nominated, appointed and chosen, are hereby commanded, together with the Church-wardens of the said Parish, to provide for their said Poor according to the Form of the Statute in such Case made. *Given* under our Hands and Seals, *&c.*

Justices neglecting to nominate, forfeit 5 *l.* 43 *Eliz. cap.* 2.

By this Statute, they are to meet every Month in the Parish-Church, if not sick, or having some other just Excuse to be allowed by two Justices; and the Intent of their Meeting is to consider of some proper Methods, not only

only to tax the People, and apply the Money for Relief of the Poor, but to raise by such Taxation a convenient Stock of Flax, Hemp, Wooll, Thread, Iron, and other necessary Stuff, to set them to Work.

If they neglect thus to meet, they forfeit 20 *s.* for every Neglect to the Use of the Poor.

We have Laws now in Force, to confine Men to certain Places of Habitation, which is a Sort of Imprisonment, not for a Fault, but for a Misfortune in being poor.

But by a late Act, the Liberty of a poor Man is a little inlarged, for now he may remove into another Parish where he may have Work; but then he must have a Certificate under the Hands and Seals of the Church-wardens and Overseers, or the major Part of them; or under the Hands and Seals of the Overseers where there are no Church-wardens, acknowledging the Person therein mentioned to be an Inhabitant legally settled in the Parish. 8 & 9. *Will.*

This Certificate must be attested by two Witnesses, and allowed and subscribed by two Justices, and delivered to the Officers of the parish to which he removeth.

And this shall oblige the first parish to receive the poor Man and his Family, when he stands in *Need* of *Relief*.

And by a subsequent Law 'tis declared, That the person who shall come into a parish by such Certificate, shall not be adjudged to have a lawful Settlement by any Act whatsoever, unless he shall take a Lease of 10 *l. per Annum*, or execute some annual Office in such parish. 9 & 10. *Will.*

In *Trinity*-Term, 2 *Annæ*, a Question did arise between two parishes in *Northampton*, upon an Order removed into *B. R.* by *Certiorari*; which was thus:

A person who was not legally settled in the parish who gave the Certificate, but who had lived there for some time, went into another parish by Virtue of the Certificate, by which the parish who gave it owned him to be settled as an Inhabitant with them: Afterwards, being poor, the parish from which he came took him again: but upon Inquiry, found that he was never lawfully settled with them, but had gain'd a Settlement in another place before they gave this Certificate, and thither they removed him: The Parish to which he was removed, appeals; because those who had given the Certificate, had owned him to be an Inhabitant setled with them; but the Certificate was held by the Court to be only an Evidence of a Settlement, and so the first Order was confirmed.

The persons to be maintain'd by a parish-Charge, are of two Sorts, *viz.* poor by Impotency, as *aged Persons*, *Infants Ideots* or persons *visited by Sickness*.

2. poor by Casualty, as *Persons maim'd*; House-keepers decayed by *Fire*, *Robbery*, or being bound for others and paying their Debts.

And every Inhabitant and Occupier of Houses, Lands, Tythes, Mines or

Underwoods, are to be taxed towards this Charge, according to the visible Estate which he hath or possesseth in the parish where taxed, and not elsewhere.

This Tax is either upon Lands or Goods, but one and the same person is seldom taxed for both.

The Farmer or Occupier, and not the Landlord, is liable to this Tax; for it arises by reason of the Land in the parish, and the Landlord is never assessed for his Rent.

The most reasonable Way of Land, is according to a pound Rate, and not according to the Quantity of the Land.

Where a Man hath Land, and a great Stock of Wares, as a Clothier, *&c.* he may be taxed for both, but not for such Stock or Goods with which he doth use to manure his Lands.

When Goods are rated, it ought to be after the Value of Lands, *viz.* Goods of the Value of 100 *l.* shall be rated at 5 *l. per Annum* as Lands are; and the person must be charged only in that place where the Goods are at the Time of the Assessment, for if he hath no Goods where assessed, and is distrained, he may have an Action of Trespass, *&c.*

If the parish is not able to maintain its own poor, two Justices may tax any other parish within the Hundred, and the Sessions may tax any parish within the County.

If a parish extendeth into two Counties, or Liberties, the Justices in such Case shall intermeddle with that part which lies within their respective Jurisdictions; but the Overseers shall act in the whole parish, and not divide themselves. 1 *Kent.* 350.

If there is a Vill, a parish which formerly had a Church or Chappel, and parochial Rites, and Officers chosen by the Inhabitants, and a separate Taxation made, *&c.* this is a parish within the Act. *Hutt.* 93. *Cro. Car.* 92.

But making Rates since the Statute, and proof of a Chappel being in a Village before, will not make it a parish with all other parochial Rites.

The Title of an Assessment for the Poor.

W. in the County of *Kent ss.* AN Assessment made on the Inhabitants of the parish aforesaid, for and towards the necessary Relief of the poor thereof for this present Year, commencing, *&c.*

A. B. }
C. D. } Church-Wardens.

E. F. }
G. H. } Overseers.

A Con-

A Confirmation of the Rate by the Inhabitants.

WE whose Names are subscribed to this Assessment, being Inhabitants of the Parish aforesaid, have seen and perus'd the same, and the several Sums above-mentioned are, by our Approbation, rated upon the respective Persons according to the best of our Judgment.

Confirmed by Two Justices.

RAtified and allowed by us, Two of His Majesty's Justices of the Peace for the County aforesaid.

J. M. P. L.

The Rate being thus confirmed, if any Person shall refuse to pay, *&c.* it may be levied by Warrant from two Justices by Distress, *&c.* and if that cannot be taken, then two Justices may commit without Bail till Payment, *&c.* The Form is,

A Warrant to distrain for the Poor's Tax.

To the Overseers of the Poor of the Parish of, &c.

Kent ss. WHereas Complaint upon Oath hath been made unto us, That *A. B.* and *C. D.* both of your Parish, Husbandmen, being duly and severally assessed; that is to say, *A. B.* in 2 *s.* and *C. D.* in 4 *s.* for and towards the necessary Relief of the Poor of the said Parish, have and do refuse to pay the same as by Law they ought: *These are therefore* to command you, That forthwith you, or one of you, do levy the said respective Sums of Money upon the said *A. B.* and *C. D.* by Distress and Sale of their respective Goods: and in Default of such Distress, that then you certify the same to us. *Given* under our Hands and Seals, *&c.* *A. B. E. G.*

A *Mittimus* where a Distress cannot be had.

To the Keeper, &c.

WHereas *A. B.* and *C. D.* both of, *&c.* were lawfully and duly assessed the respective Sums of, *&c.* for and towards the necessary Relief of the Poor of the said Parish, and that they refused to pay the said Sums, and thereupon a Warrant was directed to the Church-wardens and Overseers of the Poor of the Parish aforesaid, under the Hands and Seals of, *&c.* two of His Majesty's Justices of the Peace for the said County, to levy the same by Distress and Sale of the Goods of the said Offenders; And whereas it appeareth unto us, That the said *A. B.* and *C. D.* have no Goods and Chattels upon which a Distress may or can be made, and that the said *A. B.* and *C. D.* do still refuse to pay the respective Sums upon them assessed: *We therefore* herewithal do send you the Bodies of the said *A. B.* and *C. D.* commanding you to receive them into your Custody, and that they remain therein without Bail or Mainprize, until they pay the said respective Sums. *Given* under our Hands and Seals, *&c.*

But if any one thinks himself grieved by a Tax, he may appeal to the Sessions, whose Determination is final.

Sometimes the Sessions refer the Matter back again to two Justices, to examine the Equality of the Taxes, and then those Justices may confirm it, if they see Cause.

These Overseers must within Four Days after the End of their Year, and after other Overseers are nominated, give up their Accounts before two Justices in these Particulars:

1. What Money they have received, or what is assessed and not received.
2. What Stock either they or the Poor have in their Hands.
3. What Apprentices they have put out.
4. What Poor they have Relieved.

If they refuse to account, two Justices may commit them to Gaol, there to remain without Bail till they account, and pay the Money in their Hands to succeeding Overseers.

If they make a false Account, they may be bound over to Sessions, and there indicted.

If they refuse to deliver over what remains in their Hands, two Justices, by Warrant directed to succeding Officers, may appoint them to levy it by Distress, *&c.* and if that cannot be taken, then may commit them, *ut prius.*

A Warrant to make the Overseer account.

To the Constable of, &c.

These are in His Majesty's Name to command you, That you forthwith give Notice to the Church-wardens and Overseers of the Poor of the Parish of, *&c.* in the County aforesaid, for the Year last past, personally to appear

appear before us at, &c. on, &c. to give us a true and perfect Account in Writing of Things by them done relating to their said respective Offices: *And you are hereby required to signify unto them, that they do then and there certify unto us the Names of such other Inhabitants within your said Parish as are thought fit to be Overseers of the Poor there for the Year ensuing.*

This last Clause may be left out where other Overseers are already appointed.

A Warrant to levy the Arrears in the Hands of former Overseers.

To the Overseers of the Poor of the Parish of, &c.

Kent ss. WHereas it appeareth unto us upon your Complaint upon your Oaths, That *A. B.* and *C. D.* Church-wardens, &c. and *E. F.* and *G. H.* Overseers of the Poor of the said Parish for the Year last past, were in Arrear to the said parish in the Sum of 10 *l.* for Monies by them collected and received, and not disbursed, in the Execution of their Office, and have not yet paid the same to you; *These are therefore* to command you, That you, or some of you, do levy the said 10 *l.* by Distress and Sale of the Goods of, &c. rendring to them respectively the Overplus; and in Default of such Distress, that then you forthwith certify us of the same. *Given* under our Hands and Seals, &c.

A Warrant to Overseers to pay what is in Arrear to a poor Person, and to continue to relieve him.

To the Overseers of the Poor, &c.

Kent ss. WHereas Complaint hath been made unto me by *S. M.* of your Parish, Widow, that the former Overseers of the Poor of the said Parish, did pay unto the said *S. M.* the Sum of 2 *s. per Week*, for and towards the Relief of her self and Children, and that you do refuse to pay the said Weekly Allowance unto her, so that she is utterly disabled to make any Provision for her self and her said Children; *These are therefore* to require you, upon sight hereof, to pay unto the said *S. M.* all such Arrears as are become due since you have forborn to pay the same, and that you continue unto her the former Allowance of 2 *s. per* Week, or forthwith shew Cause why you refuse so to do. *Given* under my Hand, &c.

A Warrant commanding the Overseers to relieve a poor Person.

To the Overseers of the Poor of the Parish of, &c.

Kent ss. WHereas Complaint upon Oath hath been made unto me, That *A. B.* of your Parish, Labourer, is very poor and impotent, and utterly disabled to provide for himself and Children, so that they are likely to perish for want of Relief; *These are therefore, &c.* that forthwith you do relieve the said *A. B*, and his Children, and that you make such an Allowance Weekly, as may be convenient for and towards the Support of himself and Children, or forthwith shew Cause why you refuse so to do.

Grantfather and Grandmother, Father and Mother, if of Ability, are bound to relieve their Children, as the Sessions shall think fit, under the Penalty of 20 *s. per* Month.

The Husband of the Grandmother is a Parent within the Meaning of the Act, especially if she was of Ability at the Time of the Marriage, or if she had an Estate afterwards. The same Law for a Father-in-Law. *Stiles* 283.

By the Statute of 13 & 14 *Car.* 2. *cap.* 12. upon Complaint by the Church-wardens and Overseers of the Poor to any Justice within Forty Days after a poor Person came to settle in a Tenement under 10 *l.* two Justices might remove him to the Place where last settled for Forty Days, 13. *Car.* 2.

This Statute did not prevent clandestine coming into Parishes, for People would conceal themselves for Forty Days, which made a settlement; and therefore by another Statute of 1 *Jac.* 2. *cap.* 17. the Forty Days was to be accounted from the Time of the *Delivery of Notice in Writing* to one of the Church-wardens or Overseers; and this must be of the House of his Abode, and the Number of his Family, if any.

But this Act was not a sufficient Remedy against such Settlements; and therefore by 3 & 4 *Will.* & *Mar.* the Forty Days *Anno* 1692. Continuance is to be accounted from the Time of *Publication of Notice in Writing* of the House of Abode, and Number of his Family.

This is to be read in the Church by the Overseer or Church-warden next *Lord's-Day* after Divine Service, who neglecting to read, forfeits to the Party grieved 40 *s.* Neglecting to register such Notice, forfeits the like Sum, to be levied by Distress, &c. and for want of Distress, may be committed for a Month without Bail.

Proof must be before One Justice by Two Witnesses upon Oath.

But there are some Exceptions out of this last Act, which will make a Settlement,

Settlement, without ſuch notice, as (1.) If on his own Account he execute any publick Yearly Office or Charge for a Year. (2) If he pay any Share of Taxes or Levies of the Pariſh.

But it muſt not be Taxes to the King, for theſe grow due, and are to be paid by reaſon of the Reſidence of the People. (3.) If an unmarried Perſon, not having a Child, ſhall be hired for a Year, ſuch Service, that is, not the Forty Days, but his continuing in the Service for a Year, ſhall be a Settlement. 8 & 9 *William* 3. (4) Being bound an Apprentice, and inhabiting in a Town, ſhall be a Settlement.

The Act of the 13 & 14 *Car.* 2. Intituled, *An Act for the further Relief of the Poor of this Kingdom*, is made perpetual, by 12 *Annæ*.

And, after reciting the Act of the 9 & 10 of *W.* 3. it is further enacted, That if any Perſon, who ſhall be an Apprentice, or Hired Servant to any Perſon whatſoever, who did come into, or ſhall reſide in any Pariſh, &c. by Means of a Certificate, and hath not gained a legal Settlement in ſuch Pariſh, &c. ſuch Apprentice, by Virtue of ſuch Apprenticeſhip, or ſuch Servant by being hired to any ſuch Perſon, ſhall not be adjudged to have any Settlement in ſuch Pariſh, &c. by reaſon thereof; but every ſuch Apprentice or Servant ſhall have his Settlement in ſuch Pariſh, &c. as if he had not been bound Apprentice, or had not been Hired Servant to ſuch Perſon.

Church-wardens and Overſeers refuſing one ſent by Order of two Juſtices, forfeit 5 *l.* to the Uſe of the Poor of the Pariſh from whence he was removed, 3 & 4 *W.* & *M.* *cap.* 11.

Proof muſt be by two Witneſſes upon Oath, before one Juſtice of the County to which he is removed.

Forfeiture muſt be levied by Diſtreſs by Warrant of one Juſtice of the County to which he is removed, directed to the Conſtable where the Offender lieveth, &c. and for want thereof, be committed for Forty Days.

He may appeal to the next Seſſions of the Place from which removed.

Giving Notice to a proper Officer to appeal, and not proſecuting the ſame; or appealing, the Seſſions may order Coſts for whom the Appeal is determined or to whom Notice was given, to be paid by the Overſeers of the Poor, or other Perſon againſt whom 'tis determined, or by the Perſon who gave Notice, &c.

And if he lived out of the Juriſdiction of that Court, one Juſtice where the Perſon dwelleth, upon Requeſt to him made, and upon producing a true Copy of the Order proved by one Witneſs upon Oath, ſhall by Warrant, &c. cauſe the Money mentioned in the Order to be levied by Diſtreſs. &c and for want thereof, commit the Perſon for Twenty Days.

Appeals muſt be determined at the Seſſions of the County, or Place wherein the Pariſh doth lie, from whence the poor Perſon is removed, and not elſewhere.

None are to be relieved, whose Names are not registred in a Parish-Book kept for that Purpose, unless by Authority under the Hand and Seal of a Justice of the Parish, or if none there, by a Justice in the Parts adjoining, or by Order of Sessions.

But in Cases of Pestilential Diseases, *viz*. Plague or Small-Pox, in respect of their Families only, they are excepted, 3 & 4 *W.* & *M. cap.* 11.

He and his Wife and Children cohabiting in the same House, must have on the uppermost Garment, and upon the Shoulder of the Right Sleeve, a large *Roman* P. and the first Letter of the Parish; or otherwise, one *Justice*, &c. upon Complaint, may cause his Allowance to be abridged or suspended, or may commit Offenders to the House of Correction, not exceeding Twenty one Days.

Officers relieving such who do not wear the Badge, forfeit 20 *s*. for every Offence; one Moiety to the Informer, the other to the Poor.

Proof is to be before one Justice upon Oath of one Witness; Forfeiture is to be levied by Warrant of one Justice,

A Warrant to apprehend a Person returning into a Parish from whence he was removed.

To the Church-wardens and Overseers of, &c.

WHersas *A. B.* being in *July* last lawfully settled in the Parish of, &c. did come into the Parish of, &c. in the County of, &c. not having given Notice to the Overseers of the Poor of the Parish of F. of the place of his Abode, the Number of her Family, nor otherwise acquired a lawful Settlement there; and upon Complaint made by the Officers of the said parish of F. that the said *A. B.* was likely to be chargeable to their parish, they obtained a Warrant to remove her, and accordingly did convey and remove her to the said parish of, &c. since which the said *A. B.* did of her own Accord return to the parish of, &c. from which she was *Removed*. *These are therefore* to require you, or one of you, to bring the said *A. B.* before me, or some other Justice of the peace of, &c. to shew Cause why she returned to the said parish of, &c and farther to do and receive as to *Justice* doth appertain. *Given* under my Hand and Seal, &c.

The punishment is, To be sent to the House of Correction to be whipt as a Vagabond. The *Mittimus* is as followeth:

A *Mittimus*

A *Mittimus* for Returning.

To the Constable of, &c. *and To the Keeper, of,* &c.

Kent ss. AS in the former Warrant to the Word (*Removed,*) *These are therefore* to require you, That you, or some or one of you, do forthwith convey the said *A. B.* to the House of Correction, and there to deliver her to the Keeper thereof, requiring you also the Keeper to receive her into your Custody, and punish her as a Vagrant. *Given* under my Hand and Seal, *&c.*

A Warrant to send a Wife and Children to her Husband, *&c.*

To the Church wardens and Overseers of the Poor of the Parish of, &c.

Kent ss. WHereas Complaint hath been made unto us, That *A.* the Wife of *C. B.* an Inhabitant in the parish of, *&c.* in the said County, is lately come into your parish, of, *&c.* and hath brought with her Three Children of the said *C. B.* being all Infants, and that the said *A.* and Children are likely to be chargeable to the said parish: *These are therefore* to require you, or some of you, forthwith upon sight hereof, to convey the said *A.* and Children, to the parish of, *&c.* aforesaid, and to deliver them to the said *C. B.* there to be settled with him according to Law; and if you do not find him there, then to deliver the said *A.* and Children to the Overseers of the poor of the said parish of, *&c.* requiring you the said Overseers to provide for them as Inhabitants of your parish. *Given* under our Hands and Seals, *&c.*

Posse Comitatus.

THE Justices, in levying the power of the County, may have the Assistance of all Lay-men under the Degree of Knights, and above Fifteen Years of Age, and able to travel, upon pain of Imprisonment, and Fine to the King.

But 'tis in the Discretion of the *Justice* how many or how few he will have, and after what Manner they shall be armed.

One Justice may take the power of the County to suppress Rioters.

Process.

THIS is usually after the Indictment found, and is always in the Name of the *King*, directed to the Sheriff, and *Teste* by the Justice: The Justices have power by the express Words of their Commission to make process upon Indictments of Felony, or Trespasses; but where a Man is indicted in one County who liveth in another, there must be an *Alias* after the first *Capias* before he can be *Outlawed*, and there must be Three Months between the *Teste* and Return thereof. 8 *H*. 6. *cap*. 10.

There is a *Proviso* in this Statute, That process shall go out as usual when the party is indicted in the same County where he liveth; that is, if it be for Felony, and the party not in Custody, the Justices may award a *Capias*, and then an *Exigent*; but if in Custody, they may award process to try the Offender the next Day.

If it is for Trespass, then there must be a *Venire facias*, &c. and if *Nihil habet*, &c. a *Capias*, *Alias*, & *Pluries*, and so to the *Exigent*; but if he is returned Summoned, then a *Distringas* must issue if he doth not appear, and so *Infinite* till he come.

Sometimes process is given by particular Statutes; as *per* Statute of 5 *Eliz. cap*. 4. the Justices may award several *Capias*'s to a Sheriff or Officer of another County where a Servant or Apprentice in Husbandry departs from his Master.

Per 5 *Ed*. 6. *cap*. 11. *Justices* may award process to a Sheriff of another County, in Cases where Offenders are indicted for Felonies in Counties where the Facts were done, but not where they live.

If any Man is indicted for *Murder* there shall be but one *Capias*, and then an *Exigent*.

But *per* 25 *Ed*. 3. *cap*. 14. If for Robbery, there shall be two *Capias*'s before the Outlawry.

These processes may be stayed by *Supersedeas* issuing from the Justice, setting forth that the Defendant came before him, and hath found Sureties for his Appearance to answer the Indictment, or to pay his Fine.

Prophecies.

PUblisher or Setter-forth of any fantastical or false prophecy, with Intent to raise Sedition, being lawfully convicted, shall be imprisoned for a Year without Bail, and forfeit 10 *l*. 5 *Eliz*. *cap*. 15.

For

For the Second Offence, being convicted, &c. shall be imprisoned for Life, and forfeits all his Goods. One Moiety of these Forfeitures to the *King*, the other to the Prosecutor. Prosecution to be in six Months.

Purveyance.

BY the Statute of 12 *Car*. 2. *cap*. 24. no Person by colour of Purveyance for the King, *&c*. shall take any Thing from the Subject without the Owner's Consent.

Any *Justice* of the Peace, or the Constables of the Place, may commit the Offender who by colour of any Warrant under the Great Seal, or otherwise, shall make Purveyance, *&c*. there to remain till the next Sessions, and the Party shall recover treble Damages and treble Costs.

Quaker.

NO *Quaker* shall be permitted to give Evidence in any Criminal Causes, or serve in *Juries*, or bear any Office or Place of Profit in the Government. *&* 8 *Will*. 3. *cap*. 34.

By this Act, their solemn Affirmation is to go for an Oath, which is as follows, *viz*.

The Affirmation.

I *A. B.* do in the Presence of Almighty God witness the Truth of what I say.

And if what he affirms is false, he shall be punished as in Cases of Perjury. *This Act* is made Perpetual in *Great Britain*.

Rape. *vide* Rape in Felony.

THis is Felony at Common Law, committed *by Force* upon a Woman, by Carnally knowing her, she never consenting thereunto, either before or after the Fact.

For if she consent after the Fact, 'tis still a Rape; and tho' she will not prosecute, yet the Husband may; and if she have none, then the Father or next of Kin may appeal.

In *Scotland*, the Woman ought to complain the same Day or Night in which she was ravish'd; and by our Law, she ought to complain in Forty Days afterwards, but rather immediately; for Concealing it, implies a Consent before the Fact.

Those who assist in committing a Rape, being present, are Principals, 11 *Rep.* 37. *Savil* 42.

In *Bracton*'s Time, the Punishment was loss of Eyes and *Genitalia*, because *calorem stupri induxerunt*.

It was a Doubt, Whether a Rape could be committed on a Girl of Seven Years old: but if she had been nine Years, it was no Question, *Dyer*, 304.

Anno 9 *Car.* 1. One *Martin Page* was indicted at the *Old-Baily*, for that he *Carnaliter cognovit* an Infant, under the Age of Ten Years. At his Trial the Jury would not find him guilty, because it was not proved he entered the Body of the Child; but he having very much abused her, the Court ordered an Indictment of Battery to be exhibited against him, which was tried at the Bar; and he was found guilty, and fined 100 Marks, and ordered to stand in the Pillory, *&c.* and to be bound with Sureties for his Good Behaviour during Life, and committed during the King's Pleasure. If under Ten years, then tho' she consent 'tis a Rape, by 18 *Eliz. cap.* 6. if above Ten years, then not consenting at first, tho' she consent afterwards, is likewise a Rape.

A Warrant upon a Rape.

To all Constables, &c.

Kent ss. WHereas we have received Information and Charge upon Oath against *A. B.* of, *&c.* touching a certain Felony, that is to say, with the Carnal Knowledge and Ravishment of *N.* the Wife of *C. D.* of, *&c.* *These are therefore* in His Majesty's Name, to require you to bring the said *A. B.* before me, or some other of His Majesty's Justices of the Peace for the said County, to be examined touching the Premisses, and to be further dealt with according to Law. *Hereof* fail not at your Perils. *Given*, &c.

Recognizance.

THIS is a Bond of Record, testifying, That the Party oweth to the King a certain Sum, *&c.* upon the Non performance of a Condition.

Tis

'Tis Matter of Record as soon as it is taken or acknowledged, tho' it be not made up, but only entred in the Justices Book; and therefore for a Breach of it an Indictment will not lie, but a *Scire Facias. Raym.* 196.

When you take a Recognizance, the Name, the Place of Abode, and the Trade or Calling both of the Principal and Sureties, are to be punctually set down, and the Principal is to be bound in double the Sum which his Sureties are bound in.

When 'tis entred or made up, you read the Condition to the Parties bound, calling them by their Names, thus:

You A. B. *acknowledge to be indebted unto our Sovereign Lord the King*, &c.

These Recognizances are to be ingrossed in Parchment or Paper, to which the Justice subscribes his Name, but the Persons bound need not set their Hands to it.

Where a Justice has Power to take a Recognizance, if the Party refuse to be bound, he may commit him. 11. *Rep.* 52.

'Tis expedient for the Justice to keep a Book, in which he ought to enter his Recognizances, thus,

A. B. *de*, &c. *in* 20 *l. ad comparend' ad proximas Assisas* or *Session' Pacis* (as the Case is) bound over for the suspicious stealing of an Horse from *C. D.*

Sureties { W. W. *de*, *&c.* / W. N *de*, *&c.* } 10 *l.*

The Number and Sufficiency of the Sureties is Discretionary in the Justice, before whom the Recognizance is acknowledged: and when once taken, if he is deceived in the Ability of the Sureties, he may compel the Party to put in more; but this is when the Recognizance is taken *ex Officio*, and not by Virtue of a *Supplicavit*.

Feme-Covert and Infants may not enter into Recognizance, but their Sureties only, if 'tis for *keeping the Peace*.

Justices cannot award Process, but these Records must be certified into *B. R.*

These are to be certified, notwithstanding the Demise of the King, or Death of the Cognizor, or of the Party at whose Suit they are taken; nay, though they are released.

If they concern any Evidence against Felons, they must be certified the next Gaol-Delivery. 2 & 3 *Phil. & Mar. cap.* 10. *vid.* Tit. *Behaviour.*

All whatever is a Breach of the Peace, is a Forfeiture of a Recognizance. See *Good Behaviour, Page*

But Opprobrious Words, as to call a Man a *Lyar*, *Knave*, &c. are not a Breach of the Good Behaviour, so as to make a Man forfeit his Recognizance; for though such Words may be provocations to break the Peace, yet they do not immediately tend to it, as Assaulting and Threatning do. *Cro. Eliz.* 86. 4 *Inst.* 180, 181.

So a Person Beating, in Defence of his Child, Father, Goods, Master, Mother, Possessions, Way, in Defence thereof, if ancient, is not a Breach of the Peace.

A Condition of a Recognizance for a Misdemeanor.

THe *Condition* of this Recognizance is such, That if the said *C. D.* shall Personally appear before the *Justices* of the Peace at the next General Quarter-Sessions of the Peace, to be held for, &c. and shall then and there answer unto such Misdemeanors which shall be objected against him, and that he do not depart without Leave of the Court, then this Recognizance to be void.

Rescous.

THIS is a Resistance against a lawful Authority, and by Violence taking away a Prisoner, or procuring his Escape.

If the Person rescued hath committed *Felony*, and was *arrested* for it, then *rescuing* of him is *Felony*; but if he was not arrested, then the opposing or hindring any Person to apprehend him is a *Misdemeanor*, but no *Felony*.

But the Rescuer shall not be arraigned of the Felony till the Principal is attainted; and if he die before Attainder, the Felony is discharged; but he shall be indicted, fined and committed for rescuing him. *Hale's Pl. Coron.* 116.

Indictment for a Rescous was *quod arrestavit*, without saying, & *in custodi sua habuit*, and for this Reason it was quash'd; tho' in the same Indictment it was alledged, That the Defendant rescued him *out of the Possession* of the Bailiff.

A Warrant of Rescous.

To all Constables, and others His Majesty's Officers of the Peace, whom these may concern

Kent ss. W*Hereas* Complaint upon Oath hath been made before me, by *C. D.* That

That on the 27th Inſtant *E. F, G. H.* & *J. K.* in a Riotous and Violent manner in the ſtreet, did Reſcue out of his Cuſtody one *L. M.* after he had arreſted him by Virtue of a Warrant from, *&c.* at the Suit of *T. M.* for Ten Pounds debt, *&c.* *Theſe are therefore* in his Majeſtys Name to Require you to bring the ſaid, *&c.* (of whom you ſhall have notice) before me or ſome other of his Majeſties Juſtices of the Peace, to be examined and dealt with according to Law. *Hereof* you are not to fail. *Given under, &c.*

Perſons oppoſing or reſiſting any Officer, *&c.* in the Execution of any Proceſs, to be committed to the County-Gaol without Bail, until the next Aſſizes or Goal-delivery. 8 *&* 9 *W.* 3. *cap.* 27.

Reſtitution of Stolen Goods.

AT the Common Law, the Owner of Goods ſtolen could not have Reſtitution upon an Indictment againſt the Felon, though he was freſhly purſued, becauſe the Proſecution was at the Suit of the *King*; it was otherwiſe upon an Appeal, becauſe that was at his own Suit.

But this is now remedied by the Stat. of 21 *H.* 8. *cap.* 11. for if the Felon be found guilty, or attainted of the Proſecution of the Party robbed, or Owner of the Goods, the Juſtices have Power to award Reſtitution *of the Goods ſtolen.* *Noy.* 128.

A Man ſtole Cattle, and ſold them in *open Market*, the Sheriff ſeized the Thief and the *Money*, and he was convicted and hanged at the Proſecution of the *Owner* of the Cattle, and he had Reſtitution of the *Money*: For though the Statute gives Power to the Juſtices to award Reſtitution, *&c.* of *the Goods ſtolen*; and though the *Money* in this Caſe was not *ſtolen*, yet becauſe it did ariſe by *ſtealing*, it ſhall be within the Equity, though not in the very Words of the Statute. *Noy.* 128.

This my Lord *Coke* call a *Beneficial Law*, becauſe it giveth a Party robbed a more ſpeedy Remedy than by Way of *Appeal*, which before this Statute he ought to bring, or he could have no Reſtitution: And becauſe 'tis beneficial, therefore it hath been held to extend to the Executors or Adminiſtrators of the Party, though they are not mention'd in the Statute. 3 *Inſt.* 242.

In ſome Caſes there can be no Reſtitution, as if the Felon ſells the Goods in a Market, *&c.* and is afterwards convicted, the Property is altered by the Sale; or if he waive them and eſcapeth, and 'tis not known who he was, the Lord having ſeized, the Owner cannot have Reſtitution, becauſe the Felon cannot be indicted or attainted; but if Plate is ſold in a Scrivener's Shop, it ſhall be reſtored upon Conviction, *&c*, becaufe fuch a Shop is not a proper Market for fuch Goods. 1 *And* 344. *Moor* 360.

But notwithftanding the Cafes above-mentioned, the Practice hath been otherwife ever fince 4 & 5 *Car.* 1. for if the Criminal is convicted at the Profecution of the Party who loft the Goods, he fhall have Reftitution, though they were fold in a Market-Overt; and if the Party who bought them pleads it to a Writ of Reftitution brought, the other upon a Demurrer to fuch Plea will have Judgment.

This Refolution tends to the Advancement of Juftice to make Men vigilant in profecuting Offenders, and it will difcourage Perfons from buying Goods for a fmall Value in a Market, of fuch whom they have Reafon to fufpect. *Keeling* 48. *Coke's Magna Charta* 714.

But if Goods are ftolen, and not waived in Flight, or feized by proper Officer, there the Party may take his Goods again though he doth not profecute; but if waived or feized, the Party fhall have no Reftitution till Conviction at his Profecution, and even in fuch Cafe he fhall have no more than what is mentioned in the Indictment, though other Goods where' ftolen at the fame Time; and the Reafon is, becaufe by fuch Omiffion the Offender might have efcaped.

Riot.

A Riot is where *Three Perfons, or more*, meet to do an Unlawful Act with Force, and accordingly execute the fame; for if they do not, 'tis only an Unlawful Affembly. But it can be no *Riot*, except there is a *Precedent Intent* to do an Unlawful Act, and that with *Force*.

Riots, *&c*, fhall be fuppreffed and enquired of at the Kings Charge, which the Sheriff is to disburfe by Indenture between Juftices and him.

What Perfons meeting in Numbers fhall not make a Riot.

An Affembly meeting together, and they know not for what.

A Bailiff or Conftable requiring Perfons to affift him, *&c*.

A Jury falling out and fighting.

Infants meeting in Numbers, not incited by a Man of Difcretion.

Perfons meeting together to Dance, or to be Merry on *May-Day*, *&c*. or to Play at any Sport.

A Number of men meeting to carry away a Thing of Burthen, to which one claims a Right, tho' he hath none, provided they ufe no threatning words.

All thefe are no Riots.

'Tis no Riot in Servants, if they go with their Mafter (who intends to commit

a Riot)

a Riot) and they are ignorant of his Intentions. But a Stage-Play, causing a great Number to meet, is a Riot. *Rol.* 109.

A Justice having Notice of a *Riot*, he must endeavour to remove it; he may bind the Rioters to the Good Behaviour, and if they have no Sureties, or refuse to be bound, he may commit them; and if the Justice neglects, he is to be fined; and the Two next Justices to the Place where the Riot was committed, forfeit 100 *l.* to the *King*, if they neglect (*having Notice*) to suppress a Riot. 13 *H.* 4. *cap.* 7.

The Record of One Justice is Traversable, but not of Two, because 'tis pursuant to the Statute.

But One Justice sitting in a Judicial Place, and seeing a Riot, may Record it upon his own View, which is not Traversable, because he then acts as a Judge; but 'tis otherwise if he do not sit in such place.

When a Riot is over a Justice cannot meddle, but only proceed against the Offenders, as Trespassers against the Peace.

One Justice cannot Fine them, for this must be done by two Justices, by virtue of the Statute of 13 *H.* 4. *cap.* 7. And they ought to send to the Sheriff or his Deputy, who by the Statute seem to have a concurrent Jurisdiction with them in Fining the Offenders; and therefore upon a Writ of Error brought, the Judgment was Reversed where a Fine was set without the Sheriff. *Raym.* 386.

But yet, 'tis the Opinion of Mr. *Lambert*, That the *Justices* without the Sheriff, if they see a Riot, may Commit the Rioters, take away their Weapons, and appraise them for the use of the King, and justifie the Beating and Killing, if Opposed.

If Rioters escape being taken by the *Justice*, this Record being Certified, as aforesaid, Process shall issue out against them out of *B. R.*

The *Justices* may likewise grant Warrants to take those who escape, and bind them to good Behaviour, or Commit them, when taken.

Several were indicted for a Riot in rescuing a person arrested near *Charing-Cross*, and were fined 500 *l.* and to stand in the Pilory. *Cro. Car.* 300.

A Warrant against Rioters.

To all Constables and other his Majesties Officers of the Peace, whom it may Concern.

WHereas Complaint, upon Oath, hath been made before me by *C. D.* That yesterday, as he was going about his lawful Business, *E. F.* met him in the Street in his Way, with two Men in his Company, unknown to the said *C. D.* who in a Riotous, Inhuman and Barbarous Manner did Assault, Beat, Bruise and Wound him:

These

These are in his Majesty's Name to Require you to bring the said *E. F.* and the other two Persons (of whom you shall have Notice) before me, or some other of his Majesty's Justices of the Peace, to be examined and dealt with according to Law. Hereof you are not to fail. *Given* under my Hand and Seal, &c.

The Form of a Record of a Riot upon View.

MEmorandum, That on the 27th Day of *September*, in the sixth year of the Reign of our Sovereign Lord *George*, of *G. Britain*, *&c.* King, *Annoq; Dom.* 1719. We *C. D.* and *M. W.* Esqrs. Two Justices of the aforesaid Lord the King, the Peace in the County aforesaid to preserve and keep, assigned; and *G. C.* Esq; then Sheriff of the said County, At the grievous Suit and humble Supplication of *W. S.* of *H.* in the County aforesaid, Yeoman, in our proper Persons did come to the dwelling House of *W. S.* in the County aforesaid, and then and there did see *M H.* of *H.* aforesaid, Yeom. and *H. P.* of *C.* in the County aforesaid, Labourer, and other evil Doers and Disturbers of the Peace of our said Lord the King, unto us unknown, (to the Number of Persons) with Swords, Daggers, *&c.* and Unlawfully and Riotously at the same House were gathered together, and much Harmes upon him the said *W. S.* did commit, to the great Disturbance of the Peace of our said Lord the King, and Terror of his People, and against the Form of the Statute in such Case made and provided. *And Therefore* We the aforesaid *C. D.* and *M. W.* then and there the aforesaid *M. H.* and *H. P.* did Arrest, and to the next Goal of our said Lord the King, in the County aforesaid, did cause to be sent, of our own View and Record Convict of that Illegal Assembly and Tumult, *&c.*

This Record must be Certain, as to the Time, Place, Number, Weapons, Manner, and other Circumstances, because tis a Judgment and not Traversable, for if upon Examination it appears to be no Riot, or that the Justices did not see it, yet the Parties are concluded.

But for Committing without Recording, or making a Record without Come the Justices forfeit 100 *l.*

Information

Information against *two Justices* for not enquiring into a Riot, and found against one of them, is good. *Roll. Rep.* 109.

After the Riot is Committed (if not within the View of the *Justices*) and the Rioters are gone, the two Justices, within a Month, may make a Precept to the Sheriff to summon a Jury to enquiry of it; and if 'tis found, then they may Commit the Offenders, and Certifie the Inquisition into *B. R.* that they may be fined, which should not be less than 10 *l.* for the Principal. *Stiles* 303.

The Form of the Inquisition.

INquisition of our Lord the King, taken at *L.* in the County aforesaid, the 27th Day of *September*, in the sixth year, &c. *Anno Dom.* 1719 by the Oath of (*the Jury*) honest and lawful Men of the County aforesaid, before *H. P.* and *W. N.* Esqrs. two Justices of the aforesaid Lord the King, the Peace in the County aforesaid to preserve, and also for divers Felonies, Misdemeanours and other Transgressions in the same County perpetrated, to hear and determine assigned, which same Jurors upon their Oath, aforesaid, say, That *M H.* of *H.* in the County aforesaid, Yeoman, and other Malefactors and Disturbers of the Peace of our said Lord the *King*, to the Jurors aforesaid unknown, the 20th day of *September* last past, with Force and Arms, *viz.* with Clubs, Swords, Daggers, *&c.* and other Unlawful Weapons, in the Messuage of *W. S.* in the County of *H.* aforesaid, between the hours of ten and eleven in the fore-noon of the same Day, Unlawfully and Riotously did enter, and in and upon him the said *W. S.* did make an Assault, and him did Beat and wound to the great Disturbance of the Peace of our said Lord the *King*, and Terror of his People, and against the Form of the Statute in such Case made and provided, *&c.*

This Inquiry within a Month must be intended of great Riots; for by virtue of their Commission the Justices may inquire into small Riots at any time afterwards, so that the Limitation of a Month seems to prevent the Forfeiture of 100 *l.* by the two next *Justices*, in case of great and notorious Riots, they neglecting to make Inquiry within that time.

But if they enquire afterwards, the Indictment shall not be Quashed for that Reason, because a Riot is an Offence at Common Law, and the Statute is not Penal, but only Directory to the Punishment. *Sid.* 186.

After the Riot is found upon this Inquisition, the Justices may award a *Venire facias*, directed to the Sheriff of the County, under their own *Teste*, Commanding him to cause the Offenders to appear before them (*The Form whereof you may see before in Process on Indictments.*)

This is only where the Offenders cannot be taken, and so if the Sheriff return *Non est Inventus*, you may proceed to the Outlawry. But if they appear, the Justices may fine them, and Commit them till paid, or may take Sureties by Recognizance to pay the Fine, or may accept a Traverse; which Inquisition and Traverse must be sent to the next Sessions, or into *B. R.* there to be tryed.

The Charges of the Justices and Jury are to be paid by the Sheriff out of the Fines, and therefore by the Stat. of 2 *H.* 5. *cap.* 8. the Fines may be encreased, and an Indenture being made between the Justices and the Sheriff, he is to be allowed it in passing of his Accounts in the Exchequer.

If t e Truth of a Riot cannot be found by Inquisition, then within a Month afterwards, the same Justices and Sheriff must Certify into B. R. so much of the Fact as appears to them, together with the Names of the principal Offenders, and Circumstances and Impediments why the Truth was not found, *sub pœna* 20*l.* This Certificate may be in *English*, by way of a Letter, comprehending the whole Truth, with the Time, Place, *&c.* and if any thing material be left out of the Inquisition, it may be supplyed in the Certificate. But if the Sheriff dye, or the Justices are put out of Commission before the Certificate made, it cannot be done afterwards.

A Mittimus to the Goal upon View, *&c.*

To the Keeper of, &c.

UPon Complaint upon Oath made unto Us *P. L.* and *L. M.* Esqrs. two of his Majesty's Justices of the Peace for the County aforesaid, by *H. C.* of *E.* we did this present 30th day of *August*, go to the House of *M.* and there did see *P. Q. W. M.* and others assembled together in a Riotous and Unlawful Company, at *H.* aforesaid, to the Terror of the People, and against the Peace of our Sovereign Lord the *King*, and against the Form of the Statute in that case made and provided: *We do therefore* herewithal send you the Bodies of the said *P. Q.* and *W. M.* they being Convicted of the said Riot, and Unlawfully assembled, by our own View, Testimony and Record, Commanding you the said Goaler to receive them into your Custody, and safely to keep them until they shall from thence be delivered by due Course of Law. And hereof fail not. Given under, &c.

Robbery,

Robbery is a Felonious and Violent taking Money or Goods from the *Person* of another, to any value, *putting him in Fear*; for without putting in fear tis no Robbery. *Dyer* 224.

My Lord *Coke* tells us, That tis *Robbery*, because Goods were taken *Quasi de la Robe*, that is, from the *Person*, as he calls it. But the Learned Sir *Henry Spelman* gives us a different account of the Word, *viz*. That in the time of the *Saxons* it was usual for Travellers to lodge in any Mans House for one Night (for in those days they had very little Money, and no Inns) That *Reab* in the *Saxon* Language signifies a *Garment*; and because Rogues did steal the Cloaths of such Travellers (for they had nothing else to lose) therefore they were called *Robatores*, and the Crime it self *Roberie*; so that at first it was not a taking from the *Person*, for the Cloathes were usually stolen in the Night after the Traveller was at rest: But now it must be a taking from the *Person*, and 'tis the Violence and putting in Fear that distinguishes this Offence from a Cut-purse or Pick-pocket, which is *Calm & Secrete*.

Now an Assaulting, without taking any Thing, is no Robbery. But Commanding the Person to *Deliver*, and he doth it, this is a Taking and Robbery, tho' the Thief doth deliver the Thing taken back again. So is Compelling one to Swear to bring him Money, and he doth it; if the Wife receives it, this is a Taking. And all that are in Company (tho' the Fact is done by one alone) are Principals.

Three Persons come to Rob *M*. and one doth the Fact out of the sight of the other, who afterwards returns to them, 'Tis Robbery in all. 1 *And*. 116.

If being pursued, and endeavouring to escape, the true Man let his Hat or Money fall, and the Thief takes it up, This is a Taking from the Person. So is taking in his Presence; for in Law this is a Taking from his Person.

Assaulting one, and putting him in Fear, and then driving away his Cattle in his Presence; This is taking from his Person, and Robbery.

By a late Statute, he who apprehends and prosecutes a Highway-Man to Conviction, shall, within a Month after, receive of the Sheriff of the County where the Robbery was committed, 40 *l*. producing the Certificate of the Judge or Justices, before whom the Person was Convicted. And if any one is killed in taking of a Highway-Man, those who have a right to administer shall have the 40 *l*. and he who takes, Prosecutes and Convicts, shall have the Horse, Furniture, Money, and other Goods of the Highway-man, unless stolen, 4 & 5 *W*. & *M*.

The Hundred is Chargeable if the Robbery is committed in the Day-time; and therefore if its done in *January* after Sun-setting, or if a Highway-man compel a Waggoner in the Day-time to drive his Waggon out of the Way, and then robs him in the Night, this shall likewise be a Robbery in the Day, because the first Seizure was a Robbery, and the Hundred in both Cases shall answer it. *Sid*. 263. See *Hue-and-Cry*.

SEssions is a Court of Record held before Two or more Justices, *Quorum unus.* Formerly it was Discretionary in the Justices at what Time to keep this Court, which made it Uncertain; but now by the 2 *H.* 5. *cap.* 4. 'tis appointed to be kept four times in a year.

If the Justices should happen to be divided in Opinion about the Conveniency of the Place of holding or keeping the Sessions, and some should appoint one place and some another, and the Sessions should be held at both places, 'Tis void in both, because the Authority of the Justices being equal, their several Appointments must be so likewise; and by the Nature of the Service, there can be no Priority of Time.

Two sorts of Persons ought more especially to attend this Court, *viz.* Those who are to serve there by virtue of their Office, and those who are lawfully Summoned. And these are the *Justices of the Peace*, *High-Sheriff* & *under-Sheriffs*, *Coroners*, *Clerk of the Peace*, *Constables*, *Goaler*, *Jurors*, and those who are bound by Recognizance to Answer, give Evidence or Prosecute.

Freedom of Access is incident to a Court of Record, as this is; so that if any Person come Voluntarily thither about any business of the Sessions, as to prefer a Bill of Indictment, &c. or is Compelled to appear to save the Forfeiture of his Recognizance, he shall be protected from Arrests upon mean Process; and if he happen to be arrested, the Court may discharge him upon Examination of the Matter, and Oath of the party himself. 1 *Lev.* 159.

Justices of the Sessions may hear and determine Trespasses against the publick Peace, and upon Conviction give Judgment of Fine, or otherwise, as the Case requires.

It was the Policy of our Ancestors to establish several Courts in every County, not only for the speedy Administration of Justice, but to suppress Disorders in the first Motion, before they should arrive to such Power as to disturb the Neighbourhood. This was the business of County-Courts of Sheriffs, and of Tourns, and of Leets. The Authority of those Courts declining for several years, seems now to be devolved on this of the Quarter-Sessions, which yet maintains a Form of Judicature, tho' by Custom and Usage, 'tis abated, as particularly in Cases of Felony. For the Power which the Justices have, is either by Acts of Parliament, or by their Commission, and by both they have Authority to try Felons; for by 4 *Ed.* 3. *cap.* 2. they have Power to hear and determine *Felonies*, and to inflict Punishment according to Law; and by the second *Assignavimus* in their Commission, which relates only to the Sessions, they have Authority to enquire by a a Jury, &c. of all *Felonies*, &c. and likewise of several other Articles therein mentioned, and may send out Process against the Offenders to bring them in, and then Try them, and give Judgment according to Law. Now though they have this Power, yet the common Practice is to Try only *Petit-Larcenies* at Sessions, and the Felons are, of course, carried to the Assizes by the Goaler, who takes no Notice of this Court without particular Order.

'Tis

'Tis true, where a Statute creates a Crime, and appoints before whom it shall be Tryed, in such Case if the Sessions is not named, they have no Jurisdiction; as in *Forgery* upon the Stat. 5 *Eliz.* cap, 14. which provides that the Indictment shall be taken before Justices of *Assizes* and Justices of *Oyer* and *Terminer*, for they have an express Clause in their Commission *To Hear and Determine*, yet they cannot proceed in their Sessions against Offenders of this Nature, because there is another Commission of *Oyer and Terminer*, which is distinctly known by that Name; This was adjudged in my Lord *Sanchar*'s Case. 9 *Rep.* 118. *B.*

But there are many Things and Offences which by particular Statutes ought to be done and prosecuted in this Court, as,

Inn-holders, Whether they sell Victuals or Drink at unreasonable Prices, 21 *Jac.* cap. 21. 2 *Edw.* 6. cap. 15. or forfeited their Recognizances, 5 & 6 *E.* 6. cap. 25.

Buggery and *Bastards*, 25 *H.* 8. cap. 6. 13 & 14 *Car.* 2. cap. 12.

Weights and Measures, 9 *Hen.* 5. cap. 8. 11 *H.* 7. cap. 4. 8 *H.* 6. cap. 5. 11 *H.* 6. cap. 8.

Counterfeit Letters, and getting Money by them, 33 *H.* 8. cap. 1.

Escapes of Felons, 1 *R.* 3. cap. 3.

Estreats of Sheriffs, Controuling them by Justices, 11 *H.* 7. cap. 15.

Fore-stalling, regretting and ingrossing, 5 & 6 *E.* 6. cap. 14.

Forging of Deeds, &c. 5 *Eliz.* cap. 14.

Jurors levying Issues lost by them, 27 & 30 *Eliz.* cap. 7 & 18.

Money false, to suppress it, 3 *H.* 5. cap. 7.

Moss-Troopers, to suppress them, 29 & 30 *Car.* 2. cap. 2.

News false, telling it, 2 *R.* 2. cap. 5. 22 *R.* 2. cap. 11. 1 & 2 *P.* & *M.* cap. 3.

Perjury upon the Stat. of 5 *Eliz.* cap. 9. 29 *Eliz.* cap. 5.

Prophesies, false and fantastical, publishing them, 5 *Eliz.* cap. 15.

Riots, Routs and Unlawful Assemblies.

Rogues, Vagabonds, 13 & 14 *Car.* 2. cap. 12. 1 *Jac.* cap. 7. 39 *Eliz.* cap. 2.

Servant Assaulting his Master, 5 *Eliz.* cap. 4.

Usury on the Statute of 13 *Eliz.* cap. 8.

These and many more Crimes and Offences against the Law are Cognizable before the Justices in their Sessions.

Strict Words are not required in an Order of Sessions, as they are in an Indictment; but Forms are necessary in the Proceedings. And as to Fines imposed there, R. B. may mitigate them. 1 *Ven.* 37.

The Sessions may fine a Jury for not finding a Bill upon plain Evidence: The Jury in this Case was fined 10 *l.* *Sid.* 219.

And now I have mentioned Fines, it may not be improper in this place to inform the Reader what grievous Fines and Punishments have been inflicted on Persons for Striking in *Westminster-Hall*. And as the Court of Sessions should act in Conformity

formity to the great Courts there in the Diſtribution of Juſtice, ſo where they are Interrupted in the peaceable Adminiſtration thereof, by Fighting in the preſence of that Court, the Puniſhment for ſuch an Offence ſhould bear ſome proportion to that which is inflicted on Offenders for Striking in the Preſence of the Courts above, which is thus, *viz.*

For ſtriking a Man in the face, and threatning to hang him, if he give Evidence againſt a Felon, who was then to be Tryed in B. R. he was Impriſoned during Life, to forfeit all his Lands during Life, Goods and Chattels, and that his Right Hand ſhould be Cut off; which was done accordingly.

For drawing his Sword on the Stairs, going up to the *Court of Requeſts* (tho' it was out of the View of the Courts) Judgment to perpetual Impriſonment.

For Aſſaulting another in the *Palace-Yard*, the Court ſitting, Impriſonment during the Kings pleaſure, and fined 100 *l.* *Cro. Eliz.* 405. 3 *Inſt.* 140. *Cro. Car.* 373.

In theſe two laſt Caſes there was no Judgment for Cutting off the Right Hand, becauſe the Facts were not done in the Preſence of the Juſtices.

Then if before the Tryal the Offender is bailed, it muſt be Body for Body; and formerly this Offence was puniſhable with Death.

Superſedeas.

To the Sheriff, Bailiffs, Conſtables, and other his Majeſty's Miniſters within the ſaid County, Greeting.

WHereas P. *M.* of *H.* Carpenter, hath Perſonally come before me *C. M.* Eſq; one of his Majeſty's Juſtices of the Peace for the County of *M.* and hath found ſufficient Sureties, that is to ſay, *W. C.* and *H. P.* of *L.* Yeomen, either of which hath undertaken for the ſaid *P. M.* under the Penalty of Twenty Pounds, and he the ſaid *P. M.* hath undertaken for himſelf under the Penalty of Forty Pounds, That he the ſaid *P. M.* ſhall well and truly keep the Peace towards our Sovereign Lord the King and all his Leige People, and eſpecially towards *W. N.* of *Q.* Baker, and alſo that he ſhall Perſonally appear before his Majeſty's Juſtices of the Peace at the the next General Quarter-Seſſions of the Peace to be held at *N.* for the ſaid County of *M.* *Therefore*, on the behalf of our Sovereign Lord

Lord the King, *I Command you and every of you*, That you utterly forbear to Arrest, Attach, Take or Imprison, or otherwise by any means, on the said occasion, to molest the said *P. M.* And if you have for the said occasion. and no other, taken or Imprisoned him the said *P. M.* That then you do forth-with cause him to be delivered and set at Liberty, without further delay. Given under, *&c.*

Note, A Supersedeas of this Nature is held good, though the Sureties are not named, nor the Sum they are penally obliged in, yet it is better to express them both; for if in such Case it shall appear the Sureties are not sufficiently Responsible, nor bound in sufficient Sums, better Sureties may be taken, and accordingly all the *Supersedeases* issuing out of the Court of Chancery, Queens-Bench and Common Pleas do mention the Names of the Sureties, and the Sums they are obliged in for the Delinquents forth-coming to answer, *&c.*

So upon good Security taken, a *Supersedeas* may be taken for Good Behaviour, *Mutatis mutandis*. *Cromp.* 237.

Squibs.

THe People having got a foolish Custom of throwing Squibs during the time of any publick Solemnity, and some having lost their Eyes thereby, and other Damages being done, a Law was made, prohibiting the *Making, Selling, or offering or exposing to Sale any Squibs*, &c. *or Fire-works*, or any Cases, Moulds or Implements for making Squibs, *&c.* And prohibiting persons to suffer any Squibs, *&c.* to be cast out of their Houses, or out of or from any part thereof, into any publick Street, or into any Street or House, 9 & 10 *Wm.* 3.

The *Offence* is declared to be a Common Nusance, and the Maker of the Squibs or Moulds, or Seller, *&c.* is to forfeit 5 *l.* He that throws or assists in throwing or firing any *Squibs, &c.* or that permits any *Squibs* to be thrown out of his house forfeits 20 *s.* for every Offence. The Conviction to be before one Justice, by Confession of the party or Oath of two Witnesses. The Forfeitures to be levied by Warrant from the Justice before whom the Party is Convicted, by Distress and Sale of the Goods, one moiety to the Poor of the Parish, the other to him who prosecutes to Conviction.

But Commissioners of the Ordnance, or any person authorized by them, may order Fire-works to be used and fired, and so may the Artillary Company in *London*, and the Militia of *England*, in the Exercise and Practise of Arms only.

Suspicion

Suspicion.

Communis vox & fama, that such a Person did the Offence, is sufficient Cause of Suspicion; but then the Fact must be actually done, otherwise not.

In many Cases evident Proofs are not to be had, and therefore probable Presumptions are good Causes of Suspicion, and sufficient for a Justice to commit the Person suspected.

Presumptions are thus divided by Lord *Coke*.

1. *Violenta*, which, he tells us, is *plena Probatio*.
2. *Probabilis*, which moveth a little.
3. *Levis*, which is of no Force.

Some Presumptions of the first Sort are so violent, that no Proof can be admitted to contradict them; as if a Man is taken with a bloody Knife upon a murdered Person, or flying from the dead Man; though no Body saw the Stroke actually given, yet there needs no further Proof.

When a Felony is committed, any Man may arrest suspicious Persons, and carry them before a Justice of Peace, who may commit them, or take a Recognizance to appear at the Assizes or Sessions.

Swearing.

By the Statute of 21 *Jac. cap.* 20. the Punishment of one prophanely Swearing or Cursing, was one Shilling to the Use of the Poor.

The Prosecution was to be within Twenty Days after the Offence.

The Conviction by the Oath of Two Witnesses before One *Justice*; and this Penalty was to be levied by Warrant and Distress, *&c.* and if that was not to be had, then the Offender, being above Seventeen Years old was to be put in the Stocks for Three Hours; and if under that Age, then he was to be whipp'd by the Constable, who was to have a Warrant from a Justice for that Purpose, or by the Parent or Master in the Presence of a Constable, if the Penalty was not Paid.

But some Alteration was made of this Law by that of 6 & 7 *W*. for by this Law the Forfeitures of 1 *s*. is confin'd to Day-Labourers, common Soldiers, Sea-men and Servants; but other Persons are to pay 2 *s*. for each Oath or Curse.

And

And for the second Offence double the Forfeiture; and for the third Offence, three Times as much as the first; and in Default of Distress, if the Offender be above Sixteen Years of Age, he shall be set in the Stocks for one Hour for a single Offence, and for more than one, (if convicted at the same Time) two Hours.

If under Sixteen, and do not pay the Penalty, he shall be whipp'd by the Constable, by a Warrant from the Justice, or by the Parent, Guardian or Master, in Presence of the Constable.

The Prosecution must be within Ten Days after the Offence. And the Conviction before One Justice by the Oath of One Witness. The *Justice* who omits his Duty, forfeits 5 *l.* one Moiety to the Informer, *&c.*

This Act is to be read by Parsons in the Church the next *Sunday* after every Quarter-day, yearly, or he forfeits 20 *s.*

Justices must keep a Book wherein they must register these Convictions, and certifie them to the Quarter-Sessions.

A Warrant to levy the Money for Prophane Swearing.

To the Constable, &c.

WHereas it was this present Day duly proved before me upon Oath, That *A. B.* of, *&c.* did on *Wednesday* the 20*th* Day of this Instant *November*, being then above Sixteen Years of Age, prophanely offend, by Swearing Four Oaths in the Parish of *&c.* in the said County, by Reason whereof he hath forfeited to the Use of the Poor of the said Parish, 2 *s.* for every Time he did so offend: *These are therefore* to require you forthwith to levy the said Forfeiture, being in the whole 8 *s.* upon the Goods and Chattels of the said *A. B.* by Distress and Sale thereof; and that you pay the same, when levied, to the Church-wardens or Overseers of the Poor of the said Parish of, *&c.* where the aforesaid Offence was committed, for the Use of the Poor of the said Parish: And if no Distress can be taken as aforesaid, and in case the said *A. B.* shall not pay the said Forfeiture, or give Security for the same, that then you do set him in the Stocks, there to remain the Space of two Hours. *Given*, &c.

Treason.

THis is a *Crime* of so *Transcendent a Nature*, that it hath not yet been defin'd; 'Tis *Malum in se*, and therefore an Offence at Common Law, before the Statute of 25 *Edw.* 3.

'Tis true, before that Statute, the Judges did usually determine what Treason was, which made it some-what Incertain; but since that time it hath been generally reduced under *Six Kinds*; and though more Treasons were introduced by many subsequent Laws, yet that old Stat. of *Edw.* 3. was Re-inforced by first *Mariæ* 1. So that all made between these two Laws are abrogated, and the Stat. of *Edw.* 3. is the Standard at this Day.

The Six Kinds of Treason, are these:

BY Compassing or Imagining the Death of the *King*, *Queen*, or *Prince*, and declaring the same by some Overt-Act.

By Killing the *Chancellor*, Treasurer, Justices of either Bench, or of Assize, *Oyer* and *Terminer*, in the Administration of Justice.

2. To violate or Carnally know the *Queen*, the *King's* eldest Daughter unmarried, the Prince's Wife.

3. Levying War.

4. Adhering to the King's Enemies.

5. Counterfeiting the Great Seal, the Privy-Seal, the King's Coyn.

5. By bringing Counterfeit Money into *England* like the King's Coyn.

Any open Act manifesting a Design to depose or imprison the King, is a sufficient Declaration of compassing or imagining, &c. as providing Arms to effect it, sending Letters to incite wicked Persons to attempt it, writing to Foreign Princes to invade the Kingdom, assembling the People to take the King into their Custody: These, and such like, are Overt-Acts to make one guilty of High-Treason within this Branch of the Statute, especially if there is any Proof of Words signifying to what Purpose such Acts were done.

And even Words themselves may be laid as an Overt-Act of Treason, for tis the natural Way to express our wicked Intentions; and this was *Cro. Car.* 332

332. *Crohagan*'s Case, who being beyond Sea, said, *I will kill the King if I can come at him.* This Person afterwards came into *England*, and was indicted for Compassing the King's Death, and those Words were laid as an Overt-Act, and being proved, he was convicted of High-Treason. 'Tis true, my Lord *Coke* was of a contrary Opinion in his *Pleas of the Crown*, *fol.* 14. But in the Case of the Regicides, that Opinion was denied to be Law, *Keel.* 13. However, he agreed, That Words set down in Writing may be an Overt-Act to prove the Compassing the King's Death.

Twyn's *Case*. So is Printing any Treasonable Positions.

So is the gathering Men together to compel the King to comply with their Demands, or to remove Evil Counsellors, or to conspire with a Foreign Prince to invade the Kingdom. *Keeling* 21.

But a Man, *Non compos Mentis*, cannot be guilty within this Branch, &c. because he is depriv'd of his Reason; but he may be guilty by attempting any Violence upon the Person of the King, &c.

This Overt-Act must be alledged and proved in every Indictment, &c.

And because a Civil War, and the Destruction of the People, are the natural Consequences hereof, therefore this was Treason at Common Law.

A King before his Coronation, a King *de facto*, is a King within this Act; but the Husband of the Queen-Regent, or the Right Heir to the Crown not in Possession, is not so.

A Queen must absolutely be so, and not a Dowager.

The Second Son after the Death of the Eldest, the Eldest Son of the Queen *Regnant*, *Prince*, but the Collateral Heir Apparent is not within this Statute.

Violating the Queen doth not extend to a Dowager; if the Queen consents, 'tis Treason in her; but there must be some open Act to manifest it, which must appear by plain and not conjectural Proof; and the Offender must likewise be attainted in his Life-time, for if he die before Conviction, he cannot be attainted but by Parliament.

This Offence was likewise High-Treason before this Statute, because it utterly destroyed the Certainty of the King's Issue, and by Consequence raised Contention about the Succession.

A Conspiracy, or compassing to levy War, is no Overt-Act, &c. unless a War is actually levied: This appears by the Statute of 13 *Eliz. cap* 1. Which made such Conspiracy Treason during the Life of that Queen; but if a War is levyed, then the Conspirators are all Traytors, tho' not actually in Arms.

And yet the Meeting and Consulting to levy War, tho' no War is actually levied, will be a sufficient Overt-Act to prove the Compassing and Imagining the Death of the King.

'Tis true, there is an Opinion in my Lord *Coke*'s *Pleas of the Crown* to the contrary; but that Opinion has been denied to be Law. Now

Now if a Meeting and Consulting to levy War, tho' no War is afterwards levied, shall be a sufficient Overt-Act to prove the Compassing the King's Death *a fortiori*, 'tis so where War is actually levied. *Keel*. 20.

Raising Forces for any publick End or Purpose, is Treason; this was the Case of *Cotton*, and other *London* Apprentices, who assembled to pull down Bawdy-houses: They chose Captains among themselves, and marcht in a posture of War; they wounded the Constable and opposed the Guards: All which was found specially at the *Old-Baily*; and upon Consideration of the Fact, some of them were executed, *Sid*. 358.

Several Conspired in *Oxfordshire* to pull down Inclosures, and to go to the Lord *Narris*'s House for Armour, Horses, &c. and from thence to *London*, and to joyn with more: This was held Treason.

Two or more Conspired to levy War, and one of them afterwards actally raised Forces; This was held Treason in all, by the Opinion of the Judges in Sir *Nich. Throgmorton*'s Case, who Conspired with *Wyat*.

Some *London* Apprentices were committed for a Riot, and some other Apprentices Conspired to Release them, and to kill the Lord Mayor, and provide themselves with Armour, by breaking open two Houses near the Tower; They had a Trumpet, and a Cloak on a Pole, instead of a Flag, and were going towards the Lord Mayor's House, but were opposed by the Sheriffs, whom they Resisted; And this was held Treason, by levying War, and within the Stat. 13 *Eliz*.

Adhering to the King's Enemies, is Aiding or Comforting them, by surrendring any Fort or Castle to them for Reward.

If the King's Subject becomes a Rebel, he is not properly called an Enemy, but a Traytor, and shall have Judgment against him as such, and not as an Enemy, because an Enemy is out of the Allegiance of the King; and if such Person is succoured out of the Realm, This, my Lord *Hales* tells us, is not an *Adhering* to an Enemy, within this Clause. But I can see no Reason for the Difference between an *Enemy* and *Traytor*; for I think one and the same Man may be both.

An Enemy coming into *England* in a War-like Manner, shall be Executed by Martial Law, but a Subject assisting him is a *Traytor*.

Treason done beyond Sea. As to this matter, at Common Law, the Person was to be Tryed in the County where he had Lands; but now by the Stat. of 35 *H*. 8. *cap*. 2. it may be Tryed in B. R. or in any County where the King appoints, and so shall Treason committed on the Sea; and this is by Virtue of the Stat. of 28 *H*. 8. *cap*. 15. tho' by the Civil Law it must be Tryed before the Admiral.

Compassing to Counterfeit the great Seal, is not Treason, for it must be actually Counterfeited, and it must be like the Great Seal.

If the Chancellor put the Seal to a Patent without a Warrant, this is no Treason now; but it was otherwise before the making of this Statute, as appears by the Old Lawyers, *Briton* and *Bracton*, who wrote before that time.

Putting

Putting the Great Seal to another Patent, is not Counterfeiting, (as my Lord Coke ſays) but a great Miſpriſion; and this was one *Leak's* Caſe, who glued Two Parchments ſo cloſe that it could not be perceived, and put a Label through both; and upon the uppermoſt he wrote a Patent, and got the Great Seal affixed to the Label, then he took off the written Parchment, and left the Label hanging to the Blank: This was held to be a Miſpriſion.

But I can ſee no Reaſon why it ought not to be High-Treaſon, becauſe it produceth the ſame Miſchief with Counterfeiting, which is ſo; and if it creates the ſame Miſchief, it ſhould in Reaſon have the ſame Puniſhment.

Thoſe who Aid and Conſent to Counterfeiting, are within this Statute.

But the Counterfeiting of the Privy Signet is not Treaſon within this Act, but it is declared ſo to be by a ſubſequent Statute, *viz.* by 1 & 2 *Phil.* & 2 *Mar. cap.* 11.

One *Robinſon* counterfeited the Privy Seal, but he omitted ſome Words in the Style, and added other Words, on purpoſe that there might be a Difference between the true Seal and the Counterfeit: He likewiſe counterfeited a Grant, and by the Help of this counterfeited Privy Seal, he obtained the Great Seal to his Patent: This was declared to be High-Treaſon; for having collected Money by theſe Counterfeits, he had Uſurped Regal Authority. 2 *Roll. Rep.* 52.

To Forge the Coyn, was Treaſon at Common Law, tho' the Offender did not utter it; and to Counterfeit it, is made ſo by this Statute. But *Clipping, Waſhing, Filing, &c.* was no Counterfeiting it within this Statute; yet it was made High-Treaſon by a ſubſequent Act of Parliament, *viz.* by 5 *Eliz. cap.* 11. but it was no Corruption of Blood or loſs of Dower.

So likewiſe *Impairing, Diminiſhing, Falſifying, Scaling, &c.* is not Counterfeiting, but 'tis made Treaſon by 18 *Eliz. cap.* 1. without Corruption of Blood or Loſs of Dower.

By *Money* is intended only the *proper Money* of this Nation; but now Forging or Counterfeiting any *Foreign Money*, (if made current here by Proclamation) is High Treaſon *per* 1 *Mar. cap.* 6.

And Forging it, if not current here, is a Miſpriſion of Treaſon in the Principal Forgers, their Aiders and Abettors.

Bringing counterfeit Money into the Realm, is meant ſuch as is made in *Imitation* of *Engliſh* Money, and brought from Foreign Parts, not within the Dominion of the *King*.

It muſt not barely be *uttered* here, but it muſt be *brought in and uttered* by one and the ſame Perſon; if ſo, 'tis Treaſon.

Trial. By the Statute of 7 *Will.* 3. *cap.* 3. ſome Alterations are made in Trials of Traitors; for before that Statute, Men were committed for Treaſon, and Friends were not ſuffered to come near them; they had neither Pen,

Ink or Paper, and did not know for what Treason they were committed, or by whom accused; if by chance any Person advised them without Leave of the Court, he was punishable; and if upon the Arraigment the Prisoner desir'd Councel upon any Point of Law, those Councel must be ready to argue it *instanter*, and the Court did give Judgment as soon.

'Tis true, he had Liberty to except against any of the Jury, but that could be no Advantage to him, because he never had a Copy of the Pannel to consider against whom to except.

When he produced any Witnesses, they were not to be examined upon Oath, which (as it hath been observ'd) is either too great an Advantage for the Prisoner, or none at all; for if his Witnesses not sworn shall have equal Credit with those which are upon Oath, the Prisoner has too great an Advantage; but if they are not to have Credit, because not sworn, then why is he suffer'd to have any Witnesses on his Side?

2 *Bulst.* 147. My Lord *Coke*, so long ago as in *Anno* 11 *Jac.* told us, That the Jesuits had slandered our Common Law in the Case of Trials of Offenders for their Lives, because they had neither Councel, nor were their Witnesses examined upon Oath. For Truth cannot appear but upon the Testimony of Witnesses; and therefore 'tis absolutely necessary to put the highest Obligation on them on both Sides, which is an Oath.

7 *W.* 3. *cap.* 3. By this Statute it is provided, That a Person indicted for Treason, whereby Corruption of Blood may be made, or for Misprision of such Treason, shall have a Copy of the whole Indictment Five Days before his Trial, he desiring the same; and this is that he may advise with Councel, by Two of whom he may make a full Defence, and his Witnesses shall be upon Oath: He is not to have the Names of the Witnesses for the King.

That no Man shall be Indicted, Tried or Attainted of such Treason or Misprision, *&c.* but upon the Oaths of Two lawful Witnesses, who shall both speak to the same Overt-Act of Treason, or to different Acts, but of the same Treason, unless the Party is mute, refuseth to plead, or challengeth above 35 peremptorily, or confesseth his Fault.

But such Offender may be outlawed; and if attainted by Outlawry, yet he may come in and be tried by Law after such Outlawry, and he shall upon his Trial have the Benefit of this Act.

And where distinct Treasons of divers Kinds shall be alledged in one Indictment, one Witness to one Species of Treason, and another Witness to another, shall not be two Witnesses within the Meaning of that Law, and no Evidence shall be given of an Overt-Act, unless expresly laid in the Indictment.

The Prosecution must be within Offence 3 Years after the Offence committed, except it be for a Treason in designing or attempting the Assassination of the King.

No

No Indictment, &c. shall be quashed for Mis-writing, or for false or improper *Latin*, unless Exception be taken to the same before the Evidence given in Court; neither shall any such Matter be a sufficient Cause to arrest the Judgment after Conviction, yet it may be reversed by Writ of Error.

When a Peer is tryed, all the Peers who have a Right to sit and vote in Parliament, shall be summoned 20 Days before the Trial: They must take the Oaths. But the Act doth not extend to any Indictment for Counterfeiting the Coin, the Great Seal, &c. After Examination of the Offender, and of the Witnesses who are to be upon Oath, the Criminal must be committed.

Dyer 286. *b.* Indictment for Treason must be found in that County where the Fact was done, which may afterwards be removed into *B. R.*

3 *Lev.* 396. If it is for levying War, Conspiring the Death of the King, or adhering to his Enemies, it must conclude *contra Legiantiæ suæ debitum*; and 'tis not sufficient, tho' the particular Facts set forth therein do shew that what was done by the Offender was against his Allegiance: This was Mr. *Walcot*'s Case, who was executed for High-Treason, and his Attainder was reversed in the House of Lords by one Vote.

There is a late Statute, 2 & 3 *Ann.* Which makes it Treason for any Officer and Soldier *out of the Realm*, either on Land or Sea, to hold Correspondence with any Rebel or Enemy to the *King*, or to give them Advice or Intelligence, by Letters, Messages, Signs or Tokens, or any other Way whatsoever, or to enter into any Condition with them without the King's Leave, or Lisence of the General, Lieutenant-General, or Chief-Commander. *Vide Act* 12 *Ann.* in Tit. *Soldiers*. The tryal is to be by a Jury of *Middlesex*, or by a special Commission.

And by a Law 3 & 4 *Anne*, 'tis made Treason, during the War with *France*, to send, or cause to be sent, loaded, transported or deliver'd to the use of the *French* King, or any of his Subjects residing within his Dominions, these Goods following, *viz.* *Arms*, *Powder*, *Bullet*, *Salt Peter*, *Coardage*, *Hemp*, *Iron*, *Masts*, *Ordnance*, *Pitch* or *Tar*.

Any Person since *May* 4. 1705. going voluntarily into *France*, or any of the *French Kings* Dominions in *Europe*, without Lisence, or who have bore Arms for the said King since that time, and shall Return or Continue here without Lisence, shall be guilty of Treason.

There is likewise another Treason made by the Act, entit. *An Act for the better Security of his Majesty's Person and Government*, That if any Persou after 25 *March*, 1706, shall maliciously, advisedly, or directly, *by Writing or Printing*, declare or affirm, That the King is not lawful King, or that the *pretended Prince of Wales* hath any title to the Crown, or that any other Person hath a Right to it, otherwise than according to the Act of Settlement made 1 & 12 *Wm.* 3. or that the Kings and Queens of *England* are not able, by the Authority of their Parliaments,

to

to make Laws sufficient to limit and bind the Crown of this Realm, shall be guilty of High-Treason. And if any one by *Preaching*, *Teaching* or *advised Speaking* shall declare, maintain or affirm, as aforesaid, such Person being lawfully Convicted, shall incur the Penalty of a *Præmunire*. But if the Prosecution be for Words, there must be Information given of such Words, upon Oath, to one or more Justices of the Peace within three days after the words are spoken; and then the Prosecution must be within three Months after such Information; and the Conviction must be by Oath of two Credible Witnesses.

The Form of a Mittimus.

To the Keeper of the Common Goal &c.

I Send you herewith the Body *H. M.* who was brought before me this present Day, and Charged with High-Treason. These are therefore to Command you to take the said *H. M.* into your Custody, and him Safely to keep in your Goal, till he shall be from thence delivered by due Course of Law. Given under my Hand and Seal, *&c.*

Then the Justice must take a several Recognizance of every Witness to appear at the Assizes, and give Evidence against the Prisoner.

In High-Treason there are no *Accessaries*, but all are Principals; and therefore my Lord *Coke* tells us, That what will make a Man Accessary to a Felony before the Fact, the same will make him Principal in High-Treason.

Petty-Treason.

PEtty-Treason consists in three Particulars, *per Stat.* 25 *Edw.* 3. As, 1st. *A Servant Killing his Master.* This extends likewise to the Mistress who hath no Husband, and to the Wife of the Master. If a Servant have Malice against his Master whilst he is in his Service, and afterwards, going out of his Service, *Killeth* him, this is *Petty-Treason*, but killing him upon a suddain Quarrel is *Manslaughter*.

2dly. *A Wife Killing her Husband.* If she procure another to Murder her Husband, she is only *Accessary*, unless she was present in the House when the Fact was Committed, tho' not in the same Room, and she shall be hanged, and not burnt, because she, as *Accessary*, cannot be guilty of Treason, where the *Principal* is guilty of Murder; but if the Person prosured is a Servant, then 'tis *Petty-Treason*

Treason in both. If she, and another not being her Servant, killeth the Husband, 'tis Petty-Treason in her, and Murder in the other.

3dly, *Ecclesiastical Persons killing their Ordinary.* Petty-Treason doth not suppose a Trust and Obedience in the Offender, which is either Civil, as in the Cases abovementioned, or Ecclesiastical, as in this Case.

But this Statute shall not be construed according to Equity, and therefore if the Son killeth the Father or Mother, 'tis not Petty-Treason, unless he was a Servant receiving Wages, as well as a Son.

Aiders, Abettors and Procurors, are adjudged to be within this Act.

Misprision of Treason.

THIS is when one knoweth of any Treason, and concealeth it; but it must be a *bare Knowledge* only, for if the Person consents to the Treason, he is a Traitor. Therefore the Person ought, as soon as may be, to reveal it to some Magistrate. But receiving a Traitor, and comforting him, knowing him to be such, he is a principal Traitor himself.

If one knowing upon what Design Persons meet, and hear them discourse of Treason, though he says nothing himself, or doth any Act towards it, yet this is Treason; for 'tis more than a Concealment, because, by his Silence, he gives consent to what was then doing. But if he did not know upon what Design they met, and he casually hears their traiterous Discourses, and says nothing, and never comes again to their Consultations, this Concealment is only *Misprision* of Treason; but if he comes into their Company again, and hears their Discourses, and then conceals it, this is High Treason, for it sheweth his Approbation of their Design: And this was Sir *Everard Digby*'s Case, who was present at the Powder-Treason, met with the Traitors, and heard their Discourses, but neither said or acted any thing. For to make *Misprision* of Treason, there must be a *Knowledge* of the Design (as already hath been observed) and of the Persons, or some of them, and likewise a Concealment of it, for a Man cannot be said to conceal what he doth not know: And therefore if I tell a Man, that there will be a Rising at such a Time, and do not mention the Persons who are to be in Arms, or the Nature of the Plot, and this is concealed by that Person to whom I told it, 'tis but Misprision of Treason, because he had no Knowledge of the Treason it self.

But if a Man knows the Conspirators, and then in general Discourse tells the People there will be a Rising, and doth not discover the Plot, or the Traitors, this is Misprision of Treason; for notwithstanding such general Discourse, he conceals both the Treason and Traitors. The safest Way in these Cases, would be to discover the Treason to some Magistrate; for if to a Person who hath not Authority to take an Exa-

 mination

mination, it may be a Question, Whether such a Discovery will acquit him from Misprision of Treason. *Keeling* 22. *Vid. Misprision.*

Trial.

THE Trial of an Alien, who lived here under Protection of the Laws, if it be for Treason, it shall not be *per medietatem Linguæ*; but 'tis otherwise in Petit-Treason, Murder or Felony. 1 & 2 *Phil. & Mar.*

But such a Trial *per medietatem Linguæ*, is not to be allowed *ex Officio*, or *ex debito Justitiæ*, but at the Instance of the Party; for if he doth not desire it, 'tis to be as at Common Law by a Jury of *English* Men.

If a Man commits Treason in *Ireland*, he may be tried here; and this was *Orork*'s Case. *Dyer* 1 and 262.

By the Statute of 33 *H.* 8. 'tis enacted, That if a Person is examined by three of the King's Council, upon *Treason*, *Murder*, *&c.* and confesseth it, or is suspected by the Council to be guilty; in such Case, the King, by a special Commission, may have the Offender tried in any Place. 33 *H.* 8. *cap.* 23.

One *Grevel was examined* before the Council as *Accessary* to a Murder in *Warwickshire*, and it was adjudged, that he should be tried *there*, because he was examined as an *Accessary*, and not for the Murder it self. 1 *and* 194.

But regularly Indictments must be found in the proper County, and the Trial must be by Jurors of that County.

Stroke in one County and Death in another, the Offender shall be tried where the Party died. 2 & 3 *Ed.* 6. *c.* 24.

A Trial cannot be had the same Sessions in which the Party is indicted, unless in Criminal Cases, and that is in *favorem Libertatis.*

But then the offender must be in Custody; but this seems not to be agreeable to Reason, that a Criminal should have a longer time allowed him to advise in trivial Matters, than in those which concern his Life.

Yet the Defendant was indicted and tried the same Sessions for a *Barretry*, and held good, because he appeared; and in such Case, upon his Appearance, he may be tried as well then as afterwards. 2 *Cro.* 404.

Vagrants.

FOR reducing the Laws relating to Rogues, Vagabonds, Sturdy Beggars and Vagrants, into one Act; and for the more effectual punishing them, and sending them

them whether they ought to be sent, it is enacted, That from the first of *Augusto*, 1714 (12 *Annæ*.) All Persons pretending to be Patent-Gatherers, or Collectors for Prisons, Goals or Hospitals, and wandring abroad for that Purpose.

All Fencers, Bearwards, common Players of Interludes, Minstrels and Juglers.

All Persons pretending to be Gypsies, or wandring in the Habit or Form of counterfeit *Egyptians*; or pretending to have Skill in Physiognomy, Palmestry, or like crafty Science. Such as pretend to tell Fortunes, or like fantastical Imaginations, or using any subtil Craft, or unlawful Games or Plays. All Persons able in Body, who run away and leave their Wives and Children to the Parish; or not having wherewith otherwise to maintain themselves, use Loytering, and refuse to work for the common Wages: And all other idle Persons wandering abroad, and begging, (except Soldiers, Mariners, or Seafaring Men, licensed by Testimonial under the Hand and Seal of a Justice of Peace, setting down the Time and Place of their Landing, and the Place to which they are to pass, and limiting the Time of their Passage, while they continue in the direct Way, and during the Time so limited;) shall be deemed Rogues and Vagabonds.

The Constables, and other Parish-Officers, are to apprehend all such Persons as shall be found Wandering, Begging, or Misordering themselves as above, and convey them before the next Justice; who is to inform himself as well by the Oath of the Person apprehended as otherwise, in Writing, to be subscribed by the Party, and transmitted to the Quarter-Sessions to be kept on Record: And to send him to his last legal Settlement or Place of Birth; if under the Age of 14 Years, to the Abode of Father or Mother, if known; if not known, then to the Place where found last begging or misordering themselves and pass'd unapprehended.

The Form of the Examination of a Vagrant.

The 10th Day of *Octob.* 1720.

THis Examinant upon his Oath saith, That he was born in the Parish of, &c. *and that since his Birth he hath obtained a legal Settlement in the Parish of,* &c. *in the said County of,* &c. *wherein he lived near 7 Years, and during that Time paid* 20 l. per Annum *Rent for a Tenement in the said Parish of,* &c. *That it is about five Years since he rented the said Tenement, but hath not obtained a legal Settlement in any other Place or Parish since.*

Jurat Die & Anno A. B.
supradict' coram

J. L.

It is provided in the said Act, That no Constable shall be obliged to receive such Vagrant by any Pass or Order, unless it appear by the Pass, That such Vagrant was whipped, or sent to the House of Correction through which he last passed, (except Women with Child, Soldiers wanting Subsistence, having Certificates, or such Persons as the Justices, *&c.* shall judge not able to undergo such Punishment) which must be inserted in the said Pass.

The Form of the Commitment.

To the Keeper of the House of Correction at *M.* in the said County.

I Send you herewith the Body of A. B. *a Vagrant, taken wandring and begging in the Parish of,* &c. *and upon his Examination upon Oath, he appears to be a Vagrant, (confessing that he begged, as aforesaid;) and therefore is within the Meaning and Intent of the late Act of Parliament: You are to set him to Labour for the Space of two Days, and omit Correction, (he being Sixty Years of Age, and very infirm:) And at the End of the said Time, you are to deliver him to* C. D. *one of the Constables of the said Parish of,* &c. *(who took him up) to be by him conveyed to the Parish of,* &c. *in the said County of* K. *it appearing to me upon his Oath to be the Place of his last legal Settlement.*

Given under my Hand and Seal this 10th Day of *October*, 1720.

The Form of the Pass to the last Settlement.

To *C. D.* one of the Constables of the Parish of, *&c.* in the County of, *&c.* and to all other Officers whom it may concern.

WHereas A. B. *being (as he informs) about the Age of* 60 *Years, was apprehended in the said Parish by the said* C. D. *begging Alms, and brought before me* P. L. *Esq; one of his Majesty's Justices of the Peace for the said County. And upon Examination of the said* A. B. *taken before me upon Oath, it doth appear that he was found begging as abovesaid; and that he hath obtained a legal Settlement since his Birth in the Parish of,* &c. *wherein he lived Seven Years, and during that Time paid* 20 l. per Ann. *for a Tenement in the said Parish of,* &c. *and that it is about Five Years since he rented the said Tenement; and that he hath not obtained any other legal Settlement in any other Place or Parish since as I can find:* These are therefore *in His Majesties Name, to will and require you to convey the said* A. B. *on Foot to the said Parish of,* &c. *and him deliver to the Constable, or other Officer of the same Parish, to be there provided for according to Law: And I do allow the Space of one Day for his passing there.* Given under my Hand and Seal, *&c.*

Then the Justice who makes the Pass, is likewise to deliver to the Constable a Certificate, as followeth:

To *C. D.* one of the Constables, *&c.*

WHereas *by a Pass under my Hand and Seal, bearing Date this 10th Day of* October *Instant, I do hereby order and direct you the said* C. D. *one of the Constables of the Parish of,* &c. *in the said County; That you convey on Foot* A. B. *(by* (by You taken up begging Alms in the said Parish) to the Parish of, &c. in one Days Time from the Date hereof, it appearing to me upon his Oath to be the Place of his last legal Settlement; for which you are to be allowed the Sum of 1 s. and no more: And you are to give the Bearer a Receipt for him on the Backside hereof. Given under my Hand, &c.

The Receipt to be endorsed on the Back of the last mentioned Order.

Received this 10th Day of October, 1720. *of* C. D. *one of the Constables of the Parish of*, &c. *the Person of* A. B. *a Vagrant, by him taken up in the said Parish begging of Alms. I say received.*

If the Place of Birth or last Settlement of such Vagrant be not in the same County &c. where apprehended, then the Pass is to direct him to be delivered to the Officer of the first Town of the next County, &c. named in such Pass or Certificate, through which such Persons are to be conveyed in the direct Way to the Place whether they are to be sent, and take such Receipt as above; and the Officer to whom the Vagrant is delivered, is to apply to a Justice of Peace of his Precinct, &c. who shall cause the Vagrant to be stripp'd and openly whipped, or sent to the House of Correction for two or three Days, and afterwards conveyed with the former Pass and a new Certificate in like Form; and so to be done from one County or Precinct to another, till brought to the Place first ordered to be sent.

The above Precedents will serve, *mutatis mutandis*, for Persons misordering themselves, or committing any other Acts of Vagrancy.

Constable not using his best Endeavour to apprehend Vagrants, it shall be deemed a Neglect of his Duty.

If any other Inhabitant refusing to apprehend a Vagrant, or assist therein, forfeits 10 *s.* to the Poor, to be levied by Distress. Oath of one Witness.

The Justice may order the Constable to pay two Shillings to the Person who apprehends such Vagrant; upon Refusal may make him pay 20 *s.*

The Justices of Peace of every County, City, &c. or any two of them some Time before or after the Quarter-Sessions, shall meet, and command the Constables in their several Divisions (who shall be assisted with sufficient Men of the same Places) to make a general privy Search in one Night for Rogues, Vagabonds and sturdy Beggars.

A Warrant for a general privy Search.

To the Constables of the Parish of, &c.

Whereas *by Virtue of an Act of Parliament made in the Twelfth Year of the Reign of our late Sovereign Lady Queen* Anne, *intitled*, An Act for Reducing the Laws relating to Rogues, Vagabonds, Sturdy Beggars and Vagrants into one Act

Act of Parliament, and for the more effectual Punishing them, and sending them whither they ought to be sent. *These are therefore in His Majesty's Name, (taking to Your Assistance a sufficient Number of Persons) to make a general privy Search on* Wednesday *the 15th Day of this Instant* October *in the Evening and Night of the same Day, for Rogues, Vagabonds and sturdy Beggars, and other Persons misordering him or her self; and if any such You find to apprehend, and the next Morning following such Your said Search, You bring them before Us, and others His Majesties Justices of the Peace that will be assembled at*, &c. *by Nine of the Clock, to be there examined and dealt withal according to Law: Hereof You are not to fail, as You will answer the contrary at Your Perils.* Given under our Hands and Seals, *&c.*

If the Justices shall see cause to judge any Rogue or Vagabond to be dangerous to the People, and unlikely to be reformed, may commit him to the House of Correction or common Goal to be kept at hard Labour till the next Quarter-Sessions.

Mittimus *for an incorrigible Rogue.*

To the Governour of the House of Correction.

WE *send You herewith the Body of* A. B. *who was this Day taken up drunk asleep in the Street in the Parish of*, &c. *by* C. D. *Constable of the said Parish (and who was some short Time before committed to Bridewell for Pilfering) and by us is adjudged to be a dangerous and incorrigible Rogue, and unlikely to be reformed: Keep him to hard Labour until the next Quarter-Sessions of the Peace to be holden for the said County, there to be dealt with pursuant to a late Act of Parliament relating to Rogues, Vagabonds, sturdy Beggars and Vagrants: And for Your so doing this shall be Your Warrant.* Given under our Hands and Seals this 16th Day of *October*, 1720.

If the major Part of the Justices at the Quarter-Sessions shall adjudge such Person a dangerous and incorrigible Rogue, they may cause him to be whipped Three Market-Days successively, and kept to hard Labour, during such Time as they shall think meet; and if he shall before the Time expired, break out, and make his Escape, he shall for such his Offence, be guilty of Felony.

The Pass as per *Act* 12 ANNÆ.

To the Constable of the Parish of, *&c.*

WHereas —— *being, as he informs, about the Age of* —— *Years, was apprehended in the Parish of* —— *aforesaid, there wandring and begging, pretending as a Fencer*, &c. (as the Case shall require) *and brought before me, one of His Majesty's Justices of the Peace for this County; and upon Examination of the said* ——

and

and of —— taken before me, upon Oath, it doth appear, that the said —— was born at ——, in the County of ——; or, *That the said —— was found begging in the Parish of —— where he last passed unapprehended, and the Place of his or her Birth cannot be discovered; and it doth not appear to me, that the said —— hath obtained any legal Settlement since his or her Birth:* **These are therefore** *to require You to convey the said —— in the next direct Way to the said Parish or Town of ——, and there deliver him to the Constable or other Officer of the same Parish or Town, to be there provided for according to Law;* or else, *to convey the said —— to the Parish or Town of —— that being the first Town in the next Precinct through which he ought to pass to the said Parish or Town of —— to be thence conveyed on according to the Directions of this Act, to the said Parish or Town of ——. And I do hereby allow the Space of — Days for his or her passing to the said Parish or Town of ——* **Given** *under my Hand and Seal this —— Day*, &c.

The Order as *per* Act.

WHereas *by a Pass* (reciting the Substance or Effect of the said Pass) *I do hereby order and direct, That the said Person or Persons is or are to be conveyed on Foot,* (or, *in a Cart*, or, by *Horse*, &c.) *to the said Parish or Town of —— in —— Days time, for which the said Constable*, &c. *is to be allowed the Sum of —— and no more.* **Given** *under my Hand this —— Day*, &c.

Verdict.

IN Capital Cases, the Jury cannot be discharged before the Verdict is given.

And it must be given openly in Court, for no privy Verdict is allowed in such Cases.

But the Jury may find Matter specially, *viz.* If the Indictment is for Murder, they may find the Defendant guilty of Manslaughter, Chance-medly, or *se Defendendo*; but then they must find in what manner, that the Court may judge of the Law arising upon the Fact.

A. B. was indicted for Murder. The Fore-man of the Jury said he was guilty of Man-slaughter; the rest of the Jury informed the Court, That they did not agree to that Verdict. Then the Court asked *A. B.* Whether he would be discharged of that Jury. He consented, and the Prisoner was tried by another upon the same Indictment, and found guilty of Murder, and had Judgment to be hanged. *Yelv.* 15.1 *&* 103.

The Verdict must be perfect; and therefore if upon the Statute of 8 *H. 6.* the Jury find, *si Domus predict' not fuit in possessione Dom' Regis*, then *Billa vera*; this is void, for 'tis a conditional Verdict.

There is no Necessity of finding the Value of any thing as laid in the Indictment: More they cannot find, but less they may.

Watch

Watch.

IN walled Towns, the Gates ought to be shut from Sunset to Sunrising, and none shall lodge in the Suburbs except the Host will answer for him. 5 *H*. 4. *c*. 5. 5 *Ed*. 3. *cap*. 5.

Any Justice may cause the Watch to be set; but no Man is compellable to watch, unless he is an Inhabitant in the Town.

If a Person who ought to watch, and is commanded by the Constable so to do, refuseth, 'tis a Question whether he may put him in the Stocks; but he may complain to a Justice of Peace, who may bind the Offender over to the Sessions, or the Constable may present him there. *Cro. Eliz*. 204. 3 *Leon*. 208. same Case.

A Warrant to appoint a Watch.

To all the Constables and other his Majesty's Officers whom these may concern within the Parish of, *&c*.

THese *are (in His Majesties Name) to will and require You from Time to Time to appoint and settle sufficient Watches (to meet at Nine at Night, and not to depart till Six in the Morning, amongst whom a competent Number of good House-keepers are always to be present.) And You, and every of You, are to bring us the Names and Conditions of Your respective Watches at our said weekly Meetings, that the performance of your Duties herein may be the better known and taken Notice of, His Majesty (in Council) having given us strict Command herein. You are likewise to give us an Account of all such as arm themselves beyond their Qualities, and to use Your utmost Endeavours by all the Ways imaginable to preserve His Majesty's Peace during his Absence from this City*. Dated this 8th Day of December, 1720.

A Warrant for Watch and Ward, and to apprehend idle Persons.

To the High-Constable of the Hundred of *A*. and to the Petty-Constables, *&c*. within the said Hundred.

WHereas *Information hath been given unto us, That very many suspicious idle Persons do wander about the Country without Controulment or Question; For the better prevention thereof for the Future, and of Robberies, and other Misdemeanours often occasioned thereby:* These are therefore *(in His Majesty's Name) to charge and command You, and every of You, to take care of Your Officers herein, and to see that you keep and cause Watches to be duly kept in all Parishes and Places within Your said Hundred of* A. *by able and well-armed Men every Night, and Ward by Day from Sun to Sun, and command them that they do apprehend all such* Rogues, Vagabonds *and* sturdy Beggars, *and other wandering and idle suspicious Persons as you shall apprehend by Day or Night and conceive to be more than ordinary dangerous, and bring them before us, or some other of his Majesties Justices of the said County, to be examined and dealt with according to Law. And all Persons whatsoever are hereby commanded to be aiding and assisting, and obedient to you herein. Hereof fail not,* Given *under our Hands*, &c.

A Warrant by Order of Sessions to keep Watch and Ward.

To the Constable and Headburrough of the Hundred of L.

WHereas several Robberies, Felonies and other Crimes have been lately committed in the County aforesaid; it was therefore ordered at the last General Quarter-Sessions of the Peace, held at *M.* for the said County, That Watch and Ward be duly set and kept in all and every usual Place and Places within your Hundred. You are therefore to take Care, that the same be done pursuant to the said Order; you are likewise to apprehend all idle and suspicious Persons, and bring them before us, or some other of his Majesty's Justices of the Peace for the said County, in order to proceed against them according to Law And hereof fail not at your Perils. Given under our Hands and Seals, *&c.*

A *Mittimus* to the House of Correction of one apprehended by the Watch.

To the Keeper of the House of Correction

WHereas A. B. *was this present Day brought before me* P. L. *Esq; one of his Majesty's Justices*, &c. *the said* A. B. *being taken last Night by the Watch set by the Constable of* &c. *and charged with wandring abroad at unseasonable Times of the Night, and also with other disorderly Behaviour*: These are therefore *to require you to take the said* A. B. *into your Custody, and him safely to keep, until he shall be delivered by due Course of Law from thence, and in the mean Time to make him labour, allowing him such Maintenance as he shall earn thereby, and you are to punish him as by Law is required. You are likewise to bring him to the next Quarter-Sessions*, &c.

Weights and Measures.

THERE are two sorts of Weights, *viz.* *Troy* Weight, and *Averdupois*.

Troy Weight hath 12 Ounces to the Pound; and by this are weighed, Gold, Pearl, Jewels, Silks, Silver, Wheat, *&c.*

Averdupois hath 16 Ounces to the Pound, and by these are weighed, Bread, Butter, Cheese, Drugs, Flesh, Flax, Grocery Ware, Hemp, Iron, Steel, Lead, Pitch, Tar, Tallow, Wool, Wax, *&c.*

These, and all Commodities which are garbled, and of which any *Refuse* is made, are weighed by *Averdupois* Weight, and to every Hundred there is an Allowance of 12 Pounds, and so *pro Rato*.

The Bushel must contain 8 Gallons, or 64 Pints of Wheat, and must be kept sealed in every City, Burrough or Town. 11 *H.* 6. *cap.* 8. 31 *Ed.* 1. 12. *H.* 7.

Eight Bushels make a Quarter of Corn striked. 15 *R.* 2. *cap.* 4. The Standard of Bushels, Gallons and Ells, must be signed with an Iron Seal of the King's; and if any sell or buy with Measure unsealed, he shall be amerced. 31 *Ed.* 1. the Statute *de Pistoribus*.

This Standard must be kept by the Mayor and Bailiffs of the Town, and Six Persons must be sworn, before whom all Measures must be Sealed. 31 *Ed.* 1.

Every Measure is to be according to this Standard, and shall be Striked, and not heaped. 25 *Ed.* 3.

A Tun of Wine is 252 Gallons. The Pipe is 126. A Barrel of Herrings is 30. A Butt of Salmon is 40 Gallons, 2 *H.* 6. *cap.* 11. 1 *R.* 3. *cap.* 13.

Vessels made contrary to that Statute, the Owner forfeits the Commodities therein contained to the Lord of the Town where found; but the Prosecutor must have a 4th Part.

Every City, Burrough and Town must have a common Ballance, and sealed Weights, in the Keeping of the Head Officer or Constable there, otherwise the City forfeits 10*l.* the Burrough 4 *l.* and the Town 40 *s.* to the King.

Justices of the Peace have Power to hear and determine these Offences. 8 *H.* 6. *cap.* 5.

The Mayor shall have one Penny for *sealing* a Bushel, and for every other Measure a Half-Penny.

If he refuse or delay to seal, he forfeits 40 *s.* to be divided between King and Party grieved. 7 *H.* 7 *cap.* 4.

Two Justices (*Quorum unus*) have Authority, as well by Examination as by Inquiry, to hear and determine Faults of Mayors and Head Officers, and of Buyers and

Sellers

Sellers otherwife than by the Standard, and fet Fines at Difcretion ; defective Weights and Meafures are forfeited, and muft be burnt. 11 *H.* 7. *cap.* 4.

But now by the Statute of 22 *Car.* 2. *cap.* 8. 'tis prohibited to fell Corn, Grain or Salt, otherwife than by the Standard, and the Bufhel muft be *ftruck even with the Brim*, and fealed : The Forfeiture for every Offence is 40*s.* the Conviction to be by Oath of One Witnefs before One Juftice, Mayor or Head Officer; and muft be levied by Warrant directed to the Church-Wardens and Overfeers of the Poor, for the Ufe of the Poor of the Parifh where the Offence was committed ; and if no Diftrefs can be had, the Party may be committed without Bail till he pay the Penalty.

If Head Officers of Cities, Burroughs or Corporations, fuffer any Perfon to fell or buy by other Meafure, and if upon Complaint do not punifh the Offenders, then if they are convicted at *Seffions*, they forfeit five Pounds to the Poor and Informer ; and if no Diftrefs can be had they may be committed till Payment.

Conftable may fearch and examine if any Perfon ufe other Meafures, *&c.* and if they find any unfealed, may break them, and may prefent the Offender at the next Quarter-Seffions.

By 22 *&* 23 *Car.* 2. *cap.* 12. buying or felling Corn or Salt without meafuring (if required) or in any other Manner than is directed by the former Acts of 22 *Car.* 2. forfeits befides the 40 *s.* all the Corn or Salt, or the Value thereof, to the Perfon grieved ; and upon Complaint to One or more Juftices of the Peace, the Proof fhall lie upon the Perfon accufed, who muft make it appear by Oath of One Witnefs, That he did buy or fell according to this or the former Statute.

If he fail in fuch Proof, he forfeits all the Corn or Salt, or Value thereof, which is to be divided between the Informer and Poor where the Offence is Committed.

This is to be levied by Warrant from One or more Juftices, *&c.* before whom committed.

A Warrant to warn in all Tradefmen, and others, to have their Weights and Meafures examined by the Standard.

To the Borfholder of the B——— of *A.*

These are to will and require you, and (in His Majefty's Name) to charge and command you, That you warn all Perfons inhabiting within your faid Borrough, which have or ufe any Weights or Meafures, *to be tried and examined by the Standard, at the late Market-place near* H. *in the County of* Kent, *on* Thurfday *the Twenty Eighth of this Inftant* December, *by Eight of the Clock in the Forenoon ; and that you alfo warn to be at the Time and Place aforefaid, Fifteen fufficient Men of your faid Burrough, that they, and every of them, perfonally appear before me to do and perform fuch Things as for His Majefty's Service fhall be then and there injoyned them : And that your felf be there*

there present with this Precept, and have there the Names of all Artificers, Tradesmen, and other Persons whatsoever within your said Burrough, having or using any Weights and Measures whatsoever: **Hereof** *fail not at your Peril.* **Given** *under my Hand and Seal,* &c. 11 *H.* 7. *cap.* 4. 12 *H.* 7. *cap.* 5.

The Clerk of the Market's Warrant.

To the Constables of the Parish of *A.* &c.

These *are in his Majesties Name,* &c. *to will and require you, and every of you, upon sight hereof, to summon and cause the several Inhabitants within your respective Wards that buy and sell by* Weight *or* Measure, *to have their respective Weights and Measures to be tried and examined with the Standard on* Munday *the Fifth Day of* April *next, by Eight a-Clock in the Forenoon, at the* George Inn *in* A. *in the County aforesaid; and at the same Time and Place you deliver unto me in Writing the Christian Names and Sirnames of every such Inhabitant, with their respective Callings.* **Whereof** *you, and every of you, are not to fail,* &c. **Dated** under my Hand the 28*th* Day of *March*, 1721

Millers.

His *Toll-Dish* ought to be according to the Standard, and he ought to take but One Quart for Grinding One Bushel of hard Corn brought to his Mill; but if he fetch it, and carry it home, then two Quarts.

For *Malt*, he is to take but half the Toll he taketh for other Corn, because that is easily grinded.

These Offences are punishable in the Leet; but for *changing a Grist*, a Miller may be indicted at the Sessions, for tis a Wrong done by Deceit, and is *contra Pacem*.

Bakers

Bakers.

A Table of the Aſſize of Bread, according to the Act of the 12*th* of Queen Anne.

		Penny Loaf.				Six Penny Loaf					
		White		Wheat.		Wheaten.			Houſhold.		
s.	d.	Ounces	Drams	Ounces	Drams	Pounds	Ounces	Drams	Pounds	Ounces	Drams
2	6	18	9	27	13	10	6	13	13	14	7
3	0	15	7	23	3	8	11	00	11	9	6
3	6	13	4	19	14	7	7	3	9	14	14
4	0	11	9	17	6	6	8	4	8	11	00
4	6	10	5	15	7	5	12	11	7	11	9
5	0	9	4	13	14	5	3	7	6	15	4
5	6	8	7	12	1[illegible]	4	11	13	6	5	2
6	0	7	1[illegible]	11	9	4	5	8	5	12	11
6	6	7	2	10	11	4	00	3	5	5	9
7	0	6	1[illegible]	9	15	3	11	9	4	15	7
[illegible]	[illegible]	6		9	4	3	7	10	4	10	2

The

The Form of an Affidavit againft a Baker for felling Bread lefs than Weight, to be left with the Juftices; upon which he makes the following Summons.

A. B. *of the Parifh of &c maketh Oath, That on the fifth Inftant he bought of C. D of the Parifh of &c. Baker, One Half-quarter of a Peck Wheaten Loaf of Bread, and paid the faid C. D. Two Pence Half Penny for the fame; which faid Loaf weighed, when new, but Two Pounds* 2. *Ounces, and* 4 *Drams, whereas it fhould have weighed Two Pounds and four Ounces, according to the Affize of Bread made the* 27 *Day of* January *laft.*

Jur' coram me 6° *die Marti, anni* 1721. P. L. A. B.

A Summons thereupon,

To C. D. Baker at his Houfe in, *&c.*

These *are to Summon you perfonally to appear before me* P. L. *Efq; one of His Majefty's Juftices of the Peace for the faid County, at my Houfe in* &c. *To morrow Morning by* 9 *of the Clock, to fhew caufe why you fhould not be convicted for felling Yefterday, One Half-quarter of a Peck Wheaten Loaf of Bread to one* A. B. *which weighed but Two Pounds* 2 *Ounces and* 4 *Drams, whereas it fhould have weighed Two Pounds and* 4 *Ounces, according to the laft Affize of the* 27th *of* January *laft: otherwife a Warrant of Diftrefs will be Iffued out againft you for the faid Offence.* Given *under my Hand the* 6th *Day of* March, 1721.

The Warrant of Diftrefs.

To the Conftables, *&c.* of the Parifh of, &c.

Whereas *it appears unto me, whofe Hand and Seal is hereunto fet, one of his Majefty's Juftices of the Peace for the faid County, upon Information on Oath of* A. B. *That on the Fifth of this Inftant March,* C. D. *of* &c. *In the Parifh of* &c. *Baker, did then and there fell to him the faid* A. B. *One Half-quarter of a Peck Wheaten Loaf of Bread, and received Two Pence Half Penny for the fame; which faid Loaf weighed but Two Pounds* 2 *Ounces, and* 4 *Drams, whereas it fhould have weighed Two Pounds and* 4 *Ounces, according to the laft Affize of Bread of the* 27th *of January laft, contrary to the late Act of Parliament, Intituled,* An Act to regulate the Price and Affize of Bread: *For which faid Offence he the faid* C. D. *hath forfeited the Sum, of* 40 *s. to the Informer, as in the faid Act is mentioned;* And being duly fummoned, did not appear to anfwer the faid Offence:) These are therefore *in his Majefty's Name, to charge and command you upon Sight hereof, to demand of the faid* C. D. *the faid Sum of* 40 *s. fo by him forfeited as aforefaid, (he being duly profecuted within the fpace of* 3 *Days after the faid Offence committed:) And if he fhall refufe or Neglect to pay the fame, That then you forthwith levy the fame by Diftrefs and Sale of the Goods and Chattles of the faid* C. D. *Which faid Monies, when received, you are hereby ordered and required to pay to the faid* A. B. *the Informer in this Cafe.* Hereof *you are not to fail, as you will Anfwer the contrary.* Given *under my Hand and Seal,* &c.

Wrecks

VVrecks.

A *Teſtimonial* for one who hath ſuffered Ship-wreck.

R. K. of *M.* in the County of *Kent*, Eſq; one of His Majeſty's Juſtices, *&c.* To all Conſtables, Borſholders, *&c.*

FOraſmuch *as the Bearer hereof* A. B. *aged about*, &c. *having lately been at Sea in a Ship called*, &c. *hath ſuffered Shipwreck, and got to Land at* G. *in the ſaid County of* K. *upon the Tenth Day of March laſt paſt, as I am credibly informed, as well by the Report of the ſaid* A. B. *as alſo by the Teſtimony of divers of the Inhabitants of* G. *aforeſaid; and for that the ſaid* A. B. *hath not wherewithal to relieve himſelf in his Travel homewards to* T. *in the County of* S. *where he ſaith he was born, or hath a Dwelling*, &c. These are therefore *to will and require you, and every of you, to whom theſe Preſents ſhall come, not to moleſt or trouble the ſaid* A. B. *in his Travel to* T. *aforeſaid, where he is limited to be within Twenty Days next after the Date hereof, but to deſire you rather to relieve him in his Neceſſity, as you ſhall ſee meet; and withal, you the ſaid Conſtables and Borſholders of every Town where he ſhall come, to help and aſſiſt him with Lodging in convenient Time, ſo that he travel the direct Way to* T. *aforeſaid, and behaving himſelf according to Law.* Given, *&c.*

For preſerving all ſuch Ships, and Goods thereof, which ſhall happen to be forced on Shore, or ſtranded upon the Coaſts of this Kingdom, or any other His Majeſty's Dominions, It is Enacted, *per* 12 *Annæ*, That all the Sheriffs, Juſtices, *&c.* upon Application to them made, That any Veſſel is in Danger of being ſtranded, or run on Shore, or that is ſtranded or run on ſhore, ſhall command the Conſtables neareſt the Sea-Coaſts where ſuch Ship ſhall be in Danger, to call together as many Men as ſhall be neceſſary for the preſervation of ſuch Ship.

And all Officers of Men of War, *&c.* ſhall be aiding and aſſiſting on the Penalty of 100 *l.* Forfeiture.

VVomen. *ſee* Felony.

A Woman taken away by Force, is a Crime which is not mitigated, tho' the Marriage is by Conſent afterwards.

The Preamble of this Statute is, *viz. That Maids, Widows and Wives, having Subſtance in Goods, Lands and Tenements*, and ſome being Heirs at Law, have been taken *away for the Lucre of ſuch Subſtance* againſt their Wills, and married or defiled; and then 'tis Enacted, That he who taketh any Woman ſo againſt her Will, ſhall be a Felon. Alſo the Procurer, Abetter, and wilful receiver of ſuch Women, Clergy taken away *per* Stat. 39 *Eliz. cap.* 9.

A Woman inticed the *only* Daughter of her Father (who would be worth 5000 *l.*) to see a Ship, and when she had her on the *Thames*, carried her by Force and Threats into the Country, and there she was Married; but the Truth was, she had a *Brother*; and this was held not to be within that Statute, because the Preamble mentions the Estate and Condition of the Woman taken away, *&c.* and restrains the Purview to to these particular Cases.

(1.) There must be a Taking by Force. (2.) She must have Substance in Lands, Goods, *&c.* (3.) Or she must be Heir *Apparent*. (4.) She must be married or defiled.

Now in this Case the Woman had not a present Subsistence in Goods, for her Father was living; and she was not Heir Apparent, for she had a Brother then alive. *Hob.* 182. *Hurt.* 2.

But admitting a Woman hath Substance, *&c.* or is Heir Apparent, another Question hath been made upon this Statute, Whether the taking such a Woman by Force and Threatning her to make a Contract for Marriage, is Felony or not? and held in the Negative; for tho in the Body of the Act 'tis said, That the Taking by Force is Felony, yet the Intention of the Law is afterwards expounded, *viz.* it must not only be a Taking by Force, but marrying or defiling. It's true, Justice *Croke* was of a contrary Opinion, but other is Law at this Day. 1 *And.* 115. *Savil.* 59.

There is another Statute, and 'tis the last of *Phil.* and *Mar.* which relates to the taking any *Woman Child* under the Age of 16 Years out of the Custody, and against the Will of the Father or Mother, or the Person to whom the Father devised the Child: The Punishment in such Cases is 2 Years Imprisonment without Bail, or to pay such Fine as shall be imposed on him by *B. R.* 4 *&* 5 *Phil. & Mar. cap.* 8.

If he *defile* or *marry* such *Child*, he shall be imprisoned 5 Years or pay a Fine, *&c.* to the King and Party grieved.

If such Child is above 12, and under 16 Years, and consenting to Marry, then the next of Kin, to whom her Inheritance should come, shall enjoy it during her Life; and after her Decease, it shall go to the Heir at Law, but never to the Husband.

A Freeman of *London* devised the Custody of his Daughter to *C.* and died, the Daughter being then in the Country: *C.* gets a Warrant from the Chief Justice to take her, which he did, but she was then married to *B.* This was held to be out of the Statute because the Child was never in Possession of the Guardian. *Sid.* 363.

This last Statute seems to be an Affirmance of the Common Law; for if (before the Statute) a man came to the Father's House and contracted with his Daughter under 15 Years of Age, and by appointment meeting and marrying him, this is punishable by Fine and Imprisonment. *Sid.* 387.

An Information was exhibited against the Defendant for a lawful Practice and Combination in procuring a clandestine Marriage in the Night, between a Servant Maid and a young Gentleman who was Heir to an Estate; and this was without Banes or Licence: And the Parson being drunk, they were fined 100 Marks, and committed till paid. *Mar.* 12. *Cro. Car.* 557.

THE

THE

Office, Duty and Authority

OF

SHERIFFS,

How and in what Manner to execute the ſame, according to the Common and Statute Laws of *Great-Britain*, which are now in Force and Uſe.

LIKEWISE,

Of *UNDER-SHERIFFS* and their Deputies; and where the *High-Sheriff* ſhall be anſwerable for their Defaults, and where not, *&c.*

Together with the

Office and Duty of CORONERS.

PHILADELPHIA:
Printed and Sold by *Andrew Bradford*, at the *Bible* in the Second Street, MDCCXXI.

An Explanation of several Writs and Law-Terms used in the following Treatise, viz.

CAPIAS, a Writ before Judgment.

Scire facias, a Writ to call a Man to shew cause to the Court, why Execution of Judgment passed should not go out.

Fiere Facias, a Writ for the Sheriff to levy within a Year and a Day, the Debt or Damages recovered.

Habeas Corpus, A Writ to remove a Man that is indicted or imprisoned for a Trespass.

Audita Querela, A Writ that lies against him who has taken out a Statute Merchant or Recognizance, why Execution should not be granted.

Exigent, A Writ where the Defendent cannot be found, for the Sheriff to call him five County Days to appear, under Pain of Out-lawry.

Vendicioni Exponas, A Writ to the Sheriff commanding him to sell Goods in his Hands, taken in Execution.

Capias ad satisfaciendum, A Writ where a Man has recovered an Action personal, as for Debt, Damages, Detinue, *&c.*

Latitat, A Writ where a Man in personal Actions is called to the King's Bench.

Capias Utlagatum, A Writ against one out-law'd; and by special *Capias utlagat*, the Sheriff is commanded to seize all the Defendants Lands, Goods and Chattels.

Elegit, A Writ for him that hath recovered Debt or Damages, or upon Recognizance.

Distringas, A Writ to distrain one for a Debt to the King, or for his Appearance at a Day.

Venire facias, A Writ to cause Twelve Men of the County to come and say the Truth upon the Issue joined.

Tales, A Book of Jury-Mens Names.

Habeas Corpora, A Writ to bring such Jury-men as refuse to come upon the *Venire facias*.

Array, A Ranking or setting forth a Jury.

Accedas ad Curiam, A Writ that lies for him that has received false Judgment.

Redesseisin, is a Disseisin made by him who before was adjudged to have disseised the same Man of his Lands and Tenements.

Habere facias seisinam, A Writ commanding the Sheriff to give a Man that hath recovered Lands, Seisin.

Habere facias Possessionem, A Writ to give a Man Possession of Lands.

Rescons, An illegal taking away, and setting at Liberty.

Disseisor, He that disseiseth, or putteth another out of his Land.

Non est inventus, He is not to be found.

Cepi Corpus, I have the Body of such a Man.

B. R. *Bancus Regius*, The Court of King's Bench.

Dies Juridicus, The Day of the Court.

Per Curia, By the Court.

THE

THE OFFICE and DUTY OF SHERIFFS.

AS to the Time when and by whom the Realm of *England* was divided into Counties, Authors seem to differ. The Word *County* or *Shire* are certain Circuits or Parts of the Kingdom, into which the whole Realm was divided, for the more convenient Government thereof, and is governed by an Officer which we call *SHERIFF*, signifying *Præpositus*, or Governor. And it appears by History, That *Earls of Counties* had the Guard of the Counties long before the Conquest, and which was derived from the *Romans*; and the *Sheriff* was Deputy of the *Earl*, and the *Romans* called him *Vice-Consul*, 1 *Inst.* 168. By the *Stat.* 14 *Ed.* 3. *c.* 7. The Judges are to nominate three Persons of every County to be presented to the King, that he may pick one of them for *Sheriff* or Governor of the County. But the *Stat. of* 9 *Ed.* 2. restrains not the King's Power, but he may constitute a *Sheriff* without Election, or grant it in Fee; for all the Acts of Grace flow from him; and the *Stat. of* 14 *Ed.* 3. was made to ease the *S*overeign of Labour, and not to deprive him of Power; the Election being meerly in the King, and the Office Ministerial only.

The *Sheriff* takes Place of every Nobleman in the County during the Time that he is *Sheriff*; and though the *Sheriff* be not a Justice of the Peace, yet he is a *Conservator of the Peace*, and may imprison Persons upon good Cause, as Breach of the Peace, suspicion of Treason, Felony, Fresh Suit or Hue-and-Cry. Upon foreign Invasion he may raise the County, so upon Rebellions and Insurrections, and may command any Number he thinks fit to aid him. But by his own Authority he shall not arrest a Man upon suspicion of Felony, except there be a Felony committed in Fact, and he himself have Suspicion of him. But the *Stat.* 17. *Ric.* 2. *c.* 8. The Sheriff may raise the *Posse Comitatus* to suppress Rioters, and commit them to Prison, 13 *H.* 4. *c.* 7. And if the Rioters resist, the Sheriff and his Assistance may justify the Killing them, and may arrest and imprison all such Offendors. If the Sheriff

Sheriff see a Person carry Weapons in the High-Way, *in Terrorem Populi*, he may commit him, though he doth not break the Peace in his Presence. And though the King constitute a Sheriff *durante beneplacito*, and may determine it at will, yet he cannot determine it in part, nor abridge him of any thing incident to his Office, during the Time he is Sheriff.

The Sheriff is an Officer of that Eminence, that he ought to have all Right pertaining to his Office, and to be favoured in Law before any private Person. And therefore though Escapes are so penal to Officers, the Judges have always made a benign Construction, as the Law will permit in favour of them; and to the intent that every One may bear his own Burthen, they will never judge an escape by strict Construction. If a Sheriff be slain in doing his Duty, it's Murder in him who kills him, although no former Malice was between them; and if there were Error in awarding Process, or in the Mistake of one Process for another, and the Officer be slain in the Execution thereof, the Offender shall not have Advantage of such Error, no more than a Sheriff who suffers a Prisoner to escape, shall take any Advantage thereby. Nor is an Officer, if he be resisted, bound to fly to the Wall, as a private Man is. Every Man is bound by the common Law to assist the Sheriff, or his Deputy, in the Execution of the Kings Writs, according to Law, (for the Deputy hath the same Power as his Master.)

Every Sheriff is to be resident in his own Person within his County, during the Time he is Sheriff, except he be Licensed by the King, 4 *H*. 4. *c*. 5. A Sheriff of one County hath no Power within another County, yet the Sheriff by Force of the King's Writ may carry the Prisoner through several Counties. And yet though the Sheriff be much favoured and respected in the Law, and in the Execution of Criminals, yet he shall be guilty of *Homicide* for not observing the Order of Law in putting a condemned Man to Death, 7 *Rep*. 13. 1 *Jac*.

The Sheriff must take the Oath and Sacrament (as is now usual for all Officers and Ministers of Justice (*Stat*. *Car*. 2.) and the Oaths appointed by *Stat*. *William and Mary*.

Here follows the Oath of a Sheriff.

YOU shall swear, That you shall serve the King well and truly in the Office of Sheriff of A. *and do the King's Profit, in all that belongs to you to do by way of your Office, as far forth as you can or may. Ye shall truly keep the King's Rights, and all that belongeth to the Crown, Ye shall not assent to decrease, to Lessenings or to Concealments of the King's Right, or of his Franchises; And whensoever ye shall have Knowledge that the King's Rights, or the Rights of his Crown be concealed or withdrawn, be it in Land, Rent, Franchise or Suits, or any other things, ye shall do your true Power to make them be restored to the King again; and if ye may not do it, ye shall certify the King or some of his Council thereof, such as ye hold for certain will say it to the King. Ye shall not respite the King's Debts for any Gifts or Favour, where you may raise them without great Grievance of the Debtors. Ye shall truly and righteously*

teously treat the People of your Sheriffwick, and do Right as well to the Poor as to the Rich, in all that belongeth to your Office. Ye shall do no Wrong to any Man for any Gift or Benefit, or Promise of Goods, for Favour nor Hate. Ye shall disturb no Man's Right. Ye shall truly acquit at the Exchequer all those of whom you shall any thing receive of the King's Debts. Ye shall nothing take whereby the King may lose, or whereby that Right may be disturbed, letted, or the King's Debt delayed. Ye shall truly return, and truly serve all the King's Writs, so far forth as shall be within your Cunning. Ye shall not have to be your Under-Sheriff, or any of the Sheriffs Clerks of the last Year past. Ye shall take no Bailiff into your Service, but such as ye shall answer for. Ye shall make each of your Bailiffs to make such Oath as ye make your self, that belongeth to their Occupation. Ye shall receive no Writ by any of You or Yours unsealed, or any sealed under any Seal of any Justice, save of the Justice in Eyre, *or Justice assigned in the same Shire where ye be Sheriff, or other Justice having Power or Authority to make any Writs unto you by the Law of the Land. Ye shall make your Bailiffs of the true and sufficient Men in the County. Ye shall be dwelling in your proper Person in your Bailiwick, for the time ye shall be in the same Office, except ye be otherwise licensed of the King. Ye shall not let your Sheriffwick, nor any Bailwick thereof to farm to any Man. Ye shall truly set and return reasonable and due Issues of them that be within your Bailiwick, after their Estate and their Honour; and make your Pannels your self of such Persons as be most next, most sufficient, and not suspected or procured, as it is ordained by the Statutes; and over this, in Eschewing and Restrainder of the Man-slaughters, Robberies, and other manifold grievous Offences, that have been done daily; namely, of such as name themselves Soldiers, and by other Vagrants, the which continually encrease in Number and multiply, so that the King's true Subjects may not be safe; yea, ride or go to do such things as they have to do, to their intollerable Hurt and Hinderance. Ye shall truly and effectually, with all Diligence possible to your Power, execute the Statutes, as the Statutes of* Winchester, *and of Vagabonds. These things all ye shall truly keep. So help you God.*

The old Sheriff is Sheriff of the County until the New Sheriff be sworn: For it is the Taking of his Oath that doth compleat him in his Office. And the Arrest is good by the old Sheriff, till a new Commission be shewed him, or other sufficient Notice, or a Writ *De Exoneratione Officij* come to his Hand. And upon his Receipt of such Writ, if a new Sheriff be not commissioned, the Coroner of the County supplies the Vacancy.

When the New Sheriff is compleat in his Office, he must take over from his Predecessor all his Prisoners and Writs precisely by View, and by Indenture to be made between them, wherein all the Causes that he has against every Prisoner must be set forth and delivered, or else the new Sheriff is not chargeable with them. But if the old Sheriff die, the new Sheriff in such Case shall at his Peril take Notice of all Executions which are against any that he finds in Goal, and of all Writs

Dalt.

Dalt. 17. *Moore* 688. *Pop.* 85. *Mesme Case.* Nor is the new Sheriff obliged to receive Prisoners from his Predecessor but in the common Goal of the County. And if upon the New Sheriff's refusing to receive such Prisoners as are not in Goal, the Prisoner escape, an Action will lie against the old Sheriff. And if the old Sheriff die, the Party who sued Execution may help himself, *viz.* By a remanding the Body by a *Corpus cum Causa*, whereby he may be brought to be duly in Execution.

The Form of an Indenture for Setting over Prisoners and Writs, &c.

This Indenture *made*, &c. *between* A. B. *Esq*; *late* Sheriff *of the County of* Essex, *of the one Part*; *and* C. D. *Esq*; *now* Sheriff *of the said County, of the other Part, Witnesseth, That the said* A. B *by Virtue of his Majesties Writ of Discharge (of his late Office) to him directed, hath delivered and set over unto the said* C. D. *these following Writs: That is to say, A* Capias *against* W. H. *returnable at the supreme Court at*, &c. *to answer* J. Smith, &c. *together with the Bodies of* J. N. *in Execution, at the suit of* G. H. *for the Debt of* 22 l. *and* J. H. *at the suit of* E. F. *In Execution for* 12 l. *and* R. G. *in Execution as well at the suit of* L. M. *for a Debt of* 50 l. *as also at the suit of* N. K. *for a Debt of* 40 l. &c. *In Witness*, &c.

All the Writs which are set over in the Indenture between the Sheriffs, if they have been executed by the old Sheriff, then they must be returned by him, or in his Name, and endorsed under by the New Sheriff, thus,

This Writ, as endorsed, was delivered to me by A. B. *Esq*; *late* Sheriff, *my Predecessor, at the going off his Office.*

p. C. D. *Vice Com'*

Process in some Cases may be to the old Sheriff, to bring the Body of a Prisoner, and that is, where before he hath made a Return of *Cepi Corpus & parat' habeo*, and afterwards he is removed, and a new Sheriff made; on Non-Appearance of the Prisoner, Process shall go to the old Sheriff, as *Distringas*, &c. The Difference is, if the Sheriff, at the Day, return *Cepi Corpus*, and have not the Body ready, he shall be amerced, and a *Distringas* shall be awarded to the Coroners. But if the old Sheriff at the Day return *Cepi Corpus*, and before the Day of Return he is removed, and a new one is made, the *Distringas* here shall be awarded to the new Sheriff, if it appear on Record that he has taken the Body.

A Sheriff on a *Fieri facias* seized Goods in his Hands to the Value of the Debt, and paid part of the Debt, and the Goods not being sold, nor the Writ returned, the Sheriff was discharged; and afterwards sold the Residue of the Goods without any

any *Venditione exponas*; and *per Curia*, the sale is good; for the Writ *Fieri facias* gave him Authority to sell without any other Writ, 2 *Cro.* 73. *Ayer & Aden.*

If Money be paid to the old Sheriff, and he is dischargen before the Return of the Writ, the Party shall not be compelled to pay it again, and the Plantiff may have his Remedy against the old Sheriff, *Cro. El.* 209. *Rook & Wilmot.*

If an Attachment may be granted against a Sheriff for Contempt, after he is removed out of his Office, the Justices said, they could not do it; for now he is no Officer, and cannot now be fined, and without Fine they do not use to imprison, 2 *Browl.* 141.

Of UNDER-SHERIFFS.

As in former Times the *Earls* had the Jurisdiction of the Counties, and the Sheriff was their Deputy, so now the *High-Sheriff* comes in the Place of the *Earl*, and has his Deputy or *Under-Sheriff*, if he see cause to depute one, and may discharge such Deputy, and appoint another when and as often as he sees Cause.

Every Under-Sheriff, before he meddles with his Office, shall, before one of the Justices of Assize, or two of the Justices of the Peace of the County (*Quorum unus*) take the Oaths appointed by Law, and sign the Test, on Pain to forfeit treble Damages to the Parties grieved, if he commit any Act contrary to the said Oaths, or either of them.

The Oath of an Under-Sheriff.

I, A. B. *shall not use nor exercise the Office of Under-Sheriff corruptly, during the Time that I shall remain therein; neither shall nor will accept, receive or take by any Colour Means or Device whatsoever, or consent to the taking of any manner of Fee of any manner of Person or Persons for the Impannelling or Returning of any Jury, Inquest or Tales, in any Court of Record for the King, or betwixt Party and Party, above two Shillings, or the Value thereof, or such Fees as are allowed and appointed for the same by the Laws and Statutes of this Realm; but will, according to my Power, truly and indifferently, with convenient Speed, impannel all Jurors, and return all such Writ or Writs touching the same, as shall appertain to be done by my Duty or Office, during the Time that I shall remain in the same Office.* So help me God.

The

The High-Sheriff in making an Under-sheriff doth implicitly give him Power to execute all the ordinary Offices of the Sheriff himself, that be transferred by Law, as serving Process, Execution, and the like. But in Cases where the Words of the Writ are, *That the Sheriff shall go in his own Person*, as on a Writ of *Partition*, *Waste*, *Redisseisin*, *Accedas ad Curiam*, there the Under-sheriff cannot do it, that is, if Exception be taken at the Bar before the Return be received; but if the Sheriff return, That he was there in proper Person, and this Return be received, and the Writ filed, then the Court cannot examine it, and the Party can have no Averment against the Return, nor can have any Error. *Cro. El. Clay's Case*, *Hob. p.* 13.

And though the High-Sheriff may make an Under-Sheriff, or not appoint one; or when made, remove him at Pleasure, yet during the Time he is Under-Sheriff, he cannot abridge his Power, no more than the King can in the Case of the High-Sheriff himself. If the Sheriff will make an Under-Sheriff, provided he shall not serve Executions above 20 *l.* without special Warrant, this Proviso is void. Nor can the Under-Sheriff restrain himself by Covenant.

If the Under-Sheriff make a Return amerceable, there the High-Sheriff shall be amerced; for the Return is made expresly in his Name; but if it be a false Return, whereupon an Action of Debt lies, in that Case it may be brought against the Under-Sheriff. *Dr. and Stud. cap.* 42.

As to serving Writs, it's said, a known Sheriff need not shew his Warrant at first, although it be demanded, nor a special Under-Sheriff without demand; but when he has peaceably submitted to the Arrest, he ought to read the Writ, or tell him the Contents, that he may know at whose Suit the Process is, out of what Court, for what, and of what Return, that the Party may know what to do, 6 *Rep.* 52. The Sheriff must not dispute the Authority of the Court, though the Process be erroneous.

If the Officer come to Arrest a Man, and he flyeth, the Officer may pursue him and take him in another County, but he can't beat him, because he was not arrested.

If a special Sheriff, by Force of a Warrant, on a *Capias* in Process, enters into the House of *J. S.* the Door being open, and there takes *J. D.* against whom the Writ is, the Process is well served as to *J. D.* and all Strangers. And if any Stranger rescue him, he at whose Suit he is arrested shall have Action against him, 2 *Rol. Abridg.* 272.

A *Capias* was returnable on *All-Souls-Day*, which is *non Dies Juridicus*, which the Sheriff returned, and so let the Party go; it is a bad Return: The Writ was good, and the Detaining of the Parties lawful, and he was commanded to bring him into Court. *Pop.* 205.

If a Sheriff arrest a Man before a Writ be delivered to him, it is a trespass. If a *Latitat* returnable the 10th of *July*, comes to the Sheriff to arrest *J. S.* he may arrest him on the said 10th of *July*. But upon a *Capias* in Process, he may not arrest the Party after the Day of Return.

As

An Arreſt in the Houſe, the Door being open, at ſix a Clock at Night, is good enough.

By the late Act of Parliament none can be arreſted on a *Sunday*, except for Treaſon, Felony, or Breach of Peace.

As to Arreſting one Perſon for another; the Sheriff had Proceſs againſt one *Adderly*, and he took one *Adderby*; if he were known by one Name or the other, it is good, otherwiſe not, *Moore* 407. *N.* 548.

If a Sheriff executes a *Capias*, and there is no Original to warrant it, he is excuſable; but he muſt take Notice, at his Peril, of the Perſon and Goods that he arreſts; for he is not to examine whether the Original be ſued out or not. But if he arreſts *J. S.* inſtead of *J.* N. he does it without Warrant.

An Under-Sheriff who had two Warrants againſt one at the Suit of *J. S.* laid his Hands on him, and ſaid, *I arreſt you by Force of a Writ that I have*, but did not ſhew it him, nor had it in his Hands, nor told him at whoſe Suit; yet the Court reſolved,

1. This Arreſt, without ſhewing the Warrant and telling at whoſe Suit till the other demanded it, was good and legal.

2. This Arreſt, without having the Warrant in his Hand, and having both Warrants about him, is well enough, although he did not ſhew by which of them he arreſted him.

If the Sheriff, Bailiff, or other Officer, ſay to the Perſon againſt whom he has a *Capias* or Warrant, *I arreſt you in the King's Name*, though he lay no Hands on him, it ſeems this is a good Arreſt, eſpecially if it be a known ſworn Officer, and the Party at his Peril ought to obey him; and if the Officer hath no lawful Warrant, the Party may have an Action of falſe Impriſonment againſt him, *Co.* 5. 66, 69.

An Arreſt in the Night is lawful, be it at the King's or anothers Suit, *Co.* 9. 65. *Shep. Abr. Part.* 2. p. 302.

Where Sheriff, Bailiff, Conſtable, or other ſuch like Officer or Miniſters of Juſtice, in the Doing of their Offices, as in the *Execution of Writs, Warrants of the Juſtices of the Peace, Keeping the Peace, Apprehending of Felons*, or the like, do require or command others that are no Officers, to aſſiſt them in that Work or Service, ſuch Perſons muſt aid and aſſiſt ſuch Officer; and then what they do is lawful and juſtifiable therein, as if the Officer or Officers had done it, 11 *H.* 7. *cap.* 15. *Weſtm.* 1. *cap.* 9. *Winton* 3. *H.* 7. *Co.* 8. 96. *Shep. Abr. part* 2, *p.* 302.

The Sheriff or Bailiff is bound at his Peril to arreſt the right Perſon againſt whom the Warrant is, otherwiſe he is liable to an Action of falſe Impriſonment. *Shep. part* 2. *p.* 308. *Mine Caſe.* 600, 602. *Brow. falſe Impriſ.* 38. *Law* 49.

Of BAIL.

BAIL is ſo called, becauſe the Party bailed is delivered by Law into the Cuſtody of thoſe that are his Bail, and who are to anſwer the Party, if they do not produce the Principal to do it.

At Common Law, if the Sheriff had taken any Man by the King's Writ, he must not be delivered but by *Breve de Homine replegiando*, and was not compellable to take Bail. But by the Statute of 23 *H. 6.* he is compelled to take Bail, and the Design of the Statute is to prevent the Extortion of Sheriffs, who used to extort great sums for granting Bail. And this Statute prescribes the Form of the Bail-Bond, and enacts, " That no Sheriff nor any of his Officers shall take or cause to be taken, or " make any Obligation for any Cause aforesaid, or by Colour of their Office, but " only to themselves, of any Person, nor by any Person which shall be in their " Ward, by the Course of the Law, but by the Name of their Office, and upon " Condition written, *That the said Prisoners shall appear at the Day contained in the* " *Writ or Warrant, in such Places as the said Writ shall require*; And any other Obligation taken by them in any other Form shall be void.

The Sheriff is Judge of the Sufficiency of the Sureties, and he may take one or two.

A Condition was, That if he appeared at *Westminster* such a Day to answer, *&c.* The Defendant pleads, That before the Day of the Return of the Writ, the Term was adjourn'd to *Hartford*, and that there he appeared. The Plantiff demurs *Per Cur'* he ought to conclude his Plea, *Prout patet per Recordum*; for though he appeareth, yet if his Appearance be not entered of Record, he forfeits his Obligation, and he ought to conclude his Plea so, otherwise the Plantiff cannot Answer thereunto, as to say, *Nul tiel Record, Cro. El.* 466. *Corbit and Cook.*

After the *Stat.* 23. *H.* 6. the Sheriff cannot make a special Return in a *Capias*, but only a *Cepi Corpus* or *Non est inventus*. And though the Statute compels him to take Bail, yet it does not alter the Return.

The Return of a *Paratum habeo*, is, in Effect, no more than he hath the Body ready to bring into Court when the Court shall command him. And for such Return he is amercible to the Court till he bring in the Body.

If a Sheriff refuse to take reasonable Bail, an Action of the Case lies against him. Or if a Sheriff refuse to take Bail, he is liable to an Action of false Imprisonment. But if he take insufficient Bail, no Action lies against him by the Party, for he is Judge of the Bail.

An Action of the Case against the Sheriff for not taking reasonable Sureties, not having sufficient Estates in the County, and returning *Cepi Corpus*, and yet not having the Bodies ready by the Day, lies not; for he is compelable to let to Bail; and if he have not the Body, he shall be amerced. And because he shall be amerced, the Statute gives him Advice to take sufficient Sureties for his own Indempnity, 2 *Sand.* 59. *Postern and Hansen.*

By these Words in the Statute, That *if the Sheriff return a* Cepi Corpus, *he shall be chargeable to have the Body by the Day of the Return*, &c. it is intended only, that he may be amerced to the King for not having the Body at a Day. 2 *Sand.* 60.

If the Defendant appear not to the Sheriff's Bond according to the Condition thereof,

thereof, the Plantiff may, (by Leave of the Sheriff) sue the Bond in the Sheriff's Name; but it's in the Plantiff's Election to sue the Sheriff; and the Sheriff shall be amerced, till he assign the Obligation to the Plantiff. But by the *Stat.* 4 *&* 5 *of Q. Anne*, the Plantiff upon the Sheriff's Assignment may sue the Bail-Bond in his own Name, if he see Cause so to do.

A Bond given to be a true Prisoner (as by Law he ought) is good, and not within the Statute of 23 *H.* 6. But a Bond of one in Execution, to be a true Prisoner, is within the Statute and void. So also a Bond or Covenant for Fees is void. And so is a Bond for Chamber-Rent, 3 *Keb.* 133.

But by the Statute of 13 *Car.* 2. *c.* 2. Persons arrested by Process out of the King's Bench or Common Pleas not expressing the Cause of Action in the Writ, Bill or Process, and which are Bailable by the Statute of 23 *H.* 6. shall give Bail Bond not exceeding the Sum of 40 *l.* If the Sheriff take Bond for more, the Party shall have an Action upon the Statute against the Sheriff; but the Bond is not void. And upon the Defendants Appearance at the Return, he shall discharge such Bail-Bonds. But this Statute extends not to Arrests upon *Capias utlagat'*, *Rescons*, *Contempt* or *Privilege*; nor to Popular Action, or Action on any Penal Law, Indictment or Information. See more *Tit. Bail.* pag.

Of Return of Writs.

A Return is but a Certificate made by the Sheriff to the Court from whence the Writ issued, of that which they have done touching the Execution of the same Writ.

There is a Difference between the *Teste*, and the Return of Writs. A Return may be on the Essoyn Day. A Writ shall not abate if the Return be *quarto Die post*. If a Man be bound to appear the First Day of the Term in Court, if he appear the first Day of the Essoyn, and then have his Appearance recorded, this is good. 2 *Bulst. Bedo & Piper.*

Deputies are allowed in all Ministerial Offices; but all Returns made by them, are to be made in the Name of the principal Officer. And the Sheriff is to put his Name to every Return made by him, or the Return is to be void, 3 *Bulst.* 78. None can make the Return of a Writ, but such a Person who at the Time of the Return remains an Officer to the Court.

Against the Return of a Sheriff there is not any Traverse, Averment or Answer.

Generally all Writs of Execution, (except *Elegit*) as *Capias ad satisfaciend. Habere fac' Seisinam*, *Habere fac' Possessionem*, *Fieri fac*, *Libertate*, &c. which are the final Process, and after which no Judgment is given, nor no further Process, and when Matters *en fait* are only to be done, as, Land to be delivered, seisin had, Goods sold, *&c.* are good, though the Writs be not returned or filed, if the Execution be duly made.

But in Case of an *Elegit* otherwise, because the Extent is to be made by Inquisition, to the Intent that the Court may be Judge of the Sufficiency of it, and every Inquisition ought to be of Record.

If a Writ directed to the Sheriff be executed, and after a New Sheriff is chosen, the new Sheriff ought to return the Writ in this Manner, *viz. Recepi hoc breve Prædecessori meo directum, sic indorsatum*; i. e. *I received this Writ directed to my Prædecessor, so indorsed.* But if a Writ be not executed by the old Sheriff before he is removed, the Writ must be delivered to the New Sheriff, and by him executed and returned without any Mention of his Predecessor.

If a *Capias* comes to the Sheriff to take a Man, its no Return that he was not found within his Bailwick after the Delivery of the Writ, *Prout sibi constare poterit.* This is not good, but he ought to return expresly, *Quod non est inventus*, 9 *H.* 6. 57.

The Sheriff returned a Resistance on *Habere fac' Seisinam*, and he was amerced 20 Marks, because he did not take the *Posse Comitatus*, and an *Alias awarded*, *Hill.* 19 *Ed.* 2. *Execu.* 147.

Its no good Return for the Sheriff to say, The Party will not pay his Fees, and therefore he would not serve the Writ, 34 *H.* 6. because he may recover his Fees by Action, when he has done his Duty.

The Sheriff of *Yorkshire* returned a Protection on Arrest. It was set aside *per Cur'* in Regard the Sheriff can return nothing else but *Non est inventus*, or *Cepi Corpus*, at his own Peril, and the Sheriff was ordered to return his Writ on Pain, 2 *Keb.* 168.

Where the Sheriff takes Bail, according to the *Stat.* 23 *H.* 6. and returns *Cepi Corpus*, though the Party do not appear at the Day, yet the Sheriff shall not be charged in an Action on the Case for a false Return, *Siderfin, p.* 22.

Note. A *Venire* ought to be delivered to the Sheriff four Days before the Return of it, if the Jury dwell Forty Miles off, and eight Days if they dwell further from the Place where the Tryal is to be. *Pract. Reg.* 87. 333.

The Name of the Sheriff ought to be to the *Distringas*, and *Tales* are of Necessity, and to the Return of the *Habeas Corpora*, 12 *Ed.* 2. *c.* 5.

Tales not returned by the *Sheriff* or his Deputy, but by a Clerk of the Court by general Appointment of the *Sheriff*, it is well enough, and the *Sheriff* is answerable for it, 1 *Keb.* 357.

Of

Of Juries, and Their Returns.

JURORS are of two sorts, Juries to enquire are *Grand Juries* at the Assizes or the Quarter-Sessions. So *Juries* returned before Justices of the Peace, to enquire of *Riots, Forcible Entries*, the Sheriff is to summons them.

If it be conceived an indifferent Jury will not be returned, the Court on Motion will order the Sheriff to attend the secondary of his Office with his Book of the Free holders, to have an indifferent one returned. *Pract. Reg.* 163.

When Tryal is to be for a Thing which concerns the Under-Sheriff, there the High-sheriff shall return the Jury; but if the Tryal concern the High-sheriff, the Coroner shall return the Jury, *Pract. Reg.* 164.

The Sheriff ought not to return *Privilege* to be exempt from Juries, but to return them summoned, and the Party claiming *Privilege* ought to appear in Person to claim the same, and not the Sheriff for him.

But Peers in Parliament are not to be impannelled, nor Tenants in Ancient Demesn.

By *Stat.* 11 *H.* 7. No Indictment shall be found by any Persons named to the Justices, without due Return of the Sheriff, and by Inquest of lawful leige People returned by the Sheriff.

The Justices of Goal-Delivery, or Justices of the Peace (*Quorum unus*) in open Court, may alter the Pannel returned by the Sheriff, to enquire of the King only, by Addition or Substraction of any of the Jurors so returned; and they have Power to command the Sheriff to put other in the Pannel, according to their Discretion. And the Sheriff ought to return the Pannel so reformed, upon Penalty of the said Act. *Coke* 12. *Rep.*

By the *Stat.* 4 & 5 *W. & Mary*, all Jurors are to have *Ten Pounds per Annum*. It is very needful for the Sheriff to have a Book containing the Names of all the Freeholders in his County, and their Sufficiencies, that he may be able to make the Pannels according to his Oath, and better know Pledges and Sureties.

If any Person be returned on a Jury of less Estate than *Ten Pounds per Annum* he may be discharged by Challenge, or upon his own Oath; and the Sheriff, Coroner, or other Officer, returning any one of lesser Estate shall forfeit *Five Pounds* to their Majesties, for every Person so returned. And a Jury must be summoned six Days before the Day of their Appearance. And none shall take a Reward to excuse a Juror's Appearance, on Pain to forfeit Ten Pounds to their Majesties. But this Act extends not to Cities, Burroughs, or Towns corporate.

If any one or more of the Jury be returned at the Denomination of the Party, Plantiff or Defendant, the whole Array shall be quashed.

If

If the Plantiff or Defendant have an Action of Battery or Debt against the Sheriff, or if the Sheriff have a Parcel of Land depending on the same Title; or if the Sheriff or his Deputy be either of Counsel or Attorney, or Servant, or Gossip of either Party, all the Array shall be quashed.

Consanguinity or *Affinity* are the Principal Causes, but its no Challenge to the Array, if all the Jurors be of Affinity.

Malice between the Sheriff and one of the Parties, or that one of the Parties has brought an Action of Debt against the Sheriff, is good Cause of Challenge.

Challenge to the Polls, *i. e.* to the particular Jurors, are of four sorts; 1. *Peremptory*, without shewing any Cause, and this for Treason is Thirty Five, Felony Twenty. 2. *Principal Challenge* to the Polls; so called, because it stands of it self, without leaving any thing to the Conscience or Discretion of the Tryers. 3. Challenger to the Poll must shew Cause *presently*. After one hath taken Challenge to the Poll, he cannot challenge the Array. 4. If the Plantiff alledge a Cause of Challenge against the Sheriff, the Process shall be directed to the Coroner; and if any Cause against the Coroner, then the Court shall appoint *Elisors*. Sometimes the Court appoints two of them that be impannelled.

All Challenges must be taken before the Jurors are sworn. No Challenges shall be admitted against the Tryers appointed by the Court.

Of a Writ of Enquiry of Damages.

IF upon the Executing of a *Writ of Enquiry of Damages*, the Sheriff refuseth to swear and examine some of the Witnesses produced on either Part, and yet doth execute the Writ, the Court will grant a New Writ to the Party grieved, for the Old Writ was not well executed. *Pract. Regist.* 348.

A *Writ of Enquiry of Damages* cannot be executed by a Deputy, or Bailiff, but by an Under-sheriff it may.

If a *Writ of Enquiry of Damages* be returnable the 29th *Sept.* the Sheriff may take the Inquest and enquire the Damages the Day of the Return, and after he returns it the same Day; this Writ is well executed. If the Inquest be impannelled the Essoyn Day, and hear their Evidence two or three Days after; yet this Writ is well executed, *Mich.* 11. *Car.* 1.

The Jury cannot find *That no Trespass is done*, neither may the Sheriff make such Return; but if the Jury will find no Damages, the Sheriff must make his Return accordingly.

Return

Return of a Writ of Enquiry of Damages, viz.

Executio istius brevis patet in quadam Inquisitione huic brevi annex'.

INquisitio indentat' capta apud C. *in Com.* Warwick *(tali Die & Anno) coram* A. B. *Armig' Vicecom. ejusdem Com. Virtute cujusdam brevis Domini Regis, eidem vic. direct. & huic inquisitioni consut' per Sacrament'* R. S. F. G. *&c. (ad numerum* 12 *Jurores) qui dicunt super Sacramentum suum quod* A. P. *in brevi Inquisition' huic consut' nominat' sustinuit damna occasione (Transgres. prædict.) per* H. *in prædict brevi nominat' prout in eodem brevi fit mentio ad* 40 *s. & pro mis' & custag' ipsius* A. P. *per ipsum circa sectam suam in hac parte appositis ad* 40 *s. In cujus rei*, &c.

Of Returns of a Devastavit.

THE Defendant pleads *plene Administravit*, and the Verdict is for the Plantiff, this estops the Sheriff of the County where the Tryal was to return *Nulla bona*; for he is concluded by the Verdict to make any return contrary to it; but the Sheriff of another County shall not be so concluded. But the Sheriff of the County where the Writ is brought ought to return a *Devastavit*, and thereupon the Plantiff shall have Process into another County. 2 *Leon. N.* 90. *p.* 67.

Of PRISONS.

ALL Prisons are the King's, but a Subject may be Keeper. The Custody of County Goals is incident to the Office of Sheriff, and inseparable from the Sheriff; and therefore if the King grant the Custody of such Goal to another, it's void; for the Sheriff is the immediate Officer of the King's Courts, and shall be answerable for Escapes and be subject to Amerciaments, and therefore he shall put in such Keepers as he shall answer for.

The

The Sheriff may remove his Goal from one Place to another within his Bailiwick, but not in a particular Place without Prescription.

No Prisoner shall be put in Irons, but Traytors, or those taken for Felony or Trespass *in parcis & vivariis*, &c. A Prisoner in Execution shall not be in Fetters, but for Criminal Causes. A Prisoner (while he is such) is under the Protection of the Law, and accordingly is to be used. And therefore where a Prisoner, by Duress of the Goaler, comes to an untimely End, it is Murder in the Goaler, 3 *Inst.* 52. 91. And the Law implies Malice in him, in respect of the Cruelty. And therefore if a Man die in Prison, the Coroner ought to sit upon him, to the End it may be inquired, if he came to his Death by the Duress of the Goaler. 3 *Inst.* 91.

If the Sheriff or other Officer, where he ought to hang the Party attainted, according to the Judgment and Charge, will burn or behead him, *&c.* The Law in this Case implies Malice in him.

By the *Stat.* 14. *Edw.* 3. *c.* 10. If a Keeper, or Under-Keeper of a Prison, by too great Duress of Imprisonment, or by Pain, make a Prisoner become an Appellor, *viz.* An Approver against his Will, it's Felony.

If a Prisoner is in Execution, and the Goaler or Sheriff die, he is in Abeyance and Custody of the Law.

A *Goaler* is not bound to deliver his *Prisoner*, who is discharged by the *Court*, until he pay his Fees.

Every *Sheriff*, and other *Person*, having *Authority* of Keeping Goals, or of *Prisoners* for Felony, shall certify the Names of every such *Prisoner* in their Keeping at the next general Goal-Delivery in every County, there to be Kalandered before the Justices of the *Delivery* of the same Goal, whereby they may, as well for the King as the Party, proceed to make Delivery of such Prisoners, according to the Law, on Pain of Five Pounds. 3 *H.* 7. 3.

If the *Goaler* suffer an Escape, the *High-Sheriff* or *Goaler* are chargeable *therefore*.

Of Fieri Facias.

FIERI *facias* is a Judicial Writ lying for him who hath recovered Debt or Damage, directed to the *Sheriff*, commanding him to levy the same of the Defendants Goods: And it lies within a Year and a Day; but after a Year and a Day there must be a *Scire facias*.

This Writ of *Fieri facias* is only against the Goods and Chattels of a Man, *viz.* Leases for *Years*, Corn *growing* or sown upon the Land, or moveable Goods, as *Corn in the Barn*, *Houshold Goods*, *Money*, *Plate* and *Apparel*. *Co.* 1. *Inst.* 296. 6

Goods pawned shall not be taken in Execution for the Debt of him which pawned them, during the Time they are pawned. *Kitchin* 226.

The

The Sheriff upon a Writ of Execution may not seize and sell to the Party a Furnace annexed to the Freehold, for this would be Waste in the Lessee. 37 *El. B. C. Day & Austin.*

If one sell any Goods to another in the Time of Action depending against him; these Goods shall not afterwards be taken in Execution; for they were lawfully bought (if done *bona Fide*, and for valuable Consideration.) But if a *Fieri facias* be directed to make Execution of Goods, and after the *Teste* of the Writ, and before the Sheriff executes it, the Party sells his Goods *bona Fide*, they may nevertheless be taken in Execution (*aliter* now by the *Statute of Frauds* and *Perjuries*) *Cro. El.* 174.

If the Party dies after the Writ of Execution awarded, and before it be served, the Sheriff may serve it on the Goods in the Hands of the Executor; for by the Execution awarded, the Goods are bound, and the Sheriff needs not take Notice of his Death, *Cro. El.* 181. *Parker & Moss.*

The Plantiff (being Sheriff) seizeth the Goods in Execution by Force of a *Fieri facias*, and after, before the Sale of them, the Defendant takes an Opportunity to remove them, and converts them to his own Use; and the Plantiff (being Sheriff) brings his Action of *Trover*; and adjudged the Action lies well. For by the Seizure of the Goods in Execution, the Sheriff hath a Property in them, so that he may reseize them and sell them, as well when he is out of his Office, as before. *Mod. Rep.* 2. *Sand.* 47. *Willbaham & Snow.*

After the Debt levied, the Sheriff is Debtor to the Plantiff, and capable of a Release from him, the Action ceasing against the Defendant, is *ipso facto* by the Law transferred to the Sheriff, having both the Judgment to make it a Debt, and the Levy to make him answerable; and though the Action of Account will properly lie in this Case, yet the same will many times bear both Actions, though the Money be received by *Auter Manis*, or the like, *Hob.* 206, 207. *Speak & Richards.*

If the Sheriff in executing a *Fieri facias* doth not misbehave himself, he shall not be charged in Debt, or *Scire Facias*, but if upon the *Fieri facias* the Sheriff return, That he hath levied the Money, and doth not pay it to the Plantiff at the Return of the Writ, the Plantiff may have a *Scire facias* against the *Sheriff*, to shew Cause wherefore the Money should not be levied of the Goods of the Sheriff, 2 *Sand.* 344, 345.

So if in *Fieri facias*, to levy 200 *l.* Debt, the Sheriff returns, That he had made his Warrant to his Bailiff, who had seized divers Goods to the Value of 160 l. and that they were rescued out of his Custody, *ita quod*, he could not levy the Debt, and that *S. nulla alia habuit bona.* The Plantiff may bring a *Scire facias* to have Execution against the Sheriff for the Monies, according to the Value returned, and the Sheriff shall pay it out of his own proper Goods, 1 *Anders.* 247.

On *Fieri facias* the Sheriff seized several Goods, which were Mercery Ware, and returned *Fieri facias ad Valentiam*; which Return was filed. The Sheriff appears, and prays to amend the Return, because some of the Goods were impaired by lying, and he could not get Buyers. *Per Curia.* 1. Such Return may not be altered, after it is returned and filed. 2. Where the Sheriff returns *Fieri facias ad Valentiam*, this shall be no Excuse of his Payment of the Money, because he might have returned, he had seized the Goods, and that they remain *pro defectu emptorum*, and then he may be excused, if *Bona peritura* they perish. *Siderfin. p.* 40. *Needham & Bennet.*

As to Amendment of Returns, Matter of Form in a Return is amendable, but not Matter of Fact; which goes to Justification of Imprisonment. 2 *Bulst.* 259.

If the Sheriff have a *Fieri facias* against a Man's Goods, and before Execution he pay him the Money; in this Case he cannot do Execution after, and if he do, an Action of Trespass or false Imprisonment lies against him, *B. R.* p. 12. *Jac.* 1.

The Sheriff upon a *Scire facias* cannot deliver the Defendants Goods to the Plantiff in Satisfaction of the Debt, but must return the Execution in Court, *Cro. El.* 504.

On *Fieri facias* against *J. S.* who has the Goods of *A.* in his Possession, if the Sheriff sells these Goods, Trover or Trespass will lie against him; and to prevent this, all the Sheriffs in *England* take Security, *Keb.* 693. *Sander's Case.*

Therefore in this Case the safest Course is for the Sheriff to enquire by a Jury, in whom the Property of the Goods is, or else not to meddle with such Goods which do not plainly appear to him to be the Defendants; and it being found by a Jury, that excuseth the Sheriff.

If Goods remain in the Sheriff's Hands for want of Buyers, and there perish, the Sheriff shall not be chargeable; but if the Sheriff refuse a Buyer, Action on the Case lies, 2 *Keb.* 464.

There is a Difference between the Sale of a Term on a *Fieri facias*, and Extent on an *Elegit*; for the *Elegit* is, That they appraise the Goods and Chattels of the Debter, and extend his Lands; and therefore if they are not appraised by the Jurors, he cannot sell them (*vid. Dyer, fol.* 100. and so in 5 *Rep. Palmer's Case.*) Execution by *Elegit* ought to be *per Inquisitionem per Stat. W.* 2. *c.* 18. which saith, (*per Rationabile Pretium*) which extends to Chattels, and *per Extentum*, which refers to Lands. In *Elegit* the Goods are to be delivered to the Party *per Rationabile Pretium*, but in *Fieri facias* the Sheriff must sell the Goods. 1 *Keb.* 566. *Glaswel & Morgan.*

In *Elegit* the Term may not be extended without shewing the Certainty of the Commencement; for after the Debt satisfied, the Party is to have his Term and Remainder. But upon *Fieri facias* the Sheriff may sell, and his Return is general, *quod fieri feci de Bonis & Catallis*, 5 *Rep. Palmer's Case.*

Now

Now the Sheriff is to be careful in the Sale of a Term in *Elegit*, if he make particular Recital, that there be no Miſtake. But a general Recital is better. As,

In *Ejectment*, it was found by ſpecial Verdict, That the Sheriff upon an *Elegit* impannelled a Jury, who found that the Defendant was poſſeſſed of a Leaſe for a Hundred Years, which began *Mic.* 2 *&* 3 *Phil. & M. ubi revera*; as it was found it begun *Mich.* 3 *&* 4 *Phil. & M. Cujus quidem H. Statum intereſſe & terminum in Tenementis prædictis pædict. Juratores appretiarunt ad* 80 *l.* and the Sheriff ſold it to the Leſſor of the Plantiff for 80 *l.*

Now the Inqueſt found one thing, and he ſells another (as this Caſe was) and the Sale not being warranted by the Inqueſt, is void. But had the Inqueſt found he had been poſſeſſed of ſuch Land generally for the Term of divers Years to come, and they had appraiſed it for ſo much, without ſhewing the certain Beginning or Determination, it had been well enough; for they ſhall not be compelled to find a Certainty, not having Means to be informed thereof. Or if the Sheriff ſells all ſuch Intereſt which the Defendant had in the ſame Term, the Sale had been good. 5 *Rep. Palmer's Caſe.*

So in *Sr. Sidenham*'s Caſe in *B. R.* the Inqueſt on a *Fieri facias* found that the Defendant was poſſeſſed of ſuch a Term, and miſtook the Date, and the Sheriff ſold it; the Sale was not good. And on the new *Fieri facias* the Court directed that it ſhould be found, That he was poſſeſt of a Leaſe for Years generally, and yet continuing, and that he ſold it. *Cro. El.* 584.

W. had Execution out of the King's Bench by *Scire facias* of a Term, which was ſold by the Bayliff of a Liberty. After, upon another Judgment, the Bayliff delivers this Term to another, pretending that the firſt Judgment and Execution was fraudulent. But *per Curia*, it is not well done; for he is not a Judge of Fraud, and the Court will not allow ſuch Pretence to Sheriffs and Officers. *Latch.* p. 53. *Warrington's Caſe.*

If a Sheriff extend or ſell a Leaſe, this Sale ſhall bind the King (as to his Debt) becauſe it is but a Chattel, and there was no Coven, 8 *Rep.* 171.

Of Writs of Poſſeſſion.

IN all Caſes where the Execution of a Judgment, in which the Demand is of a Thing *certain*, if the Sheriff do this Thing, he is not any *Diſſeiſor*. But where the Execution is in the Generality, without mentioning of any thing in *particular*, there the Sheriff ought to make Execution of the right Thing, at his own Peril, otherwiſe he ſhall be a Diſſeiſor; for he is bound to take Notice of it. As if a Man recover in Aſſize divers Houſes, and after the Tenant reverſeth it in a *Writ of Error*, and a *Writ of Execution* iſſues to the Sheriff, to put him in Poſſeſſion of the

Houses, which he had lost by the Judgment, although the Tenants are Strangers to the Recovery; and for this they ought not to be ousted without *Scire facias* against them; yet if he do Execution by putting them in Possession by Force of this Writ, he shall not be any Disseisor, for that he hath the direct Authority of the Court to do it. *Pasch.* 15. *Jac. Lloyd & Bethel.*

So in Judgment for the casual Ejector for seven Houses, and on *Habere facias Possessionem* turns out these seven Tenants, and eight other Tenants, without any Process or Plea against them. *Per Curia*, We will not grant any Writ to supercede the Execution against the eight Tenants; for if it should be, it ought to be *quia Erronice*, and there was not any Error in the Proceeding against them, because there was not any Proceedings. But they did advise, that every one should bring Trespass against the Sheriff, 2 *Siderfin.* 155. So Trespass lies against the Sheriff, if he does not execute on the right Places.

If the Sheriff do deliver more Acres than are in the Writ, this makes not the Writ erronious, but in such Case, Action on the Case lies against the Sheriff for doing it; or an Assize against him that hath the Possession delivered to him for the surplusage of the Land. But if the Writ of *Habere facias Posses.* to deliver Possession to the Plantiff, of Lands recovered by him in Ejectment, contains more Acres of Land than were in the Declaration, the Writ is erronious. *Pract. Regist.* 131, 132.

If a Man brings *Ejectione firma* of Forty Acres of Land, and recovers Thirty, and not the Residue, upon the Writ of Execution the Sheriff may deliver to him any three or more, in the Name of all, without setting out the Land in Metes and Bounds, although the Plantiff had not recovered all the Acres, whereof he had brought his Action, and whereof he had supposed the Defendant Tenant.

But if a Man be to be put in Possession of divers Messuages upon a Writ of Execution, and the Houses are in Possession of several Men, he ought to go to every House particularly, and to deliver Seisin of it; for the Delivery of Seisin of one, in the Name of all, is not sufficient; for he ought to deliver *Plenariam Seisinam, Trin.* 15 *Jac. Floyd & Bethel's Case.*

In *Formedon* on Non-Tenure of three Messuages, the Jury found he was Tenant of one of the Messuages, and not of the other, the Plantiff may have Judgment, and a Writ to the Sheriff to deliver Seisin; and the Plantiff at his Peril is to shew to the Sheriff what Messuage it was the Jury did intend; for the Jury is not tied to set Bounds to it. *Cro. Eliz.* 256. *Scriven & Prince.*

Upon *Habere facias Possessionem* the Sheriff returned, That in Execution of the said Writ he came to the House recovered, and removed out all the Persons he could find. and delivered to the Plantiff Possession, and departed; and soon after, three Persons secretly lodged in the House, expelled the Plantiff: On Notice whereof he returned again to the House, to put the Plantiff in full Possession, but the others resisted him, so that without Peril of his Life he could not do it.

1 *Leon.*

1 *Leon, p.* 145. *Upton & Wells.* On this Return the Court awarded a New Execution.

A Writ of *Habere facias Possessionem* was directed to the Sheriff; a *Writ of Error* was brought, and a *Supercedeas* granted, directed to the Sheriff to stay Execution; and the *Supercedeas* was shewed to the Sheriff as he was going to do Execution, yet he refused to obey it, and did Execution notwithstanding. This is a great Contempt in a Sheriff, and the Court ordered a Writ of *Restitution* to be granted. 2 *Bulst.* 194. *Thomas & Owen.*

N. B. The Sheriff in Cases where Land is revered, is to put the Party in Possession and Seisin by a Twig, Clod, *&c.* of an House by a Key, *&c.* of Rent by Corn or Grass growing on the Land, out of which the Rent issues. 6 *Rep.* 52.

It is no good Return, That another is Tenant of the Land by Right, or that he has nothing in the Land.

Seisin of the Land in one Vill, in the Name of all the Land in three Vills is good.

A Return of a Fieri facias.

BY *Virtue of the within Writ, I have caused to be made of the Goods and Chattels of the within named* A. B. *the within named* 200 l. *the which* 200 l. *I have ready at the Time and Place within contained, to render unto the within named* C. D. *as within I am commanded.*

J. S. Vice Com'.

A Return of a Scire facias.

BY *Virtue of the within Writ to me directed, by* A. B. *and* C. D. *good and lawful Men of my Bailwick, I have made known unto* J. S. *That he be before his Majesties Justices,* &c. *at the Time and Place within written, to,* &c. *as within I am commanded.*

J. S. Vice Com'.

A Return of a Habere facias Possessionem.

BY *Virtue of the within Writ to me directed (such a Day and Year within written) I have caused the within named* A. B. *to have Possession of his within written Term of, and in, the Tenements within written, with the Appurtenances, as I am within commanded.*

J. S. Vice Com.

A Return of a Habere facias Seisinam.

BY *Virtue of the within Writ to me directed, I do hereby make known unto the within Justices, That (such a Day and Year within written) I have caused the within named* A. B. *to have full Seisin of one Messuage with the Appurtenances in* S. *within named, in all things as by the said Writ I am commanded.*

J. S. Vice Com.

The Sheriff makes his Warrant to a Bailiff, to take the Body of, *&c.* upon a *Capias satisfaciend.* and before the Warrant executed, the Sheriff receives a *Supercedeas*, and the Bailiff having Notice, proceeds; yet the Arrest is not lawful, but the Bailiff is excusable in Trespass. *Moore, p.* 677. *Prince & Allington.*

Of ELEGITS.

ELEGIT is a Judicial Writ, given by the *Stat. W.* 2. *c.* 18. either upon a Recovery for Debt or Damage, or upon a Recognizance in any Court. By this Writ the Sheriff shall deliver to the Plantiff *Omnia Cattalla Debitoris (exceptis Bobus & Afris Carucæ) Mediatatem Terrarum*, and this must be done by Inquest taken by the Sheriff for the Valuation of the Goods and Lands ought to be first found by the Inquisition of a Jury. *W.* 2. *c.*18. gives the *Elegit*; so that in *Elegit* the Sheriff may take in Execution the Moiety of the Lands of the Conizor, *&c* and all his Goods and Chattels, (except as aforesaid) and was to deliver them to the Conisee, or he who recovers, upon a reasonable Extent or Price, until the Debt be satisfied; and the Sheriff shall deliver him the Seisin of the Land, and he is called *Tenant by Elegit*, and shall do no Waste, 4 *Rep.* 47.

The *Elegit*, as to Goods, is in Effect but a *Fieri facias*; and therefore if there be no Lands, and Execution be upon Goods, and they are not sufficient, he may have a *Capias*, *aliter* if Lands be extended.

As to what Things may be extended, or not, you must know, That all Goods and Chattels, in which are included Leases for Years, shall be exended (except Oxen and Beasts of the Plow) the Moiety of the Lands.

Rent seck, where there is not any Reversion, cannot be delivered *ut liberum Tenementum.*

Annuity certain is extendable by *Elegit. Cro. Jac.* 78.

Lands in *Antient Demesne* may be delivered in Execution by the Sheriff, by force of an *Elegit* out of the King's Court.

If

If Lands descend to an Infant, the Sheriff may cease to extend.

Two Inquisitions taken at several Days, by several Juries, upon one Statute Merchant, were adjudged naught; one was taken of the Land, and the other for the Lands and Goods. 1 *Brownl.* 38.

A Lessee had a Lease of the Value of 100 *l.* and after the Teste of the *Elegit*, and before the Sheriff had executed the *Elegit*, assigns his Term to one, who assigns over to the Plantiff in the *Scire facias*; and afterwards the Sheriff executes the *Elegit*, and delivers the Lease to the Plantiff *Tenend.* &c. for the Satisfaction of the Debt, which came to but 43 *l.* *Per Cur.* The Sheriff could not deliver the Lease at another Value than what the Jury had found it at. And the Sale made by the Sheriff is as strong as if it had been made in open Market, and all the Goods and Chattels are bound after the *Teste* of the *Elegit*, and cannot be sold by the Owner after. 1 *Brownlow* 38. *Conyers & Brandling.*

Upon *Elegit* there needs no *Liberate*. *Aliter* upon a *Statute.*

In every *Elegit* the Sheriff must return, and set out the Moieties distinctly, unless they be Tenants in common, and in that Case he must return the special Matter.

On Inquisition of a Lease, which is but a Chattel, the Sheriff may sell it as Goods; but if he extends it, there shall be no other Benefit than as of a common Extent.

Two Persons recovered severally against one in Debt; he who had the first Judgment sued first an *Elegit*, and had the Moiety of the Land delivered in Execution; afterwards the other sued the *Elegit*, and the Sheriff prayed the Advice of the Court. *Per Cur.* He shall deliver but the Moiety of that Moiety which he had at the Time of the Writ awarded. *Cro. Eliz.* 482. *Hitt & Cogan.*

Actual Possession ought not to be delivered on *Elegit*, the Sheriff ought only to deliver Seizure, to enable the Plantiff to maintain an Ejectment, and the Tenant may plead on the Ejectment, else the Tenant would be turned out unheard, and be remediless; yet if actual Possession be delivered, it is remediless. 3 *Keb.* 243. *Jefferson & Dawson.*

In *Elegit* the Sheriff ought to deliver the Moiety by Metes and Bounds, *Hutton*, p. 16.

Upon *Elegit*, the Sheriff ought to return the Extent, and also that he hath delivered the Lands.

Elegit needs not to be returned: Therefore if the Sheriff by Force of an *Elegit* delivers to the Party the Moiety of the Lands of the Defendant, and does not return the Writ; if now the Plantiff will bring Action of Debt, *de Novo*, the Defendant may plead in Bar the Execution aforesaid, though the Writ of Execution was not returned. *Earl of Leicester's Case*, 1 *Leon. p.* 280.

The Sheriff returns upon *Elegit*, that the Party had not any Lands, but only within the Liberty of St. *Alban's*, and that *J. S.* Bailiff there hath the Execution and Return of all Writs, who enquired and returned an Extent by Inquisition, and

and that the Bailiff delivered the Moiety to the Party, and the Plantiff by Virtue of the Extent entered.

Per Cur. 1. The Bailiff may make such Inquisition by Warrant from the Sheriff. 2. When a Jury by the Inquisition find the Seisin and Value of the Land, the Jury shall extend all the Land; and the Bailiff in a Franchize, and the Sheriff where there is none, shall deliver the Moieties, and not the Jury, *Cro. Car.* 317. *Sparrow and Mattersech.*

On an *Elegit*, averring no Goods were seized, it hath been held, no *Scire Facias* lieth; but upon a *Fieri facias*, bare Seizure is an Execution. 2 *Keb.* 789, 821. *Smith and Mildmay.*

An Extent upon a *Statute Merchant.* The Plantiff put the Conisee in Possession of Parcel of a House and Lands, and suffered the Conisor to continue in the Rest of the House; by reason whereof the Conisor kept the Possession of the whole, and held the Conisee out. The Conisee, to the Intent he might have a full and perfect Possession of the whole, caused the Sheriff that he did not return the Writ of Extent, on which it is entered on the Roll, *Quod Vicecomes nihil inde fecit nec misit breve*; An *Alias breve extendi facias* may well be awarded. And the Sheriff cannot Return, that the Land was formerly extended by the old Sheriff, because by the Entry upon the Roll it appears, that no Execution was done; but if the Entry be not, the same is an Execution for the Party, tho it be not returned; 2 *Leon.* 12. *N.* 20. *Coleshill & Hastings.*

If more than a Moiety be delivered upon the *Elegit*, 'tis for the whole. *Siderf. p.* 91.

The Sheriff may extend or sell a Lease, and this Sale shall bind the King, because but a Chattel, and no Coven in the Case, 8 *Rep. Sir George Fleetwood's Case.*

Where the Sheriff extends a Mannor by the Name of Acres, Land, Meadow, Wood, no Advowson passeth.

If one extends a *Statute Staple* at the Suit of *A.* the Sheriff extends the Lands, and takes the Goods, and seizeth them into the Hands of the King; but does not make Livery; and after a *Writ of Prerogative* of the King issues out of the Exchequer, and commands the Sheriff to levy the King's Debt of *B. viz.* 100 *l.* of the Goods of the Debtor; and if he had not sufficient, then to extend the Lands; and this is delivered to the Sheriff after the first *Writ of Extent*, but that was not returned. The Sheriff ought in this Case to execute the *Extent* for the King's Debt, because the Property of the Goods and Lands were not in *A.* before they were delivered to him by *Libertate*; and the Goods being seized into the Hands of the King for the Use of the Party, were priviledged from all other Executions but that of the King. 2 *Roll. Ab.* 158. *Dyer* 67.

Where the Officer without any Warrant or Authority, shall levy any Duty for the King, and after shall account for the same in the Exchequer, or otherwise pay the same to the King's Use, there the Officer seemeth chargeable but as a Trespasser; but if he shall convert the same to his own proper Use, it is Felony.

N. B. When

N. B. When Lands are extended and the Debtor in Prison, the Creditor out of the Profits of the Lands is to find the Debtor Bread and Water in Prison.

By Virtue of the Writ on the *Statute Merchant*, the Sheriff may deliver the Lands and Goods presently, upon the *Extent*, to the Party. But by the Writ on *Statute Staple*, or Recognizance in the Nature of it, he is to extend the Lands and Goods, and to seize them into the Hands of the King; but not to deliver them to the Party without a *Libertate*.

The Proceedings in a *Statute Merchant* is a *Capias*, and if the Sheriff thereupon return a *Cepi Corpus*, then he shall remain in Prison a Quarter of a Year, within which Time he may sell his Goods and Lands to pay his Debts, and this by the express Words of the *Statute* of 13 *H.* 7. *c.* 16. But if the Sheriff return *Non est inventus*, Execution shall be granted of his Lands and Goods.

But in a *Statute Staple* and Recognizance, the first Process is to take his Body, Lands and Goods, all in one Writ, which is a more speedy Remedy than the *Statute Merchant*.

Now on a *Statute Staple* and Recognizance, the Writ of Execution upon the Return of the Conisor dead, is to extend the Lands, *nec non Catalla*, which were of the Conisor at the Time of his Death: And this is the constant Course, as appears by the Records of *Extents*, which are in the Rolls.

On *Extent* of a *Statute Merchant* the Sheriff returns, That the Body cannot be found, and that he had extended the Lands, and delivered them to the Plantiff, *Reg.* 146.

Extent on a *Statute Merchant* issued out against *R.* the Conisor, the Sheriff returned, That the Conisor was possest of divers Goods, and seized of Lands, which he delivered to the Conisee, and that the Conisee accepted the Land. But because the Sheriff did not return, That he had not any other Lands, Goods or Chattels, it was adjudged insufficient, and a New Writ awarded; though some held it was well enough in the Case of a Conisor, but not in the Case of a Purchasor, 1 *Brownl.* 37. *Fletcher and Robinson.* If the Conisor be returned dead, Execution shall be granted against his Executor, without *Scire facias* to have Execution of his Goods, so against the Heir and Tertenants.

If the Sheriff does not return the *Capias*, or return *Tarde*, or that he directed it to a Bailiff of a Franchise, he shall be punished, and yield Damages to the Party grieved, according to the *Statute de Mercatoribus*, *W.* 2. *c.* 39.

Two Inquisitions taken at several Days by several Juries upon one *Statute Merchant*, were adjudged naught. One was taken of the Lands, the other for the Lands and Goods, 1 *Brownl.* 38.

If another had these Lands in Execution by *Elegit*, or is in by Descent; in such Cases the Sheriff shall return the special Matter, *i. e.* In the first Case, That he hath extended the Land of the Defendant, but he cannot deliver the same to the Plantiff, for that another had the same in *Extent* before.

The Sheriff having an *Extent* upon a *Statute*, may gather the Goods all into One Place, to be viewed and appraised by the Jurors, and he is not a Trespassor, *Mo.* 563.

Of Returns on Scire Facias.

SCIRE *Facias* is a Judicial Writ directed to the Sheriff, *&c.* and is usually to warn a Man to come and shew the Cause to the Court, why Execution of a Judgment shall not be done.

Conisor in a Recognizance dies, *Scire facias* goes against his Executors and Heirs of his Land, *&c.* The Sheriff returns, That he had no Executor, *& scire feci W. H. Filio & Hæredi prædict. M. (le Conisor.)* This Return agrees not with the Writ, yet it may be good, 3 *Rep.* 15. *Sir W. Herbert's Case.*

Scire facias on a Recognizance in Chancery against *C.* who was returned dead: Then a second *Scire facias* issued against the Heir of *C.* and against the Tenants of the Land of *C.* which he had *Tempore Recognitionis, vel postea.* The Sheriff returned *C.* Tertenant, and omitted to return any thing against the Heir. This is a Non-Return of the Sheriff, and not a Mis-Return, and is not aided by any of the Statutes.

The Tenant without the Heir ought not to be charged: Therefore the Heir ought to be summoned, for the Heir may have a Release to plead, or other Matter to bar the Execution. Or if the Heir be within Age, the Parol shall demur, and the Tertenant shall have the Advantage thereof: And a new *Scire facias* issued *ad informand. Curiam*, and the Return was, That he had not any Lands in his Bailiwick that descended to his Heir, nor any Heir within his Bailiwick, and good enough; though it had been better if he had returned who was Heir, and that he was warned, or that there was not any Heir within the said County. *Cro. Car.* 295. *Eyres and Taunton.*

The Writ commands the Sheriff to give Notice to the Tenants of the Land in Fee-simple, and the Sheriff returns not, *That those which he had returned were Tenants of the Land in Fee simple*; and so the Words of the Writ are not answered. 1 *Brownl. Rep.* 145, 146.

The Sheriff may return Twenty Four Tertenants of the Whole, and every Tenant may plead in Discharge of himself, or he may return, That each is Tertenant of so many Acres.

Of

Of Refcous, *and in what Cafe Action lies againft the Sheriff for a* Refcous.

IF in the Arrefting, the Party is refcued be in on Execution or mean Procefs, no Action for this lies againft the Sheriff. And if the Prifoner be arrefted on mean Procefs, and as he is bringing to the Goal is refcued, no Action lies againft the Sheriff, for the Sheriff cannot be fuppofed to have the *Poffe comitatus* upon every mean Procefs; *aliter* if it be upon Execution, there *Caveat Vicecomes.* But if he be arrefted upon mean Procefs, and brought to the Goal, then its no good Return for him to fay, *The Goal was broken, and he was taken away from him.*

The Refcuer fhall be doubly punifhed by the King, and by the Party, or Sheriff; he fhall be fined to the King, and Attachment fhall iffue out againft him; and the Party fhall have a Writ of *Refcous* againft him, and fo fhall the Sheriff too. 2 *Keb.* 240 *Hopping's Cafe. Cro. Car.* 109. *Myn and Coughton's Cafe.*

No *Refcous* can be on a *Scire facias* for Goods, but in fuch Cafe the Party fhall have Action on the Cafe. And a Refcous lies only on a *Capias*, which lies againft the Perfon, for which *Vide Cro. Car. Sly and Finch's Cafe*; which is as follows.

Scire facias was brought againft *Finch* Sheriff of *Gloucefter*, for that the Plantiff having brought a *Fieri facias* directed to *Finch*, he returned, That he had taken Goods into his Hands to the Value of 72 *l.* and had fold as much of them as amounted to 11 *l.* and the Refidue remained *pro defectu emptorum* till fuch a Day, at which Time he putting them to Sale, they were refcued from him. Upon which Return the *Scire facias* was brought, to fhew Caufe why the remaining Debt fhould not be levied on his Goods. To this the Defendant demurs. All agreed that the Return is not good. And *per Curiam* he is chargeable by this Return, If he had returned only *quod remanent pro defectu emptorum*, therein he had done his Office; and in fuch Cafe, on the Election of a New Sheriff, a *Diftringas Vicecomitas* fhall iffue to fell the Goods, and to deliver the Money to the New Sheriff. But when he faith further, That they were refcued out of his Hands, therein he hath mifdemeaned himfelf. And by *Dodderige* the Sheriff hath charged himfelf by this Return, as well in Regard of his Mifdemeanor, as alfo that he hath his Remedy againft the Refcouffers; nor can the Court award a Writ of *Venditioni exponas*, becaufe it's againft his own Return.

By *Hutton*, upon mean Procefs the Sheriff never had Remedy for the Refcous, but he fhall return the Refcous. And upon Execution he fhall not return the Refcous, but have an Action, and the Party is not prejudiced; for he fhall have an Action againft the Sheriff, though in Point of Law the Party is liable.

 The

The Rescouser shall be doubly punished, by the King and by the Party; upon the Return of the Sheriff he shall be fined to the King, and Attachment shall issue out against him, and the Party shall have a Writ of Rescous against him, and so shall the Sheriff too.

Of ESCAPES.

ESCAPE is, where One Man that is arrested, or imprisoned on the Arrest, comes to his Liberty before he is delivered by Order of Law.

If a Man in Execution be suffered to go at Large out of the County, or within the County, or within the Town where the Prison is, and though it be upon Bail, it is an Escape; for he ought to be kept *in arcta Custodia. Plowd. 36. b. Plat's Case.*

If a Sheriff remove Prisoners without Command, for Ease, Delight or Benefit of them, it is an Escape. To suffer a Prisoner to walk in the Town, though with a Keeper, it is an Escape, unless it be by a *Habeas Corpus* from a Court of Justice.

Upon this Point of the Prisoners going at large, there is a Diversity to be well heeded, *viz.* Between One in *Execution*, and One only taken by a *Capias*; for when the Sheriff is commanded by Writ to have the Body at *Westminster* such a Day, he may be Keeper of him in another County, or in what Place he please.

But if one in Execution at the Suit of the King, or of a common Person, and (by the Lisence of the Lord Chancellor or Treasurer) be suffered to go into the Country with a Keeper, to gather Money, the sooner to pay the King; this is an Escape, for the King himself cannot lisence a Man in Execution to go so at Large. *Dyer 12 & 13 Eliz.* 297.

If One be in Execution at the Suit of the King in the *Fleet*, the Warden may suffer him to go to his Council with his Keeper, but not so in the Case of a common Person.

A Man is in Execution for Debt, and a Woman being Warden of the *Fleet*, Marries the Prisoner; This is an Escape, for that he cannot be his own Prisoner, nor a Prisoner to his Wife.

It was referred by the King to the Judges, *Trin. 12. Car. 1.* Whether in regard of the Plague, *Habeas Corpora* may be granted for the Prisoners in Execution, in the Prisons of the *King's Bench* and *Fleet*, upon Judgment in the *King's Bench* and *Exchequer?* And it was certified by them to the Lord Keeper, That if upon *Habeas Corpus* granted, the Goaler suffers the Prisoners to go at large, that this is an Escape, and

and that no *Habeas Corpus* ought to be by Law for that Purpose. Which the King well approved of.

The Sheriff delivers a Prisoner upon a void *Audita Querila.* This is no Escape, and there the Prisoner may be taken again in Execution. But if a *Scire facias* had in it the Words of *Audita Querila*, it's against Law, and is an Escape. *Mo.* 344, *N.* 479. *Collins Case.* 1 *Roll. Rep.* 383.

If a Man recover against *Baron* and *Feme*, and take both in Execution, and the Wife is suffered to escape; though the Husband continues in Prison, yet Debt lies in this Escape against the Sheriff; in which all the Debt shall be recovered. 2 *Bulst.* 320. 1 R ll. *Abr.* 810.

If a Sheriff arrest a Man upon a *Latitat*, or other mean Process, and the Prisoner is rescued from him before he be carried to Prison, and the Sheriff returns the Rescous against the Rescousers; this shall excuse the Sheriff in *Action for Case* upon Escape, because he is not bound, nor is it convenient for him to bring a *Posse Comitatus.* But if he bring him to Goal, and after he is rescued out of Prison (though he returns Rescuous) yet this shall not excuse the Sheriff; for he ought to keep his Goal at his Peril.

But if the Sheriff takes a Man in Execution, as on a *Capias ad satisfaciend.* and he is rescued before he brings him into Prison, though he returns the Rescous, yet this shall not excuse him, for that he is to take the *Posse Comitat.* and the Party cannot have a new Execution. *Proby and Lumly.*

If the Prison be broken by the King's Enemies, this shall excuse the Sheriff from Escape, for the Goaler could not resist them; and he can have no Remedy over. But if a Prison be broken by Rebels and Traitors within the Realm; so as the Prisoners escape, this shall not excuse the Escape; for the Goaler may have his Remedy over.

But if Prisoners escape by suddain Fire, this shall excuse the Sheriff, for it is the Act of God. *Dyer. Pl.* 66.

If a Man upon a *Capias ad satisfaciend.* be taken in Execution, and after rescues himself from the Sheriff, and escapes, the Plantiff may have a new *Capias* against him, and take him again, the first Writ not being returned or filed, nor any Record made of the Award; and this on a *Scire facias* after a Year; because he shall not take Advantage of his own Wrong. 1 *Roll. Abr.* 904. *Mounson* and *Clayton.*

So if one in Execution escape, and the Sheriff makes fresh Pursuit after him, and takes him again, although it be a long Time after and in another County, yet he shall be in Execution, because he shall not take Advantage of his own Wrong.

A Prisoner escapes, the Goaler makes fresh Pursuit, and before he hath taken him the Prisoner dies: This is the Act of God; and yet because it was once an Escape, the Action of Escape lies against the Goaler, *Poph. p.* 186.

Upon

Upon Escape, the Sheriff may not in fresh Pursuit, enter into the House of *J. N.* and break the Chest of *J. D.* to search for the Prisoner. 2 *Roll. Abridg.* 564.

All Prisoners are such, either by Matter of Record or Matter of Fact.

By Matter of Record, when one present in Court is committed to Prison by the Court. There, if the Goaler have him not ready, it's an Escape without more Enquiry (unless he has reasonable Excuse) and the Judges will set the Fine presently.

By Matter *en Fait*, a Man is a Prisoner when he is arrested by the Sheriff, Bailiff, Constable, *&c.* and escapes, there the Jury ought to find it, and present it before the Justices, and then the Justices assess the Fine.

Upon a *Capias* for Felony, the Sheriff returns *Cepi Corpus*, and hath not the Body at the Day, the Sheriff was amerced 50 *l.* for the Escape.

By some it is Felony in the Sheriff to suffer a Prisoner to escape. *Vid. Stat. de frang. Prisonam.* If the Goaler suffer the Escape, its Felony in him, and a Forfeiture of his Office. 6 *H.* 7. 11. 10 *H.* 7.

If a Prisoner in the Goal attempt to escape, and having broke his Irons, strike the Goaler (coming in the Night to his Prisoner,) and the Goaler slayeth him, it is no Felony, 22 *Ass.* 35.

The *Stat.* 4 *Ed.* 1. *de frang. Prisonam*, mitigates the Rigour of the Common Law; for before that Statute, the Breaking of Prison was Felony in every Case; but now it is not Felony, but where the Party was committed to Prison for Felony. 2 *Leon. p.* 161. *Holcroft's Case.*

What Acts of the Sheriff shall amount to false Imprisonment.

If a Bailiff arrest one after the Writ is returned, false Imprisonment lies.

A Precept to arrest from an illegal Court, will not save an Officer from an Action of false Imprisonment, *Hob. p.* 61.

Trespass, *&c.* will not lie against the Sheriff for Executing Process, though it was erroneous.

Sheriff asks another if his Name be *J. S.*? He says, Yes: On which he arrests him by a Warrant which he had to arrest *J. S.* yet false Imprisonment lies, if he be not the Right Person, *Mo.* 457.

One

One had a *Capias ad satisfaciend.* delivered to the Sheriff, who made a Warrant to his Bailiff to do Execution, Afterwards a *Supercedeas* was awarded, and delivered by the Sheriff, the Defendant being his Bailiff, who escaped, and the Defendant retook him, and detained him in Execution. This second is a false Imprisonment: for though the first Imprisonment was legal (he having taken him by Virtue of a Warrant made before the *Supercedeas* awarded and delivered) he not having Notice of a *Supercedeas*, was excusable. But the Detainment in Prison was afterwards a Wrong. For he being the Sheriff's Servant, and by Intendment having Time given him sufficient to have Notice from his Master, ought at his Peril to take Notice thereof. *Cro. El.* 918.

If a Man be in the Hands of the Under-Sheriff in Execution for Debt, and the Debtee tells the Sheriff, That the Prisoner has satisfied him; If the Sheriff release not the Prisoner, it's false Imprisonment, as in the Case reported in *Bulst.* 3. 96, 97. *viz.*

A. in Execution at the Suit of *B.* afterwards *B.* comes to the Sheriff, and tells him, He had made and sealed a Release of the Debt to the Prisoner, and that therefore he shou'd deliver him out of Execution. The Sheriff does not so, but keeps him still in Prison. *B.* brings Action of false Imprisonment. It lies.

By *Coke*, Detainure after this by the Space of one Hour, is false Imprisonment.

Remedy against SHERIFFS, &c.

IF the Sheriff in his Court quash an *Essoyn* erroneously, without the Consent of the Suitors, Action on the Case lies against him. 26 *Assize* 45.

If a *Distringas* issues to the Sheriff to distrain the Defendant in the Action, by all his Lands and Chattels, *&c.* and the Sheriff returns *Too small Issues*, although an Averment lies by the *Stat. W.* 2 c. 44. yet the Plantiff may well have his Action on the Case against the Sheriff, because it appears by the Words of the Statute, that this is a false Return. The Statute ordains, That the King shall have the Issues, but restrains not any Remedy that the Plantiff had at Common Law. 3 Car. 1.

If the Sheriff embezel an *Exigent* delivered to him at my Suit, Action on the Case lies *tam pro Dom. Rege, quam pro meipso.* 14 *Assize* 12.

Action on the Case lies against the Sheriff, for that he levied such a Sum of Money on a *Fieri facias*, at the Suit of the Plantiff, and brought not the Money into Court at the Day of the Return.

The

The Sheriffs Office about Partition.

TO execute a Writ of Partition, the High-Sheriff must be upon the Land in Person: And if Exception be taken at the Bar before the Writ be returned and filed, a New Writ shall be awarded; but if the Sheriff in such Case returneth, *That he was there in proper Person*, and this Return be received, and the Writ filed, the Party cannot aver against the Return, nor shall have Error. Cro. *El.* 9. Clay's Case.

Omitted, in English, *in Pag.* 247.

A Return of a Writ of Enquiry of Damages.

THIS *Inquisition indented, taken at* C. *in the County of* W. (such a Day and Year) *before* A. B. *Esq; Sheriff of the said County, by Virtue of a certain Writ of our Lord the King, to the same Sheriff directed, and to this Inquisition annexed, by the Oath of* K S. T. G. *&c.* (*to the Number of Twelve Jurors*) *who say upon their Oaths, That* A. P. *in the Writ to this Inquisition annexed, named, hath sustained Damage by Occasion* (*of the within named Trespass*) *by* H. *in the aforesaid Writ named, as in the same Writ is mentioned, to* 40 s. *and for the costs and Damages of the same* A. P. *about his Suit in that Behalf expended, to* 40 s. *In Testimony whereof*, &c.

N. B. The Sheriff and all the Jurors must sign and seal this Inquisition.

The

The Office and Duty of the Clerk of Assize and Clerk of the Peace:

SHEWING,

The Manner and Form of Proceedings at the Assizes and General Goal-Delivery, and at the Court of General Quarter-Sessions of the Peace.

WHEN the Judges set out for any County, to hold the Assize, the Sheriff sends his Bailiff to the Edge of the County, to bring them the best Way to the Place where the Assize is to be held; and before they come there, the Sheriff with his Under-Sheriff and Bailiffs, with their white Staves, and his Livery-Men with their Holberts in their Hands, and attended with the chief of the Gentry of the County, do wait upon the Judges at the usual Places, and conduct them to their Lodgings at the Town where the Assizes are appointed to be held. When the Judges have reposed themselves at their Lodgings, the Sheriffs and Bailiffs with their white Staves, and Livery-men with their Holberts, two by two, wait on the Judges to Church, where the Minister reads Prayers, *&c.* and from thence to the usual Place, where the Assizes or General Goal-Delivery are held.

When the Court is set, the Clerk of Assize must make three Proclamations, and cause the Cryer to say as follows, *viz.*

O Yes, O Yes, O Yes, My Lords the King's Justices do straitly charge and command all Manner of Persons to keep Silence, and hear the King's Majesty's Commissions of Assize and Nisi Prius *openly read, upon Pain of Imprisonment.*

Which being read, the Clerk must say, *God save the King*, and the Cryer with a loud Voice repeat it after the Clerk,

Then the Clerk delivers a Roll of all the Justices of the Peace to the Judge, and then causes the Cryer to make Proclamation and say, *All Justices of the Peace for this County of H. answer to your Names at the first Call, and save your Fines.*

Then the Clerk must name them as they are returned in the Calendar.

When the Justices are all called, the Clerk shall cause the Cryer to make Proclamation and say, *All Sheriffs and Coroners of our Sovereign Lord the King, within this County of* H. *answer to your Names as you shall be called, every Man at the first Call and save your Fines.*

Then the Clerk shall cause the Cryer to call the chief Constables, Petty-Constables, &c. which being done, the Clerk must cause the Cryer to make Proclamation and say, *All Justices of the Peace, Sheriffs, Coroners and other Officers, that have taken any Inquisitions or Recognizances, whereby you have let any Man to Bail, put in your Records thereof forthwith, that my Lords, the King's Justices may proceed thereon.*

Then the Goaler must give the Clerk of Assize an Account what Prisoners have been bailed by any Justices of the Peace after they were committed, that the Clerk may call to the Justices that bailed them for their Recognizances.

Then must the Clerk cause the Cryer to make another Proclamation and say,

You good Men that be returned to enquire for our Sovereign Lord the King, and the Body of this County of H. *answer to your Names, every Man at the first Call, and save your Fines.*

If there do not appear enough to make up a Jury, then must the Clerk call them over again, *A. B. Gent.* (the Cryer repeating the same after him) and if he do not appear; the Sheriff or his Bailiff certifying the Court, upon Oath, that he was summoned, and no reasonable Excuse appearing to the Court, he must be fined. But if any reasonable Excuse appear to the Court, the Clerk shall mark him *spared.*

If it so happen, that a full Jury do not appear at the second Call, the Sheriff must return some of the Freeholders of the same County, that are present, or such as he shall meet with.

Note, There ought to be at least Thirteen upon a Grand Jury, that there may be a casting Vote, and there is commonly Fifteen, Seventeen, Nineteen, and so from that Number to Twenty three.

Then the Grand Jury must be called in Order, every Man by his Name, and Addition, as they are returned. When the Jury is full, the Clerk shall Swear them, after this Manner: The Foreman by himself must lay his Right Hand on the Book, and the Clerk shall give him the Oath, as followeth, *viz.*

You, as Foreman of this Inquest, for the Body of this County of H. *shall diligently enquire, and true Presentment make, of all such Matters and Things as shall be given you in Charge, The King's Counsel, your Fellows and your own you shall keep secret; you shall present no Man for Hatred, Envy, or Malice, neither shall you leave any Man unpresented for Love, Fear, Favour or Affection, or Hope of Reward; but you shall present Things truly, as they come to your Knowledge, according to the best of your Understanding.* So help you God.

The

The rest of the Grand-Jury, by three at a Time, in Order, are Sworn as followeth.

The same Oath which your Foreman hath promised to observe and keep on his Part, you, and every one of you do promise to observe and keep on your Parts. So help you God.

When the Grand-Jury are all thus Sworn, then the Clerk doth say to the Cryer, *Count these.* And as the Clerk doth name them, the Cryer shall count them. Which being done, the Clerk shall say, *Good Men and True, stand together and hear your Charge.*

Then the Clerk shall direct the Cryer to make Proclamation and say, *The King's Justices do straitly charge and command all manner of Persons to keep Silence whilst the Charge is in giving to the Grand-Jury, upon Pain of Imprisonment.*

Then the chief Justice gives the Charge to the Jury.

Whilst the Charge is giving, the Clerk shall file the Recognizances and figure them in order to prosecute, and those to answer upon another File, and the Informations and Examinations upon another File.

When the Charge is given, two Constables are ordered to attend upon the Grand-Jury.

Then the Clerk shall order the Cryer to make another Proclamation, and say, *All Manner of Persons that are bound by Recognizance to prosecute, and prefer any Bills of Indictment against any Prisoners, or others, let them come forth and prosecute, or else they shall forfeit their Recognizances.*

When any Persons are to give Evidence to the Grand-Jury, the Clerk shall swear them after this Manner.

The Evidence which you shall give to the Grand Inquest shall be the Truth, the whole Truth, and nothing but the Truth. So help you God.

And if upon the Evidence given, the Grand Jury have cause to find an Indictment, they write on the back Side thereof, *Billa vera*; but if they have not sufficient Evidence to find the Indictment, they write on the back Side thereof, *Ignoramus.*

When the Court rises, the Clerk directs the Cryer to make three Proclamations, and say, *All manner of Persons that have appeared here this Day before the King's Justices, at these Assizes and General Goal-Delivery, may take their Ease at present, and attend here again at Two a Clock in the Afternoon,* (or to Morrow in the Forenoon). And then he says, *God save the King.*

When the Court sits in the Afternoon, (or the next Morning) the Clerk shall cause the Cryer to make three Proclamations, and call the Court after this Manner.

All Manner of Persons, who are adjourned over to this Hour, and have any thing here to do before my Lords the King's Justices of Assize and General Goal Delivery, Let them now draw near and give their Attendance, and they shall be heard.

 Then

Then (if the Court see Cause) they send for the Grand-Jury, and when they appear, the Clerk shall call them by their Names, and then ask them, if they be agreed of any Bills of Indictments, or Presentments? If they say, *Yea*, the Clerk shall bid them present them to the Court, and upon the Delivery of them the Clerk shall say, *These Indictments or Presentments you do find and are content the Court shall put the Presentments into Form, altering no Matter of Substance?* Then the Grand-Jury shall say, *Yea*; And so they shall go together again. Then the Clerk, out of Respect to them, shall bid the Constables to *make Way for the Gentlemen of the Grand Inquest*.

Then the Cryer makes Proclamation again, and shall say, *My Lords the King's Justices do straitly charge and command all Persons to keep Silence, for now they will proceed to the Pleas of the Crown, and the Arraignment of Prisoners upon Life and Death. And all Persons that are bound by Recognizance to give Evidence against any Prisoners that shall be at the Bar, draw near and give your Evidence, upon Pain of Forfeiting your Recognizances.*

If any Prisoners be let to Bail, and not in Prison, then the Clerk shall cause the Cryer to call him on this Manner.

A. B. *of the Parish of* C. *Labourer, come forth, save thee and thy Bail, or else thou forfeitest thy Recognizance.* If he appear not, then call the Sureties on this Manner, D. E. *and* E. F. *bring forth* A. B. *whom you undertook to have here this Day, or else you forfeit your Recognizance.*

If he appears not, then the Clerk passeth by that Indictment, and calleth to the Goaler to set forth the Prisoner named in the next Indictment. And when he is at the Bar the Clerk saith unto him,

A. B. *hold up thy Hand*. Which done, he then shall say, *Thou standest here indicted by the Name of* A. B. *of*, &c. *for that thou*, &c, (And so read all the Indictment) And then ask him, *What sayest thou? Art thou guilty of this Felony whereof thou standest Indicted, or not guilty?* If he saith, *Not guilty*, the Clerk shall say, *Culprest*, and then shall ask him, *How wilt thou be tried?* If he say, *By God and the Country*, The Clerk shall say, *God send thee a good Deliverance*; and shall write in the Indictment, *Po. Se.*

If the Prisoner upon his Arraignment shall confess his Fact, the Clerk shall write over his Head in the Indictment, (*Cogn.*) and so he is set by till the Time of giving Judgment.

And if the Prisoner upon his Arraignment will not confess the Felony, whereof he stands indicted, nor plead *Not guilty* thereunto, but stand mute; or otherwise will plead such Matter, as shall be no direct Answer to the Offence. In these Cases he shall be put to his Pennance for contemning of the Law, and refusing the ordinary Tryal devised by the Law, and the Clerk shall write over his Head in the Indictment *Stat Mutus*, and he must be set by till Judgment be given, unless he will plead in the mean time *Guilty*, or else put himself upon his Country.

Upon

Upon the Prisoners pleading *Not guilty*, and putting himself upon the Country, the Cryer, by Direction of the Clerk, shall call the Petty-Jury thus:

You good Men that are returned to enquire between our Sovereign Lord the King, and the Prisoner at the Bar, answer to your Names, every Man at the first Call, upon Pain and Peril that shall fall thereon.

And then he shall call every one of them in Order by his Name.

The Jury appearing, the Clerk says, 'You the Prisoner at the Bar, Hear what 'is said unto you: These good Men that were last called, and do now appear, are 'those that shall pass between our Sovereign Lord the King, and you upon your 'Life and Death. If therefore thou wilt challenge them, or any of them, thou 'mayst challenge them as they come to the Book to be sworn, before they are 'sworn, and thou shalt be heard.

If the Prisoner be Arraigned for *High-Treason*, he may challenge peremptorily, in Favour of his Life, Thirty Five, without shewing Cause; but if he be arraigned for *Pettit-Treason*, *Murder*, or *Felony*, he cannot challenge peremptorily above Twenty; but if he shall challenge above Twenty and under Thirty Six, he shall not forfeit his Goods and Chattels.

Then the Clerk shall direct the Cryer to make Proclamation, and say,

'If any Man can inform the King's Justices, or the King's Attorney, or this In-'quest now to be taken, between our Sovereign Lord the King and the Prisoner at 'the Bar, of any Treason, Murder, Felony, or other Misdemeanor, committed or 'done by the Prisoner at the Bar, let them come forth and they shall be heard; 'for the Prisoner stands now at the Bar upon his Deliverance. And all others that 'are bound by Recognizances to give any Evidence against the Prisoner at the Bar, 'let them come forth and give their Evidence, or else they forfeit their Recog-'nizance.

Then must the Clerk call the Jury to be sworn, every Man severally, and bid every one look upon the Prisoner, and swear them severally on this Manner.

'You shall well and truly try, and true Deliverance make, between our Sovereign 'Lord the King, and the Prisoner at the Bar, whom you have in Charge, and a 'true Verdict shall give, according to your Evidence. *So help you God.*

When all are Sworn, the Clerk shall say to the Cryer, *Count these*; and then he calls every one of the Jury over by their Names, and the Cryer counts them. That done, the Clerk must ask them, *If they be all sworn?* If they say, *Yea*; then he must call to the Prisoner, and bid him, *Hold up his Hand*; and then say to the Jury, 'Look upon the Prisoner, you that be Sworn, and hearken to his Cause. 'You shall understand, that he stands indicted by the Name of *A. B.* &c. *(as in the* '*Indictment)* for that he, *&c. (and reads the Indictment.)*' That done, the Clerk shall say, 'Upon this Indictment he hath been arraigned, and upon his Arraign-'ment he hath pleaded *Not guilty*, and upon his Tryal hath put himself upon God 'and the Country, which Country you are: So that your Charge is to enquire,

'whether

'whether he be guilty of this Felony whereof he ſtands indicted, or not guilty. 'If you find him guilty, you ſhall enquire what Lands, Tenements, Goods or 'Chattels he had at the Time of the Felony committed, or at any Time ſince. If 'you find him *Not guilty*, then you ſhall enquire if he did fly for it, or not. If 'you find that he did fly for it, then you ſhall enquire what Goods and Chattels 'he had at the Time that he did ſo fly for it, or at any Time ſince. If you find 'him not guilty, nor that he did fly for it, you ſhall ſay ſo, and no more. And 'hear your Evidence.

Then muſt the Clerk direct the Cryer to call the Witneſſes. That being done, and the Witneſſes for the King do appear, the Clerk ſhall bid them lay their Right Hands upon the Book, and give them this Oath, *viz.*

'The Evidence that you, and every of you ſhall give to this Inqueſt againſt '*A. B.* the Priſoner at the Bar, ſhall be the Truth, the whole Truth, and no'thing but the Truth. *So help you God.*

When all the Witneſſes for the King have been heard, then if the Priſoner deſires, that any Witneſſes ſhall be heard for him, they muſt be called alſo, but they ſhall ſpeak without Oath, unleſs the Fact be under Felony, or that ſome Statute direct the ſame.

After the Jury have heard their Evidence, and the Judge has ſummed up the ſame to them; the Clerk ſhall Swear a Conſtable in this Manner.

'You ſhall well and truly keep every Perſon Sworn of this Jury together, in ſome 'convenient Room, without Meat, Drink, Fire, Candle or Lodging; and you 'ſhall not ſuffer any Perſon whatſoever to ſpeak to them, or any of them; 'neither ſhall you your ſelf ſpeak to them, until ſuch Time as they be agreed 'of their Verdict, unleſs it be to aſk them, if they be agreed of their Verdict. '*So help you God.*

Then the Conſtable attends the Jury to ſome convenient Place, where they may conſult of their Verdict, and continue at the Door till they be all agreed.

When they have agreed on their Verdict, they return to the Court, and the Clerk calls them over by their Names, and aſks them, *If they be all agreed of their Verdict?* If they ſay, *Yea*; he aſks, *Who ſhall ſay for them?* They ſay, *The Foreman.* Then he calls the Priſoner to the Bar, and bids him hold up his Hand. Then he ſays to the Jury, *Look upon the Priſoner, you that be ſworn; What ſay you, Is he guilty of the Felony whereof he ſtands indicted, or not guilty?* If they ſay *Guilty*, Then the Clerk aſks them, What Lands, or Tenements, Goods or Chattels he had at the Time of the Felony committed, or at any Time ſince: If the Jury find any, then the Goods muſt be recorded. But their common Anſwer is, *None to our Knowledge.* Then the *Clerk* ſaith, *Look to him, Goaler.*

If the Jury ſay, *Not guilty*, then the Clerk muſt ſay to the Priſoner, *Down upon your Knees and ſay, God ſave the King and this Honourable Bench.*

When

When the Clerk has entered their Verdict, he must say to the Jury, *Gentlemen, Hearken to your Verdict as the Court has recorded it.* And then reads it to them in this Manner, *You say that* A. B. *is guilty of the Felony whereof he stands indicted. And so You say all.*

When the Judge is ready to give Judgment, the Clerk of Assize causeth the Goaler to set the Prisoner found guilty to the Bar, and saith unto him,

'*A. B* Thou mayst remember, that before this thou hast been indicted for this 'Felony by thee done and committed; Thou hast been arraigned, and pleaded not 'guilty; and for thy Tryal thou hast put thy self upon God and thy Country, 'which Country hath found thee Guilty. What canst thou say for thy self, why, 'according to the Verdict pass'd against thee, thou shouldest not have Judgment to 'suffer Death? What sayst thou, *A. B.*?

Then if he prays his Clergy, and may have it by Law, the Ordinary must be called to shew him the Book, and when he has shewed it to him, the Clerk must say, *Legit ut Clericus, vel non.* If the Ordinary says, *Legit*, then the Form of the Entry must be, *Et Tradito ei Libra, Legit ut Clericus*; and then must the Prisoner be burned in the Hand. But if the Ordinary saith, *Non legit ut Clericus*, the Prisoner must be executed.

Memorand. That all Indictments upon Riots, Trespasses and other Misdemeanours, under the Degree of Felony, must be tried after the Felons. And those that are found guilty, the Judge imposeth a Fine upon them, or other Punishment, as he findeth the Nature of the Offence.

If a Woman be indicted and arraigned of Felony, it is no Plea for her to say, she is with Child; but she must plead to the Indictment, *Guilty*, or *Not guilty.* And if she be found guilty, then she may alledge that she is with Child. And then the Clerk of Assize may order the Sheriff to return an Inquest of Twelve Women before the Justices. And when the Sheriff hath returned them, the Clerk shall call over their Names, and when they all appear, he shall Swear them severally, after this Manner.

'You, as Fore-Matron of this Jury, shall Swear, That you will search and try 'the Prisoner at the Bar, whether she be quick with Child of a quick Child, 'and thereof a true Verdict shall return, according to the best of your Judg-'ment. *So help You God.*

Then shall he give to the rest of them (every one by her self) this Oath:

'The same Oath which your Fore-Matron hath taken on her Part, you shall also 'take and observe on your Part. *So help You God.*

When they are all Sworn, the Constable shall convey the Jury and Prisoner to a Chamber, where they shall search and try if she be quick with Child, *&c.*

When they have agreed upon their Verdict, they shall return to the Court, and deliver in their Verdict in the same Manner as is before related.

If

If they find that the Prisoner is quick with Child of a Quick Child, then Execution shall be stayed till she be delivered; but if they find that she is not quick with Child of a quick Child, she shall be hanged presently, for it will not avail her to be young with Child.

Then the Clerk shall direct the Goaler to set those Prisoners only to the Bar who are to die; that done, he shall cause the Cryer to make Proclamation, and say:

'My Lords the King's Justices do straitly charge and command all Manner of 'Persons to keep Silence, while they proceed to give Judgment against the Pri- 'soners at the Bar.

Judgment being given, and other Tryals over, and the Judge having heard such Grievances as are complained of unto him, concerning Misdemeanours and the like, the Cryer maketh three Proclamations to adjourn the Assizes, and saith,

'All Manner of Persons, that have here appeared before the King's Justices at 'these Assizes and general Goal-Delivery for this County of *H.* may depart at 'present, and attend at, *&c. God save the King.*

Note, The Proceedings on the *Nisi prius* are the same with the Proceedings at the Court of Assize, only the Words *Nisi prius* must be added; as for Example, in calling the Jury, *You good Men of the* Nisi prius, *summoned to appear here this Day*, &c.

The Court of General Quarter-Sessions *of the* Peace *is held after the same Manner as the* Assizes, *only altering the Term.*

THE Justices of the said Court of Quarter-Sessions of the Peace are to hear and determine by Jury, or otherwise, according to their Power, of Causes within their Commission, and the Statutes referred to their Charge.

The Court being set, the Clerk shall cause the Cryer to make Proclamation, and say,

'His Majesty's Justices of the Peace do straitly charge and command all manner 'of Persons to keep Silence, and hear his Majesty's Commission of the Peace 'openly read, upon Pain of Imprisonment.

Then the Clerk shall cause Proclamation to be made three Times, *viz.*

'All Manner of Persons that will sue or complain, or have any thing here to 'do

'do at this Court of General Quarter-Seſſions, holden here this Day, before
'his Majeſty's Juſtices of the Peace for this County of *H.* draw near and
'give your Attendance, and you ſhall be heard.

Then he ſhall cauſe another Proclamation to be made; *viz.*

'*A. B*, High-Sheriff of the County of *H.* return the Precepts and other Proceſs
'to you directed and delivered, returnable here this Day, that his Majeſty's
'Juſtices of the Peace may proceed thereon.

Then he ſhall make another Proclamation, and call the Conſtable by their Names to anſwer at the firſt Call, and ſave their Fines,

Then the Clerk ſhall cauſe another Proclamation to be made, and ſay,

'All Juſtices of Peace, and other Officers, who have any Inquiſitions, or Re-
'cognizances, whereby you have let any Perſons to Bail, or taken any
'Examinations, or other things, ſince the laſt Seſſions, put in your Records
'thereof, that the King's Juſtices of Peace may proceed thereon.

Then he ſhall make another Proclamation, *viz.*

'You good Men that be returned to enquire for our Sovereign Lord the King,
'and the Body of this County of *H.* anſwer to your Names, every Man at
'the firſt Call, and ſave your Fines.

When the Grand Jury is full, he ſhall cauſe the Foreman to lay his Right Hand on the Book, and take the Oath, as in *Pag. 266.*

When the Jury is ſworn, the Clerk ſhall cauſe Proclamation to be made, and ſay,

'His Majeſty's Juſtices of the Peace do ſtraitly charge and command all Manner
'of Perſons to keep Silence whilſt the Charge is giving, upon Pain of Im-
'priſonment.

The Charge given by the Judge of the Court many times varies, according to the Circumſtance of the County where the Court is held. But in order to inform ſuch as may not be acquainted with it, I ſhall here ſet down a ſhort Form of a Charge to be given to a Grand Inqueſt, *viz.*

Gentlemen,

SINCE the Juſtice of a Kingdom cannot be confined within the Compaſs of a Crown; for that no one Perſon can hear all the Complaints of his People, the King has been pleaſed to derive ſome Particles of his Authority to his Juſtices in the ſeveral Counties, thereby to enable and qualify them to diſpence Juſtice to the People. And in order thereto, the Laws of this Realm have that tender Regard to the Freedom and Liberty of the Subject, that no Perſon can be impeached in their Lives and Fortunes, unleſs Twelve of their Neighbours ſhall find good Cauſe for the ſame; Therefore it behoves you all that be now concerned in this Affair, to be ſo careful in the Performance in the Truſt repoſed in you, that no Offences may eſcape unpreſented, leſt you contract the Guilt of their Vices upon your ſelves. But I ſhall not preſs your Oaths and Duties to you, ſince I view your Perſons, and know you to be Men experienced, and alſo endowed with

Principles of Honesty and Religion. However, since Custom and Necessity require me to say something to you, I shall reduce your Charge to these three Heads, viz.

You are to enquire and present,

1. All those that offend the Health of your Souls, and their Offences extend against *God and his Church*,

2. All those that offend against the Health of your Head, and their Offences extend against the *King and his Government*.

3. All those that offend against the Health of your Body, and their Offences extend against the *People, and their Peace and Quiet*.

And I do not doubt your Care and Diligence herein; for that by the Performance of this Duty, you will demonstrate to the World, that you Fear God, Honour the King, *and* Love your Neighbour. *And so I dismiss you to your Business.*

Then must the Clerk direct the Cryer to make Proclamation, and say,

'All Manner of Persons that be bound over by Recognizance to prosecute, or 'prefer any Bill of Indictment against any Person or Persons, before His 'Majesties Justices of the Peace, let them come forth and prosecute, or 'else they shall forfeit their Recognizances.

When any Evidence appears, he shall in Presence of the Court lay his Hand on the Bible, and the Clerk shall swear him in this Manner:

The Evidence which you shall give to the Grand Inquest shall be the Truth, the whole Truth, and nothing but the Truth. So help you God.

Then shall the Clerk proceed in the same Manner as is directed in Page 267.

When any Persons are discharged upon their Appearance upon Process, the Clerk of the Peace shall forthwith put such Persons out of Process, and enter their Names in his Book, and shew the same to the Court, before another Process shall be called.

When all Processes be discharged, then the Traverses shall follow next in Course.

When the Parties do appear who stand indicted of *Trespasses, Mayhems, Batteries, Riots, Routs, Conversions*, and the like Offences, the Party indicted shall not hold up his Hand at the Bar, but the Clerk shall call the Person indicted, and when he appears, shall say unto him,

Thou standest here indicted by the Name of F. E. *in the Parish of* G. *in this County, Labourer, for that thou*, &c. (And so read the Indictment.) And then shall ask him, *What sayest thou? Art thou guilty of this Trespass whereof thou standest indicted, or not guilty?*

If he shall say, *Not guilty*, and shall traverse the Indictment, then he shall enter into Recognizance to prosecute his Traverse at the next Quarter-Sessions; which Recognizance shall be taken after this Manner;

F. E. Thou

F. E. *Thou dost acknowledge thy self indebted unto Our Sovereign Lord the King in the Sum of*, &c. *to be levied of thy Lands and Tenements, of thy Goods and Chattels, and this upon Condition, That thou shalt appear at the next General Quarter-Sessions of the Peace, to be holden before his Majesty's Justices of the Peace for this County, and shalt then and there prosecute thy Traverse, which is taken with Effect; and shalt not depart the Court without Lisence.*

But if the Party will not confess the Offence whereof he stands indicted, or will not plead *Guilty*, or will plead such Matter as shall be no Answer to the Indictment, Judgment shall be entered against him, according to the usual Course used in Actions at Common Law.

Note, That the Party indicted may, by his Counsel, before Plea pleaded, take Exceptions to the Insufficiency of his Indictment; and if the Court shall quash the same for *Error*, the Clerk of the Peace ought forthwith to indorse the Cause of the *Error*, wherefore the Indictment was quashed, on the Back-side thereof; but if the Court shall see cause when the Indictment is quashed, they may give Order that a New Indictment be drawn against the Offender.

Then the Clerk shall call the Parties bound by Recognizance to prosecute their Traverse; and if any of them do not appear, then the Cryer shall call him thrice, and say,

A. M. *come forth and prosecute thy Traverse with Effect, else thou forfeitest thy Recognizance.*

Then the Clerk shall cause the Cryer to call the Prosecutor three Times, in this Manner:

D. L. *come forth and prosecute thy Indictment against* A. M. *and thou shalt be heard.*

If the Prosecutor do not appear to prosecute his Indictment, and Affidavit be made in Court that he had timely Notice of the Tryal, the Jury shall be sworn, and the Clerk shall charge them with the Indictment, concluding thus;

That to this Indictment he has pleaded Not Guilty, and for his Tryal has put himself upon his Country, which Country you are: And none appearing to prove the Fact against him, unless you do know upon your own Knowledge, that A. M. *is guilty of the Matter of Fact charged in the Indictment, you shall find him Not guilty,*

And upon such Verdict the Court shall discharge him. But if the Prosecutor do appear, the Clerk shall cause the Cryer to call the Jury in this wise;

You good Men that be returned to enquire and try this Issue of Traverse between our Sovereign Lord the King and A. M. *answer to your Names at the first Call, upon Pain and Peril that shall fall thereon.*

When the Jury is full, the Clerk shall say, *A. M. Look to your Challenges.*

Then he shall swear the Jury, every Man singly by himself, laying his Right Hand on the Book, thus,

You shall well and truly try the Issue of Traverse between Our Sovereign Lord the King.

King, and A. M. *for a Trespass whereof he stands indicted, according to your Evidence.* So help you God.

When all the Jury is sworn, the Clerk shall read their Names, and the Cryer shall count them. Then he shall ask them, *If they be all sworn?* If they say, *Yea,* he shall bid them *stand together and hear their Charge.*

Then the Clerk causes the Cryer to make Proclamation in this Manner:

If any Person can inform His Majesties Justices of the Peace, the King's Attorney, or this Inquest now to be taken, of any Trespasses or other Misdemeanor acted or committed by A. M. *come forth and give your Evidence, or else he shall be discharged.*

Then the Clerk shall read the Indictment, and charge the Jury as the Indictment is, what they are to enquire. Then shall the Indictment be opened by Counsel, and the Witnesses called to prove the Matter of Fact, which Witnesses shall be sworn by the Clerk after this Manner;

The Evidence which you shall give to this Inquest against A. M. *shall be the Truth, the whole Truth, and nothing but the Truth.* So help you God.

In all Tryals the Counsel of the Prosecutor shall conclude the Evidence, and the Judge of the Court shall give the Directions to the Jury. Then shall the Jury depart to some convenient Place to agree upon their Verdict, with a Constable, to whom the Clerk shall administer this Oath, *viz.*

You shall well and truly keep every Person, sworn of this Inquest, together in some private Room, without Meat, Drink, Candle or Lodging; and you shall not suffer any Person whatsoever to speak to them, or any of them; neither shall you your self speak to them, until they have agreed on their Verdict. unless it be to ask them, whether they have agreed of their Verdict. So help you God.

When they have agreed on their Verdict and returned into Court to deliver the same, the Clerk shall call them severally by their Names, and ask them, *If they have agreed on their Verdict?* If they say, *Yea,* then he shall say, *Who shall say for you?* If they answer, *Our Foreman,* then he shall say to the Jury,

What say you? Is A. M. *guilty of the Trespass, or Riot, or Rout,* &c. *whereof he stands indicted, or not Guilty.*

If they say, *Guilty,* or if they say *Not Guilty,* then the Clerk shall record the Verdict, and then say to the Jury, *Hearken to the Verdict as the Court has recorded it.*

And then he shall repeat it in this Manner, *You say that* A. M. *is guilty of the Riot, Trespass,* &c. *whereof he stands indicted; And so you say all.*

When a Person has entered into Recognizance for the Appearance of another, if the Delinquent do not appear, the Clerk shall cause the Cryer to call them in this wise.

A M *of the Parish of* ——— *Cordwainer, come forth, save thee and thy Bail, or else thou forfeitest thy Recognizance.*

But

But if the Delinquent do appear upon the Recognizance, then the Clerk shall enter a *Comparuit*, and then call the Prosecutor thus,

D. E. *come forth and prosecute the Peace against* A. M. *or else he shall be discharged.*

And if the Prosecutor doth not appear after he hath been thrice called, the Delinquent shall be discharged of course.

If a Person be bound to appear, or bound to his good Behaviour for a certain Time, and during that Time do keep the Peace towards the King and all his People, then Proclamation shall be made in open Court in this manner,

If any Person can shew any lawful Cause why the Peace granted against J. B. *shall be continued, let him come forth, and he shall be heard, for he stands upon his Discharge.*

And if none come to prosecute, he shall be discharged. So when any Person doth demand the Peace against any Delinquent, the Justice or his Clerk shall administer unto the Prosecutor this Oath, *viz.*

The Peace which You require against A. B. *is not out of any Ill-will or Malice which You bear to him, but meerly to preserve Your Life, House, Goods or Chattles, from any bodily Harm or Mischief, which he by himself, or any other by his Procurement, may attempt to do.* So help you God.

When the Justices proceed to give Judgment upon Offenders, the Clerk shall cause Proclamation to be made, and say,

His Majesties Justices of the Peace do straitly charge and command all manner of Persons to keep Silence whilst they proceed to give Judgment against the Prisoners at the Bar.

Note, That every Judgment which shall be given, and every Fine which shall be assessed, ought to be openly pronounced and declared by the Court, to the End it may advance the more Good to the Prince in Profit, to the Justices in Credit, and to the People in Example.

When the Justices have heard all such Grievances as are complained of unto them concerning Misdemeanors, and the like, the Cryer shall make three Proclamations, and adjourn the Sessions, saying,

All Manner of Persons that have any thing more to do at this Quarter-Sessions of the Peace, holden before his Majesty's Justices of the Peace for this County of H, *may depart hence at this Time, and keep their Day again here at*——

GOD Save the KING.

A

A Guide to Coroners.

THE Office of *Coroner* hath its Etymology or Derivation from *Corona*, being an Officer of the Crown, and hath principal Cognizance of some Pleas, called *Pleas of the Crown*.

Coroners were first established by King *Alfred*, and ordained to be Conservators of the Peace. To their Office appertains the receiving of Appeals of the whole County, of Felonies committed within a Year and a Day; to award the Exigents of Contempts, and to pronounce Judgment of Out-Lawries upon County Days.

Of ancient Time this Office was of such Estimation, that none could have it but a Knight; for this was the Policy of ancient Times, that Officers did ever give Grace to the Place, and not the Place (only) to grace the Officer. And to the Intent that the Coroner should have sufficient within the County to be responsible for all that he doth, or ought to do by his Office, and that they might execute their Office without Bribery,

The Coroners Office is both Judicial and Ministerial. And as to the View of a Body of a Man, it is his Office, That so soon as he shall be certified of any casual Death, to send the Constable of the Place to summon a sufficient Number of Men of the four next adjacent Towns, That at such a Time and Place they appear before the Coroner, where the Body is to be viewed; and if it be buried it is to be taken up; and he is to record the Names of those who buried him. And if it hath been damaged by ill-keeping, or lain so long that it cannot be Judged how it came by its Death, the same must also be recorded, that this Negligence may be punished at the Coming of the Justices of Assize into the Circuit; for the Town where the Neglect was shall be grievously amerced upon the Sight of the Coroners Rolls.

He must do his Office in Person, and see the Dead Body when he maketh Inquisition, otherwise the Enquiry is invalid.

If the Coroner be remiss and negligent in coming to execute his Office, after he is sent unto, he shall be amerced.

The

The Coroner with the Jury present are to view the Bodies of such as come to casual Deaths, make away themselves, or made away by others, or suspected to be put out of the World by violent Means, hard Usage, starving in Prison, or elsewhere; and they are to enquire how such Person came to his End, and to make strict Examination concerning the same, by sending for any Person or Persons that can give Information thereon. Then are they to give their Verdict to the best of their Judgment, setting forth the Manner of his being killed, whether he died of another's Felony, or of his own, or by Mischance, as by the Fall of a House, Wall, Timber, Kick of a Horse, and the like; and if of Blows, whether of a Staff, Stone, or any other Weapon: And he is to record in his Rolls the Names of such Jurors as were summoned and do not appear, that the same Offences of Disobedience may not pass unpunished: For by a Jury he is to certify how the King came to lose a Subject, the Strength and Power of a Prince consisting in the Force and Number of his People; and therefore it's his Interest to maintain and secure them in Peace and Tranquility.

The Method of keeping the Coroner's *Court.*

THE Coroner's Court is a Court of Record, and held after this Manner:

When the Coroner cometh to view a Party that hath hanged, killed, or drowned himself, or that hath come to his Death by any other Accident, he must either go himself, or make out his Warrant to impannel a Jury, to the Constable or Bailiff in whose Liberty the Party lieth dead, to appear before him at such a Place, Day and Hour as he shall appoint. The Form of the Warrant runs thus:

To the Sheriff (or Constable) of *York*, &c. Greeting:

THese are to will and require you, in the Name of Our Sovereign Lord the King, straitly to charge and command You, That you cause to come before me, A B. Coroner of the County of York, *at the House of* C. D. *in* Kingston, *between the Hours of One and Two in the Afternoon of this present first Day of June, Twenty Four good and lawful Men of the said Town, or the three next adjacent Towns in the said County; then and there to do and execute such Things as shall be given them in Charge on His Majesty's Behalf; (or) Then and there to enquire upon the View of the Body of* Thomas Edwards *there lying dead, how and in what Manner he came to his Death. Fail not herein at your Peril, as you will answer the contrary. Given under my Hand and Seal, this first Day of* June, *in the 7th Year of His Majesty's Reign,* Annoq; Domini, 1720.

A. B. Coroner.

When you come to the Place appointed, call the Constable or Bailiff to make Return of their Warrant.

Then command three Proclamations to be made, *O Yes, Silence is commanded.* Then call the Jury after this Manner.

You good Men that are returned to appear here this present Time, to enquire for Our Sovereign Lord the King, answer to Your Names, as You shall be called, every Man at the first Call, upon Pain and Peril that shall fall thereon.

And such of the Jury who fail to appear, shall be fined Forty Shillings.

The Jury appearing, Swear Fourteen or Fifteen of them, and give the Foreman his Oath, thus,

You shall diligently enquire and true Presentment make on the Behalf of Our Sovereign Lord the King, how and in what Manner Thomas Edwards, *here lying dead, came to his Death; and You shall deliver up to me* (his Majesty's Coroner for the County of, *&c.) a true Verdict thereof, according to such Evidence as shall be given up to you, according to Your Knowledge.* So help you God.

Then Swear the rest by four at once, thus;

All such Oath as L. M. *the Foreman of this Inquest for his Part hath taken, you and every One of You, shall well and truly Observe and keep on your Parts, according to Your Evidence.* So help you God.

If the Evidence be not ready, you may adjourn until another Day and Place to receive their Evidence, binding the Jury by Recognizance in Twenty Pound each for their Appearance.

Then send out your Warrant for the Witnesses, commanding them to come to be examined before you, and to deliver their Knowledge touching the Matter in Question. And when they appear, take their Examinations in Writing under their Hands.

If it be about the Tryal of a Man's Life, then must the Witnesses be all bound over in 20 *l.* a Piece, at the least, personally to appear at the next Assizes, to deliver their Knowledge therein.

The Recognizance must be in this Manner, *viz.*

THE 22*d Day of* August, *in the Fifth Year of the Reign of Our Sovereign Lord King* GEORGE, *of* Great-Britain, *&c.* A. B. of C. *came before me* D. E. *One of His Majesty's Justices,* &c. *and acknowledged himself to be indebted to Our Sovereign Lord the King,* &c.

'The Condition of this Recognizance is such, That if the above-bounden *A. B.* 'do personally appear before the Justices of Assize and Goal-Delivery, at the 'next Assize to be holden at —— for the said County; and then and there 'deliver and set forth his Knowledge, touching the Death of *Thomas Edwards*, and do 'not depart thence without Lisence of the said Court, that then this Recog-'nizance

'nizance to be void and of none Effect, or else to be and remain in full Force
' and Virtue.

Acknowledged before me the Day and Year above-written,

D. E.

Then command three Proclamations to be made, thus,

O Yes, O Yes, O Yes, If any Man can give Evidence on the Behalf of his Majesty, how and in what Manner Thomas Edwards, *here lying dead, came to his Death, draw near and You shall be heard.*

The Evidence appearing, give him, her or them the Oath, *viz.*

All such Evidence as you shall give to this Inquest, concerning the Death of T. E. *here lying dead, shall be the Truth, the whole Truth, and nothing but the Truth.* So help you God.

The Jury being sworn, command them to stand together and hear their Charge, which the Coroner must give, *viz.*

Gentlemen,

'YOU that are sworn, you shall by your Oath declare of the Death of this Man, ' whether he died of Felony, or by Mischance; and if of Felony, whether ' of his own, or of another's; and if by Mischance, whether by the Act of God or ' of Man: And if of Famine, whether of Poverty or of common Pestilence; and ' from whence he came, and who he was. And if he died of another's Felony, who ' were Principals and who were Accessaries; And if Hue-and-cry were made, or ' not; and whether the Men fled, or not. You are also to enquire, whether he ' died of Long Imprisonment and hard Usage there, or not; and who threatned ' him of his Life or Members: And so of all prevailing Circumstances that can come ' by Presumption.

' And in Case he died by Hurt or Fall, then you shall enquire the Names of the ' Finders, of his next Neighbours, and who were his Parents, and if he was killed ' there, or elsewhere; and if elsewhere, by whom and how he was brought: So ' also you are to enquire, if there was any *Deodand*, and to whose Hand it came.

' And in Case he died of another's Felony, then you are to enquire, who were ' the Felons, from whence they came, and where they now are.

' And if he died of his own Felony, then you are to enquire of the Manner, ' and how he came to make away with himself; and of the Value of his Goods, ' and where they are. All which you are to enquire of, and endeavour to find out.

So far the Charge to the Jury.

You are also to observe, if one Man wilfully kill another, or if a Man kill or drown himself, the first doth forfeit by that Fact both his Lands and his Goods; and the other forfeits but Goods and Chattels, and no Lands.

And if any Homicide happen to be wilful Murder, (which Offence cannot be too severely punished) the Offendor herein ought to lose both Life, Lands and Goods.

But if it be found Man-slaughter, and the Offender can read, then he may, in Favour of his Life, by the King's Mercy, have the Benefit of his Clergy, and so save his Life. But in this Case he shall forfeit both his Lands and Goods. The Goods being found must be appraised, and left in the Town or Village where such Offender dwelt, and there safely kept, until the Offender be acquitted, or convicted by due Course of Law; In the Interim, the Offender must be maintained with his Goods, so that he may be kept alive to answer his Fact, And when he is convicted, such Goods as remain must go to those to whom they belong by the Law, and not before. And as for the Offender's Free Land, immediately after Conviction, his Majesty must have *Annum, Diem* and *Vastum* therein, and after, the Lord of whom it was holden, shall have it as an Escheat.

Thus having in brief declared these things incident to my Office, and to you to enquire of, I will conclude. Therefore now stand together and hear your Evidence.

Having heard the Evidence, they must give in their Verdict, upon which the Coroner draws up the Inquisition, thus,

An Inquisition of Murder.

Middl. ss.

AN Inquisition indented, taken at the Parish of *S.* in the County of *Middlesex*, the 25th Day of *March*, *Anno*, &c. before *T. E.* Gent. Coroner of the County aforesaid, upon Sight of the Body of a certain *W. F.* then and there lying dead, by the Oath of *J. W. R. W.* &c. honest and lawful Men of the Parish aforesaid, and four other Villages in the County aforesaid, next adjoining the same Parish, being sworn, tried and charged to enquire on the Part of our Sovereign Lord the King, after what Fashion and how the aforesaid *W. F.* came to his Death, upon their Oath do say, That the aforesaid *E. L*, late of the Parish of *S.* aforesaid, in the County aforesaid, Labourer, the Twentieth Day of *March*, *Anno*, &c. aforesaid, not having the Fear of God before his Eyes, but being moved and led by the Instigation of the Devil, with Force and Arms, *&c.* at the Parish aforesaid, in the County aforesaid, in and upon the aforesaid *W. F.* then and there in the Peace of God and of our said Lord the King being, feloniously an Assault did make, and that the aforesaid *E. L.* him the said *W. F.* then and there on the Earth did cast and throw down; and the aforesaid *E. L.* with his Left Hand, and with both the Feet of him the said *E. L.* the aforesaid *W. F.* (so as he lay flat on the Earth) in and upon his Breast with his Hands and Feet feloniously did strike, beat and tread down. And the aforesaid *W. F.* then and there with his Left Hand, and with both the Feet of him the said *E. L.* in and upon the Breast of the said *W. F.* a Mortal Bruise

Bruise did give, in Length Six Inches and in Breadth Four Inches; of which said mortal Bruise the aforesaid *W. F.* then and there instantly languished, and languishing did live, from the said Nineteenth Day of *March*, *Anno*, &c. until the Twentieth Day of the said Month of *March*, then next following, on which Day the aforesaid *W. F.* at the Parish aforesaid, in the County aforesaid, of the aforesaid Mortal Bruise died; and so the Jurors aforesaid upon their Oath aforesaid say, That the aforesaid *E. L.* the aforesaid *W. F.* feloniously did kill and Murder, in Manner and Form aforesaid, against the Peace of our said Lord the King, his Crown and Dignity; and what Goods and Chattels the aforesaid *E. L.* had at the Time of the Felony aforesaid, in Manner and Form aforesaid by him committed and done, the Jurors aforesaid do not know.

In Testimony whereof I the said Coroner have, as well as the Jurors aforesaid, to this Inquisition interchangeably set our Seals, the Day, Year and Place aforesaid.

An Inquisition for Manslaughter, *where one was starved, and perished for Want of Sustenance.*

Middlesex ss.

THE Inquisition indented, taken at *Hamstead* in the County of *Middlesex*, this Twentieth Day of *December*, *Anno*, &c. before *J. G.* Gent. Coroner of our Lord the King for the said County, upon Sight of the Body of *W. T.* then and there lying dead, by the Oath of *W. P. T. E. J. M.* &c. honest and lawful Men of *Hamstead* aforesaid, and of Four other Villages in the County aforesaid, next adjacent the Town of *Hamstead* aforesaid, which being charged and sworn to enquire in what Manner, when and how the aforesaid *W. T.* came to his Death, upon their Oath do say, *That* J. B. *of* W. *in the County aforesaid, Taylor, and* S. *his Wife, not having God before their Eyes, but being seduced and led by the Instigation of the Devil, the* 20th Day *of* November, Anno, *&c. aforesaid, with Force and Arms,* &c. *at* W. *aforesaid, in the County aforesaid, in and upon the said* W. T. *then an Apprentice of the said* J. B. *in the Peace of God and of Our Lord the King then being, feloniously, voluntarily, and of his Malice forethought, an Assault did make, and that the aforesaid* S. *then, to wit, the aforesaid Twentieth Day of* November, *in the Year aforesaid, and divers other Days and Times, as well before as after, at* W. *aforesaid, in the County aforesaid, feloniously, voluntarily, and of her Malice forethought, detained and kept —— from the said* W. T. *and to him the said* W. T. *did not exhibit and give good and sufficient Aliments, Victuals, Cloaths, Bedding, Medicine, and other Necessaries, with an Intent the said* W. T. *through Want, then should miserably languish, starve and die:*

Of which Detention and Want of Aliments from the aforesaid W. T. *and no Exhibition and Allowance to the said* W. T. *of good and sufficient Aliments, Victuals, Cloaths, Bedding, Medicines, and other Necessaries, by her the said* S, *unto the said* W. T. *from the aforesaid Twentieth Day of* November, *in the Year aforesaid, until the Fifteenth Day of* December, *then next following, in the Year aforesaid, at* W. *aforesaid, in the County aforesaid, miserably languished, and languishing miserably lived, upon which said Fifteenth Day of* December, *in the Year aforesaid; the aforesaid* W. T. *for want of good and sufficient Aliments, Victuals, Cloaths, Bedding, Medicines and other Necessaries, at* W. *aforesaid, in the County aforesaid, miserably starved and died: And that the aforesaid* J. B. *together with the aforesaid* S. *his Wife, at the Time of the Felony and Murder aforesaid, by the said* S. *in Manner and Form aforesaid, done and committed, feloniously and voluntarily, and of her Malice forethought was present, assisting, aiding, procuring, comforting and helping, the aforesaid* S. *the aforesaid* W. T. *in Manner and Form aforesaid, to starve and murder:* And so the Jurors aforesaid say upon their Oath aforesaid, *That they the said* J. B. *and* S. *his Wife, the aforesaid* W. T. *in Manner and Form aforesaid, feloniously, voluntarily, and of their Malice forethought, starved and murdered, against the Peace of our said Lord the King, his Crown and Dignity,* &c. And so the said *W. T.* came to his Death, and not otherwise, neither any other Manner besides what abovesaid. But what Goods and Chattels, Land or Tenements, the aforesaid *J. B.* and *S.* his Wife, at the Time of the Felony and Murder aforesaid, by the said *J. B.* and *S.* his Wife, in Manner and Form aforesaid done and committed, or at any other Time afterwards (until the taking of this Inquisition) had, the said Jurors do not know.

In Testimony, &c.

Inquisition where one is slain by Misfortune, by a Cart loaden with Hay.

Middlesex ss.

INquisition indented, taken at, *&c.* ——— who say upon their Oaths, *That the aforesaid* A. B. *the Tenth Day of* May, Anno, *&c. aforesaid, at* S. *aforesaid, in the County aforesaid, going with his Cart from* S. *aforesaid unto* L. *in the said County, by the Way between* S. *and* L. *aforesaid, to wit, at,* &c. *aforesaid, in the County aforesaid, his said Cart loaden with Hay, fell upon the Body of the aforesaid* A. B. *and so did slay and break his Body, of which the aforesaid* A. B. *then and there incontinently died.* And so the Jurors aforesaid, upon their Oath aforesaid, say, That *the aforesaid* A. B. *in Manner and Form aforesaid, by Misfortune is come to his Death.* And farther the Jurors aforesaid upon their Oaths aforesaid say, *That*

then

then and there Four Horſes, with the Cart and Load of Hay, containing in Weight by Eſtimation Fourty Stone, did move at the Death of the aforeſaid A. B, *and that the ſaid Four Horſes are of the Price of Eight Pounds Ten Shillings, and that the aforeſaid Cart is of the Value of Twenty Shillings; and that the aforeſaid Cart remaineth in the Cuſtody of* C. D. *of* S. *aforeſaid, to wit, late Wife of the aforeſaid* A. B. *And that the aforeſaid Fourty Stone of Hay are of the Value of Fourty Five Shillings and Ten Pence, and remain in Cuſtody of* D. F. *of* S. *aforeſaid, Gent.*

In Teſtimony whereof, as well the Coroner as the Jurors, *&c.*

An Inquiſition where One drowns himſelf.

Middleſex ſſ.

INquiſition indented, taken, *&c.* ——— ——— who ſay upon their Oath, *That the aforeſaid* A. B. *the Second Day of* May, Anno, *&c. aforeſaid, about Eight of the Clock in the Forenoon of the ſame Day, not having God before his Eyes, but being ſeduced and led by the Inſtigation of the Devil, of his Malice forethought, at* M. *aforeſaid in the County aforeſaid, then and there alone being, in the common River there himſelf voluntarily and feloniouſly did drown.* And ſo the Jurors aforeſaid upon their Oath aforeſaid do ſay, *That the aforeſaid* A. B. *in Manner and Form aforeſaid, then and there voluntarily and feloniouſly, as a Felon of himſelf, did kill and murder, againſt the Peace,* &c.

In Teſtimony whereof, as well the Coroner aforeſaid as the aforeſaid Jurors, *&c.*

If One hang himſelf, then the Inquiſition, thus;

Middleſex ſſ.

INquiſition indented, *&c.* (the Hour, *&c.*) not having God before his Eyes, but being ſeduced and led by the Inſtigation of the Devil, at *S.* aforeſaid, in a certain Wood, adjoining to the ſaid *S.* then and there alone being, with one Rope made with Hemp, of the Price of one Penny, which he then and there in his Hands had and held, and one End then about his Neck then and there he put, and the other End then about a Branch of a certain Oak Tree he tied, and himſelf then and there with the Rope aforeſaid voluntarily and feloniouſly did hang and ſtrangle; and ſo the Jurors aforeſaid upon their Oath aforeſaid ſay, *&c.*

No Forfeiture of Lands.

Of Homicide *and* Manslaughter, Felo-de-se.

HOMICIDE is Killing of a Man by Man, *Dalt.* 339, 349. *Exivi Termini* comprehends Treason, Murder, *&c.* It is no Difference whether the Party slain be a Denizen, Alien or Englishman, if he lives under the King's Protection. *Dalt.* 340. *Lamb.* 237. *Cromp.* 21. *a Numb.* 1.

To kill one attainted for Treason or Felony, or Outlawed for Felony, or attainted in Præmunire, is Felony, by 4 *Eliz. Stamford* 13. *Dalt.* 342. *Crompt.* 24. *a Num.* 29.

Homicide is either killing himself, *Felo-de-se*; or by another, and *Felo-de-se*. A Man by killing himself forfeits to the King his Goods and Chattels, Real and Personal, and his Debts due by Speciality, *Dalt.* 341. But no *Lands* nor Blood corrupted, *ibid.* But his Goods are not forfeired till his Death, *ibid.*

An Infant, or One *Non compos Mentis*, does not forfeit; but a Lunatick killing himself out of his Lunacy, doth forfeit his Goods, *Dalt.* 340.

Homicide of another, is either voluntary or involuntary: voluntary is Murther, *Vide Murder or Manslaughter.*

Manslaughter is when two Men, *&c.* fight together on a sudden without precedent Malice, and one of them kill the other, *Dalt.* 349. *Lamb.* 248. *Crompt*, 16. *a.*

Manslaughter is either by *Chance medly*, or *Se defendende*, House and Goods.

By *Chance-medly* is *Felony*, but may have Clergy. *Dalt.* 349.

One Fighting breaks his Weapon, another standing by puts one into his Hand, or otherwise lends it him, and with it he kills another, it is *Manslaughter* in the Lender. *Dalt.* 134. *Crompt*, 16. *b. Numb.* 12. *Lamb.* 252.

The Servant fighting in his Master's Defence, though there were Malice in the Master, and not told to the Servant, and one be killed. *Lamb.* 240. So a Stranger taking Part, *Lamb.* 238. is Chance-medly. *Dalt.* 348

If two that were in Malice are reconciled, and fall out upon a new Occasion, and one is killed, it is *Manslaughter* only, *Dalt.* 350. *Lamb.* 250.

Se defendendo, is where one killeth another in the necessary Defence of himself, or his, thereby to save himself, or his Possessions or Goods, or some other Person which he is bound to defend from Peril, and it is either against a Felon, Murtherer, Thief or Loyal Subject, *Dalt.* 356. *Lamb*, 152.

Against a Loyal Subject, if he be assaulted by another Man, he must fly so much as he may, till he be letted by some Wall, or other material Hinderance, that his Necessity of Defence may seem inevitable; and he shall be committed till the Time of his Tryal, lose his Goods, and sue out his Pardon, *Lamb.* 253. *Dalt.* 35. It is not material, if he strikes again before he gave any deadly Wound, if he flies to the Strait. *Dalt.* 357, 358.

If

If a Man fly to a Wall, and hold out his Weapon, if the Pursuer run upon it and is killed, it is *se defendendo*, and forfeits his Goods. *Crompt.* 28. *a Num.* 7. *Dalt.* 349. But if he had fallen on the Ground, and the other fall on it and kill himself, there is no Loss of Goods; for he could not fly, and the Slain is in a Sort *Felo-de-se*, ibid. *P. R.* 122. *b Stam.* 16. *a.*

If a Man fall to the Ground, there his flying to a Strait is not necessary, because he might be there inevitably killed, if he did not defend himself, *Dalt.* 347, 358.

An Officer or Minister of Justice executing his Office, is not bound to fly, *Dalt.* 358. *Coke* 98, 99.

If a Servant kill one that robb'd or kill'd his Master, so it be done presently, or in Defence of his Master's Person or Goods, if he could not otherwise have avoided the same, *Dalt.* 358. *Crompt* 28. *Num.* 2. So to shoot at one that comes to burn a Man's House, is justifiable in him or his Servants. *Dalt.* 356, *&c.*

In the Defence of the Possession of a Man's Goods or House, he may justify to beat him, but may not kill him, though the Party come wrongfully to take his Goods, unless he be a Thief, *Dalt.* 358, *&c.*

To kill a true Man in Defence of House, Goods or Land, is Manslaughter, *Dalt.* 338. *Crompt.* 27, *b. Num.* 4.

Involuntary Homicide.

THis is either by *Misadventure* or *Necessity*. The first is, when a Man doing a lawful Act, killeth a Man: This is not Felony of Death, but he shall have his Pardon of Course for Life and Lands, but forfeiteth his Goods, *Lamb.* 254, *Dalt.* 351.

For Example: A School-Master, Father, Mother, or Master correcting a Child Scholar or Servant. Moderately shooting at Pricks, Butts or lawful Marks: A Workman casting Tiles, Timber or Stone from off a House or any thing from off a Cart, and giving Warning, or doing other lawful Things, giving Warning.

But the Killing of a Man in doing any unlawful Act without evil Intent, is Felony; as shooting Arrows, casting Stones into High-ways where People resort, or unto other Places or usual Resort, *Dalt.* 35 .

If a Man be slain by the Fall of a House or Tree by a Beast, *&c.* Any Party by a wilful Default, causing it, it is Felony, *Dalt* 351.

The Thing that causes the Death is a *Deodand*, and forfeited to the King, *Dalt.* 253, *Crompt.* 35. *a.*

Deodands are not forfeit till the Matter be found on Record.

If a Man be slain under Fourteen Years of Age, nothing is forfeited as a *Deodand. Dalt.* 353. *Lamb.* 21, *&c.*

Of

Of Appeals in Case of Murthers, &c. *fit to be known by Coroners and others; with the Manner of proceeding in such Cases.*

THE Word *Appeal* is derived from the Verb *Appello, to call*, because the Party bringing it, calls the Delinquent to Judgment; it is the same with an Accusation, and they are of three Sorts, *viz.*

(1.) *An Appeal brought by an Heir for some Injury done to his Ancestors, whose Heir he is.*

(2.) *An Appeal brought by a Wife, for Wrong done to her Husband; and by her only it can be brought, if it be for his Death, who has the Right to prosecute it.*

(3.) *A Wrong done to the Appellants themselves, as some Robbery, Maim, Rape,* &c. *Coke Instit. Sect.* 500.

And where a Murder is committed, it must be brought within a Year and a Day; for after that Time it cannot be brought at all. And by a Statute of *Hen.* 7. it is enacted, That the Coroner shall do his Office, and the Offenders may be attainted at any Time within the Year, at the King's Suit; but if acquitted, yet the Party within the Year and Day shall have Liberty to bring an Appeal against such Person either acquitted or attainted, If the Benefit of the Clergy be not before thereof had: And in order thereunto, if any Person happens to be acquitted for the Death of a Man within a Year, the Justices before whom he is acquitted shall not suffer him to go at large, but either to remit him again to Prison, or to let him to bail after their Discretion, till that Year and Day be past, that so he may be forthcoming to answer the Appeal, if any be brought within that Time.

The Form of an Appeal of Murder.

J G. *here instantly appeals* R. B. *of the Death of her Husband* W. G. *For whereas the aforesaid* W. *was in the Peace of God and the King at* Woodbridge *in the County of* Middlesex, *on the Eighth Day of* February, *in the second Year of the Reign of our Sovereign Lord* George, *&c. At Five of the Clock in the Evening of the same Day, came the said* R. B. *as a Felon of our Lord the King, of a premeditated Assault, with Force and Arms,* &c. *and upon him the said* W. G. *then and there feloniously an Assault did make, and with a certain Sword made of Iron and Steel, to the Value of* Five Shillings, *which he then and there in his Right Hand did hold, the aforesaid* W. *upon his Head did Strike, and one Mortal Wound of two Inches long, at the fore Part of his Head, and an Inch deep, even to the Brain of the said* W. *did then and there feloniously give; of which said Wound the said* W. *for five Days after following did languish; and on the Thirteenth Day of the same Month, in the Year aforesaid he there died,*

for

(or if the Case be so, *instantly died.*) *And so the said* R. B. *as a Felon of our Lord the King, the aforesaid* W. *feloniously did kill and murder, against the Peace of our said Lord the King his Crown and Dignity. And this he did wickedly, and as a Felon against the Peace of God, and of our Lord the King; the aforesaid* J. G. *offers that the same be detained, as the Court of Our Lord the King shall think meet.*

And though a Woman can in Case of Murder, bring an Appeal for the Death of her Husband, yet otherwise may she bring an Appeal of Robbery, *&c.* for therein she is not restrained by *Magna Charta*, Chap. 34. according to the Opinion of my Lord *Coke*, *Inst.* 2. *Fol.* 68.

But if the Widow of the murthered Husband marry again before the Appeal is entered, or when it is depending, it shall abate, that is, it can be of no Force; nay, if in her Appeal she hath Judgment against the Defendant, if after she marries, before he is hanged, she can never have Execution of Death against him; but if she be not married, she may proceed to Execution, and it is held she has Power to Pardon him, or remit his Offence, even at the Gallows, and also the Time for the Year and Day limited, is to commence from the Time the Party dies, not from the Time of the Wound or Cause of his Death given, for till he dies, there is in this Case no Felony committed.

If an Appeal of Murther be brought, and the Suit depending, and after the Year and Day be elapsed, one become accessary to the Murder, the Plantiff shall have an Appeal against him after the Year and Day past; but it must be brought within the Year and Day after the new Felony of Accessary.

And thus much I thought fit to add to the Office of a Coroner; for though this is rarely practised, it is still in Force, though too often compounded by those that have Right to prosecute in Appeals.

THE Course of DESCENTS OF Lands or Estates.

Collected out of Sir Matthew Hale's *History of the Laws of* England, *Pag.* 206, 235, 236, &c.

AMONG the many Preferences that the Laws of *England* have above others, I shall single out Two Particular Titles, which are of common Use, wherein their Preference is very visible, to wit, 1. The Hereditary Transmission of Lands, from Ancestor to Heir, and the Certainty thereof: And, 2dly, The Manner of Tryal by *Jury*, which, as it stands this Day setled in *England*, together with the Circumstances and Appendices thereof, is the best Manner of Tryal in the World.

First then, touching Descents and Hereditary Transmissions, I shall premise certain general Rules; where, Note, *That in all Descents the Law prefers the worthiest of Blood*, as,

1. In all *Descents immediate*, The *Male* is preferred before the *Female*, whether in Successions *Descending*, *Ascending*, or *Collateral*: Therefore in Descents the Son inherits and excludes the Daughter; the Brother is preferred before the Sister, the Uncle before the Aunt.

2. In all *Descents Immediate*, the Descendants from Males, are to be preferred before the Descendants from Females: And hence it is that the Daughter of the eldest Son is preferred in Descents from the Father, before the Son of the younger Son and the Daughter of the eldest Brother, or Uncle, is preferred before the

Son

Son of the Younger; and the Uncle, nay, the Great Uncle, *i. e.* The Grandfather's Brother, shall inherit before the Uncle of the Mother's Side.

Rule II.] 2*dly*, In *Descents*, the next of Blood is preferred before the more remote, though equally or more worthy. And hence it is, 1, The Sister of the whole Blood is preferred in Descents before the Brother of the half Blood, because she is more strictly joined to the Brother of the whole Blood, (*viz.* by Father and by Mother) than the half Brother, though otherwise he is the more worthy.

2. Because the Son or Daughter being nearer than the Brother, and the Brother or Sister than the Uncle, the Son or Daughter shall inherit before the Brother or Sister, and they before the Uncle.

3. That yet the Father or Grandfather, or Mother or Grandmother, in a direct Ascending Line, shall never succeed immediately the Son or Grandchild; but the Father's Brother (or Sister's) shall be preferred before the Father himself; and the Grandfather's Brother (or Sister's) before the Grandfather: And yet, upon a strict Account, the Father is nearer of Blood to the Son than the Uncle; yea, than the Brother: For the Brother is therefore of the Blood of the Brother, because both derive from the same Parent; the common Fountain of both their Blood. And therefore the Father is preferred at this Day in the Administration of the Goods before the Son's Brother of the whole Blood, and a Remainder limited *proximo de Sanguine* of the Son shall vest in the Father before it shall vest in the Uncle, *Vid. Littleton, lib.* 1. *fol.* 8, 10.

Rule III.] 3. That all the Descendants from such a Person, as by the Laws of *England* might have been Heir to another, hold the same Right by Representation, as the common Root from whence they are derived: And therefore,

1. They are in the Law in the same Right of Worthiness and Proximity of Blood, as their Root that might have been Heir was, in Case he had been living: And hence it is, that the Son or Grandchild, whether Son or Daughter of the eldest Son, succeeds before the Younger Son; and the Son or Grandchild of the eldest Brother before the youngest Brother; and so through all the Degrees of Succession, by the Right of Representation, the Right of Proximity is transferred from the Root to the Branches, and gives them the same Preference as the next and worthiest of Blood.

2. This Right transferred by Representation is infinite and unlimited, in the Degrees of those that descend from the Represented; for. *Filius* the Son, the *Nepos* the Grandson, the *Abnepos* the Great Grandson, and so *in infinitum*, enjoy the same Privilege of Representation, as those from whom they derive their Pedigree have, whether it be in *Descent Lineal* or *Transversal*: And therefore the Great Grandchild of the *Eldest Brother*, whether it be *Son* or *Daughter*, shall be preferred before the

 Younger

Younger Brother; because, though the *Female* be less worthy than the *Male*, yet she stands in Right of Representation of the *Eldest Brother*, who was more worthy than the *Younger*. And upon this Account it is,

3. That if a Man have *Two Daughters*, and the *Eldest* dies in the Life of the Father, leaving six Daughters, and then the Father dies; the *Youngest Daughter* shall have an equal Share with the other six Daughters, because they stand in Representation and Stead of their Mother, who could have had but a Moiety.

Rule IV.] 4. That by the *Law of England*, without the *special Custom* to the contrary, the *Eldest Son*, or *Brother*, or *Uncle*, excludes the *Younger*; and the *Males* in an equal Degree do not all inherit; but all the *Daughters*, whether by the same or divers Venters, do all inherit together to the Father, and all the *Sisters* by the same Venter do inherit to the *Brother*.

Rule V.] 5. That the last actual *Seisin* in any *Ancestor*, makes him, as it were, the *Root of the Descent*, equally to many in *Intents*, as if he had been a *Purchaser*: And therefore he that cannot, according to the *Rules of Descents*, derive his Succession from him that was last actually seized, though he might have derived it from some *precedent Ancestor*, shall not inherit. And hence it is, That where Lands descend to the *Eldest Son* from the *Father*, and the *Son* enters, and dies without Issue, his *Sister* of the whole Blood shall Inherit as Heir to the Brother, and not the *Younger Son* of the Half Blood, because he cannot be Heir to the Brother of the Half Blood: But if the *Eldest Son* had survived the *Father*, and died before the Entry, the *Youngest Son* should inherit as Heir to the Father, and not the *Sister*; because he is Heir to the Father who was last actually seized. And hence it is, that though the *Uncle* is preferred before the *Father* in *Descents* to the *Son*, yet if the Uncle enter after the Death of the *Son*, and die without Issue, the Father shall inherit to the Uncle, *Quia Seisina facit Stipitem*.

Rule VI.] That whosoever derives a Title to any Land, must be of the Blood to him that first purchased it: And this is the Reason why, if the *Son* purchase Lands, and dies without Issue, it shall descend to the Heirs of the Part of the Father; and if he has none, then to the Heirs on the Part of the Mother; because though the Son has both the Blood of the Father and of the Mother in him, yet he is of the whole Blood of the Mother, and the Consanguinity of the Mother are *Consanguinei Cognati* of the Son.

And of the other Side, if the Father had purchased Lands, and it had descended to the Son, and the Son had died without Issue, and without any Heir of the Part of the Father, it should never have descended in the Line of the Mother, but escheated: For though the *Consanguinei* of the Mother were the *Consanguinei* of the Son, yet they were not of Consanguinity of the Father, who was the Purchaser:

chaſer: But if there had been none of the Blood of the Grandfather, yet it might have Reſort to the Line of the Grandmother, becauſe her *Conſanguinei* — were as well of the Blood of the Father, as the Mother's Conſanguinity is of the Blood of the Son: And conſequently alſo, if the Grandfather had purchaſed Lands, and they had deſcended to the Father, and from him to the Son; if the Son had entered, and died without Iſſue, his Father's Brothers or Siſters, or their Deſcendants, or for want of them, his Great-Grandfather's Brothers or Siſters, and their Deſcendants; or for want of them, any of the Conſanguinity of the Great Grandfather, or Brothers and Siſters of the Great Grandmother, or their Deſcendants might have inherited; for the Conſanguinity of the Great Grandmother was the Conſanguinity of the Grandfather; but none of the Line of the Mother or Grandmother; *viz.* The Grandfather's Wife, ſhould have inherited, for that they were not of the Blood of the firſt Purchaſer. And the ſame Rule, *e converſo*, holds in Purchaſes in the Line of the Mother or Grandmother, they ſhall always keep in the ſame Line that the firſt Purchaſer ſetled them in.

But it is not neceſſary, that he that inherits be always Heir to the Purchaſer; it is ſufficient if he be of his Blood, and Heir to him that was laſt ſeized. The Father purchaſes Lands, which deſcended to the Son, who dies without Iſſue, they ſhall never deſcend to the Heir of the Part of the Son's Mother; but if the Son's Grandmother has a Brother, and the Son's Great Grandmother hath a Brother, and there are no other Kindred, they ſhall deſcend to the Grandmother's Brother; and yet if the Father had died without Iſſue, his Grandmother's Brother ſhould have been preferred before his Mother's Brother, becauſe the former was Heir of the Part of his Father, though a Female, and the latter was only Heir of the Part of his Mother; but where the Son is once ſeized, and dies without Iſſue, his Grandmother's Brother is to him Heir of the Part of his Father, and being nearer than his Great Grandmother's Brother, is preferred in the Deſcent.

But, Note, *This is always intended ſo long as the Line of Deſcent is not broken; for the Rules of Deſcents are to be obſerved, as if he were the Original Purchaſer, and as if it had been in the Line of the Father or Mother.*

Rule VII.] 7. In all Succeſſions, as well in the Line *Deſcending*, *Tranſverſal* or *Aſcending*, the Line that is firſt derived from a *Male* Root has always the Preference.

Inſtances whereof in the Line *Deſcending*, &c. *viz.*

A. has Iſſue two Sons, B and C. B. *has Iſſue a Son and a Daughter,* D. *and* E. D. *the Son has Iſſue, a Daughter* F, *and* E *the Daughter has Iſſue, a Son* G. *Neither* C. *nor any of his Deſcendants ſhall inherit, ſo long as there are any Deſcendants from* D. *and* E. *and neither* E. *the Daughter, nor any of her Deſcendants ſhall inherit, so long as there are any Descendants from* D, *the Son, whether they be Male or Female.*

So in Descents *Collateral*, as Brothers and Sisters, the same Instances applied thereto, evidence the same Conclusions.

But in Successions in the Line *Ascending*, there must be a fuller Explication, because it is darker, and more obscure: I shall therefore set forth the whole Method of *Transversal Ascending Descents*, under the Eight ensuing Rules, *viz*.

Rule I. If the *Son* purchases Lands in *Fee-simple*, and dies without Issue, those of the *Male Line Ascending*, *usque infinitum*, shall be *preferred* in the *Descent*, according to their *Proximity of Degree* to the Son; and therefore the *Father's Brothers* and *Sisters*, and their Descendants, shall be *preferred* before the *Brothers* of the *Grandfather* and their Descendants; and if the *Father* had no *Brothers* nor *Sisters*, the *Grandfather's Brothers*, and their Descendants; and for want of *Brothers*, his *Sisters*, and their Descendants, shall be *preferred* before the *Brothers* of the *Great Grandfather*: For although by the Law of *England* the Father or Grandfather cannot immediately inherit to the *Son*, yet the Direction of the Descent to the *Collateral Ascending Line*, is as much as if the *Father* or *Grandfather* had been by Law *inheritable*; and therefore as in the Case the *Father* had been *inheritable*, and should have *inherited* to the *Son* before the *Grandfather*, and the *Grandfather* before the *Great Grandfather*; and consequently if the *Father* had *inherited*, and died without Issue, his *Eldest Brother*, and his Descendants, should have *inherited* before the *Younger Brother* and his Descendants; and if he had no *Brothers*, but *Sisters*, the *Sisters* and their Descendants should have *inherited* before his *Uncle's* or *Grandfather's Brothers*, and their Descendants. So, though the *Law of England* excludes the *Father* from *inheriting*, yet it *substitutes* and *directs* the *Descent* as it should have been, had the *Father inherited*, viz. *It lets in those first that are in the next Degree to him.*

Rule II. The second Rule is this, *That the Line of the Part of the Mother shall never inherit, as long as there are any, though never so remote, of the Line of the Part of the Father*; and therefore, though the *Mother* has a *Brother*, yet if the *Atavus*, or *Atavia Patris*, (*i. e.* The *Great-Great-Great Grandfather* of the *Father*, or the *Great-Great-Great Grandmother*) has a *Brother* or a *Sister*, he or she shall be *preferred*, and exclude the *Mother's Brother*, though he is much nearer.

Rule III. *But yet farther, The Male Line of the Part of the Father ascending, shall*, in Æternum, *exclude the Female Line of the Part of the Father ascending*: And therefore in the Case proposed, of *the Son's purchasing Lands and dying without Issue*,

Issue, the *Sister* of the *Father's Grandfather*, or of his *Great-Grandfather*, and so *in infinitum*, shall be *preferred* before the *Father's Mother's Brother*, though the *Father's Mother's Brother* be a Male, and the *Father's Grandfather* or *Great-Grandfather's Sister* be a Female, and more remote; because she is of the Male Line, which is *more worthy than the Female Line*, though the *Female Line* be also of the *Blood of the Father*.

Rule IV. *But as in the Male Line Ascending, the more near is preferred before the more remote; so in the Female Line descending, so it be of the Blood of the Father, it is preferred before the more remote.* The *Son* therefore purchasing Lands, and dying *without Issue*, and the *Father*, *Grandfather* and *Great-Grandfather*, and so upward, all the Male Line being dead Pag. 244. without any *Brother* or *Sister*, or any descending from them; but the *Father's Mother* has a *Sister* or *Brother*, and also the *Father's Grandmother* has a *Brother*, and likewise the *Father's Great-Grandmother* has a *Brother*; though it is true, all these are of the *Blood of the Father*; and though the very remotest of them shall exclude the *Son's Mother's Brother*; and though it is also true, that the *Great-Grandmother's Blood* has passed through more Males of the *Father's Blood*, than the Blood of the *Grandmother* or *Mother* of the *Father*; yet in this Case the *Father's Mother's Sister* shall be *preferred* before the *Father's Grandmother's Brother*, or the *Great-Grandmother's Brother*, because they are all in the Female Line, *viz. Cognati* (and not *Adgnati*) and the *Fathers Mothers Sister* is the nearest, and therefore shall have the *Preference*, as well as in the Male Line ascending, the *Father's Brother* or his *Sister* shall be preferred before the *Grandfather's Brother*.

Rule V. But yet in the last Case, where the Son purchases Lands, and dies without Issue, and without any Heir on the Part of the *Grandfather*, the Lands should descend to the *Grandmother's Brother* or *Sister*, as Heir on the *Part of the Father*; yet if the *Father* had purchased this Land, and died, and it descended to his Son, who died *without* Issue, the Lands should not have descended to the *Father's Mother's Brother* or *Sister*, for the Reasons before given in the *Third Rule*: But for want of *Brothers* or *Sisters* of the *Grandfather*, *Great-Grandfather*, and so upwards in the Male Ascending Line, it should descend to the *Father's Grandmother's Brother* or *Sister*, which is his Heir of the *Part of his Father*, who should be *preferred* before the *Father's Mother's Brother*, Pag. 245. who is in Truth the Heir of the *Part of the Mother of the Purchaser*, though the next Heir of the *Part of the Father* of him that died last seized; And therefore, as if the Father that was the *Purchaser* had died without Issue, the Heirs of the *Part of the Father* (whether of the Male or Female Line) should have been *preferred* before the Heirs of the *Part of the Mother*; so the Son, who now stands in the *Place of the Father*, and inherits of him primarily in his *Fathers*,

Father's Line, dying without Issue, the same Devolution and Hereditary Succession should have been, as if the *Father* had immediately died without Issue, which should have been to his *Grandmother's Brother*, as Heir of the Part of the *Father*, though by the Female Line, and not to his *Mother's Brother*, who was only Heir of the Part of his *Mother*, who is not to take till the *Father*'s Line, both Male and Female, be spent.

Rule VI. If the *Son* purchase Lands, and dies without Issue, and it descends to any Heir of the Part of the *Father*, and then if the Line of the *Father* (after Entry and Possession) fail, it shall never return to the Line of the *Mother*, though in the first Instance, or first Descent from the *Son*, it might have descended to the Heir of the Part of the *Mother*: For now by this Descent and *Seisin*, it is lodged in the *Father*'s Line, to whom the Heir of the Part of the *Mother* can never derive a Title as Heir; but it shall rather *Escheat*. But if the Heir of the Part of the *Father* had not entered and then that Line had failed, it might have descended to the Heir of the Part of the *Mother*, as Heir to the *Son*, to whom immediately for want of Heirs of the Part of the *Father*, it might have descended.

Rule VII. And upon the same Reason, if it had once descended to the Heir of the Part of the *Father* of the *Grandfather*'s Line, and that Heir had entered, it should never descend to the Heir of the Part of the *Father* of the *Grandmother*'s Line; because the Line of the *Grandmother* was not of the Blood or *Sanguinity* of the Line of the *Grandfather*'s Side.

Pag. 247.

Rule VIII. If for Defaults of Heirs of the *Purchaser* of the Part of the *Father*, the Lands descend to the Line of the *Mother*, the Heirs of the *Mother* of the Part of her *Father*'s Side, shall be preferred in the Succession, before her Heirs of the Part of her *Mother*'s Side, because they are the more worthy.

And thus the Law stands in Point of *Descents* or *Hereditary Successions* in *England* at this Day, and has so stood and continued for above Four Hundred Years past, as by what has before been said may easily appear. And, Note, The most Part of the *Eight Rules*, and Differences above specified and explained, may be collected out of the Resolutions in the Case of *Clare versus Brook*, &c. in *Plowden's Commentaries*, Folio 444.

OF

Tryals by a Jury.

Having in the former Chapter treated of the *Course of Descents*, I shall now briefly consider the Excellency of the Laws of *England*, above those of other Nations, touching *The Tryal by a Jury of Twelve Men*. I shall therefore give a short Account of the *Manner* and *Method* thereof.

1st, The *Writ* to return a *Jury* issues to the Sheriff, who is to be a Person of Worth and Value, so that he may be responsible for any Defaults, either of himself or his Officers. This Officer is entrusted to Elect and Return the Jury; which he is obliged to do without the Nomination of either Plantiff or Defendant. The *Jurors* are to be such Persons, as, for Estate and Quality, are fit to serve on that Imployment. They are to be of the Neighbourhood of the Fact to be enquired, or at least of the County.

As to the *Number*, though only Twelve are sworn, yet Twenty Four are to be returned, to supply the Defects or Want of Appearance of those that are challenged off or make Default. Their Qualifications are many, *viz*. 1. *They are to be good and lawful Men.* 2 *Of sufficient Freeholds, according to the Provisions of several Acts of Parliament.* 3. *Not convict of any notorious Crime.* 4. *They are not to be of the Kindred or Alliance of any of the Parties:* And 5th, *Not to be such as are prepossess'd or prejudiced before they hear their Evidence.*

2*dly*, *The Time of their Return.* Indeed, in Assizes, the Jury is to be ready at the Bar the first Day of the Return of the Writ; but in other Cases, the Pannel is first returned upon the *Venire Facias*, or ought to be so, and the Proofs or Witnesses are to be brought or summoned by *Distringas* or *Habeas Corpora* for their Appearance at the Tryal, whereby the Parties may have Notice of the *Jurors*, and their Sufficiency and Indifferency; that so they may make their Challenges upon the Appearance of the *Jurors*, if there be just Cause.

When the *Jurors* appear and are called, each Party has Liberty to take his Challenge to the Array itself, if unduly or impartially made by the Sheriff; or if the Sheriff be of Kin to either Party; or to the Polls, either for Insufficiency of Freehold, or Kindred or Alliance to the other Party, or such other Challenges, either Principal, or to the Favour, as renders the Juror unfit and incompleat to try the Cause; and the Challenged being confessed, or found true by some of the rest of the Jury, that incompetent Person is withdrawn.

Then Twelve, and no less, of such as are indifferent, and are returned upon the principal Pannel, or the *Tales*, are sworn to try the same according to their Evidence. Being thus sworn, the Evidence on either Part is given in upon Oath of Witnesses, or other Evidence by Law allowed (as Records and Ancient Deeds, but later Deeds and Copies of Records must be attested by the Oaths of Witnesses) and other Evidence in open Court, and in the Presence of the Parties, their Attornies, Counsel and By-standers, and before the Judge and Jury, where each Party has Liberty of Excepting, either to the Competency or Credit of the Evidence or Witnesses, which Exceptions are publickly stated, and by the Judges openly and publickly allowed or disallowed; and if in his Direction or Decision he mistake the Law, either through Partiality, Ignorance or Inadvertency, either Party may require him to seal a Bill of Exception, thereby to deduce the Error of the Judge (if any were) to a due Ratification or Reversal by Writ of Error.

The Excellency of this open Course of Evidence to the Jury, in Presence of the Judge, Jury, Parties and Counsel, and even of the adverse Witnesses, appears in several Particulars, *viz.*

1. That it is openly, and *Ore tenus*, personally, and not in Writing, wherein many times a crafty Clerk will make a Witness speak what he truly never meant, by his dressing of it up in his own Terms: Whereas, on the other hand, many Times the very Manner of a Witness his delivering his Testimony, will give a probable Indication, whether he speaks true or falsely.

2. By this Course of Personal and Open Examination, there is Opportunity for all Persons concerned, *viz.* The Judge or any of the Jury, the Parties or their Attornies, to propound occasional Questions, which beats and boults out the Truth much better than when the Witness only delivers a formal Relation of his Knowledge without being interrogated.

3. By this Personal Appearance and Testimony of Witnesses, there is Opportunity of confronting the adverse Witnesses, of observing the Contradiction of Witnesses sometimes on the same Side.

4. The very Quality, Carriage, Age, Condition, Education, Credit and Place of Commorance of Witnesses, is by this Means plainly and evidently set forth to the Court and Jury, whereby the Judge and Jurors may have a full Information of them, and the Jurors (as they see Cause) may give the more or less Credit to their Testimony; for the Jurors are not only Judges of the Fact, but, many times, of the Truth of Evidence; and if there be just Cause to disbelieve what a Witness swears, they are not bound to give their Verdict according to the Evidence of that

that Witnefs, and they may fometimes give Credit to one Witnefs, though contradicted by more than one.

5. The Judge is always prefent at the Time the Evidence is given; herein he has Opportunity, in Matters of Law emerging upon the Evidence, to direct them; and alfo in Matters of Fact, to give them Light and Affiftance, by his weighing the Evidence before them, fhewing his Opinion, and obferving where the Queftion and Knot of the Bufinefs lies; which is a great Advantage many times to the Jurors. And thus, as the Jury affifts the Judge in determining Matters of Fact, fo the Judge affifts the Jury in determining Points of Law.

6. When the Evidence is fully given, the Jury withdraws to a private Place, and are there kept from all Speech with either of the Parties, till their Verdict is delivered up, and from receiving any Evidence other than in open Court. In this Recefs of the Jury, they are to confider their Evidence; and if any Writings under Seal were given in Evidence, the Jury are to have them with them. They are to weigh and confider the Credibility of *Witneffes*, and the Force of their Teftimonies; wherein they are not precifely bound to the Rules of the Civil Law, *viz. To have two Witneffes to prove every Fact*, unlefs in Cafes of *Treafon*, nor to reject one Witnefs becaufe he is fingle; nor always to believe two Witneffes, if the *plain Probability of the Fact* does, upon *other* Circumftances, reafonably encounter them; for the Tryal is not here fimply by *Witneffes*, but by *Jury*; nay, it may fo fall out, *That the Jury, upon their own Knowledge, may know a thing to be falfe, that a Witnefs fwore to be true; or may know a Witnefs to be incompetent or incredible, though nothing be objected againft him, and may give their Verdict accordingly.* And the Verdict muft be by the whole Twelve Men, not one diffenting; then, and *not till then*, is the Verdict to be received.

7. If there be *Matter of Law that carries in it any Difficulty*, the *Jury* may, to deliver themfelves from the Danger of an *Attaint*, find it *Specially*, that fo it may be decided by the Court; and if the Judge over-rule the *Point of Law contrary to Law*, whereby the Jury are perfwaded to find a general Verdict (which yet they are not bound to do, if they doubt it) then the Judge, upon the Requeft of the Party defiring it, is bound by Law to feal a *Bill of Exceptions*, containing the *whole Matter* excepted to, whereby the Party grieved by fuch Error, may have Relief by *Writ of Error*, on the *Stat. of Weftminfter.*

Thus far Judge HALE.

The

The Form of an Indictment for Assault.

THE Grand Inquest for Our Lord the King, upon their respective Oaths and Affirmations, do present, *That* A. B. *late of the County of* Bucks, *Labourer, the Twenty Fourth Day of* May, *in the Year of the Reign of our Lord* GEORGE, *by the Grace of God King of* Great-Britain, France *and* Ireland, *Defender of the Faith,* &c. *the Eighth, with Force and Arms,* &c. *at the Township of* Bristol, *in the County aforesaid, in and upon one* C. D. *in the Peace of God and of our Lord the King then and there being, an Assault did make, and him did beat, wound and evilly entreat; so that of his Life it was greatly dispaired, and other Harms to him then and there did, to the great Damage of the said* C. D. *against the Peace of our said Lord the King, his Crown and Dignity,* &c.

The Form of an Indictment for Stealing.

THE Grand Inquest for Our Lord the King, upon their respective Oaths and Affirmations, do present, *That* A. B. *late of the County of* Bucks, *Labourer, the Twenty Fourth Day of* May, *In the Year of the Reign of our Lord* GEORGE, *by the Grace of God King of* Great Britain, France *and* Ireland, *Defendor of the Faith,* &c. *the Eighth, with Force and Arms,* &c. *at the Township of* Bristol, *in the County aforesaid, One Silver Spoon of the Value of Fifteen Shillings, of the Goods and Chattles of One* C. D. *then and there being found, then and there did feloniously steal, take and carry away, against an Act of General Assembly of this Province in that Case made and provided; as also against the Peace of our said Lord the King, his Crown and Dignity,* &c.

N. B. If any thing stolen, *viz.* A Hog, or Sheep, or live Creature, name the Priee of it, instead of Value.

Richard Burn

F I N I S.